Caring for Place

E. N. Anderson

Caring
for Place

Ecology, Ideology, and Emotion
in
Traditional Landscape Management

Left
Coast
Press
Inc.

WALNUT CREEK
CALIFORNIA

Left Coast Press, Inc.
1630 North Main Street, #400
Walnut Creek, CA 94596
http://www.LCoastPress.com

ISBN 978-1-61132-958-2 hardcover
ISBN 978-1-61132-959-9 paperback
ISBN 978-1-61132-960-5 institutional eBook
ISBN 978-1-61132-760-1 consumer eBook

Library of Congress Cataloging-in-Publication Data:

Anderson, E. N.
    Caring for place : ecology, ideology, and emotion in traditional landscape management / E. N. Anderson.
        pages cm.
    Includes bibliographical references and index.
    ISBN 978-1-61132-958-2 (hardback : alk. paper) —
    ISBN 978-1-61132-959-9 (pbk. : alk. paper) —
    ISBN 978-1-61132-960-5 (institutional ebook) —
    ISBN 978-1-61132-760-1 (consumer ebook)
    1. Landscape ecology.   2. Landscape assessment.   3. Cultural landscapes.   4. Traditional farming.   I. Title.
    QH541.15.L35A45 2014
    577—dc23

                                                            2013041026

Printed in the United States of America

∞ ™ The paper used in this publication meets the minimum requirements of American National Standard for Information Sciences—Permanence of Paper for Printed Library Materials, ANSI/NISO Z39.48–1992.

Cover design by Piper Wallis
Cover photo By Li Yaoping (1880–1937), "Ancient Temple among Mountains and Valleys," Hong Kong Museum of Art, Google Art Project, Public domain via Wikimedia Commons

Dedication
To the cause of humanity-in-nature
As opposed to humanity vs. nature
and
To my field collaborators over the years, especially
Don Felix Medina Tzuc
Doña Aurora Dzib Xihum
and
To my students in the enterprise

CONTENTS

PREFACE AND ACKNOWLEDGMENTS

In Nanjing, China, in 2005, a university offered a course in the ancient Chinese art of *fengshui*. Feng shui, "wind and water," involves planning houses, communities, and graves in accord with the ways of wind and water—both the real and tangible ways known to all the world and the supernatural or imaginary ways that Chinese cosmology postulates.

This course set off a storm of protest (Lee 2005). One professor said: "It's a fake science … It only makes money for some swindlers" (Lee 2005:1). Others denounced it as "superstition" (*mixin*). Others, however, lauded it as a glorious achievement of Chinese science and culture, and welcomed the new course.

The problem is that feng shui, as we know it today, is a single, unified field, but it has elements of what we of the Western academic world would consider "magic," "science," and "religion." The distinctions between these three realms have proved useful for anthropology, but they are confounded by traditional belief systems like feng shui. This causes intractable problems for anthropologists as well as for Chinese university administrators. These problems need unpacking.

When I was in Hong Kong in 1965, friends took me to see the site of a new hospital. The foundations required deep cuts into a hill slope.

Local people were disturbed. They told me, "This is cutting the pulse of the dragon. There will be disaster." I learned that every large hill has a dragon or tiger spirit within it. Large hills with dragon-like profiles have dragons; lower and more rounded hills have tigers. Cutting the pulse of the dragon angers him. I duly wrote this down as an interesting, odd local belief.

A week later came violent rains—usual in fall in Hong Kong. The undercut slope failed. The landslide buried several houses. The neighbors said, "See, this is what happens when the dragon's pulse is cut."

I learned from this episode that people can reason from cause to effect and can infer very strange black-box variables to connect the two. We should be alert to recognize the correctness of the cause-effect link, even if we know the assumed intervening variable is highly dubious. Even Western science, in those days, could not explain why slopes fail; engineers spoke of "angle of repose," a concept as mystical as the dragon. Conversely, many Chinese saw the dragon as metaphoric, merely an image of the lines of force or energy existing within the world. For the literal-minded, earthquakes were caused by actual dragons shaking themselves in the earth. For the more scholarly, earthquakes were correctly seen as motion along lines of force revealed at particularly dramatic cliffs and other places we can recognize as fault lines (cf. Anderson 1996, 2007).

This book explores several cases of societies that teach conservation to varying degrees and in varying ways. It also examines some cases of non-conserving. I come, at the end, to a few firm conclusions, but only a few. The subject is complex. Much more research is needed, especially on the history of particular management systems. We often have reports of systems that seem to work but lack a long record that would enable us to evaluate their success. We also have reports of systems that seem to fail—but the reports come from societies shattered by hundreds of years of colonial oppression (e.g., stories in Krech 1999). I, therefore, draw heavily herein on societies with some historical record (China, Mediterranean, Maya), or on those that were contacted late and described soon after (Australia, Northwest Coast; my research on the latter region will be a separate book, a sequel to the present one).

I will examine a few particular cases I know more or less well and also will look at larger regional systems. An annoyingly necessary restriction has been to confine myself, in the particular-case chapters, to talking about areas in which I have traveled at some length and in which I know enough of the languages to do at least a little evaluation of translations; bitter experience with relying solely on translation has convinced me this is necessary. The one exception is Australia, which I touch only very briefly; it is too important to leave out. My command of the languages drawn on for other materials cited herein ranges from good to poor, but at least I was not totally at the mercy of translators.

The present book is essentially a continuation of my books *Ecologies of the Heart* (1996) and *The Pursuit of Ecotopia* (2010). In the first of these, I looked at traditional ways of conserving the environment; I go over some of the same ground in more depth here and go on to some newer topics. In the second, I focused on political ecology: environmental justice, the politics of antienvironmentalism, and the needed fixes—which, I argued, were more in areas of justice, accountability, recourse, and freedom of conscience than in the area of conservation per se. The present book goes into more detail on the history of our present plight, as well as on the alternatives that other cultures afford.

For reasons of space and copyright, I have had to leave actual works of art, and most poems, out of this book. I give references to major relevant artworks. For some poetry, see "Environment Poetry" on my website, www.krazykioti.com.

I have spent my life looking at many cultures, generalizing, trying to find broad principles; this has had a major cost, in that I am not truly expert on any one area. Anthropologists love to shoot down generalizations by saying, "my people do it differently"—the so-called anthropological veto (Konner 2007:79). I have done my share of this, but in the present book I am sticking my neck out and generalizing.

Accounts herein are subject to limitations. I make many broad-brush generalizations about cultures, but these have to be considered tentative. The only cultures I know well are my own Anglo-American (specifically Scots-Irish) roots; southeast China (Cantonese, Teochiu, and Hokkien, with research in Hong Kong, China, and Malaysia); and the Yucatec Maya. Even here my knowledge is limited. Being a part of southern Scots-Irish culture does not make me an expert on it, though I know quite a bit. I am reasonably familiar with several California and Northwest Coast Native American peoples and have done more than a year of research in British Columbia. I have traveled widely in the rest of the world, with special research journeys to Australia, Madagascar, Scotland and Ireland, and the Mediterranean (most of the larger countries) in connection with this book. I have carried out smaller bits of research in Panama, Tahiti, Singapore, Turkey, and a dozen other countries.

I am, as usual, grateful first of all to my wife, Barbara, and children, Laura, Alan, Amanda, Tamar, and Rob, and to the rest of my family. Next most important in this book have been my colleagues, especially Alan Fix, Gene Hunn (who gave the entire manuscript a very careful reading with extremely helpful commentary), Leslie Johnson, David Kronenfeld, and J. C. Laursen, and my Maya research assistants and adoptive family members Don Felix Medina Tzuc and Doña Aurora Dzib Xihum de Cen. My students have been a constant help and inspiration and kept me going. In writing this book I have depended especially on Kimberly Kirner (Kimberly Hedrick of citations herein), Sandy Lynch, Aniee Sarkissian, Jianhua "Ayoe" Wang, and Katherine Ward. Above all, the hundreds of people I have known and worked with, for well over fifty years, have all contributed to this book: colleagues, students, field consultants, and friends in all walks of life. Everywhere, I have found hospitality, support, and generous help. All I can do to pay back is to do what I can to change the world by writing.

Research for this book was supported by a long series of intramural grants from the University of California, several grants over the years from the National Science Foundation, an early grant from the National Institutes of Health, and a grant from the MacArthur Foundation to Dr. Arturo Gomez-Pompa and associates. In particular, a grant from NSF to Dr. Christopher Chase-Dunn and myself, to study world-systems, has helped with recent research.

PART I

REPRESENTATIONS

CHAPTER ONE

Environment and Cultural Representations

We should have followed Wolf, but we followed Coyote.
Southwestern Native American saying

"The tree of humanity forgets the labour of the silent gardeners who sheltered it from the cold, watered it in time of drought, shielded it against wild animals; but it preserves faithfully the names mercilessly cut into its bark." Heinrich Heine, 1833 (as quoted in Gross 1983:323)

PEOPLE IN NATURE

Most people now realize the human race is in trouble because of resource exhaustion, biodiversity loss, global climate changes, and environmental mismanagement. Responses to the problem are inadequate so far, in spite of many congresses and treaties over the last few decades. Much of the problem is due to a failure to convince the vast mass of humanity that the environmental situation is serious and needs attention. Even more serious is a failure of uniting people to act. Typical of the environmental literature is Vaclav Smil's new book, *Harvesting the Biosphere* (2013). It consists of 247 pages of superbly marshaled and brilliantly interpreted facts and statistics about our exponentially increasing offtake of the world's biotic resources; five pages of sensible, low-hanging-fruit suggestions of what to do; and not a word on how to get from point A (rampant and increasing overdraft) to point B (sensible alternatives).

A modest suggestion might be that if people of traditional and local cultures and societies have solved these problems, or even done a little better than modern humanity has done, we can learn from those other cultures. Indeed many other societies have managed the world a great deal less destructively. One might say "better," but that would be special pleading. I am not an ethical philosopher. So I will simply record the fact that those societies supported large populations over long time periods without destroying their environments.

They did it by devising good strategies for environmental management and, more to the point, getting people united behind acting on those programs. Thousands of local societies and communities, worldwide, have successfully conserved fish and forests, farmed without huge losses of soil and fertility, and prevented urban sprawl onto prime farmland.

This book deals with the ways people think about plants, animals, and landscapes. It is about the "habits of the heart" (Bellah et al. 1996) needed to conserve the environment. Many traditional cultures found ways to motivate people to unite to sustain the environment and its services. Sometimes this meant sustaining a broadly "natural" environment, sometimes a totally human-made one, such as the rice paddy systems of Asia. Either way, some societies managed for sustainable, productive use and got everyone more or less united behind the program (Holthaus 2008; Turner 2005). This runs against the self-serving belief that "everybody" acts irresponsibly and selfishly, but, as the present book will show (and many others have shown), impeccable and thorough documentation demonstrates that people do not always act that way. This is *not* to say they are perfect—only that we can learn from them.

Everyone realizes, if they think more than a minute, that we all depend on an environment that is at least healthy enough to produce food and fiber without killing us all through pollution. Most people recognize that this involves tolerating at least some biological diversity, as well as more obvious things like keeping sewage out of the drinking water and keeping deadly poisons out of the food. People also realize that having fish or forest products in the future depends on not catching all the fish or cutting down all the trees today.

Photo on Opposite Page: Modern aboriginal art at the Australian Museum, Sydney (Hibernian, Public domain, via Wikimedia Commons).

However, these realizations are not currently affecting behavior enough to save resources. The almost universal finding that big dams' ecological damages outweigh their total benefits has not stopped many nations or agencies from building more of them (Anderson 2010; Scudder 2005).

Fisheries have been wiped out around the world, but no one seems to learn. Overfishing is worse than ever. Attempts at restraint are routinely sabotaged, whether on the community level or in the world ocean, as Vaclav Smil points out in his book. In my early career, researching fisheries development, I watched fishery after fishery collapse. In China, Malaysia, Singapore, Canada, and the United States, the story was the same: fishermen fought against regulations, saying, "there are more fish out there, they just aren't biting right now." Some really believed this, in spite of all evidence. Others tried to convince themselves of it. Others knew better, but knew that regulations would immediately ruin them, while overfishing would not ruin them until a few years down the track. Still others planned to exit the fishery in any case and had stopped caring. Very often, heavy government subsidies kept uneconomic fisheries going until total collapse ensued. Worldwide, fishing would now be a losing proposition without the subsidies.

Into my rising state of hopelessness came several studies showing that many societies do control overfishing and comparable ills. R. E. Johannes's *Words of the Lagoon* (1981), in which he shows how communities regulate fishing in Micronesia, was one of the first. He went on to work with others on such Pacific Island systems (Ruddle and Johannes 1983; Ruddle and Akimichi 1984). Soon I discovered James Acheson's work on Maine lobster fishermen's regulation of their take (Acheson 1987, 2006). Doubters were convinced; Shankar Aswani of the University of California, Santa Barbara, went out to the Solomon Islands, sure that people could not manage common-pool fisheries sustainably, and came back convinced they were doing it (personal communication; see Aswani and Weiant 2004) Studies of hunting, gathering, herding, and other common-property systems followed (as the rest of this book will show).

The common thread was always that local communities were able to marshal powerful emotional forces. The communities involved people and provided rich emotional contexts that both motivated good behavior and developed strong levels of personal conscience and responsibility. Always, this involved some form of ceremony or ritual or public participation, as well as specific training that involved highly detailed education in resource management. This education was, of course, done in the field, in the course of making a living; it was not passive classroom lecturing.

In small-scale traditional societies, conservation always seemed to involve such supranormal sanctions. In modern society, secular social morality is often adequate; we have succeeded in reducing litter along the highways, outlawing random shooting of songbirds, and preserving large tracts of desert. However, overfishing, overcutting, over-draining of wetlands, urbanization of prime farmland, and other failures of sustainability continue. All these produce short-term profits for certain interests, usually politically powerful and politically protected ones. This makes them refractory to easy answers. The opposition to powerful short-term interests has to be exceptionally unified, solidary, and motivated.

This had made many of us wonder if religion is necessary, or at least desirable, for conservation (Anderson 1996, 2010; Berkes 2008; Berkes, Colding, and Folke 2000; Holthaus 2008; Taylor 2010). Certainly, there has to be some sort of cultural institution that makes people responsible, caring, and proactive. Being "for the environment" does not help unless people will stick together to pass laws, pick up litter, volunteer at parks, support science education in schools, boycott overfished species, and do all the other thousands of things that require both active personal motivation and a desire to work for the common good.

All of this brings us to a critically important conclusion: good management of resources is a result of community solidarity expressed in individual responsibility, not of knowledge about the environment. A good citizen with very limited environmental knowledge will predictably be a better environmental citizen than an expert who is concerned only with corporate profits or scientific detachment. *Motivating people to act responsibly is the key.*

The contention of this book is that such motivation is usually done by emotionally compelling cultural representations, from religion to art to peer pressure. It requires some command of the latest statistics, but, far more, it requires sheer gut-level understanding that we humans and nonhumans are all dependent on each other and have to act accordingly. On the other hand, the message cannot wander far off target, or people will not make the connections. The need is to embed specific environmental management strategies in a wider moral discourse of tolerance and solidarity.

Environmental battles become quite emotional, often opposing Good and Evil—differently defined by the different sides in the fight. Social science models often assume "average" people are the actors, but in environmental issues, the actors are highly motivated and thus highly emotional. Almost always, they are acting for the common good; the problems occur when the "common" in question is an extractive corporation or community that is maximizing its own collective good at the expense of a much wider collective good. Even small-scale "selfishness" often resolves into a lot of people trying to keep their families alive. There is sometimes genuine selfishness, and it can get truly extreme, as when ranchers and estate owners in Brazil murder conservationists and use political connections to get away with it. But usually we are dealing with collective matters and public politics.

Social institutions must not only motivate people to be responsible about environmental use. They must also make them love nature or at least care deeply and emotionally about plant and animal resources, and make them solidary in every sense. People must be able to work together with full tolerance. An institution that allows (let alone encourages) current levels of passivity is hopeless. This means that the social institution must be highly positive, emotional, empowering, and motivating, as well as successful at making people think of the long-term consequences of their acts. Otherwise, even the most well-intentioned and environmentally moral individuals will fall back on saying, "what one person does can't possibly matter" and "it won't hurt to take just one." Serious and emotionally grounded levels of precommitment are necessary to make a person sacrifice money, time, or effort to do something that no one else appears to be doing, whether it is replacing a lawn with bird habitat, putting up solar panels, or even simply voting (a notoriously "irrational" act in terms of the chance of one vote making a difference).

In the past, religion has usually been one way—very often the only way—to motivate people to be so self-sacrificing and proactive in the cause of the environment (see, e.g., Verschuuren et al. 2010). I believe, but cannot prove, that secular morality could do the job. Neither organized religion nor "environmentalism" has a stunning track record in this regard, but more personally engaging forms of environmental concern, from working with local parks to working with small farms and food systems, have often been quite successful.

Humans work together, especially in traditional economic activities, and learn through practice how things are done. This includes learning what *not* to do as well as what to do. Farmers learn from their elders, during work on the land, to save the best kernels for seed and to breed the best livestock. They learn to leave vegetation in gullies to prevent soil erosion. They learn not to shoot pregnant game animals if they can avoid it. They learn to cooperate, to tolerate each other (at least as much as is necessary for mutual aid), and to be responsible about at least some things required by the community.

In ceremonies and rituals, usually sacred but sometimes secular, they become engaged enough in their communities to act as citizens. This extends conservation, if that is a major social teaching. Anyone not alienated from community and neighborhood must care a little how the wider social group thinks; even a sociopath has to get along, and the vast majority of humans are genuinely concerned with others around them.

Saving the environment requires four things, only the first of which is directly related to it:

First, obviously, people must actually *care* about the environment. They must not only realize they depend on it; they must be emotionally involved in it.

Second, they must want to learn specific, pragmatic, factual information about the environment and how to manage it for the long term. The current state of denial about global warming is truly terrifying, but even worse is current denial about biodiversity loss, topsoil loss, farmland degradation, deforestation … the list goes on. People know more about movie stars' marriages than about imminent threats to humanity's survival. Anti-education and anti-intellectual currents now dominate American life and are appearing worldwide. America has not only massively disinvested in education over recent years, but it has turned education into mindless drills for mindless standardized tests, a problem that has been addressed in the journal *Science* as well as many other venues (Alberts 2012a, 2012b). This is contrary to all we know about education for any real-world purpose, especially science, environmental management, and emotional engagement with social and ecological worlds (Anderson 2010, 2011b, and website postings at *www.krazykioti.com*).

Third, we have to learn to be tolerant of others and to value diversity. This is partly so we can all use each other's good ideas. It is also necessary because politicians—often in the service of environment-wreckers—are more and more dedicated to whipping up hatreds, especially ethnic, religious, and political ones (Anderson and Anderson 2012). This is moving humanity away from environmental concern and toward more meltdowns of the sort that have recently affected Somalia and Syria.

Fourth, the absolute basic realization has to be that *we are all in this together*—humans certainly, but also the other lives on the planet. We have to teach everyone to realize that, and I mean "realize" literally: to "make real" the perception and all its implications.

In traditional subsistence-oriented societies, where people usually lived in fairly tight communities held together by folkways and informal leadership, enforcing conservation was often fairly easy. Everyone could see their lives depended on the environment. The effects of overuse were rapidly apparent, and hurt everyone. Leaders could not escape; they were part of the community, and even if they could survive, they would lose prestige if they oversaw a disaster. Folkways developed accordingly: conservation and management rules, usually sanctioned by religion, developed and were maintained. Of course this ideal situation did not always hold, but it held surprisingly often, even among people living in modern European and American societies. Many local fishing and farming communities still live by such rules. On the other hand, folk and local communities may lack either the knowledge or the solidarity to form and follow wise rules.

Marxians and utopians often think, or used to think, that harmony and good management would grow naturally from egalitarian co-work and co-residence. This is not the case. We all know communities and families that are totally dysfunctional in spite of, or even because of, being stuck with each other. Living together leads to constant minor slights that tend to develop into hatreds. Conversely, many communities and families work harmoniously and well in spite of being widely scattered. (My own large but quite idyllic family is widely scattered; love, not co-work, maintains it.)

Harmonious, relatively happy communities tend to manage resources well, while fractious, poorly integrated, combative communities do not. But both harmony and management have to be worked at. They do not happen unless people put in considerable ongoing effort. This requires appropriate values. My Maya friends anchor the harmonious-manager end of this spectrum; the environmentally devastating communities in the mountain Middle East anchor the other. For that matter, even within Afghanistan, in an earlier era, I observed both harmonious good-manager communities, including Hazara ones I saw, and others, often Afghan, that were horribly destructive of both nature and other people. I have lived in Maya communities that were ecological models, but have seen Maya communities that were socially and ecologically dysfunctional. What one rarely sees is a harmonious community that is ecologically irresponsible—though even that does manifest itself on occasion, especially in pioneer situations.

Local harmony can be imposed by mutual responsibility (good, indeed necessary, for conservation), but it can be imposed by dictatorial fiat or guilt-exploiting religious authority, both notoriously bad for the environment, because they interfere with local flexibility and response. Similarly, though some harmony is obviously necessary to make ideology and management work at all, some disharmony is necessary, too, in the form of dialogue, debate, and enforcement. A community too tolerant of poachers, or too gentle with people making bad mistakes, will not survive. Solidarity has to be asserted in the teeth of trouble and maintained by constant negotiation. If it does not grow organically from the need of individuals to be responsible to each other, it will not work at all.

THE PROBLEMS

The first and most obvious sets of problems are political-economic. The famous "tragedy of the commons" (Hardin 1968) has been discussed in thousands of sources. Most traditional societies have found ways to deal with it (see below; also Ostrom 1990, 2009). Far more serious today, however, is the ability of private interests, especially giant primary-production firms (Anderson 2010), to pass on their real costs of production as "externalities." Manufacturing firms can operate inefficiently—releasing a great deal of their useful inputs or products in the form of pollution—because the costs of dealing with the pollution are born by the public. Lumber firms can fail to take care of their trees because government forestry departments take care of everything from road-building to replanting to erosion control, at the taxpayers' expense. The costs of big dams, deforestation, and pollution are disproportionately born by local people, often the least affluent ones, while the benefits go to powerful politicians and rich proprietors. Giant firms find it increasingly profitable to lobby or bribe politicians, draw subsidies, and ruin the environment, rather than practicing efficiency and sustainability (Anderson 2010).

A cycle often exists in which passing on costs to the poor releases high profits, which are then invested in lobbying for higher subsidies, which can then be reinvested in further lobbying and in public-relations campaigns that are often highly misleading.

However, the problem is not only with large firms. Ordinary foolishness, irresponsibility, laziness, and procrastination do their part. Even ordinary individuals fail to act in their obvious long-term self-interest. This is partly because of a well-recognized and well-studied feature of human cognition: the "steep discount slope." This refers to the human tendency to forget about the future, or at best to regard it as so remote and uncertain that it is of little concern. Excessively steep discounting has been the subject of thousands of papers and analytic reports (see e.g., Jon Elster's *Explaining Social Behavior,* 2007). To some extent, this is built into the human animal; we have cognitive biases in the direction of optimism, presentism, and hope. We fall easily into cheerful insouciance and overoptimism.

Another part of the explanation is *low self-efficacy* (Bandura 1982, 1986), a cover term for loss of hope and wilting of will. People in most of the world today are exposed to so much domination by governments, giant firms, and local extralegal force that they simply give up, or retreat into themselves. The failure of political action among America's young people has been much remarked; it is certainly obvious in matters of conservation. They feel a loss of agency in a world dominated by giant media corporations, giant business firms, and nonresponsive governments. University administrations have become as remote and unaccountable as the giant firms. In former times, religion and group solidarity motivated the young. Today, religion has become at best an equivocal force, and group solidarity is increasingly maintained by huge, remote hierarchies that turn the ordinary people of the world into hapless followers—"subjects" rather than "citizens," in de Tocqueville's phrasing (which goes back to ancient Greek perceptions).

When people *are* motivated, they are often motivated against nature. Most modern forms of Marxism share with conservative businessfolk and some modern religious sects an idea of "dominating" nature. This idea fits neither with traditional religious thought nor with the actual words of Marx and Engels. It is much more driven by the giant productive interests (Anderson 2010).

Lack of solidarity is often due to an even more serious problem: hate. The world is now so divided by religious, ethnic, political, and other hatreds that the common good is neglected. The environment tends to get even shorter shrift than education, international justice, human rights, and honest government—all four of which are necessary for good environmental management. Even without hate, mutual rivalries, tensions, competition, sheer ignorance of others, and extreme individualism sabotage the common good, but it seems beyond reasonable question that these would be manageable if it were not for the far deeper and more serious wounds of outright hatred.

The greatest problem occurs when giant productive interests discover that they can use hate to divide the populace and stir up loyalty (even fanaticism) for the interests that are leading the campaign. Hitler and his corporate backers such as Farben and Krupp perfected this technique in Germany in the 1930s, and it is alive and well in many countries today (a fact that sorely needs further exploration and study). This cynical ploy has been particularly effective in oil-rich nations, from Iran and Iraq to the United States and Canada. Thus hate becomes a far more serious environmental problem than selfishness, greed, capitalism, or the other favorite bêtes noires of the environmentalist media.

People worry about the long future because they love their children and worry about them, or because of powerful peer pressure, strong ideology and conscience, or religion. Religion is particularly well adapted for the purpose, because it can promise no only eternal bliss to the virtuous, but punishment to the sinful. Religions that threaten punishment by the spirits in this life may be particularly successful at encouraging conservation. Almost every philosopher has observed that hellfire after death seems even more heavily discounted than other futures. Fear for one's immediate, this-world future is thus important. Chinese fishermen believed they face storms if they catch sacred fish (sturgeons, porpoises, sea turtles, and the like). Northwest Coast people face forest "accidents," if they do not thank the spirits for berries and roots, and face famine for the whole community, if they overhunt. Yucatec Maya farmers are sure they will have little or no harvest next year if they do not thank God and the spirits of the fields for good harvest this year.

Behind this lies individual and cultural variation in what is valued in the first place. The cultural variation is, of course, often due to campaigns by powerful interests—from the landlords of ancient Mesopotamia to the medieval church and then to the capitalist firms and communist agencies of today. People can be selfish—or unselfish—about material resources, or power, or reproductive capacity, or status, or fun. "Fun" can derive from hiking, hunting, eating good food, watching the currently popular movie, or countless other culturally modified or culturally constructed pastimes. Usually, for humans, what is "fun" is what is socially defined as fun—what brings people together in a warm, social context. We are truly social animals. Thus, the delights of being alone in wilderness may have a limited appeal to most people. Some cultures define the wild as simply terrifying; others as a place of spiritual power; others as a place to enjoy. The contingent histories of these cultural views are important, but often poorly known.

A frustrating experience known to all conservation workers is that one can always have early success, attracting many highly motivated and willing people, but that this quickly levels off. The problem is that every society has a number of people motivated by moral considerations for the long term and for the general population, but a much larger number of people who either cannot afford to think in self-sacrificing terms or simply do not care. My experience in the United States and elsewhere has been that it is always easy to get a large number of volunteers or morally persuadable people to develop parks, eat organic food, buy fair trade coffee, bicycle to work, and recycle papers, but that a hard ceiling is reached when about 10 to 20 percent of the population is enlisted. Increasing the numbers of the volunteers becomes progressively more difficult as one reaches farther out. An equivalent number—about 20 percent —views all environmentalism as counter-economic. Some of these resisters are simply immoral, but many genuinely believe that they are surviving through environmental exploitation and could not thrive if it stopped.

Still others—usually the majority of potential adopters—simply find the costs challenging. The costs may not be financial; time especially is very scarce in the modern world. Cognitive costs are also involved. People are wary of change, and for good reason. A change that looks promising may turn out disastrous. It is a truism that poor people are slow to change, because any mistake would destroy them. Rich people are also conservative, because of vested interests, but at least they have the opportunity to take risks.

At the very least, any change involves learning new ways of doing things, and this may be challenging. Environmentalists should always strive to make their message not only appealing but also simple.

COLLECTIVE REPRESENTATIONS

There was a time when I thought, as many do, that immediate economic concerns determined cultural views. I learned that this is not the case. Economic and ecological templates thousands of years old dominate a good deal of modern practice. Replacing forests with cattle pasture was already deforesting Europe 7,000 years ago, as it is doing in the Amazon today. It is uneconomical, appealing only to large-scale cattle owners. Replacing natural food-producing systems with neat rows of monoculture crops is almost as old in the West. The rice paddy systems of East Asia have an ancestry thousands of years long. Basic templates—

basic knowledge about how to manage and construct an environment—change slowly and propagate widely. They resist both economic rationality and change. Modern global influences are destroying local small-scale systems, but even these prove surprisingly resilient.

One place to start is with ethnoecology (Johnson and Hunn 2010; Toledo 1992, 2002). This field deals with the ways people think about the environment and, above all, how they share their thoughts, debate them, negotiate their strategies, and eventually come up with cultural strategies for resource management. Lacking telepathy, people cannot really share thoughts and beliefs, but the recent discovery of "mirror cells" in the brain makes it clear that we have near-telepathic abilities to copy others' behavior and infer their thoughts and feelings.

Cultural systems include communication, economy, ecological practice, foodways, medical systems, religion, and similar systems. All these involve practice, discourse, and thought, and one can focus on any or all of those aspects of a cultural system (see Atran and Medin 2008; Medin, Ross, and Cox 2006; also the classic work of Darrell Posey, 1999, 2004). We must even look at physical form; people are literally shaped by their cultural activities. In a brilliant and seminal paper, Marcel Mauss (1979) described the ways that culture becomes embodied through *habitus*—the culturally learned ways of moving, working, playing, dancing, living. Muscles grow, and fat distribution changes accordingly. One can often tell a person's ethnicity by the way she moves. (The concept of *habitus* was later generalized to a much wider set of phenomena by Pierre Bourdieu, 1977; see also Latour 2005:210–211. I like Mauss's original usage better. We need it.)

Cultural representations are not pure ideas existing in a vacuum. They arise from constant ongoing interaction with the world. Environmental knowledge and belief arises from people interacting with nature and natural things (Bourdieu 1977, 1990; Latour 2004, 2005).

The view taken in this book is one of people in nature: humans as part of the whole world system. The stereotype of "people vs. nature" is so firmly established in the Western world that we have completely separated biology from the social sciences. Biology is now normally understood to be about nonhumans, social sciences normally understood to be—in Wilhelm Dilthey's phrase—the "human sciences." Fields like ethnobiology and human biology are considered "interdisciplinary." Interdisciplinary research is given much lip service in academia, but actually is normally set at considerable disadvantage, because the traditional disciplines have the positions and the budget lines. Chairs of biology and social science departments do not usually look kindly at research that draws money and power away from them.

Seeing people as part of the world, not separate from other organisms, encourages us to look at human interactions with the environment, rather than simply at how people think about the environment. Phenomenologists have always attended to interaction, and the new wave of environmental phenomenologists (e.g., Abram 1996; Ingold 2000) is moving more and more into observing how different cultures mediate interaction with environments.

At the same time, we are usually interacting with other people. Working together in hunting, fishing, or farming is the most obvious and direct case in point. Marx was right in giving it pride of place among interactive contexts, with nature as with people. But hiking together qualifies, too. So does hiking alone while thinking of Chinese poetry or German landscape painting or country-western songs. Imagined interactions, or interaction with imagined others, is closely related to interacting. Such interactions shape us and transform our knowledge, though less than real direct interactions do.

It should be obvious that actual farming, fishing, and hiking practices, to say nothing of house-building, mining, logging, and everything else we do in the wide world, inevitably shape beliefs about nature. Yet, a great deal of writing on such matters ignores practice. Such worthy and valuable books as Peter Coates's *Nature* (1998) or Bron Taylor's *Dark Green Religion* (2009) are "histories of ideas"; they chronicle what people have thought and said about nature, sometimes with scarcely a word about what people were doing at the same time. Histories of ideas are valuable, but we need histories of practice, too.

Writers often blame abstractions such as "capitalism" for our problems. But capitalism is not a thing. It is an analytic abstraction. It once had a meaning: a social formation in which big businessmen (note the gender) own more or less everything, including the politicians, and set ideologies based on self-interest. This in its simple form no longer exists in the modern world. When social scientists speak of "capitalism," they now generally refer to a world dominated by firms that are maximizing profit, production, or market share. These are often private, often public (especially the state corporations of China), and often a mix. These last include parastatal firms, such as Mexico's oil company, Pemex, and might also be taken to include oil companies that are highly subsidized by government and correspondingly powerful in political circles, such as Exxon-Mobil and the Koch brothers in the United States. Some who speak of "capitalism" mean a vast, vague, undefined complex of practices and attitudes, sometimes even including communism. Marx is presumably turning in his grave. There is a deeper problem with such usages: the roots of our antinature attitudes go thousands of years back before capitalism existed.

In the present book, I consider a number of collective representations of nature (however defined), the human-created rural environment, and the cosmos as a natural or religious entity. The coverage is uneven, depending on the level I am contemplating and on the materials available. I deal at broad and general levels with Australia and Southeast Asia. I deal with two traditional societies I know well: Chinese and Yucatec Maya. For these I provide some idea of how they conceptualize the environment, how they conceptualize learning and knowledge, and how they manage their natural resources. I deal in a quite different way with early medieval Ireland. That world is known to us almost exclusively from writings of the period, but they provide such a unique and astonishing record of knowledge and love for their world of plants and animals that I could not ignore them; however, the chapter differs from others in being based almost entirely on literary records (with some backup from archaeology).

At a more ambitious scale ("fools rush in where angels fear to tread"), I deal with the Western world, which has done far more damage, but has also done much to save and conserve. The West—here is its broadest sense, from ancient Mesopotamia to modern Europe and America—has a split personality: loving "nature" and being aware of its value, while also devastating it through development that was not only destructive but often not even economic.

BROAD WORLDVIEWS

The Western world's tendency to oppose "people" to "nature," as in "jobs vs. owls" and "progress vs. wilderness," is of imperial Roman ancestry and also has ancient Mesopotamian antecedents. It has gone through the centuries without much feedback from reality. Conversely, the "people-in-nature" view typical of Native Americans is quite similar over thousands of miles and, apparently, thousands of years. These are aspects of long-lived worldviews.

There are different levels of worldview (Kearney 1984), or, as some call it, cosmovision (Lenkersdorf 1999). A worldview is a broad, unifying vision of how the cosmos is put together and how we should interact with it. As such, it underlies a good deal of religion, but lacks the specific ritual and ceremonial prescriptions; it also underlies ordinary life, providing the general plans.

Some have used "worldview" to refer to a much more tightly structured system. Rane Willerslev (2007:156) has properly critiqued such a "consistent" culture-environment worldview implying "some kind of underlying pattern or structure" like grammar. I use the word in its usual sense, for the vague, general clusters of ideas that are *not* tightly structured by culture or society. Some academics dismiss anything that does not look formal, but Willerslev points out that the rest of humanity does not do that. We need terms for these vague ideas, just as weather experts need words for *fog* and *mist*.

Anthropologists, and others, have generally equated "culture" with language, or seen language as a core of culture: French culture, Navaho culture, Dogon culture. This is useful as a kind of shorthand idea, but not very enlightening. Consider the spread of the English and Chinese languages as opposed to Navaho or Hopi. Clearly, any statements we make about Chinese culture are going to be at a far more general level than what we might say about the traditional Hopi.

This leads to the important observation that generalizations about culture can be made at all sorts of levels, from worldwide to city block. I discuss the entirety of the Western world over 5,000 years at one level. At a very different level indeed, I talk about the practice of the Yucatec Maya of west-central Quintana Roo, a very small and tightly bounded world. Obviously these are comparable only to a limited degree, but we can find useful information about worldviews at all levels.

The stability of worldview elements across time—the association of the "people vs. nature" view with Europe and European settlers, for instance—exists because of cultural lock-ins rather than because of a lack of new ideas or a lack of human capacity for change. Beliefs about managing the environment take on a life of their own, because people lock themselves into particular strategies.

An example of such a "lock-in" is the rise of bread. If one has learned to live on baked yeast-raised bread, one develops a whole network of industries based on it, from yeast production to deli sandwich preparation. Within the yeast-raised-bread culture area (basically the Near East and Europe, plus Europe's ex-colonies), every group has its own bread traditions. Some traditions, like the traditional European Easter bread, have spread over dozens of cultures (Anderson 2005a). Others, like the bagel, were very local until they suddenly went global in recent decades. Others, like the Zuni Indian sourdough bread (inspired by Hispanic baking but now distinctive), remain confined to one tiny cultural area and are dying out even there. Still others are restricted to one family with a "secret recipe." Meanwhile, development, always path-dependent, becomes increasingly focused on producing more and better wheat, rather than diversifying to other starch crops.

Religious ideas spread with the baking techniques. Communion is the most obvious, but not the only, example. For most bread-eating cultures, every crumb of bread is God's gift. In many countries, one cannot step on a crumb. In my travels, from Finland to the Middle East and Spain, I have found that crumbs are carefully picked up and either burned or fed to poultry or wild birds. Often the children are given this task, to teach them proper behavior toward bread.

Such a lock-in, especially at the very high levels, is very difficult to change. The classic European belief that it is necessary to destroy nature utterly in order to have a "developed" society is an example of a worldview component. This idea is widespread and ancient, but variable. It ranges from the extreme attitudes of modern Brazil or Iowa, or the cotton fields of west-central California, where not a single living thing is tolerated on the land except one or two cultivated crops, to the classic mixed small farming of Italy and France, where a wide range of crops and wild plants and animals are all used. Even within my homeland of

California, there is a range. The monocropped cotton fields of Tulare County are utterly lifeless, without a bird or insect stirring and without a single plant other than cotton. Conversely, the East Sierra ranches are fairly wild and natural, with cattle worked into an essentially wild ecosystem that has to be in good shape to support them (Hedrick 2007). Still a third option is the small Italian mixed farm, introduced by immigrants to the North Coast ranges.

Worldviews are the broad, general equivalent of the narrower and more specific *cultural models* (Hedrick 2007)—general plans, learned from the wider society, for managing oneself and the world. A cultural model can be powerfully determinative of action, or can be merely a suggested alternative. The Western world has several types of cultural models for farming, ranging from the vast monocrop plantation and the small mixed farm to the home garden, the organic farm, and the demonstration farm. There are even models for small monocrop farms and large mixed plantations.

This diversity of styles is produced by a complex interaction of ecology, economics, and political power. The vast monocrop fields of the southwest Central Valley depend on enormous subsidies; they are not economic or competitive in themselves. The ranches also draw on some degree of subsidy, but less than the cotton and grain fields receive. Small mixed farming has to compete largely on its own, with little or no subsidization. The huge subsidies to ecologically devastating monocrop cultivation are the result of political power, which has gone to big farmers ever since the ancient Greeks and Romans. Large-scale landlords have always had political power in the Western world, and the politically powerful have often banked their power in land and become large landlords; it is a two-way street. Uneconomic grand-scale farming and landlordism thus prevails very widely in the world.

China, however, went the opposite way. Huge estates, owned by the powerful and worked by slaves, were characteristic of early China. They declined steadily over time, and for the last several centuries of empire, China was a land of small farms. The "landlords" denounced by Mao in the mid-twentieth century owned as little as two acres. There were many larger holdings than that, but almost nothing comparable to the thousands of acres so typical of farms in California and Brazil (among other places). The reason is well known, having been made explicit by generations of rulers: the imperial court found it expedient to join with small farmers to limit and break the power of the great families. From the very beginning of the Chinese empire, in the third century BC, this policy was stated, and became overwhelmingly dominant as policy over the last 500 years of empire. The Qing Dynasty in particular, being non-Chinese in origin and therefore hated by nationalists, did everything possible to break the power of ethnically Chinese families. Because land was always the long-term basis of power, this meant, first of all, breaking up large landholdings (see Mote 1999).

So the working principles of a society are based on tradition, but not on blindly followed tradition. Tradition, in this area at least, operates not so much by constraining minds as by constraining economic options. So many previous choices have been made on the basis of tradition that the path is smooth, well-greased, and well-lighted. A new path would have to be hacked out of the thorn brush.

The usual cause of change, which does occur and can occur quite fast, is immediate economic advantage. However, "globalization" has shown that entrenched traditions can change fast simply for reasons of status emulation. American clothes, drinks, fast foods, music, films, and TV shows have swept East Asia within my lifetime, although they are neither traditional nor economically advantageous. Conversely, Chinese and Thai food has swept the United States, for reasons of taste rather than economics. Earlier, tomatoes, potatoes, and maize became staples in Europe and China. Bringing conservation to the world could be done quickly and easily—if conservation had status comparable to Hollywood movies!

THE ROLE OF RELIGION

Most traditional cultures explain a great deal of perfectly sensible, empirical knowledge by recourse to gods. In this case, that knowledge, however pragmatic and realistic, gets called "religion" by outside interpreters. Scientists then dismiss it because it is "supernatural." Religious scholars look at "belief" without seeing the thoroughly empirical side. Scholars of literature and the arts focus on style and history, neglecting real-world effects.

Bronislaw Malinowski's minor anthropological classic, *Magic, Science and Religion* (1948), based on his field work in the Trobriand Islands off New Guinea, provides a place to start. Malinowski had a simple, straightforward take on the distinctions. Science was empirical and evidence-based. Religion was emotional and social involvement with supernatural, counter-evidential beings and forces. Magic was cut-and-dried, manipulative involvement with those supernaturals. Like religion, it involved the unseen, but like science, it was intended to be instrumental rather than worshipful.

Malinowski knew that separate categories of "magic," "science" and "religion" did not exist in traditional knowledge systems. He was quite aware that he was projecting a twentieth-century European distinction onto systems that, themselves, did not really have anything like it. Thus, being no fool, he questioned and qualified the distinction between magic, science, and religion—*problematized* it, in Foucaultian terms. However, he did not really reject it. He was at some pains to show that the people he was still calling "savages" had just as solid, experiential, and pragmatic a knowledge of the world as any "civilized" folk. He was attacking the view (he cited it to Lévy-Bruhl but pointed out that the view was widespread) that traditional people live in a "prelogical" world of mysticism, blind belief, and animal-like intuition.

He said nothing about the civilized folk, but one assumes he was, as usual, sideswiping them via the Trobriands. He never forgot his self-imposed mission to confront his elite European readers with an ironic reflection of themselves. One can also assume that, like many early-twentieth-century social scientists, he expected religion to wither away in the near future.

Malinowski was guilty of many outrageous statements, such as "The road from the wilderness to the savage's belly and consequently to his mind is very short, and for him the world is an indiscriminate background against which there stand out the useful, primarily the edible, species of animals or plants" (p. 44). This was retrograde even at the time; no Boasian would have been caught dead writing such a line. But, aside from such throwaway lines, Malinowski was on the side of the angels in this book. He was hardly the first to say that traditional people had a wealth of solid empirical knowledge and high-flown spiritual experience—anthropologists from Lewis Henry Morgan onward had said that—but he was one of the more influential people saying it.

Religion is not maintained by mere exhortation. It is maintained, as Emile Durkheim (1995) showed, through emotionally compelling symbols, rituals, ceremonies, communions, and services. It involves a whole knowledge system.

We may not be able to go back to a fundamentally religious world, and it would have its own costs if we did. The Abrahamic religions suffer from privileging humanity too much, at the expense of nature. This is not necessary, and indeed is not really part of the Abrahamic tradition. However, it has become all too general a belief.

Religion is not the only way of constructing concern for nature. Arts, language and folktale, secular ceremonies, and even foodways can serve the same purpose of constructing community and motivating people to follow moral rules. Ordinary secular pleasure and aesthetic enjoyment dominate today, and were common in traditional cultures. Modern civil society has successfully taken over this role in many realms, but has failed in regard to conservation. We rely today either on traditional moralities or on extensions of civil society by groups like the Audubon Society and the Sierra Club.

Religions conserve environments to the extent that the religions construct actual love and respect for nature as an integral core part of belief. This usually involves ideals of people-in-nature, harmony with the world, and simplicity, as in contemplative Buddhism and Daoism as well as traditional Celtic Christianity and the teachings of St. Francis. People must not only love the world but must rest lightly on it. Simplicity is not only a matter of common sense or of spiritual discipline; it is a matter of saving one's resources for the most important things that life and the world afford.

A problem for environmental religion is extreme otherworldliness that teaches the faithful to turn away from this world and give it no concern. Religious persons often feel a need to turn away from social games, status-jockeying, and competition over wealth. Some religious leaders advise turning away from *all* worldly things, including concern for human and environmental health and welfare. However, most religions have seen that curing the sick, feeding the hungry, and saving the environment are worthy goals, however evil the social order may be.

Religion, being the collective representation of the community, represents and constructs these beliefs and attitudes. Religion invariably constructs a community far bigger and broader than the human one. It gives us gods, saints, spirits, ghosts, and devils. Monotheism does not eliminate these; it merely subordinates them to the high god. (The few theologically educated monotheists that do not believe in these lesser beings are highly exceptional.) In many religions, including many folk forms of the "monotheistic" ones, the communion of souls includes trees, mountains, waters, fish, and other natural kinds, as well as supernatural beings.

As guardian of morality, religion becomes the means of enforcing environmental regulation. Polynesian societies taboo endangered resources (Firth 1959). They may also think of themselves as related to all nature: "The whole cosmos of the Maori unfolds itself as a gigantic 'kin,' in which heaven and earth are first parents of all being and things, such as the sea, the sand on the beach, the wood, the birds, and man. Apparently he does not feel quite comfortable if he cannot—preferably in much detail—give an account of his kinship whether to the fish of the sea or to a traveller who is invited to enter as a guest" (Lévi-Strauss 1964:30, citing Prytz Johansen).

The congregation is not only people, but all the organisms in the relevant part of the world. Nonhumans are "other-than-human persons," in the classic anthropological phrase. This turns on the definition of "person." The word *person* is notoriously vague and polysemous. Nonhumans are not persons in the sense of being rational creatures with whom one can have a conversation. They can be thought to be similar to babies or comatose humans (as animal-rights morality often advocates). Or they can simply be "person" in the sense of beings that are owed respect and have a will, agency, and abilities of their own, as Native American teachings hold. One may consider in this context the difference between "dehumanizing" and "depersonalizing." The former generally means the sort of insult that accompanies bias, hatred, and genocide; people are "rats, cockroaches," and the like. They are only metaphorically dehumanized; they are tortured and brutalized with full attention to their human vulnerabilities (Anderson and Anderson 2012). One does not subject actual cockroaches to fiendish psychological torture. The latter refers to treating humans as still human but as nonpersons: ostracized, cut off, ignored, treated as part of the furniture or wallpaper. This is commonly done to the world's poor (Sen 1992, 2009).

Religion depends not just on socializing but on work and livelihood. Hunters worship the spirits or guardians of the game, farmers pray for fertility of fields and flocks, craftsmen and scientists worship the Great Clockmaker, business-people pray to a God who counts up and balances their virtues and sins. Any use of religion in conservation must take account of this, constructing the whole nonhuman community (as St. Francis did within Christianity).

This begs the question of what religion is (see Atran 2002; and still valuable are Radin 1957b, 1957a). For our purposes here, we will define it as the social institution devoted to constructing and representing community, through defining it or aspects of it as sacred. Religion usually deals with unseen but transcendently important powers, through prayer, ritual, and ceremony rather than manipulation, law, or force. The key term in this definition is not *unseen powers* but *social*. Religion is a social institution. (A purely individual "religion" would be individual spiritualism, not religion.)

Emile Durkheim, in his work on religion (Durkheim 1995/1912), elaborated the concept of religion as collective representation of community. The religious order divinizes the social order. The Greek gods had roles similar to ordinary human roles (mother, blacksmith, warrior, and so on) and acted like willful humans. The Chinese heaven is organized like imperial China, with the Jade Emperor presiding over a court in which various spiritual beings—including humans who earned divine status—act the parts of ministers, local governors, and so on. For the Northwest Coast Native peoples, whose society includes nonhuman persons, the supernatural world is populated with mythic bears, eagles, wolves, and imaginary animal powers like the Thunderbird. Christianity, which took form in the Roman Empire, has a single Divine Being, as Rome had a divine emperor. This equation was clearly made by the Christian emperors. Under this divine king are apostles, saints, souls of the dead, and other super-natural citizens.

The question of how religion constructs and motivates good environmental management has now been rather thoroughly investigated (Anderson 1996; Berkes 2008; Callicott 1994; Hunn 1990; Kinsley 1995; Radin 1957a, 1957b; Sponsel 2012). Roy Rappaport did much of the foundational work, theorizing religion in two major works: *Pigs for the Ancestors* (orig. 1967, 2d ed. 1984) and *Ritual and Religion in the Making of Humanity* (1999). The greatest and most definitive effort is the series of volumes resulting from conferences organized at Harvard Divinity School by the intrepid husband-wife team of Mary Evelyn Tucker and John Grim. These produced huge volumes on all the religious tradi-tions: indigenous and local ones (Tucker and Grim 1994), Christianity (Hessel and Reuther 2000), Judaism (Tirosh-Samuelson 2002), Islam (Foltz et al. 2003),

Jainism (Chapple 2002), Daoism (Girardot et al. 2001), Confucianism (Tucker and Berthrong 1998), Buddhism (Tucker and Williams 1997), and a volume on animals in religion worldwide (Waldau and Patton 2007). Zoroastrianism has not yet received a volume, but fortunately an earlier work completely fills the gap: Mary Boyce's great work *Zoroastrians* (1979). The *Journal for the Study of Religion, Nature and Culture* continues this effort.

The conclusion of these learned scholars is that every religious tradition on earth, save those of a few tiny isolated groups that have virtually no impact on their environments, enjoins some form of good environmental management. Often, this stops at the point of advising people to keep up the irrigation system, not kill too many game animals or cut too many trees, and in general "leave some for others." However, in most religions, it extends farther, often enjoining respect for all living beings—including rocks and mountains, for those many societies that believe these are living or have living spirits within them.

Trees are sacred, revered, or respected in a great many religious traditions (Cook 1974). India's well-known tree-hugging movement was religiously motivated (Agrawal 2005a, 2005b; Guha 1990; Haberman 2013; Rangan 2000). An odd and revealing proof that all humans are psychological kin is the custom of building small stacks of stones at the crests of high mountain passes. These are offerings or prayers to the mountain spirits. My wife or I have personally encountered this belief in action among indigenous and local people in Europe, Mongolia, Tibet, Peru, Hawaii, and the Northwest Coast of North America.

It is a short step from seeing that the powers of nature must be respected and venerated to seeing that all beings are under their protection and deserve ours, too. Various forms of the latter belief exist widely and are basic to Buddhism, Jainism, and Hinduism. A sense of unity with the wider cosmos, at least in the sense that "we're all in this together," is basic to these and to Daoism, mystical Islam (Sufism), and at least some interpretations of Judaism (Tirosh-Samuelson 2002). Judaism and Christianity are caught in the endless tension between Genesis 1, in which God gives humans "dominion" over the earth, and Genesis 2, in which stewardship is the ideal and the earth remains the Lord's.

Western Christianity's teacher of creation care, St. Francis of Assisi, was probably influenced by Arabic Aristotelianism—many of his contemporaries certainly were. (The myth of St. Francis as an impoverished man of the humble people is false. He was a highly educated son of a rich family, and Assisi was a major center of trade and education. He was thoroughly in touch with the scholarly currents of his time.) Christianity since his time has displayed a complex back-and-forth pattern formed by neo-Platonist world-haters, and other, less purist currents. This affects the endless debate over dominion vs. stewardship.

With the single exception of highly dualist sects of Christianity (see Chapter 8), no religion or religious tradition enjoins actual destruction of nature or of the environment. However, many strains of religion have been put to service in the last few centuries as excuses for raping and pillaging landscapes and peoples.

Religious visionaries, poets, and sages worldwide have recognized that we not only are totally participant in nature—there is no "people"-"nature" separation—but that the unity is part of a vast order that one can contemplate with reverence. Traditionally, many mystics, especially in eastern Asia, lived to achieve full clear sight of this transcendent order, and to merge themselves into it. The Chinese concept of the Dao is the most explicit and culturally elaborated form of this idea. It occurs also in Eastern forms of Buddhism (where Daoism was an influence) and other Asian religions. It was also dominant in early Celtic religion and in the *tjukurrpa* and similar concepts from small-scale societies. Modern poets and divines have substantially lost this vision of the world, but it reappears in some modern Celtic poets who are aware of their heritage, such as Edward Thomas and Robinson Jeffers.

THE ROLE OF THE ARTS

"Arts" are things people do or make to communicate emotions, moods, or aesthetic feelings. These last are hard to define because they have not been studied to any great degree by scientific psychology. I will have to appeal to readers' intuition to know what words like *beauty* and *form* mean. Arts include music, visual arts, styled discourse from poetry to folk turns of phrase, dance, food, and even things like putting extra effort into a stone tool or a gift-wrap just to make it attractive. Stone tools considerably more beautiful than they "needed to be" (according to archaeologists who have experimented with tools and reconstructions) appear tens or hundreds of thousands of years ago in the human record. Given the nature of this book, I will be concerned largely with culturally recognized traditional art forms. I reserve the right to compare these with modern arts. (I provide a back-up discussion of the "arts" on my website *www. krazykioti.com,* posting "Anthropology and the Arts," designed to accompany the present book).

Visual arts provide the clearest and simplest cases of representing nature. They have carried out this task as far back as we can trace them. For at least 50,000 years in Australia and well over 30,000 in Europe, and for probably as long or longer in Asia and Africa (where only somewhat younger paintings survive), humans have drawn animals on cave and rock shelter walls.

The human fondness for beauty and for human creation of beautiful designs and objects, remains poorly studied. Art experts today tend to agree that "beauty is in the eye of the beholder," if even there, and that items are defined as "art" and "beautiful" by culture, not by innate human tendency. A "wonderfully bloody seminar" (Kemp 2009) between neuroscientists interested in visual perception and art historians interested in social construction broke down because the two groups could not agree on even the beginning of a topic.

In fact, humans everywhere delight in geometric patterns, bright colors arranged in interesting ways, and certain specific forms. Most obvious, and totally predictable to any Darwinian, is the universal appeal of healthy young members of the opposite sex (though some, less predictably, prefer the same sex). Pictures thereof cause reactions in the brain. However, it is also true that "beautifully" done geometric patterns cause mental reactions (Kemp 2009). Landscapes and animals evidently evoke yet different responses.

In fact, although the art historians are obviously correct about complicated and highly culture-bound art, there are universal biological primes to human appreciation of visual stimuli. The universal appeal of geometric patterns has been addressed by E. H. Gombrich (1979), who points out that we must have evolved to look for them: pattern sense allows you to tell the fruit from the foliage, the nest from the sticks, the antelope from the brush, the snake from the grass. All animals have "search images" of their prey and of their preferred habitat. Primates are incredibly good at spotting food items in the vast, varied, visually complex forests they inhabit. For the same reason, motion is always spotted immediately, by humans as by all vertebrates. Beautifully patterned motion (dance, ritual) naturally appeals. Add these and other considerations together, and one sees why animals were the first and most common things portrayed in realistic art.

Gordon Orians and Judith Heerwagen (1992) hypothesized that humans would find most beautiful the type of landscape in which humans arose, which they assumed to be the savannah country of eastern Africa. Indeed, as they point out, gardens, parks, temple grounds, and landscape paintings everywhere tend toward the same thing: a wide expanse of grass or earth, scattered tall trees, and patches of shrubbery and flowers here and there. Solid forest is rarely found in planned parks (except in Japan), and bare ground, though commoner, is not predominant.

One very odd criticism of this finding was that it predicted that people would like tacky art—"Bayswater Road art," as one critic, Charles Jencks (2000), put it. Bayswater Road is apparently a place in England where Sunday painters show off their stuff. This is the only time I have seen snobbism used as a scientific argument. Jencks seems to think that people would instinctively like Great Art. In fact, one would actually *expect* that lowest-common-denominator art would be the most revealing about innate humanity. The popularity of highly sexualized portrayals of nudes confirms this expectation.

However, anthropologists have found that traditional people everywhere love their familiar landscape. Inuit love the featureless snow and ice of the Arctic. Plains Indians loved the vast short-grass lands that seemed utterly barren desert to white settlers. African forest dwellers love the dark rainforest.

Some perspective on this came to me when I traveled through the parts of East Africa where humans apparently evolved. The fact is that there is an amazing variety of landscapes, often with an easy day's walk. I had a strong sense of homecoming when I dropped off the Rift Valley rim into Lake Manyara National Park in Tanzania. It includes near-desert plains, open savannahs, a huge lake, rivers, swamps, marshes, forests, dry woodlands, brushlands, and just about anything else you can imagine—all in a few square miles! Even Arctic landscapes were not far off, on Mt. Kilimanjaro. If we humans evolved to appreciate a particular landscape, it must be a mixed one. No wonder we can learn to like anything.

European cave art is deservedly famous; no clearly better animal art has appeared since. In spite of the jokes about kids doodling on the walls, these were clearly ceremonial and ritual paintings. Contra the cartoons, these paintings are not just in well-lighted, shallow living caves (Clottes 2008). They are far down in extremely dark and dangerous caves deep below the earth. No one would go there for any but the most serious reasons. The paintings are found in vast numbers on particular walls, often juxtaposed with handprints and other personal signs. Human-animal fusion figures (probably shamans) and geometric designs imply some sort of magic. The most economical explanation is that this was hunting magic, but there is certainly much more to it than that, and countless people have theorized that sexuality, fertility, kinship, exchange, and every other favorite anthropological theme is represented.

In Australia, hunting-gathering cultures were still strong in the twentieth century, and people still paint on rock walls. Painting not only shows and teaches the stories; it actually invokes the spirits and brings them here. Often, a particular painting is said to be the supernatural being itself; it finished its active role by transforming itself into a painting for the future. Paintings done by ordinary human hands bring at least some of this transcendent reality onto the rock. Repainting of ancient designs is still done, with due ceremony. The Australian Aboriginals have apparently always created sacred maps—abstract designs that show landscapes and routes. This tradition developed into several full-blown landscape art styles, ranging from realistic to highly abstract, in the twentieth century. Similar route diagrams in art are found among many New World indigenous peoples.

All truly ancient art, and almost all hunter-gatherer art everywhere, shows only animals, humans, supernatural beings, and geometric figures. The first plants in art (as far as I can find) show up well after the dawn of agriculture. Some of the earliest plant pictures occur at Çatal Hüyük in Turkey around 6000 BCE. They become common in the Near East by historic times. Good representations of botanically identifiable plants do not seem to appear until the age of early states.

Actual landscapes—vistas of hills or mountains, or of vegetation of some sort—do not appear anywhere until well into historic times. Ancient Egyptian landscape art apparently came first, with beautiful scenes of marshes and riverscapes. Often these are hunting pictures, showing the pharaoh or great lords hunting waterfowl and the like.

Many excellent garden murals adorn Pompeii, sadly faded now, because no one has done much to conserve them. Spectacular mosaics survive from many Roman sites, but tend to show animals, including sea animals. Landscapes per se are minor components of this art. I have visited many of these sites and am struck by the brilliance and quantity of art even in tiny, isolated country towns in the wilds of North Africa.

Chinese landscapes begin with sculptured and painted mountains, not many centuries BCE, long after highly developed animal and human representation was common. Presumably landscape art developed thereafter into the great art we know today, but all early work is lost except for tomb paintings and minor carvings. The earliest great landscape paintings we have are known only from copies, but show that landscape art reached a pinnacle by the 700s CE. In the New World, beautiful floral murals adorn Teotihuacan, and sacred mountains, trees, and maize plants were portrayed more than 2000 years ago in Maya cities.

Almost every culture uses art to display its religious and cosmological ideas, including beliefs about nature and the world. Most hunting-gathering societies are intensely involved with the animals around them—not just hunted game, but all moving life. They may represent these accurately, as many European cave artists did, or may represent them in an extremely stylized form, as is done on the Northwest Coast of North America. In the latter case, the animals are represented as spirit beings and as relatives of human groups. Thus they are shown in hieratic modes, and displayed so as to call up the most powerful aesthetic feelings in the viewer. Such impact shows that the sculpture or painting actually has spirit power. The degree of intensity of aesthetic feeling measures the spiritual power of the sculpture or painting and thus the skill and spiritual depth of the carver or painter. This belief is still very much alive today among the countless Native American artists of the region.

Architecture also expresses attitudes toward the land. Contemporary housing in the Western world is generally either mass-produced after the ground is leveled by huge machines, or is made to be as huge, visible, and unrelated to the landscape as possible. The "McMansions" of the modern world are in-your-face declarations of wealth, power, and indifference to environment. This attitude has eclipsed an earlier trend in American housing, a trend that fitted houses and buildings into their environments (exemplified by Frank Lloyd Wright's work). Other cultures almost always follow that strategy, if for no other reason than that it is the simplest and most economical way to go. (American indifference to environment seems economical only because heavily subsidized; Anderson 2010.) Traditional architecture, although lacking something in comfort by modern standards, is generally both beautiful and functional. Several excellent, beautifully illustrated books on this exist (Moholy-Nagy 1957; Nabokov and Easton 1989; Oliver 1987; Rudofsky 1965).

Music and dance, because of the constraints of the media, are farther from nature. Sacred dances representing the motions of totemic animals and other power beings are almost universal among hunter-gatherer peoples and not uncommon among settled ones. They grade into purely recreational displays, like the imitations of courting grouse among Plains Indians or courting horned owls among Maya children. Music encodes songs, chants, and hymns about nature, but here the message is the words. The romantic music of Europe that seeks to portray nature in sound is best passed over in silence (double meaning fully intended). Music, however, communicates emotionality fairly directly, and thus is involved in most ceremonies worldwide (the deep evolutionary roots of music are only now being explored; see, e.g., Mithen 2007).

Food and foodways are not usually considered with the other arts, but cooking is an art in most cultures, though often a simple one. Food is the most direct way we incorporate nature into our bodies. It falls outside the present work, if only because it is too vast and specialized a topic to consider here, and I have already discussed it elsewhere (Anderson 2005a). Suffice it to say that foods naturally and necessarily tie us to the land, and express our feelings about it. Thus chefs like Alice Waters and ethnobiologists like Gary Nabhan (2008; Nabhan and Madison 2008) have worked together to encourage environment-friendly eating. Food writers are adopting this view today. Earlier cultures had no choice but to "eat local." I do not advocate locavory, but I do advocate considering food from moral and ecological standpoints.

"SCIENCE" AND "KNOWLEDGE"

The separation of cognition and emotion in Western thought has had an unfortunate and probably unintended effect: trivializing both to some extent. Purely cognitive knowledge seems dry as dust to many, if not most, of the public. Emotion has been linked to irrational, flighty, irresponsible thought and action; calling someone "highly emotional" or calling something "an emotional reaction" are not intended as compliments. By contrast, traditional societies never seem to separate these realms strongly. The separation—"Descartes' error," psychologist Antonio Damasio calls it (Damasio 1994)—was old before Descartes. It had its uses, but we are too constrained by it now.

Our academic separation of science and religion, cognition and emotion, has a great deal of value in our world of laws and law courts. The Native Americans' integration of them has a great deal of value in their traditional world of fields, forests, and waters. Our separation has its virtues, analytic and otherwise. It was certainly not a mere function of patriarchy or autocracy, as certain academics argue. But we need to qualify it now. Native American interests were rarely considered in American law courts in colonial times, and all too often are neglected even now (see Capuder 2013), but we now need it for survival.

Other cultures, worldwide, put together knowledge and knowledges in ways very different from those familiar to the modern academy. We "moderns" (and not just in the West) oppose religion to science, fact to myth, and rationality to emotion. Other peoples of the world, including Europeans of earlier centuries, integrated forms of knowledge, representation, and experience, rather than opposing them. The Euro-American classifications of knowledge into "science," "religion," "art," "ethics," and so on, and into "rational" as opposed to "emotional," have a long and complex history. Even in Euro-American thought, there are other ways of breaking up the "knowledge" field. These include the psychologists' divisions of thought into cognition, emotion, and conation (will), or alternatively into "ABC"—affect, biology, cognition. There are also the divisions of learning into disciplines, starting from Aristotle's classic division into ethics, politics, physics, metaphysics, and so on.

Simply because I am writing in English, I use terms like *science, religion, art,* and *ethics* without scare quotes and in their ordinary current-English senses. This is *not* because I privilege such meanings. As Arturo Escobar says, "[A]n ensemble of Western, modern cultural forces ... has unceasingly exerted its influence—often its dominance—over most world regions. These forces continue to operate through the ever-changing interaction of forms of European thought and culture, taken to be universally valid, with the frequently subordinated knowledges and cultural practices of many non-European groups throughout the world" (Escobar 2008:3). My mission is to do the opposite: to rehabilitate those other ways of knowing. However, writing in English, one cannot really avoid English-language terms.

Writers on Native American thought, such as Paul Nadasdy (2004), sometimes hold that not only *science* but even the term *knowledge* is too tightly tied to narrow Western rationalism. They may have a point, but both terms have usually been used more widely in European history. Nadasdy and many others essentialize "the West" and its "rationalism," and forget that Europeans have talked about mystical knowledge, spiritual knowledge, and esoteric knowledge for centuries, and that mystical alchemy was a science once.

The contrast of religion and science deserves more attention (Anderson 2000, 2011b, and website posting "Science and Ethnoscience," www.krazykioti. com; Gonzalez 2001; Hunn 2008). I have spent a good deal of my life with people who simply have no concept of "religion" in our sense. They see the cosmos holistically; everything they do has some spiritual and some practical component, and they do not split religion off from other realms of life. They work to integrate religion, reason, emotion, art, and ethics just as hard as Euro-American academics work to separate those five realms. Religion everywhere combines personal growth and improvement with community life, an important point to keep in mind.

The ancient Romans had *scientia* ("knowledge"), but no "scientists," only "philosophers." Institutionalized science arose gradually in the seventeenth and eighteenth centuries. It was carried out by people called savants or sci-ents. Later they were *scientists,* a term coined by William Whewell in the early nineteenth century. Modern science, understood as formal activity focused on labs, big grants, and formal procedures, is even newer. Yet, it is reasonable to speak of Maya botany or Chinese fishermen's ichthyology as sciences; they are highly accurate, pragmatic, systematized bodies of expert knowledge based on cumulative experience of real things and induction from that knowledge to hypothesized causal variables. Many of the causal variables seem "wrong" to us today, but that does not make them any less scientific than phlogiston, aether, and the four humors that were within European science a couple of centuries ago.

The Western world did not oppose *science* and *religion* until quite recently. Today the former term is used for forward-looking knowledge: knowledge based on current observation and experiment, and intended to be supplemented or replaced as soon as possible. Religion is the opposite: the knowledge that is basically traditional, or even eternal. It is a backward-looking field. Yet, religion does change, and science does have its unchanging foundations (think of Euclidean geometry). Science has its beliefs and values, and religion does not lack observation and rational speculation.

Modern international science has both an enormous pressure to find *new* knowledge, and an enormously complex and effective system for checking that knowledge—replicating it or proving it wrong or inadequate. Traditional science had no formalized systems for these things, and thus did them more slowly, but it both expanded and checked facts. The results are thus valuable.

Negative judgments of traditional science are usually based on picking out the things that seem silliest to a modern Westerner, such as the idea that earthquakes are caused by a giant animal shaking himself below ground. Yet, such ideas are inferred causal mechanisms, similar to the above-mentioned phlogiston and aether. In *any* science, it is these inferences that are most apt to be wrong and to be discarded over time. Many of Western science's inferred causal ideas, from string theory to the evils of saturated fats, are under attack today. This does not vitiate the accurate data assembled by modern science. Neither does the inferred underground animal's unreality vitiate the accuracy of traditional observations of where earthquakes occurred. It so happens that the underground animal, from China to Puget Sound, always shook himself in places where we now trace earthquake faults. These faults we now see as usually due to continental drift—an inferred cause that is now proven, but was ridiculed by almost all scientists in my college days.

Other cultures often recognize epistemological differences in ways that would surprise a modern American scientist. Many Californian and other Indigenous languages, for instance, have a grammatical rule that forces speakers to mark whether they have actually seen or experienced an event (using "evidential" particles), or whether they only heard about it, or whether they learned it from myth. Clearly, this has close parallels with science as we know it. But, if this grammatical rule existed in English, it would have some surprising effects. Most of us would have to admit that our knowledge of science is largely gleaned from books and lectures—we have "heard about it," not seen it—especially when the science in question involves things like black holes and quarks. And we would have to acknowledge that our knowledge of economists' abstractions like the "free market" and "decision with perfect information" are purely mythological. We never encounter them or hear of them in the real world. Ghosts are more real, in that many people claim to have actually seen ghosts.

CULTURE AND SOCIETY

"Culture" refers herein to the terms, ideas, and behaviors that people learn from their wider social groups. Throughout my career, I have focused on individuals, local subcultures, and differences within cultures. More than most anthropologists, I emphatically reject the "idealist" and "essentialist" notions of culture. Culture is not a uniform thing telepathically transmitted into the brains of its bearers. It is a collection of hopefully useful information, learned through interaction with the real world, and picked up by individuals for their own purposes. Some anthropologists have dropped the term, because it is so misused in popular speech, implying a mental straitjacket. I sympathize, but cannot manage without it. As with *science,* I would rather use the term broadly than reject it because others use it narrowly.

One delusion to dispose of immediately is the idea that cultures or civilizations are closed, airtight cells. Quite the reverse; they are actually analytic abstractions. They exist on the ground only as broad, vague, changeable complexes of more or less shared ideas, beliefs, and practices. Because cultural groupings contrast at many levels, there cannot be the closed, steel-walled "cultures" of "cultural studies" and "multiculturalism," or the tightly bounded "civilizations" of Samuel Huntington (1996). This bizarre idea of culture derives ultimately from German nationalist idealism; bluntly, it is a racist and fascist concept. Cultures are claimed to be so totally separate that they can "hybridize," like separate species of animals—presumably producing sterile and deformed offspring. A corollary is that borrowing from other "cultures" (so defined) is evil—it is impure, it is thievery, it is colonialist. The people who maintain this go right on eating wheat, corn, rice, and potatoes—each from a different part of the world—and otherwise living lifestyles that harmoniously blend all the major cultural traditions of the world.

The lack of hermetically sealed "cultures" means that people are not uniform. One can generalize only insofar as people do agree very broadly about cultural rules. All English speakers everywhere know that "-s" is the normal pluralizing suffix, and that there are a few exceptions ending in "-en" or other forms. All Chinese speakers everywhere know that Chinese words do not change in the plural except for a few exceptions like personal pronouns. Here, we can safely generalize. At the other extreme are the preposterous stereotypes we all know so well: all Irishmen fight, all "Americans" are "individualist," all "Muslims" are "fanatics," and the "clash of civilizations" automatically sets all proper Europeans and Americans (white Anglo-Saxon Protestant ones, that is) against all those hordes of Others (Huntington 1996).

I will try to confine generalizations to things that pass two filters. First, they must be widely shared. Second, they must be established as canonical. They are the behaviors you *should* do, the behaviors that matter. These are the behaviors that leave important, major, visible traces on the landscape and the ideas lying immediately behind these behaviors. Of course, there will always be people who make a point of flouting these conventions, but they have more teeth than mere fads or passing fashions.

Language, for me, is practice (see Hanks 1990). By this I mean behavior and the ideas that guide it. When I say that Chinese has no word for *religion* in the Western sense of the word, I mean exactly that: no such word exists. We can infer from this, and from how the Chinese talk about what we English-speakers call religion, that traditional Chinese thought about religiosity rather differently from modern English speakers. But we have to test this inference by actually talking with people, at length. I have done this for China. I have done similar depth research on the Maya of Yucatan, and, to a less deep level, on Anglo-Americans and on a few small traditional groups, including the Nuu-chah-nulth (Nootka) of British Columbia. Elsewhere, I have to rely on others' ethnography and on primary source materials (especially artistic ones, if I am studying attitudes).

I am trying to draw large patterns that may be useful for the world, rather than describe the minute details of local cultural practice. To see me at the other extreme—indulging my fondness for looking at individuals and local cultural variants, and developing it theoretically—see my book *Floating World Lost* (2007). Those who object to the generalizations that follow should put them in context by reading that book, which chronicles the striking differences of

Cantonese subcultures within one tiny area of Hong Kong, and of individuals within these subcultures.

Society and *community* have rather ambiguous meanings, as pointed out by Bruno Latour 2005. Much discussion has surrounded these words, but I will have to leave the issues for Latour.

Ethics refers herein to cultural ideas of what people should do, not to formal ethical philosophy. I am interested in *why* different societies came up with these beliefs, and how they deploy them. Vine Deloria Jr. has said "Western civilization, unfortunately, does not link knowledge and morality [as Native American societies do] but rather, it connects knowledge and power and makes the two equivalent" (cited by Karen Capuder, in frequent e-mails). Broadly, this is true, and I have to agree with the "unfortunately," but the point is that there is a reason for this and for other linkages and unlinkings.

I must also clarify *traditional* and *modern.* Again in contrast to much of the recent literature, I use traditional in a strictly relative way, to refer to cultural matters that have a fairly long history without too many dramatic changes. The English language is traditionally spoken in England, but today's English is very different from Chaucer's or even from Winston Churchill's. English was not traditionally spoken in Singapore, but Singapore is now so dominated by English that in another generation English will be a (or perhaps even "the") traditional language there. Traditions need not be very old and are certainly not unchanging. This was famously pointed out by Eric Hobsbawm and Terence Ranger (1983), who were cynical about it. Their cynicism was unwarranted; who ever *expected* tradition to be stagnation? Some aspects of traditional ecological knowledge can change just as fast as modern international science, given the right conditions. The point is that most of the rules for and content of traditional knowledge has been around long enough to be tested. They work, or at least work well enough to keep.

Modern is primarily a time word, and I greatly prefer the historian's usage of modern to refer to changes that began around 1500 or 1600 (the "early modern period") as opposed to confining the term to very recent decades. I do not use the word to refer to the imaginary "modern mentality" or "modernist program." As Bruno Latour rightly put it, "we have never been modern," in that sense (Latour 1993). There was no "modernist program."

Finally, my learned colleagues will seek in vain for the terms I "should" be using in a book of this kind: *globalization, neoliberalism, postcoloniality, governmentality, imaginary* (as a noun), and so on. I fear that my experience is that, although these terms may once have been used creatively and productively, especially by their originators, they have been reduced in current literature to meaningless gibberish. In social science, the value of a trendy word rather tends to be inversely correlated with the number of syllables. C. Wright Mills's great book *The Sociological Imagination* (1959) has never been surpassed on this, as on so many issues, and I can only refers readers to it.

The original concepts behind some of those words have value, but I shall invoke them in plain English. For instance, *globalization,* before being reduced to vapidity, was a vague cover term for certain processes that have gone worldwide. I shall discuss the specific processes and their actual histories, rather than the mythic "globalization."

Seth Abrutyn (2009) has described the ways that named, formalized institutions gradually developed from the undifferentiated societies of very ancient humans. Kinship is a specific, recognized, independent domain in all cultures today, and probably has been so for tens of millennia. The arts are recognized as distinct domains to varying degrees, but normally "art" is not recognized as such. Laws, leadership, and hierarchies exist in all societies, but formal structured ones with actual written law codes exist only in civilizations. Similarly, all human societies have to educate their young, but actual educational systems—schools, colleges, and the like—are an invention of urban, literate civilizations. Religion is recognized as a truly separate realm, with its own organized priesthood and temple system, only in civilizations. Science comes latest of all. The search for empirical, useful truths is eternal and humanity-wide, but "science" as a truly separate institutional realm has come into being in the last couple of centuries.

Morality remains to be separated from religion, law, and common social practice. And the economy is *always* embedded, never really a special system, in spite of formalism and the invention of "economists."

NATURE

Much of this book is based on the concepts of "nature," "environment," "resources," "management," and "conservation."

"Nature" is taken herein to mean "stuff people didn't make," including "human nature." It is *not* intended to mean untouched virgin wilderness—a commodity that does not exist anymore. Since the Pleistocene, no humanly habitable part of the world has been virgin wilderness. Within living memory, untouched wilderness did exist in the remote Arctic and Antarctic, but even those areas are now full of scientists and adventurers on ski-mobiles.

However, there remain countless important differences between Times Square and Jasper National Park. The back blocks of Jasper are properly called "wilderness," even though they are far from virginal in any essentialist sense. Anyone who doubts this is free to experiment with trying to survive in one of those two environments using only the skills devised for the other.

There is also a great deal of difference between my biological being—my "human nature"—and my culturally acquired self. Human nature gives me the ability to learn languages; culture gives me the ability to type English on a computer. Human nature gave me the ability to learn to walk; culture gave me my slouching rural-American stride. The obvious fact that these blend into each other—that "nature" and "nurture" are not separate—does not mean they do not exist, any more than the fact of gray proves that black and white do not exist.

However, many cultures, including the nonwestern ones with which I am most familiar, lack a word for *nature*. They contrast *tame* and *wild*, or *spontaneous* and *built*, or *forest* and *farm*, or some other pair, instead. We will consider such terms, culture by culture, in the second section of this book.

Many anthropologists have suggested doing away with the entire concept, because it is a Western imposition rather than a reality out there. I sympathize with the sentiment but find it impractical. We still need some way to contrast humans and their immediate creations with the stuff humans did not make. A major theme of this book is that cultures find the words and contrasts they need. We of the modern West need the human/nature contrast.

The fact that humans have profoundly *altered* "nature" is important, but equally important is the fact that people can make cars, computers, and houses, but can never make bluebirds, firs, and whales. Once those are gone, we are impoverished forever. We can never bring them back, substitute anything for them, or heal our wounds. We will have lost something infinitely important— in Levinas's (1969) sense of that phrase—and we can do nothing to regain it.

Thus the concept of "nature" remains useful. So does the concept of "wilderness," if one remembers that "perfect wilderness" is as imaginary as "perfect city" and any other essentialized "perfection."

The word *natura*, that which is inborn (cf. *natality, native*) was used by the Romans to translate the mysterious Greek *physis*, delightfully glossed by Pierre Hadot as "the inexplicable surging-forth of reality" (Hadot 2006:314). The Greeks contrasted it with *nomos*, literally *name* or *naming*, extended to mean ordering or studying (as in astronomy and economy) and then to mean culture in general. This seems to be the original intellectual side of the opposition between "nature" and "culture" that has bedeviled the West ever since (Lloyd 2007:132–138); but there could be *nomos tes physeos*, "laws of nature," such as "might makes right"—the "law" that India at the same time called *matsyanyaya*, "fish law," because the big ones eat the little ones.

Spinoza spoke of "that eternal and infinite Being we call God or Nature" (Hadot 2006:268). This brings Spinoza very close to the Chinese Daoists and Zen Buddhists, especially when we recall that Spinoza's "being" in this sense is more like the Dao than like a rock or clod.

"Natural" in European thought (see, e.g., Coates 1998), of course, has two meanings: not human-made and morally normative. It is in the latter sense that it is "natural" for wolves to eat people, but "unnatural" for people to eat people; actually, cannibalism is quite common in human history and wolves almost never eat humans. Even someone who believed that everything objectively natural is subjectively moral could not unify these meanings, because, as David Hume said, one cannot get an "ought" from an "is." Hume was perfectly aware that humans have natural instincts about fairness, nonviolence, and the like, but he showed at length that these do not determine cultural rules of morality (Hume 1957 [1751]).

"Environment" means anything around us, including the "built environment." I draw heavily on ideas of "landscape" elaborated by Carl Sauer (1963) and his student Yi-fu Tuan (1969). They developed the idea of "landscape" as both a human-created or human-influenced external reality and a set of internal representations of the environment. I contrast the "built environment" with the "natural environment," but only as a matter of degree. Chinese and Maya rural landscapes are conscious human creations just as much as their cities are, and this fact has conditioned my views on "nature" and "environment."

"Resources" are things people use. I deal with biotic resources in this book, but "resources" can be intellectual, human, or even imaginary. Spirit power is a vitally important resource to Northwest Coast Native Americans, as "grace" is to Christians, even though the existence of these outside the human mind cannot be scientifically verified. I do not agree with an occasional anthropological claim that the word *resources* is innately economistic and thus evil. Rejecting good words because they have been used in economic or colonial contexts would soon leave us without any words at all.

"Conservation" means any deliberate use or management of resources that preserves them in such shape that there will be resources left for others. Preservation is necessary to conservation at times, but sustainable harvest of plants and animals, recycling of paper and plastic, retention of soil on hill slopes, and efficient, careful use of nonrenewable resources all count, too.

Unlike Smith and Wishnie (2000) and some others, I do not insist on proving that conservation was the actual stated goal of a practice to call it "conservation." Often, the stated goal is just good farming, or efficiency, or preventing community shortages. If conservation is integral to the stated goal, but not explicitly mentioned, I am willing to count the result as conservation. This is overwhelmingly important when we come to consider traditional paddy-rice agriculture, which is usually regarded by its practitioners as just "farming" or "making a living," but which necessarily involves extremely detailed practices of soil, water, and seed conservation. Stock-raising, similarly, is not explicitly about conservation, but requires preservation of one's stock, successful maintenance of the stock through breeding, and successful maintenance of feed sources.

The word *management* has received bad press recently in some quarters, because it is supposed to convey a Western or capitalist view of the world. Obviously, I am not using it in any such sense. I am using it to mean behavior that is intended to affect things or persons for specific reasons. A shaman dancing to make the bear and wolf spirits help him is managing animal powers, just as a modern farmer is managing seed and soil. The modern farmer is often just as emotionally and personally involved in his seeds and land as the shaman is in his animal world. Only in the fevered imaginations of mercilessly essentializing social scientists does "management" imply cold, rational capitalist detachment.

Finally, I see fewer problems with the word *sustainable* than many now do. We all know what sustainability is when we talk about fish, or forests, or farming. We may not know exactly how many fish we can take and still have a "sustainable" fishery, but we know that there is a threshold somewhere. Soil conservation, forest conservation, wildlife conservation, and water conservation were major values in the rural Midwestern and southern United States where I grew up. This could mean "sustainability," but it could also mean actual increase and improvement (as by reforestation). Sustainable water use implies using no more water than the stream with resupply. Fossil groundwater is a counter case: it can be used efficiently, but is of no value unless pumped (assuming it is too deep to feed springs and streams), so we cannot use it "sustainably." In these cases we can quite clearly distinguish "sustainability" from other forms of careful use. The word has a valuable meaning. It needs to be used precisely, not thrown out because of occasional misuse.

CHAPTER TWO

Traditional Management: Basics

> There is always a close connection between social reality, the theoretical frameworks one uses to interpret it, and the sense of politics and hope that emerges from such an understanding.
>
> *Arturo Escobar (2008:284)*

MANAGEMENT REGIMES

Environment management regimes are complex results of the interaction of people and landscapes. Possibly Marx was right to foreground the mode of production—actual production of useful goods under specific ownership regimes— as the driver. However, he also held that social systems and ideologies take on lives of their own, and feed back on actual management systems in a complex, ongoing, dynamic way. Also, people with various competing or coordinating interests interact with each other, and over time their varying attitudes, wants, and beliefs shape the development of environmental management systems.

Many today would hold that most important of all is the power structure: the ability of some people to make large-scale, vitally important decisions, while others have little or no power outside their own immediate circles. For Marx, such power had to be expressed in actual ownership or control: the person directing the production process or holding real power over the land was in the driver's seat. In today's complicated world, power can take many forms, including such things as the ability to pay public relations experts to persuade legislators of one's case. But we do well to direct our attention to the people that actually control the production process, and to their beliefs and ideas. Such people generally claim they are being rational, but in many cases their acts are so insane that they must at some level think otherwise. As Herman Melville said of Captain Ahab: "Now, in his heart, Ahab had some glimpse of this, namely: all my means are sane, my motive and my object mad" (Melville 2001 [1851]:202).

People are always bound, to some extent, by cultural precedents and lock-ins, and many of these started out as partial answers to difficult questions in the dim historic past. Power-holders are perhaps more bound by their beliefs than others, because power-holders are usually above the level of having to pay the immediate consequences of their acts, and because they are often the type of person who does not care to listen to subordinates overmuch. They can make others do the suffering and dying. On the other hand, constantly changing environments force people to change accordingly, and even power-holders can remain indifferent only so long. Thus, the historical record reveals constant adjustments, adaptations, failures, restarts, and negotiations. Today's management regimes are the result of this process.

The complexity of the world and the complexity of human needs and wants prevents us from understanding everything, let alone controlling it. All solutions are partial. Thus, people manage the environment by rational economic maximizing—up to a point. Beyond that point, they have to wing it. Sheer lack of knowledge would force this in any case, but, more to the point, the human mind takes all manner of shortcuts in deciding, and many of these shortcuts lead to errors, ranging from miscalculation of probabilities to discounting the future (Kahneman 2011). One result is belief in supra-natural beings and spirits—which then in turn can be put to use in motivating conservation and good management. This is not the only case in which dubiously justified knowledge can be turned to advantage. Humans often make mistakes trying to be rational economizers; they often save themselves through trying to be other-worldly mystics.

In general, people will naturally try to maximize material and social welfare, but there are countless ways to do this under the inevitable conditions of imperfect information. Thus, cultural differences are bound to emerge, often to become fixed customs.

Photo on Opposite Page: Well-preserved forests in Southeast Asia. Sunset over Doi Inthanon, the highest point in Thailand. Photograph by E. N. Anderson.

Traditional cultures are not simple, and almost all had enough technical competence to wipe out at least some of their major resources—local fisheries, migratory game herds, and uncommon medicinal plants, for example. Regulating a fishery or an agricultural landscape is extremely difficult and demanding, and requires constant self-conscious effort, even in a very sparsely populated landscape. Humans are far more capable of destruction than many writers have thought.

We now know, for instance, that the Northwest Coast peoples were numerous enough and good enough at fishing that they could have easily wiped out the salmon of that region (Arnold 2008; Johnsen 2009). Yet the salmon not only flourished, but increased, because they were protected and even stocked in new streams. We also know, on a sadder scale, that the Pueblo III civilization of the Southwest was able to ravage its environment. It did so, and suffered a 90 percent population decline in consequence (Diamond 2005), though much of the decline represents moving away rather than dying off.

Nor was Pueblo III a unique case. We have many similar cases from recent times, when westernization removed traditional controls and led to environmental disaster without technical change. The best-studied case is the Polynesian island of Tikopia, where missionaries caused the abandonment of population controls and of taboos on overuse of resources; disaster ensued (Firth 1959). It is impossible to argue that traditional people survived because they were too few and too simple to impact the landscape. Claims of "simple people in harmony with nature" are wrong. Traditional small-scale societies are anything but simple. All have important knowledge about environmental management. Many have caused environmental damage, usually learning from their mistakes.

The reason for some resource conflicts is simple enough: Garrett Hardin's model of the "Tragedy of the Commons" (Hardin 1968). Collective action was supposedly impossible because too many people found it irresistible to maximize self-interest in the short run (Olson 1965). But why do people not follow up on well-known, successful management strategies? Why did Hardin's qualification, that only "*unmanaged* commons" were tragic (Hardin 1991; his emphasis), not lead people to manage sensibly? Hardin's "tragedy of the commons" is often claimed to be a matter of "greed." It is actually an emergent phenomenon of unregulated social action (Hardin 1991; I was able to confirm this in discussion with Dr. Hardin at the time).

We now know that people do manage well when they have real communities. Elinor Ostrom won the Nobel Prize for Economics in 2009 for her brilliant work on this (Ostrom 1990). Conversely, many a local management regime breaks down when a government alienated control from the local communities (see, e.g., Anderson 1987, 2010). But then, unless the community was small and close, something had to maintain its solidarity and maintain the rules against cheaters—usually in the absence of a regular police force. Ostrom has provided "a general framework for analyzing sustainability of social-ecological systems" (Ostrom 2009). It involves assessing the resources, the users, and the governance systems involved, and then recording interactions and outcomes (including "externalities").

Some of the best conservation and sustainability ideology goes with the thinnest population and least capacity to do damage, and, conversely, many densely populated societies take very little care of the environment (see collections such as Ford and Martinez 2000). Population density and the human footprint do not correlate well with actual damage. Instead, cultural and agricultural traditions established in very early times seem to be more determinative. The range is from Buddhist Southeast Asia, with its religious protection of trees and animals, to nineteenth-century America and twentieth-century Brazil with their vast deforestations and hecatombs of game animals. This gap is not predicted by immediate factors—economic, political, or cultural. The origins go back in time, though recent forces have shaped and directed the strategies involved. Ideology, love for natural kinds, and general worldview matter as well as immediate economics.

I focus on traditional practices and attitudes because the modern world is well enough covered in many sources (e.g., Brockington et al. 2008), and in any case modern conservation is much influenced by international norms and by prosperity (the richer countries save more, because they can afford to look to the long term). Above all, environmental management is influenced by good government. The more honest and democratic the government, the better the management—a very striking worldwide finding. Costa Rica, for instance, stands out in Central America for both reasons, as do Botswana in Africa and (with qualifications) Thailand in Asia. Democratization brought serious attention to environmental conservation in South America in the 1990s and 2000s.

There is still a large residual component explained by cultural tradition. For one clear example, North Europe is more conservationist and environmentalist than South, and both more so than the Middle East. Thailand succeeds partly because it was never a colony; it conserves better than the more colonial-influenced Malaysia, Indonesia, or Vietnam (personal research).

There are also some odd "wild cards," contingent histories such as the success of Oman at conserving soils, wildlife, and vegetation cover when many other Middle Eastern countries fail; this is largely the result of rule by the earnestly scientific Sultan Qaboos.

POLITICS AND MANAGEMENT

A different strain of political writing on the environment has focused on the ways that societies manage common property resources. This field goes far back in time, but its modern incarnation is due to the work of anthropologist and political ecologists Bonnie McCay and James Acheson (Acheson 2006; McCay and Acheson 1987; McCay 1998). Their ideas have been widely applied (e.g., Pinkerton 1989; Pinkerton and Weinstein 1995). At the same time, political scientist Elinor Ostrom (1990) became interested in water management in southern California cities.

Ostrom and her colleagues have compiled a number of lists of essentials for collective management (Ostrom 2005, 2009). Basically, a society needs to be coherent, have enforcement capacity, have full accountability and recourse, have actual ability to control the resource in question, and have a manageable number of problems to confront. A society overwhelmed by problems cannot do much. Even two simultaneous problems with the resource base are too many, if they are serious—say, an invasion during a drought.

Theoretically related work within political science includes studies of why some environmental treaties succeed when most fail (Barrett 2003). William Ascher asked in a book title *Why Do Governments Waste Natural Resources?* (Ascher 1999). The one-word answer is *corruption,* though foolishness is also involved.

Work on common property management dramatically reframes environmentalism. It turns out that almost everyone knows enough to manage their resources wisely. Except in those cases of overwhelming problems, a society can generally figure out how to keep from overfishing, over-logging, overusing water, or overhunting game. Even if the results are not immediate or easy to see, people eventually learn. The problem is getting people to do it. Even in modern Europe and America, poaching, cheating, bribery, and irresponsible political action by selfish parties routinely overwhelm environmental protection laws. Traditional small-scale societies normally lack police, formal governments, prisons, or other enforcement powers, and yet they often do better than we do.

The extreme case is represented by "culturally modified trees" (Turner et al. 2009). Throughout the world, traditional peoples manage trees by taking what they want and leaving the tree standing. Harvesting fruit is the obvious way, but people also harvest trees for bark, twigs, shoots, roots, wood, and other purposes (Grove and Rackham 2001; Turner et al. 2009).

Throughout the Great Basin, the Paiute and Shoshone made bows by cutting appropriate staves of wood from living juniper trees. Ideal are the undersides of long, straight branches, because the wood is under stress from bearing the weight of the branch. This "compression wood" is tougher and stronger than other wood. *Very* few trees in the vast, barren Basin have long straight branches, and all such trees were well known for tens of miles around. Yet, *bow staves were harvested sustainably for thousands of years.* Philip Wilke (1988) showed that staves were taken every few years from a given tree, and the tree was allowed to recover before another was taken. People did not cheat by overusing a tree or lopping a branch. I have observed the same with yew trees in the Pacific Northwest; rare is an old yew without old bow-stave scars. This requires a level of conscience almost unimaginable to a modern individual. This, and similar cultural management of trees around the world (Turner et al. 2009), certainly disproves the narrow interpretations of "rational self-interest" common in economics (e.g., Olson 1965).

Other examples of such conservation are legion. Most traditional peoples successfully prevent overfishing, overharvesting, and so on, and, for that matter, have little thievery in their fields and farms. The Maya I study in Quintana Roo know they are free to take needed food from a field, or medicine from a forest, but know they cannot take more than a tiny amount—they know when to stop. They also did not overhunt game in traditional times (this is sadly lost in many communities; Anderson and Medina Tzuc 2005).

On the other hand, by no means all traditional people conserve. Many do not, or do not do an adequate job (Hames 2007). Thus there is nothing special about traditional small-scale societies; still less do they conform to the patronizing stereotype of simple people in harmony with nature (Kay and Simmons 2002).

PRODUCTION REGIMES AND STAPLE CROPS

Unsurprisingly, the best fit with broad environmental management regimes is actual production regimes. How people produce their food determines how they manage their environment, other things being equal. However, received cultural traditions influence how this is done, and not just by determining what food people think is "proper."

The most important and obvious difference is between peoples who depend on a very wide spectrum of resources and those who depend on only a very few, especially if the latter are agricultural. Obviously, wide-spectrum cultures will feel the need to conserve their entire ecosystems. At the other extreme, peoples dependent on a few crops may (or may not) feel the need to destroy everything except vast fields of those crops.

Most hunter-gatherers and simple agricultural peoples are dependent on a very wide spectrum. They are also directly up against environmental limits; they cannot pass costs on to other people or to future generations. Even those who depend largely on one staple (as many Northwest Coast groups did on salmon—though this has been exaggerated in much of the literature) depend also on a vast range of other wild goods and cannot destroy those to increase the salmon. They often manage by burning the landscape, from Native America (M. K. Anderson 2005; Stewart et al. 2002) to Australia (see below). This might seem destructive, but in practice the burns are managed to open and renew the landscape without destroying much of it at a time.

Traditional cultivators in many areas depend on still wider spectra of crops. The Maya of Quintana Roo have more than a hundred food crops, with only maize standing out as disproportionately vital (Anderson 2005b). Southeast Asian cultivators often grow a hundred species in their dooryard gardens.

At the other extreme is the Western world, dependent since ancient times on wheat, barley, sheep, and cattle. Today, wheat, rice, maize, sugar, potatoes, cotton, and a couple of oil crops dominate the cultivated lands of the entire planet (see, e.g., Smil 2013). Cattle, pigs, sheep, and chickens provide virtually all the meat, and even sheep are losing ground. Vegetables and fruits are relatively decreasing as people become more and more dependent on processed foods made from the few majors. The only significant fruit crop worldwide is the grape, and its main use is wine. Vineyards have displaced other kinds of cultivation in much of California.

Between these two extremes are many civilizations that succeed in some ways and fail in others, and thus have particularly interesting lessons to offer. China, India, ancient Greece, and several other areas were largely dependent on a few major crops, but had to cultivate many minors for nutritional survival. Ideology and religion were influenced by this.

PRODUCTION ECONOMY AND MANAGEMENT

Some systems require much more coordinated decision-making than others. The extremes are the totally free-and-easy hunting-and-gathering systems of the San and Hadza (who rejoice in a relative lack of wants; Sahlins 1972), and the fine-tuned rice irrigation and dryland cultivation systems of Southeast Asia. The latter are so diverse, so integrated, and so dependent on exquisite timing and maintenance that any major blows are disastrous.

Hunting and gathering seems usually to produce some sort of conservation ideology if fairly dense populations, or even dispersed and mobile but fairly sizable populations, are involved. Some impressive management ideology occurs among sparsely distributed, highly migratory subarctic hunters (see, e.g., Nelson 1983).

Fishing and exploiting marine resources, such as shellfish, seabirds, and sea mammals, is all too conducive to overexploitation, as most modern populations have found out to their cost. Yet, aquatic resources were fairly well to very well managed in earlier times. Major review volumes, with chapters covering a large percentage of the world's waters, find that traditional people either manage resources explicitly for sustainability, or at least have not greatly drawn down the resource base in most cases, implying deliberate management (see Johannes 1981, 1982; Rick and Erlandson 2008; Ruddle and Akimichi 1984; Ruddle and Johannes 1983). There are enough exceptions, from cod in ancient New England to walrus in Norse-era Iceland (Perdikaris and McGovern 2008), to show that people were quite capable of devastating the resources as thoroughly as we do today. They rather rarely did so.

Agricultural traditions differ greatly from each other. Agriculture, by definition, introduces a situation in which resources are always conserved and managed. At least the seed has to be saved and the livestock protected. Usually there must be some land modification—at least clearing and cultivating. Often it requires what geographers call "landesque capital": terracing, irrigation works, planting pits or raised beds, and the like. All this requires management of soil and water. Also, any successful agricultural system relies on a mix of species and growth forms, and thus involves quite complex management at several levels.

The oldest agriculture in the world was wheat and barley cultivation in the Near East. It began around 9500 BC and stayed very small in scale for millennia. However, with the rise of civilization 5,000 years ago, extensive wheat-barley agriculture dominated millions of acres. It generally had a relatively low labor input, as traditional agriculture goes, but needed a lot of land. This led to the growth of large estates, eventually worked by slaves.

Rice stands at the other extreme. Rice agriculture, before the invention of modern machinery, was best done with high concentration of labor on limited land (Hayami and Ruttan 1985). Only about a tenth of the land in most rice areas of the world is flat enough and well-watered enough to be farmed for irrigated rice, which comprises the vast majority of rice production. Dry-grown rice yields poorly and requires years of fallowing of the land between cropping cycles. It is better to leave slopes wild, forested if possible, to provide runoff of water and nutrients for the paddy fields.

Rice also essentially forced farmers to maximize the use of the rest of the land and all its resources, because rice supports high populations but is a very inadequate food, lacking in vitamins, minerals, and protein. Rice systems have to grow vegetables intensively, and most of them also manage forests intensively. They preserve at least some areas of dense forest for watershed protection, fruit, wild products of all sorts, and timber. Rice covers vast monocrop fields in the Po Valley of Italy, the central parts of Thailand, the lower Yangzi Valley, and central California, but even in these cases, the forested mountains are within sight.

Moreover, irrigation systems require the local people to take at least some care about the environment. Elites normally must protect the system from a distance, but rice irrigation (and, for that matter, dry-rice agriculture) depends on exquisite *local* control, so the elites cannot interfere. Rice agriculture is thus inherently centrifugal. Elites are forced to accommodate, to protect communities and irrigated systems.

Rice systems thus require extremely good management. Often there is not much explicit conservation, but, even without a self-conscious "conservation" ideology, rice-dependent areas like south China, Java, and eastern India tend to be careful in resource management. However, this is not so true in less-intensive systems like those of Madagascar and parts of Borneo (personal research).

Tuber crops like potatoes and manioc use little land and little labor but are often rather low in protein. Manioc cultivation in lowland South America produces scattered populations, often—though not always—with no conservation ideology and simple management strategies. However, highland South America had intensive, extremely sophisticated regimes, and the lowlands evidently once did also (Lentz 2000). Potatoes, and manioc in parts of Asia, go with extremely dense, impoverished populations that have poor management and usually inadequate or distant government (Africa, New Guinea, early nineteenth-century Ireland). But aboriginal Polynesia was an amazing exception, with superb management of root crops. This appears to have developed after early environmental misuse; a learning curve is evident in the archaeological records (Kirch 1994, 1997, 2007; Leach 1999; cf. Firth 1959; Lertzman 2009).

Tropical millet and sorghum systems, like the agricultural systems of the Sahel and interior south India, are apparently similar, but are poorly studied. Insofar as I have personally observed such systems in Africa, they seem capable of strikingly high levels of production and good land management when intensively practiced on good soil (as by the Chagga on Mt. Kilimanjaro, from my experience). However, there is little on this in the available literature. Most sources describe less intensive millet-sorghum systems in areas of poor soil and retail the old litany of "starving, backward Africa."

Maize is high-labor, high-skill, and quite productive per acre, and thus very similar to rice, but with the big difference that it is very unreliable compared with wet-rice or typical wheat or barley farming. The slightest drought or flooding destroys the crop. Maize is also notoriously susceptible to diseases and pests. Thus maize agriculture forces mixed systems and diversification—or else it leads to huge crashes. This happened because of prolonged drought in the cases of Pueblo III and the central Classic Maya societies (Diamond 2005; Gill 2000). Unreliability forces all maize societies to depend on a vast range of other foods, both tame and wild. Maize regions thus become like rice regions in that they often maintain a large percentage of land in a wild or semi-wild state. The vast expanses of maize monocropping in today's United States, China, and elsewhere are unsustainable and will inevitably collapse.

Borderline areas—north and central China, central India, northeast Africa, old west Europe, and so on—are exactly what one would expect: intermediate along all these dimensions.

Many areas depend heavily on livestock, sometimes to the point of nomadism. Livestock management is generally more sensitive, successful, and carefully managed in traditional areas than most of the broad and general literature suggests, though sensitive, detailed studies from the Andes, Africa, Mongolia, and elsewhere provide details. Modern capitalist ranching, however, is also perfectly capable of excellent management, as many studies show (e.g., Hedrick 2007; Hyde 1974; Perramond 2010; Sheridan 1988, 2007). On the other hand, overstocking is common and devastating in many herding systems. It has been observed from western America to the montane Middle East. Both in capitalist America and Australia and in thoroughly traditional parts of Morocco, I have seen countless cases in which a fencerow separates a fine stand of grass from a trodden desert, the difference being entirely due to differences in management by individual owners. In East Africa I have frequently seen fenced, privatized range turned to desert while grass stood tall and dense in nearby grasslands still grazed by traditional nomads. In Afghanistan I have seen whole mountain ranges eaten to the bare rock, with only a few courtyards to show that grass and trees would flourish there if any decent management were found; mismanagement here was the result of war and violence, and of feudal and modern regimes that caused the conflicts. In Mongolia I have seen "modern" grazing regimes strip the land bare while traditional pastures a few miles away had tall grass.

Thus the basic cropping pattern of a culture has some ground-level effect on management regimes. Of course, such cropping patterns are far from determinative. Every broad system shows a range from meticulous, almost obsessive-compulsive land and resource management to the opposite. Indigenous lowland South America shows a spectacular range from extremely efficient management to complete lack of regard for conservation issues (Beckerman et al. 2002; Lentz 2000). Wet-rice systems are generally the best at balancing high yields with minimal environmental damage, but I have personally studied a range from the unbelievably intricate and productive systems of south China (Anderson 1988) and Sumatera to quite low-yield and forest-wasting systems in Madagascar (see "Madagascar on My Mind" on my website *www.krazykioti.com* for full references). One could find similar ranges within the other broad categories above. Still, looking at cropping patterns gives us a start—a first approximation to an explanation, and one that can be traced archaeologically and historically.

In all of this, basic ideas of the proper food, the proper farm, the proper role of government, and the proper way to manage resources are more decisive than abstract religious concepts, which in turn seem more important than aesthetic, political, or cosmological ones. But even those last are extremely important.

In between these extremes are more traditional societies from Europe to India and from the ancient Maya to the Middle East. Their elites depended on a web of supply lines, and they could draw for varying lengths of time from many resource bases—hence, they were not always good conservers. But they generally got a rapid and condign fall when they were too careless for too long.

ELITE DECIDERS

It appears, on a quick inspection, that the degree of conservation in the more complex societies has a great deal to do with whether the elites' lives are on the line.

In all societies, some people have more decision-making power than others. At the very least, children have less authority in the group than adults. In all reasonably documented societies, some adults (usually the older ones, and often males) have more power than others (younger ones, and more often females than males). The very smallest and least technologically complex groups have almost no authority systems (Boehm 1999), but even there the elders tend to decide. In more complex societies, those with more than one or two thousand people in the social group, there is invariably some sort of dominance hierarchy and decision-making order.

Notoriously, the more decoupled the major decision-makers are from the rest, the less they decide for the common welfare, and the more they decide for their own welfare—often at the expense of the rest. This bit of lore was ancient long before Marx. In regard to the environment, it allows us to predict two things. First, the more social and political separation there is between elite and masses, the less the former will care about the latter—and, therefore, about the environment that sustains the latter. Second, the more the elite can avoid being caught up in the general wreck if the environment collapses, the worse the environment will be treated in elite decision-making.

The Northwest Coast in early times provides a good example of an area where the elite was not very separate from the rest (chiefs of chiefly lineages were not much better off than commoners) and were dependent on the same resources as the commoners (local fish and plants).

Cases in which the elite is not very separate from the commoners but does not have to maintain their environmental system are rather rare, but are found in the old-time raider peoples, like the central Asian nomads and the Vikings.

Southeast Asia, of which much more below, is a case in which the elite was far above the masses and lived a very different lifestyle, but was absolutely dependent on the great rice irrigation systems—just as most of the commoners were. The environment was consequently well managed. All decision-makers, from the lowest peasant to the king, had to work together to keep the irrigation systems up. In Southeast Asia (including south China and eastern India), dependence on the rice irrigation system forced the elites to take care of that system, to protect the forests that keep it watered and keep the soil from eroding away, and to keep the other components of the local food production world in good shape. Conservation of fauna is something of a by-product, but the whole conservation situation makes religions like Buddhism very persuasive. There was an obvious need to represent religiously the morality that Aldo Leopold called "saving all the pieces" (Leopold 1949).

The modern United States is an extreme case of decoupling. The super-rich corporate elites, who actually run the country to a great extent, increasingly get their resources and make their sales outside the country. They have virtually no interest in maintaining the American environment, or even its society or economy. Rapid shifts away from environmental protection and even from education and social services have come in consequence.

In general, in the modern developed countries, the real rulers live by extracting resources from marginal areas such as Alaska, the Gulf of Mexico, Tibet, and above all the poorest nations. As long as the world depends on oil and minerals from Nigeria, Sudan, Equatorial Guinea, Iraq, Laos, and such places, the elites will pass on environmental costs to the poor of these areas and will take no care of the environment—even of basic food systems. China's elites are rapidly destroying China's food resource base; there will be mass starvation in the near future, but the present-day elites will be gone by then, or at worst they will be able to take their money and run. The people of the poor countries have little choice; their survival often depends on taking any chance they can get, even if it means death in the long run.

The greatest contrast is provided by the libertarian, not to say downright anarchic (cf. Scott 2009), shifting cultivation systems. These depend on every family or small community being free to go off into the forest and cut new fields. It is notoriously hard to hold people together in such systems; they resist integration and are hotbeds of independence. James Scott's observations on upland Southeast Asia can be matched from south Mexico, as I can testify. Small-scale local irrigation systems are also hard to rule; they require fine-tuned local management and cannot deal with meddling by outsiders who do not know the system and therefore damage it by interference. (However, Scott seems to confuse these intensely rule-bound and cooperative systems with Western-style anything-goes anarchy like the Occupy movement; they are, in fact, exact opposites.)

Ordinary dryland agriculture is much more tolerant of meddling and thus of elite rule; it is hard to damage. It is, therefore, rather more conducive to rule by elites that do not take good care of the environment. The farmers are left to their own devices; if half of them starve, the other half can still feed the rulers.

Nomadic herding systems are somewhat similar. They produce ruling elites on occasion, and those can raid or tax or otherwise avoid herding themselves, without much damaging the herder base. On the other hand, they depend in the last analysis on that base and cannot be completely intransigent.

In short, systems that allow people to scatter widely and make their livings as families are hard to rule and control, and correspondingly hard to ruin. Systems that are so fine-tuned that the rulers are forced to maintain them are easy to control, but the elites do not dare ruin them; if they do so by mistake, they die with the peasants. Systems that have a modicum of family-level or village-level independence, but are easy to rule and environmentally fairly tolerant of meddling, tend to be loci of exploitative rule. If poor environmental management is found anywhere, it will be found in them.

These observations may explain some of the collapses of history. The medieval Khmer state collapsed when drought made the state irrigation system fail. The Maya civilization in the central lowlands of Mesoamerica may have collapsed because drought ruined stable, non-shifting agriculture in wetlands, ridged field systems, terraces, and other permanent field arrays; the Maya themselves survived by shifting cultivation and abandoned the cities to go cut fields in remote areas. My observations in Chunhuhub, Quintana Roo, certainly show that after the Classic Maya town collapsed (around 800 CE), a large but unobtrusive and dispersed postclassic population persisted on isolated farmsteads wherever moisture and good soil occurred. In the Near East, where local irrigation systems supported states and sometimes empires but where dry farming and nomadic herding dominated the hills, a constant tension existed, with weakly governed hill peoples often conquering the lowlands—sometimes with devastating effects on irrigation.

It also means that we now desperately need to make the world's ever-more-powerful, ever-more-remote decision-makers realize that their lives are on the line. A world that has crashed and burned ecologically will not be good to them. They have no escape. They must learn to love what we have, enough to decide for sustainability.

SELF-CONSCIOUS CONSERVATION

Conservation management among small-scale societies is normally done landscape by landscape and case by case. It is embedded in local religion and ritual as well as in rational economic planning. It may be very strongly taught and believed, but it usually remains within the local cultural scene. It is not generally enunciated as a general principle for all humanity to follow. Each Australian Aboriginal group has its own variant of *tjukurrpa* (see below). These variants may seem very similar to the outsider, but each group defends and clings to its own.

Conscious conservation ideology as a basic general principle—at the religious and political level—goes back to ancient India: to Hinduism, Jainism, and Buddhism around 500 BC. Here it grew from a rice-and-cattle world. The need to manage not only rice but also large herds of grazing animals was associated with this development. It was not phrased in scientific, aesthetic, or economic terms, as we do today, but in religious terms. Violence was deplored, and animals and even plants were within the realm of beings needing and deserving compassion. Animals previously sacrificed to the gods, including cows and horses, were seen as too valuable to be killed.

Surely, morals and economics were not separated in this calculation. The cow was particularly protected. Marvin Harris (1966) famously argued that the usefulness of the cow had much to do with its special status. His point had been anticipated several centuries earlier, by the great Arab polymath Al-Bīrūnī, who noted that Indians use not only the cow's milk, dung, and so on, but even its breath, by bringing cows inside on cold nights to serve as living heating units (Anderson 1977). More idealist accounts may stress the religious elements more, but must agree that the cow is protected and that it is very useful (Simoons 1979, 1994).

Hinduism and especially Buddhism spread throughout Asia, influencing systems everywhere. They had an overwhelming impact on Southeast Asia (see below). This was critical to the development of the high level of sustainability seen until recently in the agriculture of that region.

China independently developed simpler and more pragmatic conservation ideas about the same time, within Confucianism and Daoism (see below). Other Asian civilizations followed, with their own interpretations, typically based on these Buddhist and Confucian analogs.

TRADITIONAL COSMOVISION

One way of understanding knowledge that I find particularly valuable is *tjukurrpa*. This Central Desert Australian Aboriginal term (see Keen 2004:217) combines some things we in modern English separate out as "law," "religion," "morals," "science," "geography," "love," and "kinship." It separates out some other things from that pool, at least the "law" and "science" ends. It also denotes the time when the supernatural ancestral beings (*tjukurritja*) created the world. Tjukurrpa is the cultural construction of the general principles a person needs to have in order to live a good life in the world. This includes everything from conserving resources to treating neighbors decently. A person who lives according to tjukurrpa lives successfully on the land, drawing from it without destroying it. Similarly, she can live successfully in society, through following social rules without being a mindless, passive conformist. She can live with herself, knowing how thoughts and emotions combine to produce a life.

So *precisely the things that we modern academics work hardest to separate— cognition and emotion, "is" and "ought," individual and society—are what the Australians work hardest to unite.* This is not because they are philosophically "backward"; it is because they are philosophically different—perhaps even philosophically ahead of the rest of us. The Western world's Greek-derived traditions in academic thought are one way of seeing the world, and a reasonable enough way, but we should consider the quite different but equally viable Australian way of cutting up intellectual space.

Tjukurrpa developed in a harsh environment—a nearly lifeless desert where people survived by truly incredible knowledge of the land. Their success is shown by the fact that when the Anglo-Australian settlers robbed them of their land and tried to "improve" it, they failed dismally and have now given vast tracts back to the Aborigines. The Aborigines lacked cities or laboratories, so they did not create "religion" or "science" as Europe knew them. They could, however, create a system that allowed almost perfect fine-tuning of life under the harshest possible conditions.

Quite different from this and also from any European philosophical concept is the Navaho idea of *hozhoo,* which means harmony, peace, beauty, health, and good resource management (see, e.g., Witherspoon 1977). To recover health, an ill patient sits (at key points in a healing ritual) on a ground painting of supernatural and natural beings to absorb the beauty and harmony of the painting and thus the blessings of the beings themselves.

For the Hopi, good ethical and ecological practice is the Hopi way, whereas bad actions—social, personal, and ecological—are *ka-Hopi,* "not Hopi" (Brandt, *Hopi Ethics,* 1954—still the best work on the ethics of a nonwestern, kin-based society). The Chinese spoke of "harmony with the Dao," understood to be working with nature in whatever one was doing: farming, healing, meditating.

The Nuu-chah-nulth of British Columbia speak of *tsawalk,* a unity with all things that involves a complicated set of concepts of respect, gratitude, and protection, as well as a sense of being in the wide world (Atleo 2004). Once again, it crosscuts European distinctions of science, religion, philosophy, law, and economics. A similar concept is the Cherokee concept of *duyukdv* (Cozzo 2012; the "v" is pronounced "uh"), which refers to balance, reciprocity, consideration, and nondestructiveness. This is the value behind the Cherokee consideration for future generations—proverbially "seven generations."

Many other cultures have distinctive terms for their basic philosophy of interaction. We learn that those familiar ways of dividing knowledge are cultural artifacts, not God-given distinctions. There are other ways of cutting up the knowledge pie. Our familiar modern European way has its benefits; other ways have other benefits, different but none the worse for that. Anyone raised to accept, more or less mindlessly, the classic divisions can easily de-center her mind enough to learn and use other divisions.

The need to represent factual knowledge and ethical treatment of resources in one system means that Native American systems of thought cannot be separated into "religion" *and* "science." This has often been pointed out in anthropology (one of the best discussions being as long ago as 1916, in Paul Radin's study of the Winnebago), but it needs continual reassertion.

What has not been pointed out is that *this different way of organizing knowledge follows directly from the need to know almost everything about the local environment.* If one must know, and *take seriously,* every significant plant, tree, creek, patch of ground, weather indicator, and star, and must be constantly open to more and more learning, one must inevitably develop an intense emotional involvement with all the above—both as individual entities and as a totality. This confrontation—total self totally open to total fact—is the reality of survival for hunting-gathering and traditional agricultural peoples. An intense spiritual involvement with the whole landscape necessarily follows. They may or may not feel "awe," but they do not have the modern urbanite's luxury of feeling nothing.

In most traditional worldviews, humans and animals, and usually plants and even mountains and rocks, interact as persons, or did so in mythic times. That time may not have been very long ago, either. In northern Australia, I have stood in a grove of rather young trees that settled there as persons in the mythic Dreaming. For at least some Australian Aboriginals, the Dreaming is still going on, in a time that is somehow either parallel or perpendicular to ours.

"GOOD MANAGERS"

Traditional people are, in general, "good managers" (in Gene Wilken's phrase, 1987) of their resources. Some are not. This leads to controversy.

Much of the basis of everyday and pragmatic knowledge, including most of science, lies in ongoing interaction with people and the environment, through actual work. This is labor in the broad sense: for pay or for other rewards, for self or for society. (This point was made by Marx and Engels long ago and is possibly the truest thing they ever said; see Engels 1966/1894.)

Traditional small-scale societies are often astonishingly good managers of resources (Anderson 1996; Berkes 2008; Lertzman 2009). There is huge variation, however. Some groups manage very little, especially if they are highly mobile people with low population densities on the land (Beckerman et al. 2002; cf. Kay and Simmons 2002; Krech 1999). Simon Foale questions traditional conservation in Oceania, noting well-documented cases of its lack (Foale et al. 2011); I have had some of the same experiences in Polynesia and China, but I have seen good conservation, too, and there are many extremely detailed reports of good local conservation (Aswani and Weiant 2004; Johannes 1981, 1982—Foale doubts his findings, but Johannes has the evidence; Ruddle and Akimichi 1984; Ruddle and Johannes 1983; for fish conservation in other areas, see, e.g., Anderson and Anderson 1978; Nietschmann 1973).

Even within one fairly uniform cultural region, and even within the same country or cultural group at different times, there are differences. Anderson and Anderson (1978) studied a violent conflict between good managers and those they considered "poachers." Totman(1989) records dramatic changes in Japanese management over time (cf. Ruddle and Akimichi 1984). Studies in the Philippines (unfortunately unpublished; see, e.g., Randall 1977) document changes in particular groups' management from sustainable to unsustainable over quite short time frames.

Purely "natural" environments no longer exist. Several books and articles treat of resulting problems for conservationists (e.g., Janzen 1998; Wapner 2010). Dan Janzen (1998) argues that we should think of the world as a garden to tend, not a wilderness to tame or fence off. On the other hand, the antienvironmentalists have had a field day with this point, arguing that there is, therefore, no real difference between Jasper National Park and Times Square and that we might as well develop everything. Even paving over prime agricultural land does not seem to faze them.

Those who have worked with traditional and indigenous communities around the world have long known that people affect "nature," and have for millennia. Outside of Antarctica, most parts of the globe have been managed by traditional and indigenous societies. Janzen is right: preserving what is left of the truly wild is a noble task, but in most of the world the more reasonable course is to see what management strategies have been used, and then see which have worked (for whatever reason) and which have been counterproductive.

Even minor components of this knowledge base can be complicated and difficult. After more than fifty years of intermittent tropical field work, I am not bad with a machete, but I am a helpless incompetent next to the Maya. Their skills are beyond description. The same for firewood gathering, small animal management under difficult tropical conditions, and so on. It is revealing, to say the least, that the closely related Tzotzil Maya of Chiapas have a huge and successful sheep-raising practice in an area where the Spanish could not even keep the sheep alive (Perezgrovas 1990).

The fishermen of Hong Kong had a similar encyclopedic knowledge. Different individuals knew different things—expertise was distributed—and the result was a total knowledge pool that would have filled many volumes. Chinese fishermen I lived with in Malaysia knew a good deal less, having been in the fishery for only a few years and in an unfamiliar environment.

Northwest Coast Native peoples were more like Hong Kong fishers; they knew an encyclopedic store of useful knowledge about the habits of fish and how to catch them. The Northwest peoples also know an incredible amount—far more than modern botanists or foresters—about management of local plant resources, from trees to root crops (Deur and Turner 2005; Turner 2005).

So do California Natives (M. K. Anderson 2005), and, farther afield, Mediterranean peasants (Grove and Rackham 2001). In fact, natural plant cover management is one area where traditional people have a clear advantage over modern international science (cf. Johnson and Hunn 2010; Williams and Hunn 1982). This area of science has been poorly developed, falling somewhere outside of botany and crop science and being of surprisingly little immediate interest to ecology or forestry. Ecologists prefer "undisturbed" landscapes, foresters industrially managed ones. Management of animal numbers by traditional hunters and herders is similarly developed to an incredibly high level in many areas. Displacing local indigenous peoples for "conservation" has led to major disasters in many areas. Well-meaning outsider conservationists rule the "ignorant, destructive" locals off the reserves, only to find out the hard way that the local people were actually maintaining the game (Brockington et al. 2008; West et al. 2006; I have seen this happen in Yucatan and in East Africa; the "Just Conservation" Facebook page keeps a running record).

Investigations of traditional farming by agricultural scientist Gene Wilken (1987) in the Americas and geographer Gary Klee (1980) in Southeast Asia showed that local small-farm operators not only knew an incredible amount about farming, they often had more extensive and accurate knowledge than agricultural experts did. Wilken, for example, studied the practice of mounding up soil around cornstalks, dismissed as foolish by agricultural scientists. It turned out to be necessary to prevent windthrow and pest damage.

Specific kinship structures may have less to do with ecology than some have thought. My mentor in these matters, Jack Potter, worked with the idea that the Chinese patrilineage might be vital to rice agriculture, because its solid, well-grounded, well-recognized command structure allowed marshaling of a great deal of labor. This could be done quickly and easily, as is necessary for rice agriculture; irrigation, planting, and harvest require huge labor forces that can be raised almost instantly. Potter tested this idea in Thailand, where patrilineal, matrilineal, and cognatic communities exist near each other and raise rice without much in the way of cultural or agricultural differences. My students and I tested it in Malaysia and Sumatera, where the same holds true. Richard Lando studied the patrilineal Batak, Lynn Thomas the matrilineal Minangkabau, and I used my knowledge of the cognatic Straits Malays (Bumiputera). It turned out that kinship made no difference. All these societies had equal success organizing labor. They all used kinship as the main organizing dimension, but any kinship arrangement would do. My students and I never wrote our side of the story up (for personal reasons including the premature death of Dr. Lando), but Jack Potter produced a fine book, *Thai Peasant Social Structure* (1976), that referred to the general finding.

Comparable matched-comparison cases exist all over the world. The Northwest Coast fishers include patrilineal, matrilineal, and basically cognatic societies (the Nuu-chah-nulth I studied were theoretically patrilateral, but in fact cognatic). All fish with equal success. Similar lack of kinship system effect on ecosystem holds for the northern hunters, the farmers of India, and various African cultivators. The slight worldwide tendency for matriliny to go with hoe agriculture and patriliny with the plow is clearly a historical accident, or at best an indirect linkage, rather than a functional fact. (I have no space to go into detail here, but can supply on request!)

The further dimensions of kin, community, and neighborhood in cultural ecology are the best-analyzed and best-covered aspect of the field, saving me from further effort at this point (see Bates 2005; Bennett 1976, 1982, 1992, reviewing hundreds of studies; Netting 1981, 1986, 1993; Steward 1955, 1977).

There is an endless debate within philosophy and environmentalism over whether we should judge a system of thought by its hits or its misses—by its best successes or by its worst errors. Do we evaluate a particular pool of traditional knowledge by its noblest ideals, or by the worst practices of its contemporary bearers?

A classic way of winning a debate is to compare the highest ideals of one's own system with the worst practices of one's rivals. In the nature of things, ideals always outrun performance. ("Man's reach should exceed his grasp, or what's a Heaven for?"—as Robert Browning commented on this truism). Moreover, any system of thought has some noble ideals and some less noble, and almost all have chalked up some performance successes and some failures. We are aware how, in United States politics, the Republicans contrasted the virtues of Free Enterprise with the sex life of Bill Clinton, whereas the Democrats contrasted the virtues of Social Security and Medicare with the bedroom and boardroom lives of whatever Republicans were sinning at the time.

This tactic of debate has been invoked in the realm of resource management. In that area, Western thought has been set against "traditional" ecological knowledge by Martin Lewis (1994), Rob Preece (1999), and Charles Redman (1999), among others. Preece, in particular, is explicit in contrasting the highest ideals of modern Christian Europe and America with the worst practice of other cultures: the excessive whaling of Japan, the deforestation of China, the alleged (but actually improbable) Pleistocene overkill of megafauna by Native Americans, and so on for many pages. Such outrageous abuse of debating rules is unworthy of a high school student. Conversely, certain supporters of indigenous peoples, especially of Native Americans, do the opposite: they contrast the noblest Indigenous ideals with the worst Anglo-American practice (e.g., Hughes 1983). This creates a stereotypic "ecologically noble savage" (Hames 2007; Redford 1990), the simple child of nature in harmony with everything. Charles Kay and Randy Simmons (2002) correctly point out that this stereotype is belittling and patronizing rather than complimentary.

A new food crop, or a cancer or AIDS drug, may be pulled from its embedding in a traditional system of thought, as qinghaosu was from Chinese medicine to create the artemisinin drugs now standard against malaria. A strongly conservationist practice may be borrowed by one culture from another, as when modern Australian wildlife managers learn from Aborigines the burning patterns that optimize the habitat for certain rare animals (personal observation in Australia, notably at Uluru National Park; see Pyne 1991). On the other hand, if a conservationist wants to turn over a major biological reserve to its traditional inhabitants for traditional management, there is a legitimate question about their *total* management strategy. Even if they have many good ideas, their overall treatment of the reserve may be devastating. This has led to some agonizing choices, and debate about them. John Terborgh (1999), for instance, writes of the Matsigenka, one of the few groups on earth who seem to be genuinely lacking in conservationist practices. They live in the area of greatest biodiversity on earth, the relatively unspoiled parts of the Upper Amazon drainage. An ornithologist and conservationist, Terborgh asks: Do we put them in charge of nature reserves?

Traditional systems do have well-demonstrated conservation effects (reviewed in, e.g., Berkes 2008; Berkes, Colding and Folke 2000; Colding and Folke 2001). They may also manage well in one way while managing badly in another (Kay and Simmons 2002). We are best advised to learn from both their mistakes and their successes, rather than stereotyping or ignoring them.

Finally, some insight into who manages, and why, is gained from looking at some of the very few success stories of restoring a ravaged habitat. Usually, once a habitat is wrecked, it is never restored except by the fall of a civilization and the return of a Dark Age (Chew 2001, 2006). This happened cyclically in the West, and many times elsewhere, from the Classic Maya collapse to the fall of Angkor in Cambodia. Sometimes the Dark Age only makes things worse. In areas where reasonably good management was practiced, eliminating people or their management may lead to the soil eroding away before nature can reclaim and rebuild (Fisher 2005, 2009), especially in dry country.

Erosion becomes extreme in limestone country. Both careless cultivation or grazing and the removal of good cultivation will turn dry limestone country into a lunar landscape in short order, and it may never recover within geological time, judging from the current situation in northwest Africa, the Mixteca Alta of Mexico (where colonial overgrazing was guilty, though even before that there was some abuse; Melville 1997), parts of upland Greece and the Levant, and other comparable environments.

Fortunately, we do not usually have to go to such extremes to get a landscape back to productivity. The most dramatic case of restoring habitat in pre-twentieth century times was the restoration of Japan's forests (Totman 1989) and fisheries (Ruddle and Akimichi 1984) by the Tokugawa Shogunate, which adopted the no-nonsense approach that the court needed forest products and fish, and that villages not doing their bit would incur condign punishments. A few beheadings of village heads put some bite into this, and forest cover increased from a very small proportion to 90 percent of the country. Quite a few other islands around the world show cycles of ruin and rebuilding.

Another early case was the restoration of forests to Denmark, which had become totally deforested by 1700. Realizing this was leading to massive coastal erosion and wind damage as well as lack of forest products, the Danish government reforested actively in the eighteenth century (Kjaergaard 1994) and later. Germany began managing forests and planting some new ones at about the same time, with major takeoff and landscape transformation in the nineteenth century.

Twentieth-century industrialism and hi-tech farming brought massive rural depopulation in marginal areas of Europe and the United States, with correspondingly dramatic recovery of forests and other wildlands. Almost everyone interested in the environment now knows that the United States reached its lowest levels of forest in the 1920s, with recovery following, in approximately the order of deforestation—New England first, Washington state latest to turn around. (A very few states, notably Alaska, have not yet turned the corner.) Not only did forests recover much of their former range in the east, but planted or spontaneous forests occupied significant areas of the prairies and plains (this mostly from personal observation in Nebraska and neighboring states, intermittently over 70+ years). Tree farms have had something to do with recovery, but more is natural regrowth on abandoned lands.

Less well known is the similar process in Europe (see, e.g., McNeill 1992). Italy is a dramatic case; France and Spain less so but catching up (personal observation). England, however, continues to lose cover, as "clean farming" destroys hedgerows and copses.

Reforestation projects are routinely pushed in the Third World today, but only South Korea has really succeeded, going from virtually no real forests in 1955 to a healthy cover on all highlands today. To my knowledge, Japan and Korea are unique in having restored healthy, mature, diverse, productive forests to vast areas by actual government programs.

In Tunisia I have seen vast tracts of young tree cover—spindly, mono-cropped, and stressed, but at least there. Parts of China have been reforested, with quite dramatic success in some areas known to me (including the hills in and north of Hong Kong), but China's claims in this area are notoriously inflated. I have traveled over and through countless miles of "reforested" land-scapes where the only trees were a very few dying pine seedlings planted long ago and never cared for. The literature and, especially, my careful perusal of satellite photos show that this, not the healthy groves above Hong Kong, is the norm. On the other hand, perusing the satellite shots shows some unexpected successes, including rebirth of the forests of the mountains of dry and barren Shaanxi Province. And recent shots of the Great Wall show a far richer and higher cover than my own photos from 1978.

Restoration of nonforest environments—wetlands, coral reefs, healthy grasslands, and the like—remains in the experimental stage, basically confined to parks, reserves, and similar environments where it is acceptable to expend huge amounts of money and labor for very little tangible result. There are some hopeful successes, but very few. The bitter fact is that we have to take care of what we have; once it's gone, there is little hope of restoring it except by com-pletely excluding people from it, and even that is no real help in the millions of square miles where people have impacted the ecosystems for better or worse over thousands of years.

FUNCTIONALISM OUTWORN

All this has led to abandonment of earlier models within cultural ecology. Broadly, anthropology and sociology in the early twentieth century tended toward functionalist models. They explained a given cultural institution by its function—either its ostensible, "manifest" function or some inferred "latent" function that the anthropologist could detect but that the people claimed not to recognize. Thus, families existed to raise children, cooking existed to make food edible, warfare existed to get booty or protect one's goods from becoming someone else's booty, and conservation existed to conserve resources. Functions could be social (families raise children, kinship systems organize kin respon-sibilities) or biological (Malinowski 1944 argued that culture exists largely to get food, shelter, health, and the like, in the most efficient ways). This could all seem quite Panglossian, and early functionalists did make everything sound perfectly in tune, but later functionalist theories went to the opposite extreme. A range of theories in the 1960s and later explained everything in culture by the needs of the elites to manage, control, and exploit the masses. This, too, is functionalism; it explains institutions, and indeed all human society, as fairly automatic reflexes of simple functions.

The problems with these theories emerged when they were applied, especially in economic development and aid work, in and after the 1950s. People simply didn't do what was predicted. Whether one assumed that people were motivated to maximize incomes, or to maximize food or "forage optimally," or to maximize "overall utility," or to maximize social connectedness, or maximize elite dominance, everyone found that the people were doing all kinds of unpredictable things. This fed back on explanations of culture. It was found that simple functional explanations under-predicted cultural diversity and change. Marvin Harris, in particular, aggressively pursued a "research strategy" of assuming that all cultural institutions could be explained by needs for calories, shelter, and a few other simple material goods. He tried hard to explain religious food taboos as nutritionally sound (Harris 1966, 1968). Although he had some success, he ultimately failed to deal with the sheer range of cultural diversity—with things like pet-keeping (Sahlins 1976), and even with why neighboring peoples in the same habitat often have quite different staple foods.

Jon Elster throughout his career pointed out that functionalist explanations can never work for humans, because humans have so much independent agency (Elster 1983, 2007). They are just too cussedly independent, original, and complicated to be predictable from narrowly functionalist theories. Related to this work, directly or indirectly, was a long line of theories based on looking not only at structure and function but also at agency. I was initially influenced toward interactive, agency-based theories by reading the work of George Homans (1974) and Erving Goffman (1959), among others. Later, I came to draw heavily on Anthony Giddens (1984), Pierre Bourdieu (1977, 1990), Arturo Escobar (2008), and Bruno Latour (2005), but I cannot say they made my theory. I was already doing it, but needed them for their more sophisticated and intelligent fleshing out of ideas I already had.

This is not to say that biology, social structure, and economic and ecological function are irrelevant. They are not; they set the stage and set the limits for human action. People respond to environments and to economic realities. Economic factors are obviously basic in human affairs, and Marvin Harris's "research strategy" is of great value. However, people's decisions are not predictable from immediate economic ends. Intention and agency fine-tune the system, often in ways that change it permanently. One needs carbohydrates to survive, and it is, for some purposes, adequate to invoke this truth to explain why people eat rice. But to explain why some people eat rice, some manioc, and some millet, or why the central Thai eat non-sticky rice whereas the northeast Thai eat sticky rice, one has to go to more arcane considerations.

There are historical reasons for all these things—it was not mere chance that determined them—but they now shape behavior far beyond the original reasons for their adoption. And to explain why some people do not eat at all—in hunger strikes, or because of desperate poverty, or because of anorexia—requires full attention to individual agency and interpersonal dynamics. Similarly, explaining why forests are conserved in the United States is easy enough on economic grounds, but only contingent history explains why Yosemite was conserved and Hetch Hetchy was not. We also need contingent explanations based on agency to tell us why Americans love dogs and Chinese eat them (cf. Sahlins 1976).

Decisions that may have originally been mere casual chance may create whole systems, because of path dependence and lock-ins. The chance interbreeding of Azerbaijan goat-face grass with wheat produced a superior rising and baking grain (bread wheat) some 8,000 years ago; it must have been a rare and local product of a remote and isolated region. It is now the world's most important, widespread, and versatile crop. One cannot imagine the world without it. I am personally sure that its rise began when the women of that area—southwest of the Caspian Sea—noticed that certain odd wheats from odd corners of the field produced a startlingly superior bread. If they had been interested only in calories and protein, they would not have cared, but they evidently wanted a better-rising, more flavorful product. Their tastes—and their individuality, creativity, and agency—have made a good share of our modern world. We should all be grateful to them, but we have no idea what language they spoke. No more do we know who domesticated rice, or who first decided to make pets of dogs (dogs were pets originally; their hunting and herding functions depended on thousands of years of selective breeding). Most conservation seems more "functional," but even in management, people have to *decide* whether to maintain the system, improve it, or let it go and try to figure out something else.

The people who really mattered to our world are nameless and unknown, but without their proactive and interactive agency we would not be here.

POLITICAL ECOLOGY

To deal with the need to look at agency as well as function and structure, political ecology developed from cultural ecology in the 1970s and especially after 1990. Political ecology looks not only at economics, ecology, and material concerns, but also at interactions from the individual level to the global.

Dimensions of kin, community, and neighborhood were well covered within cultural ecology. They are, in fact, the best-analyzed and best-covered aspect of the field (saving me from further effort at this point, see Bates 2005; Bennett 1976, 1982, 1992, reviewing hundreds of studies; Netting 1981, 1986, 1993; Steward 1955, 1977).

Less well studied, until recently, was politics—jockeying for power. Julian Steward, in creating the field of cultural ecology, was extremely concerned with that issue (Steward 1955), devoting much attention to chiefdoms (he defined the term) and states, but his earlier students were not. They tended to confine their attentions to adaptation and functional relationships within particular societies, most often non-state ones with relatively simple political orders. His later students sharply reversed this; one of them, Eric Wolf, coined the term *political ecology* in 1972 (Wolf 1972). It has since caught on widely, especially in geography (foundational texts in that field being Blaikie and Brookfield 1987; Peet and Watts 1996; Robbins 2004).

Economic interests have recently been more and more opposed to environmental legislation and practice, partly because it really threatens some of their income streams, but more because of wider ideological, political, and emotional interests (Anderson 2010; Bunker and Ciccantell 2005; Dichter 2003; Eichenwald 2000; Ellerman 2005; Helvarg 1997; Humphreys et al. 2007; Juhasz 2008; Tania Li 2007; Stiglitz 2003). We are now aware of the emotional nature of politics (Marcus 2002; Westen 2007). This includes, among other things, commitment to a certain worldview. Economists often are so committed to economism that they fail to see enormous environmental problems—as, for instance, in the recent adulation of China as the coming world leader and great power, without any notice of China's suicidal ecological policies (Anderson 2012).

Countries trapped by debt and "structural adjustment" do worse at saving their biota, partly because they are often forced by international agencies to run down their conservation efforts; countries with more NGO activity and less dependent economies do a much better job (Shandra et al. 2010). Antienvironmental forces provide divisive rhetoric; the most obvious recent case has been the spurious science of global warming denial, produced by energy companies and often much exaggerated by both conservative and Marxist politicians worldwide (see Hoggan 2009; Mooney 2005; Oreskes and Conway 2010; Powell 2011).

Even more than war, environmental damage bears most heavily on the poor. According to a recent study, only 7 percent of India's gross national product comes directly from "nature's services," but 57 percent of the income of the poor does (Sukhdev 2009).

We need bridging as well as bonding (Flora et al. 2006). That is, groups would not only maintain their solidarity, they would put a great deal of effort into maintaining bridges to other groups. Many a project has been wrecked by attending to bonding but neglecting bridging (Flora et al. 2006).

Much sociability in this imperfect world involves social games and defensive competitiveness (Veblen 1912). This typically results in a combination of oppressive elites and passive, hopeless masses. We see this, often, in large bureaucracies (Weber 1946): people competing to be the most suave, smiling, and pleasant on the surface and the most treacherous and amorally competitive underneath. This is the world classically described by Machiavelli (2005/1515), and Kautilya's *Arthaśastra*. However, not all large bureaucracies succumb to it, and many (*very* many) small communities do succumb to it. One might wish to be an anarchist (cf. Scott 2009), but the problem is human-wide, not bigness per se. Marx was right: laboring together toward a common valued goal is the cure. Marx, however, did not realize how dangerous bigness could be and how devastating even a well-meant top-down social system could become.

An interesting case showed that the difference between good and bad community could depend on the percentages of cooperators and free riders (Rustagi et al. 2010). Among Bale Oromo villages in Ethiopia, experiments revealed an astonishing variability in cooperativeness. The government had devolved forest management on the villages, which were to manage forests as village commons. In some villages, almost everyone had strong cooperative values, and these took care of their forests, at least insofar as they could organize effective forest patrols—a difficult and rather costly endeavor, but successfully done by many villages. However, some villages were made up almost entirely of free riders, and in these, forestry failed. The few cooperators got disgusted with the free-riding majority, and, reasonably enough, stopped trying. (Rustagi et al. call them "conditional" cooperators for this, but it seems to have been ordinary common sense.) Intermediate villages did as one would expect.

Political ecologists are concerned with political relations within and between societies. Often they focus on relations of dominance by large, powerful states or international bodies over small-scale local societies. Sometimes this is done almost to the exclusion of anything else, so that we are left wondering what the small-scale societies have any autonomy or agency over at all, and even whether they ever eat. This obsessive focus has been sharply critiqued by Andrew Vayda (one of Steward's earlier students; Vayda and Walters 1999, Vayda 2008). He advocates looking at a particular situation and comprehensively surveying all things that led up to it. This is certainly useful, but political ecologists are generally more concerned with the general theory of dominance and exploitation than with specific situations. In anthropology, some of the most important early work in this area was done by Michael Dove over many years, and he continues to be a leader (see, e.g., Dove 1992, 2003, 2004, 2005, 2006, 2011; Dove et al. 2003). Many of the leading current workers in this field are his students. Recently he has been teaching (at Yale) and producing students in cooperation with James Scott (see Scott 1985, 1990, 1998), who has studied the ways that bureaucracies dragoon and discipline citizens and the ways the citizens resist and maintain agency.

Blaming climate change on deforestation, and deforestation on local swidden agriculture, has been very widespread, but turns out to be largely wrong. Climate change is due to far wider forces (notably including greenhouse gases). Deforestation is largely the result of the powerful states and their multinational firms engaging in logging, plantation agriculture, and other massive development schemes (see, e.g., Jarosz 1993). Far from causing deforestation, some small-scale swidden societies may actually increase groves and forests by protecting useful wild trees (as the Maya do; Anderson 2003), or by actually establishing "wild" groves (as the Maya also do; Gómez-Pompa 1987). The Kayapo of Brazil also do this (Posey 2004), as apparently do the inhabitants of Sierra Leone (Fairhead and Leach 1996; though see Nyerges 1997) and many other peoples.

The generalization that powerful societies almost always brutally oppress, exploit, and mistreat weak ones is such common knowledge that the ancient Greeks and Romans took it as a rule of nature. What political ecology has done that is new and different is therefore of special interest and importance; it includes detailed demonstration of the ways that apparently innocent and often genuinely well-meant rhetoric adds to ecological repression. In particular, rhetorics of modernization and development almost always devalue everything local and traditional, and disproportionately favor whatever is new and technologically stylish in the developers' home country. Because of this, the more well-intentioned the development and conservation schemes in question, the worse they often turn out in practice (Tania Li 2007; Scudder 2005).

Such discourses of development have been so pernicious that they have spawned a huge literature reaching far outside political ecology. Leading studies within the latter field include Arturo Escobar's magistral *Territories of Difference* (2008) and Tania Murray Li's *The Will to Improve* (2007). Li's title sums up her thesis: the will to improve has led to steamrolling small-scale societies, from colonial and missionary times straight through to modern development efforts. Always, the rich and powerful of the First World know what is good for the poor and bare of the Third, and act accordingly. The result is always the same, whether missionaries or World Bank are the doers: the rich get richer and the poor lose what little they had. As indigenous people around the world put it, "when the whites came, we had the land and they had the Bible. Now we have the Bible and they have the land." This brings us back to the ancient Greek perception, but Li's point is that the rhetoric of development not only sounds well-meaning, but often is indeed well-meant. Innocent presuppositions are, if anything, worse than genuinely evil scheming. A Machiavellian schemer at least has the sense to keep his victims alive, to work another day. (See comparable works on development in general, such as Dichter 2003 and Stiglitz 2003; and this has been my experience, too—see my posting "Food and Development," on my website, www.krazykioti.com).

Thus, the best-intentioned ideas can be used and misused to repress local societies. This gives one the uncomfortable feeling that we often are lulled into a false sense of confidence in our ideas, and that ideas are dangerous even when no danger was intended. This has tied anthropological studies of development discourse to wider and more cynical concerns in epistemology, as will appear below.

This line of critique can get out of hand, and many examples of "critique of environmentalism" are mere attacks on conservation and environmentalism. Some critics, in spite of being ostensibly liberal or leftish politically, have gullibly swallowed the classic right-wing lies about the environmental movement. (On sources of and corrections of these lies, see Bellant 1990; Goodstein 1999; Helvarg 1997; Oreskes and Conway 2010; Powell 2011; Stauber and Rampton 1996.)

I feel that the main contribution of modern political ecology has been to recapture agency—to show that the indigenous "victims" actually have some say in it all, even if only to make humorous and bitter comments. Moreover, purely negative, hopeless accounts are by definition conservative. They create and maintain the idea that things can only get worse, so any change is bad. The endless exposés of every good cause (no matter how ridiculous the charges) have perceptibly sapped the energy of good-doers and well-intentioned citizens. The present book thus attempts to do something almost unprecedented: write a positive book of political ecology—one largely concerned with relative successes, or with debates in which the good have not uniformly lost out.

A series of particularly fine recent books by Arun Agrawal (2005), Arturo Escobar (2008), Michael Dove (2011), Paige West (2006), Stuart Kirsch (2006), Andrew Mathews (2008, 2009, 2011), and others bring out in detail the sometimes successful and always interesting attempts by local people to cope with the rapidly expanding messes they are in. (Many of these books appear in a series from Duke University Press, under Escobar's supervision; he is a professor at Duke.) Kirsch's book is particularly sad yet heartening; he gives in detail the commentary of a Papua-New Guinea people whose land and lives have been ruined by a huge gold mine. The hope comes from their degree of insight and awareness, a trait that allowed similar people in nearby Bougainville to shut down an equally destructive copper mine. Success stories are rare in this literature, but Agrawal's and Escobar's accounts show some surprisingly successful coping on the local level. The idea that the world's indigenous peoples are hopeless victims of the global juggernaut is, in the last analysis, not only wrong but a right-wing fiction that easily becomes a self-fulfilling prophecy. If we do not believe the locals can do anything, we will not make any provisions for them to try.

EMOTIONAL ECOLOGY

Kay Milton (2002) has stressed the importance of "loving nature." She studied contemporary British and Irish ecological activists and found them motivated by love, not by economic or scientific motives. She thoughtfully expanded on this perception, in light of the fact that humans integrate emotion and cognition and cannot separate these in practice (she cites Damasio 1994). Human phenomenological reality is a harmonious, or at least thorough, integration of the two. Loving nature, insofar as it applies to religious feelings or actions, would clearly be in the "spiritual" rather than the "religious" realm. For saving nature, love is essential, and so is structured ethical practice—in short, we must use spirituality *and* religion, *and* of course science, too, to save the world.

For my Maya and Northwest Coast friends, "loving nature" is not quite the perfect description. Their emotional response is both less and more than that. The Northwest Coast people have so intense an emotional feeling that *love* is the only word. Many Northwest Coast Native people today feel that the trees, animals, and rocks of their areas are home and family—living spirit persons, who may be intensely loved, just as one loves one's human neighbors, friends, and house.

This does not require traditional religion or a long time frame. Modern ranchers in the United States and Mexico love their desert homeland (Hedrick 2007; Perramond 2010). Humans simply do not remain neutral about things they have to take constantly into account (Anderson 1996). Interactions construct our world; our very selves are born of interacting (Dilthey 1985; Levinas 1969). Interactions with beings we take seriously are powerfully emotional events, and, indeed, more than that; phenomenologically, *they construct our world* (Dilthey 1985; Levinas 1969).

The emotions raised by the forest, among the Maya and the Northwest Coast peoples, are deeper and more complex than those raised by a forest among most Americans. Yet, even the modern American will usually look at a forest with a mix of awe, concern, curiosity, and other emotions. She may desire to save the forest, yet fear the mountain lions in it. She may wonder what there is to eat, or what birds nest there. She may know enough of the English and Dutch landscape art tradition to have her reaction to the forest strongly colored by Constable's or the Ruisdaels' views of woodland. Countless other associations may occur—cognitive yet powerfully informed by emotion.

"Loving nature" is basic and essential, but most cultural representations of nature go well beyond it. They deal also with security, familiarity, and other aspects of personal involvement. Gratitude is one key concept (Atleo 2004). Traditional hunters are often grateful to the game for offering itself, and farmers are famously grateful, for rain or harvests, to God or to spirits and deities of crops and fields. Shame and guilt over damaging behavior are also part of any caring conscience.

Representations require lively community solidarity. People actively work to maintain the good situation, and everyone knows they should not cheat and should stop others from cheating. A huge problem in the modern world is that people—especially in poor countries—lack the heart, or the community support, to stop abuse of resources when they see another community member doing it. Community solidarity in turn must be maintained by cultural institutions, again overwhelmingly "religious" ones.

Children learn whatever older peers, and to a somewhat lesser extent the adults, think is important and valuable (Harris 1998). At present, electronic gadgets and games preoccupy them. The environment is neglected (Louv 2005, 2011; Nabhan and Trimble 1994). This has to change. In other cultures, not only subsistence needs but also religion and other cultural systems strongly favored learning about the environment.

TRADITIONAL ENVIRONMENTAL ETHICS

Detailed anthropological descriptions of traditional environmental ethics are surprisingly uncommon. A number of recent books (including Berkes 2008; Cajete 1994; Callicott 1994; Deur and Turner 2005; Pierotti 2011; Radin 1957a, 1957b; Turner 2005) sum up many observations and conclusions, but these works summarize a wide variety of sources, of varying quality. I have discussed environmental ethics in general in two books (Anderson 1996, 2010) and a long posting, "Ethics," on my website (www.krazykioti.com).

Today, there are various studies of Indigenous and local ethical systems (see, e.g., Anderson et al. 2000). More to the point, there are now several accounts by Indigenous authors of their own traditional ethics. For the Northwest Coast, we have several sources (e.g., Atleo 2004; George 2003; Reyes 2002). Nearby are the Yupik, subject of major research on ethical philosophy and practice, by Ann Fienup-Riordan (1994, 2005).

Native Americans speak of a concept of "respect" as applied to other-than-human persons: animals, trees, mountains. "Respect," clearly, is not the sort of thing we mean when we say that students no longer respect professors (a complaint as old as teaching). We are referring to something more egalitarian, more general, more thoughtful, and more genuine. Native American *respect* is related to several technical ethical terms: the Buddhist concept of compassion; the psychological concept of unconditional positive regard (Rogers 1961); the Protestant religious concept of the priesthood of all believers; and the ordinary folk concept of considerateness or consideration. It is a sense that we are all in this together and have to be as decent to each other as possible to keep the situation functional, whatever the situation may be. Humans and other-than-human persons depend on each other, and, because of that have to act decently toward one another. One need not believe in spirits or transmigration of souls to see the value of this claim.

At best, respect approaches Emmanuel Levinas's concept of the infinitely important other (e.g., Levinas 1969). Levinas maintained that the other people in our lives are infinitely important to us, because our whole lives are constructed through interaction with them. Some "others" are more important; for Levinas, a Jewish theologian, God was the really infinitely important one, but Levinas also argued that all the people who have deeply influenced us are infinitely important in our lives. Similar ideas seem to underlie many Indigenous concepts.

It seems reasonable to draw on traditional concepts such as Navaho *hozhon*, Nuu-chah-nulth *isaak* (respect in the wide sense), and the very widespread idea of the personhood of all beings to enrich our current ideas on environmental ethics. In regard to justice, for instance, it would clearly make a major difference if we recognized nonhuman persons as deserving respect—not necessarily total protection. Native Americans are generally quite opposed, on the basis of traditional moral teachings, to the extreme "animal rights" activists (many of whom, incidentally, show no sign of respecting the animals they liberate). But traditional Native persons are even more opposed to the wanton destruction of nature simply to destroy it.

Obviously, the core of this is an ethic of sustainability: don't take too many fish, don't cut too many trees, don't waste food, don't take too many game animals. Most societies have some form of this ethic, however badly observed. Most of those without it are small groups with simple technologies, living in vast, thinly populated realms, often tropical forests. The forests of South America are particularly noted for lack of conservation (Hames 2007), though many societies in the marginal areas support denser populations in poorer habitats and have conservation ethics that may be quite elaborate and detailed (Beckerman et al. 2002; Reichel-Dolmatoff 1971, 1976, 1996).

Other cultures have similar ethical standards, usually less well described. Some particularly dramatic and important cases come from southwest China, where Tibetans (Huber 1999), Akha (Jianhua "Ayoe" Wang 2007, 2008, 2013), and other minorities maintained excellent environmental management in spite of extremely dense populations and high cultural levels.

The term *respect* is widespread in traditional conservation. In addition to *isaak*, the Mongol *shutekh* and *khundlekh*, Akha *taqheeq-e*, and other terms also translate as respect for both human elders and the wild. Communism ended this in most of China and to some extent in Russia and Mongolia, with devastating results, showing the extreme effectiveness of the old system; once it shatters, the entire resource base can be devastated in a very few years.

Sustainability by itself is not enough. If people make a radical distinction between human and nonhuman, they will tend to choose even the lowest human good in a pinch over even the highest nonhuman good. Poachers are excused because they need to feed their families; the fate of the species they exterminate is not considered.

It is fairly common experience that recreational hunters and fishers save the animals they want to kill. Recreational duck hunters have not only saved the more edible species of duck in North America, but have essentially single-handedly brought them, or at least the more edible species, back to historic population levels, after population crashes in the mid-twentieth century. Commercial hunters and fishers, by contrast, are under so much pressure to take too much that they are faced with a classic tragedy of the commons. Thus it is that almost every sport-fishing lake in North America is full of fish (though, alas, usually introduced weedy species), but the seas, given over largely to commercial interests, are empty or emptying.

More successful in motivating conservation is the effect of regarding animals and plants as persons ("other-than-human persons"). All North American and east Asian Indigenous peoples see them this way, and my sense from wide but unsystematic reading is that the same is true in most of South America and much of Asia. In India, all creatures are sacred, at least in theory; practice is far short of ideals, but still better than the practice in less idealistic lands (personal observation). In Southeast Asia, tree spirits are extremely important, animals are regarded as worthy of spiritual consideration, and conservation flourishes to the extent these beliefs survive. Where communism and contemporary extremist Islam flourish, nature retreats, but forests and wildlife continue to flourish where the old ways flourish. In Thailand and Cambodia, my wife and I have encountered tree spirit beliefs used to persuade people not to cut trees. We were once riding in a taxi in Cambodia with a public health colleague, who was joking about the *neaktaa* "tree spirits." The taxi driver stopped the taxi, turned around, and said in a serious and worried voice: "You don't joke about the *neaktaa*."

Of course, human persons are closer than other-than-human ones, and generally get more consideration in a pinch, but there is at least some balance. It was unthinkable, in these societies, to wipe out vast populations of natural plants and animals for no reason. When the Mexican government "opened up" some land for my Maya friends by bulldozing a tract of forest and leaving a waste of useless bare rock, the Maya were morally shocked as well as disgusted with the foolishness. The government, however, duly announced with pride that they had opened the land. Simply getting rid of natural growth was a good in itself. The same is notoriously common in Europe and the United States, where development is apt to be sold as getting rid of uncontrolled nature, and where destroying nature simply to destroy it is considered virtuous, or even fun (as in off-road vehicle use in untouched places).

WAR, MORALITY, AND ECOLOGY

This brings us to a key point: *the basis of morality is social and depends on the definition of society.* The entire progress of morality from Neanderthals to Gandhi may be seen as simply an extension of normal social behavior from the family outward. In the West, it extended to the tribe, then to the territory, then to the state, and finally with Christianity to the whole human race. In Asia it was expanded by Hinduism, Buddhism, and Jainism to cover the entire biological community. In the Americas, Native societies essentially all construct society to include the local plants and animals, but not the more remote humans. The people across the mountains are enemies, and their plants and animals may be theirs, but our plants and animals on our side of the mountains are people like us. For many North American Native groups, our plants and animals are actual relatives; they are descended from the Creator's children, just as we are. The Katzie of British Columbia, for instance, believed that the Creator had a son who fathered the human race and a daughter who became a sturgeon and is incarnate in the sturgeon lineages (Jenness 1955). This explains why Katzie habitat was once the most favored place for sturgeons in British Columbia. When the Katzie caught a sturgeon, they saw it as a beloved sister sacrificing her life to feed her people. Similar beliefs about salmon, deer, and other prized game animals are widespread in North America, and peccaries occupy the same slot in much of South America.

Rapid changes in the twentieth century led to the alienation of Westerners and other urban populations from the land—from farming, hunting, fishing, and even hiking and other traditional rural recreation (see Louv 2005, 2011). The result has been the rise of an extreme form of anthropocentrism and individualism, even by Euro-American standards.

An interesting sidelight on all this is that some of the most conservation-minded and environmentally protective societies have been absolutely merciless toward their fellow humans. The Northwest Coast in pre-Columbian times was famously a land of predatory raiders, yet it practiced model conservation and wild resource management. Southeast Asia was home to many incredibly warlike societies (though also to peaceful ones); both warlike and peaceful ones managed the environment well. Medieval West Europe was surprisingly environment-conscious in spite of its social landscape of Vikings, knights errant, and robber barons, whereas the "pax Romana" was ecologically insensitive.

Yet warlike societies obviously do not always conserve. The Near East has always been problematic in both environmental management and maintaining peace. In South America, the crazy-quilt of conserving and nonconserving societies (Beckerman et al. 2002) accompanies, but does not appear to correlate with, a crazy-quilt of warlike and less warlike societies. None are really pacific, but some are more frequently at war than others.

Some peaceful societies have been environmentally friendly. And some societies have alternated between war and peace, with varying environmental effects. The Pueblos of the American Southwest and the Maya of Mesoamerica had ecological overshoots (Diamond 2005 exaggerates but is as good a source as any), but were largely good managers. Interestingly, their overshoot times seem to have accompanied or followed warlike periods, to the point that some scholars think war rather than ecological overshoot brought down the great cities (see below). Their peaceful days were more environmentally friendly.

Conversely, many more peaceful societies have totally ravaged their environments. Even more striking is the fact that the United States and Europe, in the late eighteenth and through the nineteenth centuries, fought for and institutionalized civil and human rights at precisely the time when they were most environmentally insensitive. The basic pattern is clear: care for nature and care for fellow humans are not correlated.

Solidarity is obviously a necessity for good resource management. However, there is no indication that the most solidary societies are the best managers. Societies that put a heavy burden of responsibility on the individual, and thus leave a good scope for individual independence, have the best environmental record. Consider Scandinavia, Hungary, most Native American societies, and even the modern United States, versus contemporary China, much of the Middle East, and old-time Latin America. In some areas, especially Latin America, the coming of democracy and individualism has led to a rapid rise of environmentalism. On the other hand, this correlation, too, looks shaky, because the highly communal societies of Southeast Asia had good track records until recently, and some highly autocratic societies have recently been leaders in areas such as reforestation (Tunisia), water conservation (Singapore), and similar areas.

Therefore, it appears that *care for nature is not a part of general good behavior and does not follow from it. It requires a special morality and special social rules.*

ANTI-SUSTAINABILITY ATTITUDES

The extreme importance of ideology or belief systems is shown by the effects of modernization and westernization, worldwide, and the failure of most to resist it. The overtly "religious," philosophical, and aesthetic material does not travel; what travels are the beliefs so deeply held that they are not even examined. (As the saying goes, the fish does not know about water.) What has gone worldwide is a set of rules of thumb, the first and most important of which is that destroying natural resources is the way of progress.

Thomas Buckley, while researching Native American spirituality in northwest California, heard a forester tell environmentalists, "'You keep talking about the need for wilderness, the rights of trees and so on—but that's just philosophy.

We're not talking philosophy, we're talking facts. There are millions of board feet of lumber here—that's a fact'" (Buckley 2002:181). Of course, as Buckley points out, seeing a forested wilderness as just commercial lumber is just as much philosophy as the environmentalists' view. The forester was using *philosophy* as a polite euphemism for *nonsense,* and *fact* as a dramatic word for *financial interest.* But, in fact, both sides really were talking philosophy. Whether nature is seen as in some sense worthwhile, or as something to be destroyed as fast as possible for quick cash, is a philosophical question.

PIONEER FRINGES

The idea of "development" as "using ever more stuff" is a pioneer attitude that has become institutionalized. It developed on the moving frontier of the colonial world, in the United States, in Latin America, in Australia, in Africa. Related is an idea of "development" as "eliminating everything natural," as in the concept of "progress" that has turned productive forests into housing developments in the United States and unproductive cattle ranches in Latin America (Painter and Durham 1995).

As shown by countless studies, the more long-term the stake and the more total the dependence on the resource, the better the management—unless desperate need forces immediate drawdown. Secure tenure, whether outright ownership, sharecropping, or long lease, works well, but brief tenure, whether renting or insecure ownership, does not. Those who move often lose connection with landscapes. People who plan to move every three years (as Americans did in much of the twentieth century) do not invest in the land, though they may not see any reason to destroy it, either.

Even careless pioneer-fringe management may not be permanently devastating. The moving frontier in logging in America wiped out the old-growth forests quickly, but second-growth filled in, and much of the forest area was soon restored. Much of its wildlife was gone, but this is probably due more to continued hunting than to initial logging. Only in areas where urbanization or excessively short-cycle tree farming followed did the initial logging lead to permanent disastrous changes. The main problems with pioneer-fringe overuse come when wildlife is totally shot out or when land is farmed so poorly that the topsoil erodes away.

Pioneers, everywhere, generally move fast through an area, destroying all and leaving little. There is a learning curve as they learn to deal with the landscape—often too late, after much or most of the value is gone. An interesting case from a strictly premodern, precapitalist world is presented by the Polynesian settlers of remote islands like the Hawaiian chain. They did as bad a job at first as modern colonial settlers did. Archaeology shows that, in island after island, they devastated the environment, suffered a population crash, and rebuilt in a sustainable way. They learned, and eventually created stunningly successful landscapes with introduced biota and technologies (Kirch 1994, 1997, 2007; Easter Island may have been an exception [Diamond 2005] but this is controversial).

Madagascar is another case in which pioneers impacted a landscape in a far from ideal way; alas, they have still not gotten to sustainability (Goodman and Bestead2003; "Madagascar on My Mind," posted on my website, www.krazykioti.com). Madagascar's Indonesian immigrants seem to have wiped out the larger animals by fire and hunting, cut down most of the forests, and substituted Indonesian-style rice agriculture. Many other cases could be mentioned, especially from islands, which have fragile ecosystems; even ancient Cyprus and Sicily were hard hit, losing dwarf elephants and other odd fauna (exhibits, Museo di Syracusa, Syracuse, Italy).

From Polynesia to Madagascar, from Siberia to the United States, from Brazil to China, we have archaeological, historical, or contemporary evidence that pioneers in a new and lavishly endowed country run through it with virtually no thought of conservation or sustainable management. They may even destroy everything they can find. When they run out of resources they can draw down, they usually stabilize, discovering that they have done a foolish thing and need to rebuild.

Recently, Communist states, especially the USSR and China, have managed to achieve maximal environmental damage for minimal human benefit. Damage to health by pollution, damage to irreplaceable topsoil by mass farming practices, and the like put much of the USSR and Communist East Europe into terrible shape by 1989 when communism fell. China's claims of 10 percent per annum economic growth are actually offset by environmental damage to the point that the real growth rate is close to zero (Anderson 2012; Smil 2004; Tilt 2009). The contemporary environmentalists who dream of socialism and blame "capitalism" for our plight might consider this more carefully.

CASE STUDY: SACRED GROVES

Sacred groves, and sacred gardens associated with temples and other religious sites, are found almost worldwide (Conan 2007; Haberman 2013; Malhotra et al. 2007; Verschuuren et al. 2010). Often they are extremely important, even basic, in the religion of a group. They anchor the human realm in the divine and spiritualize the landscape. They also serve the more mundane purpose of conserving forest resources—a bit of materialism openly and cheerfully admitted by traditional Chinese and Indians, among others. The Zen gardens of Japan, Hindu temple groves of India, and sacred groves of the ancient Mediterranean world are particularly famous (see Conan 2007; Verschuuren et al. 2010). The sacred gardens and landscapes of the ancient Aztecs were just as impressive and have received a surprisingly large amount of documentation—the whole of Aztec religion was expressed in its gardens (Bernal-García 2007; García-Zambrano 2007). The Maya, too, had sacred groves, poorly documented because of early missionary zeal (Landa 1937). These groves grew cacao and other food plants connected with religion and with the nobility. Chocolate was an elite privilege, though commoners apparently got some. Ceiba trees were sacred then and still are today among lowland Maya.

A particularly detailed study of sacred groves exists for India (Malhotra et al. 2007). Thousands of them exist there, both in or near villages and remote from humans. Often they are the only forests in a region (as is true for China also), and as such they protect threatened wildlife and fungi as well as plants. In Kerala alone, there are well over 1,000 plant species protected by sacred groves (full list, pp. 93–123 of Malhotra et al. 2007). The full list for India would run to many thousands of species. Hundreds of medicinal plant species are found and are locally used. Many groves have detailed histories—some real, some mythic. Most are under varying degrees of threat; one odd threat is excessive religiosity, which can lead to depleting the grove to build temples or otherwise try to appear more "properly" Hindu (see p. 61).

David Haberman (2013) discusses the religious background of these trees. They are often considered *murti*, "embodied forms of the divinity" (p. 45), physical beings in which a god resides, often for purposes of making his or her otherwise-disembodied self conveniently available to worshipers who need concrete items to revere. Trees are thus considered persons. They may be regarded as having indwelling spirits that are humanlike, or they may be regarded as ordinary trees but filled with divine essence. They may or may not be persons in the anthropomorphic sense, but they are persons in the moral sense, and locally in the legal sense (at least under traditional law; but even in the United States legal personhood is not totally denied to trees—there is a tree in Athens, GA, that "owns itself"). Worshiping such a *murti* tree can be seen as simply respecting the tree, or as worshiping the disembodied godhood it represents, or worshiping the tree literally as a spirit. The line between worship and simple respect grows perilously thin here and may be a factor of how urbanized or how skeptical the worshiper is.

As I have related at length elsewhere (esp. Anderson 1996), China had sacred or feng shui groves around most villages, tomb areas, and temples, until twentieth-century "progress" destroyed most of them. In the more forest-accessible parts of traditional China, most communities had, and maintained, sacred groves, and most people believed this was necessary for both immediate practical reasons (timber, firewood) and more tenuous, worship-related ones:

trees are sacred, and their good spirits protect the community. Obviously, not all Chinese believed all this. Far from all communities had groves. One could, however, actually see and count sacred groves (as I did in Hong Kong's New Territories decades ago) and could get a good consensus on why they were preserved. China had millions of them, and they enormously influenced the landscape and ecology. In southern China, most communities had them. But the broad-brush generalization "China had sacred groves" does not mean that everybody in China was near one.

The idea spread to Korea, Japan, Vietnam, and parts of Southeast Asia. Most Southeast Asian peoples had their own sacred forests and precincts, ranging from extremely carefully managed woodlands and forests to remote and rather thinly cared-for terrain (see Chapter 7, this text). Thailand has used Buddhist religious energy, even ordaining of trees, to preserve forests (Darlington 2013; Sponsel 2012).

Ancient Europe had sacred groves as well. Those of Greece and Rome are famous but sketchily documented (see Conan 2007 for thorough surveys of what is known). Celtic groves were working woodlots, intensively managed (Reynolds 1995). Christianity was hard on such groves, cutting them mercilessly (Anderson ms 1; Verschuuren et al. 2010), as when Charlemagne cut down and burned the Saxon sacred tree Irminsul (Lewis 2008:234). Presumably there, as in China when the Communists did the same thing in the twentieth century, loss of groves meant catastrophic loss of fuel, timber, fruit, windbreaks, biodiversity (including game), and erosion control.

Sacred groves seem universal in Africa (Nyamweru and Sheridan 2008 provide several extremely detailed descriptions of the social and cultural contexts of African groves). They are maintained by communities and overseen by elders and chiefs. Sometimes chiefly or kingly courts maintain them, and in Cameroun this has led not only to protection but even to local expansion (Fomin 2008). Communities have particularly protected some useful types of trees, such as the olive (Cocks and Dowd 2008) and many fruit and timber trees. Conservationists have worked hard with local communities to save the groves, which offer both local traditions and local biodiversity. A particularly thoughtful article details the successes and difficulties of one project in Kenya (Nyamweru and Kimaru 2008). In highland Ethiopia, the traces of natural forest are confined to the areas around churches. The Ethiopian Orthodox Tewahido Church maintains religious sanctuaries around its churches. These range from 3 to 300 hectares and are all that survives of the highland forests, but there are around 35,000 of them, a good number. However, they are under threat, from encroachment by farmers and herders (Cardelús et al. 2012), and presumably from secularism, too.

Both misguided missionaries and "superstition"-fighting Marxists have been active in Africa, as elsewhere. Benin's Marxist government in the 1970s cut down many groves sacred in the Vodoun religion and important to local communities (Juhé-Beaulaton 2008). Fortunately, the regime fell and religion rallied. The importance of traditional religion in saving biodiversity is nowhere more clearly shown.

Andrew Vayda (2009) has maintained that sacred groves need not save much; he anecdotally mentions groves far from villages or management and other groves too degraded to save resources. Obviously there are many such. Sacred groves vary across all imaginable dimensions, and there is serious need to expend the same effort in studying them that has been expended on the Chinese cases.

CHAPTER THREE

Looking Over Environmental Culture Areas

> Let us now praise famous men...
> There be of them, that have left a name behind them, that their praises might be reported.
> And some there be, which have no memorial; who are perished, as though they had never been; and are become as though they had never been born; and their children after them.
> But these were merciful men, whose righteousness hath not been forgotten....
> Their seed shall remain for ever, and their glory shall not be blotted out.
> *Ecclesiasticus 44:1, 8–13*

LOCAL MANAGEMENT, GLOBAL COMPARISON

The core of this book consists of accounts of environmental representations among various groups of people around the world. I provide general descriptions of traditional epistemology and worldview and some descriptions of how those apply in conservation and management of nature.

As mentioned above, this puts me in a place not particularly congenial to me: talking in broad-brush terms about whole cultures, as opposed to talking about individual variation and practice (Bourdieu 1977). I cannot resist putting in qualifiers about ranges of variation. On the other hand, there are some views that command an enormous degree of agreement over an enormously long time. Most of these are also self-conscious, publicly stated values. These include, for instance, Maya belief in a God-given (or gods-given) duty to care for plant resources, Chinese reverence for sacred mountains and trees, and

Northwest Coast inclusion of local other-than-human persons in one's own society. When I generalize, I usually confine myself to such genuinely shared beliefs. Otherwise, I try to give the range of variation of opinion. Of course, in a few places, for example, medieval Ireland, there is not much data, and one can only infer how much variation must have existed.

Where we do have data, we find that there is often huge variation within one society. For Chinese environmental beliefs over the millennia, there are two extremes: the Daoist extinction of self as it is absorbed and lost in nature, and the attitude of seeing nature as nothing but a mine of resources (as in some later urban-bureaucratic writings). The vast majority of Chinese are close to halfway between. With Confucius and Mencius, they see people as separate from nature, and they privilege people over other biota, but they see harmony (*he*) and balance (*bing*) between people and nature as absolutely necessary and as basic to all enterprises involving use of natural resources, from water to herbs.

In all that follows, therefore, the reader should keep in mind that broad-brush portrayals of worldviews are intended to portray the main view that most affected practice. Through affecting practice, it most affected the landscape. But in every case there were as many different versions of the view as there were people present, and some of those versions could be very far indeed from the average or norm.

ROUGH ASSESSMENTS

It should be possible to provide a rough assessment of how "good" people are at managing the landscape by looking at how many people were supported, and how well, over how long a time. The current agricultural and industrial system supports seven billion people worldwide, but is crashing already after only a generation. It comes at the end of a long history of extensive monocrop agriculture, going back at least 5,000 years.

The Middle East and Europe were problem areas for millennia, destroying a great deal for relatively little benefit. Even today, when anti-environmentalists point to "prosperity" as the result of ecological lunacy, they are reckoning not only without the future but without considering the effect on less affluent people and countries. Even by 1800, most of the Near East and a very large percentage of Europe were in varying states of ecological crisis. On the other hand, though Europe and much of the Near East in the old days did rather poorly in terms of agricultural yields (Slicher von Bath 1963) and forest preservation, at least

---

Photo on Previous Page: Surya (Thuriya), Agni, Thagyamin (Indra) along with his wife Indrani, Byamma (Brahma), and Skanda in Burmese representation. The Thirty Seven Nats, 1906, from Southeast Asia Digital Library. By Sir Richard Carnac Temple [Public domain], via Wikimedia Commons.

agriculture was sustainable and some forests were maintained; the full onslaught on nature came in the nineteenth and twentieth centuries.

At the other extreme is Southeast Asia, which has supported millions of people for thousands of years, and yet up to the late twentieth century still had most of its forests and other natural vegetation and was teeming with wildlife. Southeast Asia is the only part of the world that supported major civilizations and dense populations without significant environmental damage until recent European influences took over. Proof that this really was a matter of management strategies, including ideology, was the speed of the ecological crash when Western notions were accepted.

The Indian subcontinent seems to have done fairly well in old times, but we lack good information, because foreign conquests—the Central Asian Moguls and then European colonialism—altered the systems before much was recorded. The wildlife was preserved, by Hindu *ahimsa* (nonviolence). India has a unique history of nonviolence and sparing life. Its religions—Hinduism, Buddhism (Tucker and Williams 1997), and Jainism (Chapple 2002)—all counsel nonviolence. Jainism and some sects of the other two faiths absolutely forbid the taking of animal life. Some observant Jains wear masks to prevent accidentally inhaling insects. Protection of cattle and similar animals is universal. Even the coldly, even brutally, "realistic" *Arthashastra,* a government manual supposedly written by Kautilya around 300 BC (though much of it is later), has stringent regulations against taking protected mammals, birds, or fish, or otherwise poaching or taking too many lives of any sort (Kautilya 1967:137–138). Contemporary sects not only continue the tradition, but have incorporated modern environmentalist ideas, finding them conformable with traditional religion. The results include some of the most hopeful movements on the planet, from the Chipko "tree huggers" (Guha 1990, 2000) to less known but more mainstream groups (Jain 2011). These movements, far from being some sort of ancient spirituality that can be dismissed as irrelevant to the modern world, are highly aware of economic realities and the hardheaded reasons to conserve resources; the Chipko tree-huggers were protecting their livelihood as well as their religion.

Oceania, from Micronesia to aboriginal Australia, broadly sorts with Southeast Asia in this regard. People managed well (see excellent reviews in Wagner and Talakai 2007).

New Guinea is a partial exception; it is heavily deforested in spite of low population density. However, Paul Sillitoe, possibly the most expert and certainly the most prolific writer on highland Papua-New Guinea human ecology, concludes from a lifetime of research: "Regardless of their apparently casual attitudes to forest, these people have acted as sound custodians of their environment. What is surprising is not forest destruction but that it is not more extensive … given the time humans have inhabited the region." (Sillitoe 2010:246).

Agriculture is at least 6,000 and probably 8,000 years old in the Highlands. He is referring to one group, the Wola, but from all I have read (and seen, but my experience of New Guinea is brief) it is fairly typical. Some other areas are, however, much more short of land, including forest, though even they are not close to ecological collapse (Sillitoe 2010:248–250). Vast areas have been cleared for sweet potatoes, but in traditionally managed parts of the island, tall forests survive in large patches, on ridges and elsewhere, and succession is managed to allow regrowth to a fairly tall size after cropping swidden fields. Valley centers are generally in permanent cultivation.

East Asia in general has done fairly well, considering the dense population over millennia, but with much biodiversity loss (see esp. Marks 1998; Elvin 2004). Japan managed resources reasonably well up into the twentieth century, in spite of dense population and high levels of economic activity. Not until they self-consciously Westernized did they seriously damage the environment in irrevocable ways. Serious deforestation in the sixteenth century was remedied under the Tokugawas (Totman 1989), showing an astonishing capacity to fix the environment. However, Japan recently has slipped enormously, and is prey to pollution, overfishing, and other ills (Kirby 2011).

Korea today is doing very well, being one of the more successfully reforested countries in the world, but it, too, had a very uneven past. Tibet was exemplary until Chinese Communist rule devastated age-old management systems along with the Tibetan people. However, north China has been an ecological and environmental disaster for centuries, contrasting sharply with south China and Japan.

North America, insofar as we know much about its aboriginal societies, was excellent, though not perfect, at developing sustainable management systems. Truly model systems included at least some recent Maya ones and many others in Mexico, as well as the Northwest Coast and Northwest interior systems. Successes in other parts of North America are debatable at the very least (see, e.g., Kay and Simmons 2002). Much of the eastern fringes of the New World, from Labrador through the Caribbean to Argentina, were so devastated by European settler impact in the sixteenth century that we have little knowledge of them. They had very small populations. The high civilizations of Mexico—the Aztec, Maya, Zapotec, and others—seem to have had fairly heavy impacts. Still, many rare and vulnerable animal and plant species and habitats survived, only to be decimated or exterminated by European societies.

South America provides a truly confusing situation. Many societies were extremely careful with resources, managing them sustainably and adding to wild stands; others were completely indifferent to even the most minimal ideas of management (Beckerman et al. 2002). The small and dispersed groups in the lush, rich forests of the Upper Amazon did no environmental managing worthy of the name, having no need for it. Thanks to low population density and limited technology, they had rather little ability to manage resources in any case. The same seems to be true of the societies in much of the Gran Chaco (dry forests of Paraguay and adjacent areas), where hostile conditions keep human population densities very sparse indeed. Our knowledge of this region is limited; European-brought changes devastated populations and cultures long before 1800. Some clearly did not conserve; others were good managers of at least some resources (Reed 1995, 1997).

Beckerman et al. (2002) produced a model showing that an immediate cause of management is wide sharing of meat and fish. Where people share with the community, they have an incentive to manage on a community level, and thus to manage on a wide-flung basis. Societies that share on only a family level have no incentive to manage above the family level. However, some Chaco societies share widely but do not conserve game. I suspect that long-continued dense population, with relatively little devastation by post-European forces, is the variable that matters. Such populations tend to develop sharing. Thinly dispersed populations like those of the Chaco may share, but have little reason to conserve.

The Quechua and Aymara, and some other highland South Americans, remake and reshape the land more than the Romans ever did—but then manage sensitively and sustainably the world of terraces, platforms, channels, raised fields, and stone fabrics that they have constructed (Denevan 2001).

Yet another way of dealing with nature seems to exist in Africa, but I am less familiar with the continent and hesitate to make generalizations. Ancient Egypt had animal gods and powers, but seems to have lacked the full shamanic interpenetration of animal and human. Animal transformations in African myths and tales are usually scary: lion-men, leopard-men, and other savage were-beasts seem to dominate. In general, from ancient Egypt to modern Nigeria and Botswana, there is a clear sense of closeness to nature and constant use of animal and plant symbols. Reverence for natural places, powers, and beings is widespread. Sacred groves, sea and mountain deities, and theriomorphic powers abound. The "fetish groves" of west and central Africa are major refuges for species now endangered elsewhere. Claims of deforestation in some of West Africa are at best controversial.

African societies may have done well, or may not; we have poor descriptions from the days before slaving wrecked the continent. Some groups now have definitely unsustainable practices. Marie-Dominique Ribereau-Gayon writes me (e-mails of Jan. 14 and 18, 2010; used by her kind permission) that the Wanande of eastern Congo (D. R.) "derived huge pleasure and prestige" from clearing forests for fields; as of the 1990s, "forest was fast disappearing and everyone could see that within a few more years the whole of it would be gone." The Wanande ("people who hunt for forests") were happy about this, like the American settlers of the nineteenth century, who took such pride in clearing the forests. In fact, the Wanande regard cutting forest as an erotic pleasure, and a standard phrase for sexual conquest is "cutting forest." Francesco Remotti (1987) has provided an extremely detailed and valuable analysis of Wanande phrases for sexual conquest—and "conquest" is the Wanande word; a whole semantic field related to "forest-cutting" and "conquest" is involved. They and many other groups have deforested large parts of Africa, leading to major economic and political problems in nations such as Rwanda and Burundi.

In very sharp contrast, many societies have successful management (see, e.g., studies in Beinart and McGregor 2003). Many groups conserve sacred groves and may even expand forested areas significantly (Fairhead and Leach 1996; their account has been challenged [Nyerges 1997], but satellite photographs show that the area in question has a mosaic of forest, indicating at least conservation management). East African pastoralists are models of ecological adjustment (as noted since early work by Dyson-Hudson 1966 and Goldschmidt 1969; for recent work, see, e.g., Fratkin 2004; Gray et al. 2003; McCabe 1990, 2003, 2004; Ruttan and Borgerhoff Mulder 1999).

The Maasai, with whom I have had enough contact to speak with some knowledge, do not hunt wildlife for food; they do not eat anything they do not raise. They kill lions and other predators that threaten their herds, but otherwise they depend on their livestock. They traditionally moved these around from place to place according to where the grass is growing well, thus eliminating overgrazing on any one spot. They knew every species of plant, including its value for cattle feed and medicine as well as for humans. I was impressed with Maasai ability to pick up practically any tiny dried shred of vegetation and reel off several ways cattle used it. They burned to open up country and thus kept fresh grass available. This benefited wildlife, and when Maasai were excluded from places such as Ngorongoro Crater, the brush grew up and the wildlife populations plummeted (this from my own and my wife Barbara Anderson's observations and interviews there and elsewhere in East Africa, but confirmed in the literature, e.g., McCabe 2003).

Today, towns, roads, private ranches, and—ironically—conservation lands are reducing this mobility and thus forcing the Maasai to overgraze or abandon their lifestyle. Conservation by preservation, locking out herders, has been a disaster for both the Maasai and the wildlife (West, Igoe, and Brockington 2006 and ongoing research by the latter two since). All the above appears to be true for many other cattle nomads of Africa, though there is evidently variation. The ideology of dependence on cattle, care for them, nonuse of wild animals, and high mobility is supported, as usual, by religious traditions and ethics.

Overall, these varying successes and failures are predictable. Fairly densely populated societies confined to limited areas, especially if these are ecologically fragile, will normally develop sustainable, carefully managed regimes. Extremely sparse and mobile populations, especially if they have low environmental impacts, usually show little conscious conservation—though the Australian Aboriginal peoples, confined to an exceptionally fragile environment, are a spectacular exception.

Imperial, expansionist peoples tend to lose their sustainable ways, because they can simply move in on open lands or take lands and resources from weaker peoples. Thus the Roman and Mongol Empires, and *magna forte* the European and American empires of the last 500 years, were often environmentally irresponsible. Worst has been the modernizing, global society of the past fifty years, which combines individualism (frequently to the point of total irresponsibility about others) with a belief that all resources are either infinite or infinitely substitutable. Mixed situations, like China, bear out the general prediction here.

Worldviews of environmental management sort with culture areas, to a great extent and can be classified in a general way under broad headings. Two short case studies follow; both desperately need more attention, which I hope to give them in later books, but I cannot leave them out of the present book; they are critical to its message.

THE OLD NORTHERN WORLDVIEW

In East Asia and throughout northern Eurasia and Native North America, a very old set of ideas can be seen as forming a worldview in a very general sense. It is based on intense interaction with the natural world. It provides a rather uniform basis for the local indigenous cultural variations. It seems to have spread with Arctic culture traits such as skis and snowshoes, sleds, bark lodges, hunting dogs, and, more significantly, shamanism, many thousands of years ago. Continued contact, migration, and information flow around the circumpolar land masses has remained rather uniform in key aspects. There is no deep identity, but there is a broad similarity in environmental management ideas. (I hope to discuss this at length in a book on Northwest Coast Native environmental management, so I will be brief here.)

Widespread among Indigenous and long-resident cultural groups of northern Eurasia and North America (extending into South America) is a view that animals (and sometimes plants, mountains, and rocks) are persons ("other-than-human persons") with their own integrity, volition, and agency. As such, they deserve full respect, a concept that implies anything from ordinary respect (such as we owe strangers) to a reverent, caring attitude. (For a particularly fine discussion of this concept in one Native American group, see the writings of the Nuu-chah-nulth anthropologist Richard Atleo [2004, 2011]. A similarly valuable Native account from Siberia is provided by Kenin-Lopsang 1997. For particularly sensitive and thorough "outsider's views," see Metzo 2005 on the Mongols; Willerslev 2007 on the Yukaghir of Siberia. Joseph Campbell 1983 holds that all hunting cultures have something like my Old Northern worldview, but I find this hard to support from the ethnographic record.) Tree worship, a worldwide habit (Cook 1974), is well developed in many areas, especially the Eurasian world.

The Old Northern societies are or were hunters (whatever else they may have done; they include gatherers, fishers, pastoralists, and farmers). They almost always see the game as sacrificing itself to the hunter if it wants to be killed—it voluntarily offers itself. Usually, the assumption is that game animals and humans are reincarnated. If a hunted prey animal is treated well—its body treated with respect—it will, in its next incarnation, offer itself to the hunter again. Respect means not only reverent treatment of the body; it means that every part of the body must be used. Throwing away a body part is disrespect-ful. Also, taking an animal when one does not seriously need it is disrespectful. So is taking too many animals or fish and thus endangering the survival of the resource stock.

Of course, *too many* is a negotiable term, as every fisher knows. All well-studied Old Northern societies have stories of people who pushed the limit too hard and starved in consequence. Typically, this is explained as due to the animals leaving because they were not treated respectfully, but often people realize that the animals were in fact hunted or fished out. Similar strictures apply to plant foods.

Typically, enforcement of morals is partly through activities of shamans. The word *shaman* comes from the Tungus, in the Old Northern heartland of eastern Siberia. The farther away from the Tungus the groups get, the less their religious officiants act like Tungus shamans, but the term still merits use for at least the peoples of Siberia and western North America. (The loose extension of it to all Native American, or even all tribal, religious practitioners is not one I follow.) Shamans often explain illness or accidents, and especially misfortunes that affect the whole group, as being due to disrespectful treatment of animals and plants. There are many myths upholding this idea.

Shamans typically go into trances and send their souls to the lands of gods and dead, or take on animal forms and personas. They often can transform into animals. These abilities give rise to very widespread myths. The ancient Greeks came from a shamanic background (see, e.g., Dodds 1951), and their story of Orpheus and Eurydice is a version of a myth commonly known and told all over the Old Northern world (see, e.g., Ramsey 1980 for a classic Native American version). Stories about constellations such as the Great Bear, animal transfor-mations, and people or animals becoming trees also link ancient Greece with

Indigenous cultures from Siberia to Canada. The ancient Chinese were also shamanic (Sukhu 2012; Waley 1955), as were other East Asian societies.

On the Northwest Coast of North America, salmon people live under water and have shining skins, mountain-goat people can run up sheer cliffs, and so on. When the whites first came to Vancouver Island, they appeared in ships, and some Nuu-chah-nulth thought the salmon people had decided to come in their humanoid form, complete with their houses. The fish-belly-white skins of the strangers were one giveaway (Kirk 1986). Whites are still called *mamałni,* "floating house people," in Nuu-chah-nulth. Salmon are highly spiritual beings, not just fish (and not just people).

Strong and effective conservation and management ideas prevailed, and still prevail among the most traditional peoples (Arnold 2008; Blukis Onat 2002; Deur and Turner 2005; Turner 2005; and several recent Northwest Coast Native writers, including Atleo 2004 and George 2003). The Katzie of British Columbia, living in an area where sturgeons came to spawn, believed that the Creator had two children, a boy who became the ancestor of the Katzie and a girl who became the ancestor of the sturgeons (Jenness 1955). Hence the sturgeons' preference for Katzie territory. Thus, when a sturgeon allowed itself to be caught, it was a beloved sister sacrificing herself for her brothers. Sturgeons were treated with respect, accordingly—and thus not fished out. The Anglo-Canadian settlers, without a more sophisticated fishing technology but unhampered by such beliefs, wiped out the sturgeons in a few years.

Modern environmentalists are often surprised to find that Native Americans, "in harmony with nature" though they may be, are enthusiastic hunters, and sometimes even regard vegetarians and other non-meat-eaters as not only foolish but morally wrong. ("Vegetarian: Indian word for lousy hunter"—bumper sticker on countless Native American-owned trucks in the United States.) The Northwest Coast view (insofar as there is such a thing) regards humans as natural hunters, other animals as natural prey or as fellow hunters, and life as one of mutual dependence. The prey animals give their lives for us; we take care of them by respectful hunting and respectful use of the prey we hunt. Hunted animals are reincarnated and, if treated with due respect, they offer themselves again to the hunter. The European hunter merely kills; the Native American one must interact with game and persuade them to offer themselves. Native American anthropologist Richard Atleo says it best: when European "religious people pray to God for a supply of meat ... the meat has no say in the matter" (Atleo 2004:85). For Native Americans, the meat does have a say.

Part of respect—usually the most important part—is not taking too much. The proper hunter takes no more than he (or occasionally she) and his family can use, except when sacred ceremonies demand more food for more people. Conservation thus motivated is famously more successful than mere preservation.

Some authors have suggested that the fantastic game richness of North America at European contact was due to the fact that Native Americans were too few and too technologically "backward" to impact game and fish numbers. This is not the case. Native Americans were perfectly capable of doing major damage to game, fish, and other resource stocks, and were numerous enough to have incentives to do so. These points were very effectively made by Charles Kay and Randy Simmons (2002) and David Arnold (2008). (Kay exaggerates—see Wolverton et al. 2009—but the point is still valid.) Native American abilities as hunters, fishers, gatherers and managers of vegetation, and makers of landscapes have been amply proved not only by their accomplishments, but also by their failures. Most, if not all, groups have stories of past overhunting or overfishing episodes that were followed by disaster and starvation. These were learning experiences; they are used to explain and justify explicit conservation teachings (of the "limit one's take to sustainable levels" type, not "preservation" of all animals).

It is depressing to see otherwise excellent scholars, like Shepard Krech (1999) and Peter Coates (1998:84 ff.), agonizing over whether Native Americans were simple, happy children of nature or wanton destroyers. Of course the Native Americans were neither. As pointed out by Native American scholars Ray Pierotti and Daniel Wildcat (1999; Pierotti 2011), Indians were ordinary people. They were good managers most of the time, not so good a lot of the time; never perfectly good, never perfectly bad. As stewards of the game, for example, they were hunters like hunters everywhere; they tried to manage sustainably, usually did it fairly well, but sometimes succumbed to temptation and overhunted.

Exaggerated accounts seem to force themselves on investigators in this area. Krech is a good enough scholar not to buy the idea that Native Americans single-handedly exterminated the Pleistocene megafauna, but both he and Peter Coates (1998) accept fantastically exaggerated accounts of "buffalo jumps" in which bison herds were driven over cliffs. Coates, for instance, cites the Head-Smashed-In jump site in Alberta as proof of Native American waste, apparently thinking that millions of buffalo a day were driven over. In fact the site was used only once in a generation at peak periods, and usually very few bison went over; very rarely did a whole herd fall (according to displays at the site, observed by the present author in 1992). The scholars who think Native Americans drove a million buffalo over a cliff every time they wanted a light lunch have not been following the literature on the difficulty of herding these wary and defensive animals, or on the actual rarity of such sites and kills given the enormous amount of time and space involved (see Bamforth 2011). We are not talking about tame cattle.

There is a large literature on Native American ecological sins. Much of it is simply racist and does not deserve consideration here. (Krech and Coates, by contrast, are serious scholars.) Many writers switch from arguing that a few tiny bands of hunters killed off all the Pleistocene megafauna (a claim disproved in Krech 1999 and Wolverton et al. 2009 and sources therein) to arguing that the 125,000,000 Native Americans found at European contact were too incompetent to kill off anything afterward. Suffice it to say that there were countless fish in even the tiniest streams, though a single individual with a simple net can fish out a small stream in a single night. There were millions of pronghorn, though pronghorn are sensitive, very slow in reproducing, and easy to trap and kill.

Krech and Coates suggest that Native Americans often changed their minds and overhunted after European society came. This should hardly surprise us; everybody in the world has changed in the last couple of centuries as capitalism, communism, and industrialism have gone global. The Indians were not allowed to maintain their lands or traditions. They were usually forced into missions and boarding schools and deprived of livelihood sources other than trapping. How could they avoid change? The surprising thing is that in many Native societies, from the Nuu-chah-nulth of British Columbia to the Maya of Mexico, conservation values still prevail (Anderson 2003, 2005b; Anderson and Medina Tzuc 2005; Atleo 2004; Atran and Medin 2008; Bray et al. 2003; Hunn et al. 2003; Thornton 2008). Even the remote desert Seri, reduced to near-extinction by persecution in the nineteenth century, maintain a powerful conservation ethic (Felger and Moser 1985).

AUSTRALIA

"Spirituality is more than the awareness of one's self. It is the awareness of and responsibility for knowing your place and role in the world. It is about being aware of the interrelatedness of all that was, is and will be. It is about knowing your responsibilities for the past, present and future." Adrian Tucker (Aboriginal, 1997; quoted in display, Australian Museum, Sydney, observed Aug. 2005).

Australia was, famously, a continent of hunter-gatherers when settled by Europeans (Keen 2004). No agriculture was practiced. On the other hand, Australians cultivated wild resources, including replanting of yam stems to grow new tubers after harvest. It now appears that they may have acquired some farming or crop management (of taro, yams, and bananas) from New Guinea far in the dim past, abandoning it later as sea levels and possibly climate changed (Denham et al. 2009).

Their knowledge of the environment was typical of hunting-gathering peoples: it was superb. Wendy Telfer and Murray Garde (2006) filled twenty-seven densely packed pages of a learned journal with one small local group's knowledge of rock kangaroo ecology.

More than 200 languages, many with marked dialects, were spoken in Aboriginal Australia. All were related. Most were of the Pama-Nyungan language family; only a fringe in remote parts of the north were more distinct. The Pama-Nyungan family spread over the continent about 3,000 years ago, absorbing or blending with earlier languages that (as we know) were there (Evans and McConvell 1999). No one knows why this process occurred.

In Indigenous Australian thought, creation is an ongoing process. One can, through dreams, experience the original creations of the world as happening now, and can see the landscape being changed and re-created by contemporary processes. The basic concept of *tjukurrpa* has been discussed previously. Closely related to it, if not a version of the same concept, is *alcheringa,* which means something like "of dreams" or "belonging to dreams" in the Arrernte language (Spencer and Gillen 1889, 1904; Howitt 1904). This is the word translated as "Dreaming" or "Dreamtime" in English-language literature. Related is the word *altyerre,* Creation Time. The creation time and the myth-world are revealed to people in actual this-world dreaming. So are songs and teachings, sometimes from one's ancestors.

The Dreaming is in some sense perpendicular to our world, in another sense parallel, but in the deepest sense it is simply a present part of our world. The stories—myths, Dreamings, songs—allow Aboriginal people to live the creation in real time. They also serve the practical function of teaching people about the environment. As Richard Gould observed long ago (Gould 1969), a story in which the Rainbow Serpent travels through a series of adventures, creating waterholes as he goes, is much more easily remembered than a dry list of the waterholes. In an environment where one error is fatal—where getting two waterholes mixed up means certain death to a lone traveler—all children had to know the holes perfectly, and an adventurous story is the best way to make sure of that.

Knowledge is stratified by age, gender, and degree of initiation. Men and women have different Dreamings. So do different kinship and locational groups. Knowledge includes a vast range of lore about what bird, cloud formation, or other natural occurrence signifies what event. These range from obvious accurate signs (rainclouds and their associated phenomena mean rain) to religious beliefs based on cosmic interactions (birds that signal avenging spirit-beings and the like; owls, as usual worldwide, are bad omens). The pleasant song of one small bird is verbalized "two ritual avengers are walking past." Apparently the song of the bird really does sound like this rather morbid Arerrnte phrase, the way the killdeer's and whippoorwill's cries sound like their English names (Turpin et al. 2013).

Deborah Bird Rose, one of the most insightful and empathetic anthropologists working in Australia, writes of sacred sites: "A site is a place. The power that created the world is located here, and when a person walks to this place, they put their body in the locus of creation.... To stand here is to be *known by* that power.... The significance of sacred sites lies in the connections between the life of today and the creation of the conditions and purpose of that life" (Rose 2000b:40; see also Rose 2000a, 2005).

Sacred sites include mountains, rock outcrops, rock art sites, groves, and any other landscape feature (see, e.g., Rumsey and Weiner 2001). Particularly important, as one would expect in this driest of continents, are sacred waterholes (*jila* in emerging pan-Indigenous Australian usage). One local word is *djang*: A sacred site where a being of the Dreaming transformed into its final form—rock, pool, or rock art painting. This is the usage of the Yolngu groups of the Kakadu National Park area. One such place that I encountered there was a grove of not-very-old trees that (according to the park display, observed Aug. 2005) had been a supernatural being until transformed into the grove.

A critically important concept is *country,* an Aboriginal English word based on local words such as Central Desert *ngurra.* It means the traditional habitat of a particular group (Uluru is in Pitjantjatjara country), but implies not only geographic territory but human interaction with it. *Country* is more than dirt and rock; it is alive, it is part of interaction, it has its myths and songs and traditions that are proper to it and necessary to its continued health. It is humanized landscape. Unlike the English word *country,* but like English *city* or *town,* it implies human creative management and maintenance and a history of creative construction. Unlike city and town, however, country was created not only by humans but—more importantly—by the Rainbow Serpent and other mythic beings in the Dreaming time. Nonhuman beings, visible and invisible, are still affecting and even re-creating country, along with humans. Country is so tightly involved with its inhabitants that "damage to a person's country could make the person sick, a country and its ancestors could recognise a person by their smell, and a person could have intuitive insight into the state of a country and its resources" (Keen 2004:211). Ownership of country is complex but strict and elaborately worked out; it entails a firm requirement for the owners to manage the landscape as well as they can to maintain productivity (Keen 2004:275–305).

Country is crossed by countless tracks ("songlines") of mythic and historic creators. These tracks were well known, as were the stories associated with them, which often included detailed recommendations about treatment and management of particular areas.

One example involves Wolfe Creek meteor crater, one of the largest in the world. It is the subject of extensive mythology in its area (northwest Australia near the Kimberlys). Peggy Reeves Sanday (2007) investigated the area and its stories, originally because her father discovered the meteoric origin of the crater. Local knowledge indicates full awareness of its meteoric origin, but this may be a recent addition to stories that originally ascribed its origin to Dreaming-time yam-diggers or to the Rainbow Serpent. In any case, the Serpent, or several serpents, have greatly influenced the development of the crater and the surrounding scenery. A passage supposedly connects the crater floor with local creeks, explaining why water disappears from the crater and appears in nearby drainageways. (Sanday thinks this is a supernatural passage, but it appears to me like a perfectly factual observation of the flow of groundwater.) Notable is Sanday's very detailed account of the distribution, transmission, and cultural embedding of the knowledge and the stories that teach it. She records verbatim the accounts of many people, whose stories differ according to their own backgrounds and relationship to the "country" that includes the crater.

On Cape York, aboriginal management was so diligent that Aboriginals see the landscape has having been a garden, and say the country has become wild because white men have driven the managers away: "'Poor old country, come *wild* now. No-one to look after him'" (quoted in Hynes and Chase 1982:41). Many of the management techniques familiar to a Californian researcher were found: tending wild plants, burning to open the land, managing and caring for useful trees, and so on.

As in many traditional groups around the world, much of the kinship system, including its intimate relationship with country, was expressed by food sharing rules and totemic restrictions on eating certain things (see, e.g., Keen 2004:342–343).

At Uluru National Park, controlled burning under Indigenous (Aboriginal) direction has been restored. I visited Uluru ("Ayer's Rock") in August 2005. At that time, an active program of controlled burns had begun, with local Indigenous people directing and participating. Excellent displays and presentations by Indigenous and non-Indigenous personnel provided the following information.

Uluru is a huge rock outcrop in the center of Australia. The area is desert, receiving about 6 to 12 inches of rain per year. Vegetation is surprisingly complex. The rounded rock creates orographic rain, which runs off, producing quite moist conditions all around the rock. Some slopes run large waterfalls during rains; these are important sites in Aboriginal religion. Dense woodlands of fig, eucalyptus, acacia, and other trees grow wherever water concentrates.

Away from the rock, the country is rolling and sandy. Stable dunes alternate with sandy to clayey flatlands. Vegetation is a complex mosaic. The park lists some 200 species of "prominent" plants. Very dry, open areas have little beyond spinifex grassland (dominated by species of *Plectrachne* and *Triodia*), with various small bushes. Better soil and water bring acacia savannah. Dunes and sandy areas are savannah dominated by desert oak (*Allocasuarina decaisneana*, a flowering tree that looks like a pine, has wood like an oak, and is related to neither). Almost 200 plant species grow in the immediate vicinity of the rock. Many bear edible fruit, some of which is very good. Relatives of fig, sandalwood, and tomato figure notably among fruit sources. Edible seeds, leaves, and tubers abound. Larger animal life is largely marsupials, birds, and lizards. Various snakes occur. Insects are incredibly abundant and diverse.

The area is "country" for the Pitjantjatjara people; other closely related groups live nearby and visit the rock. The Pitjantjatjara still do considerable hunting and gathering. They share with related desert groups an elaborate social system based on complex kinship and family relations and a fantastically elaborate and intricate knowledge of the environment, which enabled them to live in an area where water and food are notably sparse (see Latz 1995). They also have a long-established and rich ritual involvement with Uluru rock. The whole rock is sacred, and many areas along its edge are particularly sacred initiation, ceremonial, and ritual sites. These are now closed to non-Aboriginal visitors. The rock was popular with climbers, but that is also halted, because the climbers were not only in sacred territory but were often less than respectful to it, littering, taking chunks for souvenirs, and otherwise defacing it.

Ritual involvement with the site included rules for respectful interaction with it. This included restrictions on hunting and gathering; resources were not harvested enough to deplete them. Burning was carefully managed, apparently with religious representation of the rules.

Without human agency, the area would burn irregularly in large wildfires, because of lightning, abundant during the summer rainy season and not unknown at other times. The Indigenous people have burned the area, probably for 50,000 years or more, creating more frequent, smaller fires. These local ground fires burn off overgrown spinifex and brush, producing new, healthy growth. Like most perennial bunchgrasses, spinifex becomes overgrown and unhealthy unless regularly cropped or burned. Another benefit of burning is its suppression of introduced pest plants, especially weedy alien grasses (though in worst cases—notably when they take over lush spots with good soil—these have to be pulled by hand, a difficult, slow, annoying job). A fine mosaic of burns of various ages is created; it is different from the large burns caused by lightning in unmanaged areas (Bliege Bird 2008).

Controlled burns occur during the cool season. They are set in dense vegetation and flash rapidly through the spinifex. They do not give "clean" burns; many tufts of grass, bases of bushes, and tree trunks survive. The desert oaks, in particular, are adapted to frequent fire. They lose their twigs and foliage, but immediately grow back. Fires cover a few to a few tens of acres, reaching limits set by firebreaks, previous burns, or naturally open sandy places. The result is a fine-grained mosaic of burns of different ages.

Burning has not only made the vegetation healthier, it has reversed the ongoing decline of animal life, especially of the small marsupials (displays and presentations,

Uluru National Park, observed Aug. 2005). Some species had been declining steadily since the national park was set up, because—as Aboriginals explained over the years—the animals depend on fire, largely because it causes fresh, tender, lush shoots to appear in large quantities. Apparently these animals are highly sensitive to burning regimes, not thriving unless fires are frequent, light, and in cool periods. This is all familiar territory to a Californian like me. California's grasslands, brushlands, and woodlands have a similar fire-dependent, fire-mosaic ecology (Minnich 1988), though burning was more often in early to midsummer (the cool season in California is too wet for burning to be practical; see M. K. Anderson 2005).

Similar patterns of Indigenous burning existed throughout Australia and have been restored in Kakadu National Park and elsewhere in recent times (see Kohen 1995 for general background). For the Tiwi of the islands off northwest Australia, there is "a duty to burn dry grasses." It clears the land, restores the grass, and drives away pests (Grau 2000:357). They like the resulting clean appearance of the land. The Tiwi view sacred sites and spaces as persons, or at least as beings needing and deserving care as a person would.

Studies of hunting by the Martu of western Australia (Bird, Bliege Bird, and Codding 2009; Bird, Bliege Bird, and Parker 2005) show how necessary fire is in hunting. Lizards are almost impossible to find and catch in long grass. Regrowth of burns provides vegetation eaten by game (and often by people). Running down animals is easier; humans are not built to run through thornscrub or even bunchgrasses. Ease of pursuit is a major consideration, because the animals the Martu catch are small and fast.

THE ARTS

Australian Aboriginal arts provide important examples of collective representation of community. Community resource use and management led to religious beliefs sanctioning the art. The beliefs were part of a wider religious and ethical shell that produced ceremonies and art. The art showed, taught, and motivated specific management systems, strategies, and tactics. (The best introduction is Kleinert and Neale 2000. For some particularly noteworthy and insightful local studies, see Buku-Larrngay Mulka Centre 1999; Caruana and Lendon 1997; Isaacs 1989; Morphy and Boles 1999; and above all Myers 2002.)

Australian Aboriginal art is at least 50,000 years old—perhaps even more—and there is surprising continuity over the whole time (Flood 1997, 2004; Morwood 2002). Red paintings on rocks are the main surviving form, but ceremonial art applied to boards, fabrics, the earth, and above all, human bodies, is far commoner today and presumably was in the past. Because the oldest art known on earth is 70,000 to 75,000 years old, Australia's art apparently covers most of the human artistic career (see New South Wales Art Gallery 2004).

Rock art and other, less permanent art forms provide charters, ownership marks, interpretations (Morphy 2000a, 2000b). Rituals, repeated annually or every several years, are part of ongoing creation. Without singing and appropriate dances and ceremonies, the land would not be healthy and would not function normally. Aesthetic and emotional expression, coordinated in these "corroborees," is necessary maintenance. People must dance their proper roles according to kin, gender, and initiatory status. A dancer's ability demonstrates not just athletic prowess, but knowledge of the country, the traditions, and the religion of the dancer. In northern Australia a ceremonial leader will say to shirking participants: "What's the matter with you lot? Are you people sitting without the Law?" (Tamisari 2000:149).

For the Ngarinyin of the far north, and for many other groups: "Songs, dances, and images all come from the time when everyone was lawless, when all the animals and birds were humans.... All these animals who created ideas are our ancestors. They started ceremony, song, and the *wunnan* ... which gives us our marriage system and a network for sharing out resources to all the different clans in our country.... During Walungarri (initiation cycles) we act out the part of the animals who are our relations in the kinship system, all our family.... A composer, *banman,* gets songs from these animals.... Wunggurr (rainbow serpent) ... might deposit her egg in the belly of the *banman* and this egg will breed and grow inside the composer's body, as though the stomach of the composer is a pouch. Sometimes a male and female Wunggurr will mate inside the body of the *banman* and breed inside him in order to give him power. This power is easily lost.... " (David Mowaljarli in conversation with Anthony James Redmond, 2000:347–348). The presence of the mythical creator serpent in the singer is a dream or vision, but taken most seriously indeed.

Australian Aboriginal art has gone international in the last few decades (for the first worldwide show, see Sutton 1988). Already well known among anthropologists for its beauty, evocativeness, and expression of religion and landscape, it has been more widely accepted on the art market. Paintings that originally brought a few dollars as curios or were traded for food, now bring six-figure sums in international auctions[1].

Notable and indeed critical in the wide acceptance of Australian art was the art movement around Papunya in the early 1970s (Bardon 2004; Benjamin 2009; Myers 2002). A wider study of the whole phenomenon, *Painting Culture,* has been written by Fred Myers (2002), who has studied the Pintupi for several decades. This work is a major study of the anthropology and aesthetics behind the story and is one of the greatest studies of traditional art in the world.

Papunya was something close to a concentration camp: a settlement where nomadic desert groups were brought together. People from Pintupi, Anmatyerre,

Arrernte, and other groups gathered around a small cluster of school, clinic, and mission buildings. Conditions were as bad as could be expected, and pressure to assimilate—on the very lowest level, of course—was strong; severe racism with overt racist acts were reported.

Into this came Geoffrey Bardon as art teacher. He quickly discovered major talent in the people—largely the senior males, because he had less access to others—and developed a school of painting that rapidly moved from tentative, fledgling efforts to production of world-class masterpieces. Of course this did not appear in a vacuum. For thousands of years, Aboriginal people had painted designs on rocks, ground, and human bodies. An extremely complex, sophisticated, multiply-meaningful art had developed. All that was needed was to learn to use acrylic paints and boards (later canvas). Bardon encouraged more: he wanted full portrayal of stories, themes, and landscapes. The results must have surpassed his wildest expectations, for the people soon began painting huge and intricate pictures that are some of the greatest spiritual art on earth.

Bardon, however, seems to have had the artistic temperament and clashed with the white power structure of the place; he maintains they were racist, oppressive, and out to suppress the whole movement (Bardon 2004); an objective story of the sequence of events does not seem to exist. The failure of the local power structure and of the whole assimilation policy seems clear enough, and certainly Bardon as art teacher was successful enough to launch a quite incredible movement, but so far the rest is *not* history—at least not recorded history.

Bardon also encountered ill health; he died sadly young in 2003. Health issues caused him to leave Papunya after only two years, though he returned periodically. The great artistic period at Papunya was therefore brief, but fortunately Bardon and the elders of the community succeeded in creating an artists' association that continued. It provided some protection and help for the ongoing movement.

One of the key painters, Clifford Possum Tjapaltjarri, became the first Aboriginal painter to be the subject of an entire art book: Vivien Johnson's *The Art of Clifford Possum Tjapaltjarri* (1994). He was a highly talented Anmatyerre painter. His name, incidentally, consists of his European given name, the English name of his totemic animal, and his "skin name," that is, the name of his position in the kinship system; most Central Desert people use their skin name as a last name.

The art of Papunya shows the landscape, artistically abstracted and conceptually mythologized. Tracks of Dreaming beings are shown, hills and water are schematically indicated, and "bush foods" (wild food resources) are portrayed. A typical painting is something like a map, something like a diagram of mythic relationships, and something like a religious painting. Unlike the religious art of the West, it is intensely original, no two paintings being the same and most being highly innovative and creative. The art uses abstract signs that Bardon called "hieroglyphs" to represent particular mythic events, characters, and landscape features. Thus a whole myth can be portrayed in symbolic forms.

Common themes include water, fire, bush food, women's ceremonies, and animals. Most of these involve origin stories, especially the travels of the mythic beings as they went through the landscape creating its features. The land is constantly being created and re-created by such acts; the travels of the spirit beings go on, invisible to us.

These myths were and are teaching stories, and young people learned them. Recall Richard Gould's point that learning the sequence of water holes in the desert was easier to learn in the context of a dramatic story than as a dull list. This practical aspect of stories was evidently appreciated by the Aboriginal people, but the stories are much more; they are true sacred literature, passed on by word of mouth as the Bible and the Vedas originally were.

The early art showed some mythic themes that were not for the uninitiated. This attracted criticism, and thereafter only public themes were portrayed. This is not mere secrecy. Uninitiated individuals can sicken and even die from the raw power of spiritual art. There are reliable accounts of Aboriginal people dying from fear when they felt themselves bewitched, and sickening from fear when they found they had broken taboos, so this is no idle concern.

The Papunya experiment was not unique, and indeed similar painting explosions have taken place at several other remote stations. Aboriginal painting has now become established all over the continent, with local themes, motifs, and styles emerging.

The relations of art to country may also be seen in the sculptures of John Dodo of far northwest Australia. He works with pieces of rock that result from a titanic event. In his words: "A family from ancestral times ... were hunting near Eighty Mile Beach, or Mt. Payarr. The young son killed a female goanna heavy with eggs and ate them—an act which was taboo. This angered Pulanj, the rainbow serpent, who sought revenge first by unleashing violent storms and then by setting out to devour the boy. However the boy's father was a medicine man and had the power to seal the cave in which his family took refuge to withstand repeated attacks by the serpent. Enraged and with gaping jaws it attacked the mountain itself, biting off large chunks of rock. This continued throughout the night whilst the petrified family huddled inside. Finally, at dawn, the Serpent withdrew and the rain stopped" (cited in Kleinert and Neale 2000:576–577). The taboo on catching lizards in breeding condition is typical of the strong conservation ethic embodied in the Laws of Aboriginal groups.

A CASE STUDY IN DIFFERENT KNOWLEDGES:
FIVE CULTURES IN NEW MEXICO

When I was an undergraduate, several of my teachers were involved in a study of five cultures in central New Mexico (Kluckhohn and Strodtbeck 1961; Vogt and Albert 1966). The interest—aside from the fact that it was the home of the most active researcher, Evon Vogt—stemmed from the fact that five cultural groups shared the same area, yet could not possibly have been more different. At the least, it certainly shows that environmental determinism is a hopeless argument; all the five had totally different adjustments, yet all of them (with the partial exception of one) were doing well in this harsh landscape. (I benefit in what follows not only from the published sources, but from learning from the participants; Vogt's undergrad anthropology courses are my main source. I have subsequently traveled widely in the area and done a great deal of reading on all the cultures, as well as discussion, including discussion with anthropologists from all five cultures!)

The five were the Zuñi, the Navaho, the New Mexico Hispanics, the Mormons, and the Texans.

The Zuñi lived in one huge pueblo, basically a single apartment complex, though they had begun to scatter out, and some had settled not far from Vogt's home ranch near Ramah, New Mexico. The Zuñi had lived in northwest New Mexico since time immemorial; they believed they had been created there, and certainly their culture had. Their language is not obviously related to any in the world, and archaeology reveals no breaks in the cultural record of the area over many millennia. They were thus genuinely autochthonous, but their culture was always influenced by other pueblos and indirectly by the high cultures of central Mexico. A superb description of their ecology by John Landgraf (1954) was one outcome of the five cultures study.

The Navaho were a herding group, living in scattered "outfits" (family or clan settlements) and roving widely with their flocks of sheep. They descended largely from hunting-gathering Canadian people who moved down the Great Plains not long before Columbus.

The Hispanics were settled agriculturalists, the descendants of a monumentally diverse group of converted Moors (Nabhan 2008) and Jews (Hordes 2005; genetics proves the Jewish link), central Mexican indigenous people, and Spanish that had settled in New Mexico in the 1600s. The Mormons were a strongly communitarian religious sect; the Ramah settlement consisted of pioneers striking southeast from Utah in the nineteenth century. The Texans were the most recent immigrants; they were Scots-Irish and similar rural white southerners who had moved into the area in the early twentieth century, seeking land or escaping the Dust Bowl. Though both groups were theoretically

Anglo-American, the Mormons and Texans were as different from each other as from the three other groups. The Mormons' compact, carefully planned, tree-shaded village contrasted dramatically with the scattered, informal, often treeless ranches of the Texans.

The "five cultures" study showed that these groups differed dramatically. They all idealized the most basic human social needs—generosity, mutual aid, reliability, general nonviolence, sense of social place and honor, and so on—but they differed greatly in how they achieved these. Values on time ranged from obsessive up-to-the-minute promptness among the Mormons to New Mexico's proverbial "land of room enough and time enough" attitude among the Hispanics. Space organization ranged from compact villages to dispersed pastoralism, and note that the former links the Zuñi and Mormons, the latter includes the Navaho and Texans—cutting right across classic "ethnic" division lines! The same was observed in regard to tight mutualism versus rugged individualism. The Zuñi and Mormons were both religiously zealous to follow the letter of the rule, the Navaho and Texans more self-determined. However, the Zuñi and Mormons differed on what they were conformist about; the Zuñi stuck with ancient tradition when possible (though they were incredibly adaptive in many ways), whereas the Mormons were apparently the most dynamic of the five in picking up new ideas from the outside world. And so it went.

This provided a wonderful test case for the relative roles of tradition, environment, and genetics. The original authors dropped this opportunity for several reasons. Probably the most important were that the original leader, Clyde Kluckhohn, died suddenly at a relatively young age. Vogt became totally involved with the Highland Maya of Chiapas and devoted the rest of his life to them. However, I understood from some participants that another problem was the basic similarity in values, wants, and needs among all five. They may have differed on what to eat and how faithfully to keep appointment times, but they all were thoroughly human in basic values, and they all had to face a hard reality of drought, heat, and economic uncertainty.

The investigators had been hoping for really basic differences. But biology—common human genetics and the logical corollaries of genetic predispositions—eliminated much of the variance. Humans simply cannot subsist on grass, and in a grassland like this one, they had to use animals to make the landscape produce much that they could eat; no vegetarians here. They want to reproduce, and in the harsh and lonely conditions of New Mexico, that meant they had to marry and raise children in a family environment. No one could survive and raise children alone. Humans also need society, security, and mutual aid, and they have evolved to maintain relations of trust and generosity balanced by condemning cheaters and defending social position ("honor"). These and many other constraints made the search for truly basic differences rather sad. Even the Hispanic ease about time could go only so far in a world where one had to depend on neighbors and often on their split-second timing when a blizzard or whirlwind or other catastrophe struck. Some genetic differences in sun tolerance, diabetes proneness, and so on did exist between these groups, but were relatively minor.

Today, from the perspective of very much more research, we may look more seriously at the differences. Biology being more or less a constant, and the environment being broadly the same, all differences are cultural, and have a history.

The most obvious, of course, lies in the *use* made of the environment. The Zuñi and Mormons were irrigation farmers, sticking to fertile land near good water and relying on using it intensively. They kept a few animals, but usually without herding long distances, though some Mormon families (including Vogt's) had more extensive ranches. The Navaho and Texans were extensive stockbreeders—the one a seminomadic sheep-herding group, the other a ranch-based cattle culture that also went in for extensive dry farming and some irrigation farming. The Hispanics combined all approaches: they irrigated, they ran stock, and they dry farmed small plots.

The differences in settlement patterns followed fairly logically from the needs of irrigation versus dry farming versus stock-raising. But the choice of irrigation or stock actually followed from the prior style of settlement pattern. People who want to live together have to farm intensively if they want to make a living from their immediate lands, and people who love to live scattered out can gravitate to extensive stock-rearing. The Mormon ancestors had owned small intensive farms in the northeastern United States. The Texans' Celtic-American ancestors had been scattered farmers in the Appalachians, the Navahos' ancestors had been scattered hunters in the Canadian forest.

One fascinating item not clear at the time was the extent of intercultural borrowing. The Zuñi and Navaho had acquired their livestock from the Spanish, of course, as well as their metal and metalworking skills, their basic wool-weaving knowledge, and their dryland crops. The Zuñi are famous for their "waffle gardens," small plots irrigated in a particular way. I used to think these were a Zuñi invention until I saw the same arrangement in a reconstructed medieval Arab farm in Sicily. Apparently the converted Moors introduced it (and essentially all the rest of New Mexico's small-scale irrigation technology) to New Mexico, and the Zuñi apparently borrowed it. They were preadapted: archaeological gardens not totally dissimilar predate Columbus.

Foodways display complex borrowings, especially from Hispanics to the Native groups. The latter naturally adopted bread and mutton stew when they acquired wheat and sheep. Zuñi sourdough bread, baked in medieval Spanish-style beehive ovens, is the best bread I have eaten in North America. They also adopted chiles, which had never made it that far north before the seventeenth century. The Mexican indigenous component in the Hispanic village world had broadly determined their foodways, so they lived to a great extent on tortillas and other Mexican maize preparations and on chiles, squash, tomatoes, and other New World foods. However, New Mexico in those days was also an incredible museum of Arab food, and I kept running into recipes traceable to Baghdad and the Levant (see Jaramillo 1980, a book of recipes collected in 1942 from an elderly New Mexico Hispanic; it is full of Arab recipes, including a dish of mutton stewed with chickpeas and flavored with cinnamon that is known all over the Arab-influenced world; the Jaramillo family traces descent from "Moors" converted to Christianity after the Reconquista in Spain). An extreme case of Arabism is *boromia,* an eggplant dish that commemorates Princess Burum of medieval Baghdad and her love for that vegetable. I have not run into it in New Mexico, but it is common enough in Mexico.

Similarly, the Mormons and Texans had been more influenced than they often admitted by Native American foods; their gardens and cupboards were full of corn, beans, squash, tomatoes, potatoes, peanuts, and so on and on, and they ate turkey for festive occasions.

Since the study, American fast food has made major inroads, with the sad result that the area now has skyrocketing rates of diabetes and heart problems.

This fed into particular kinds of representation of environment. The Zuñi were perfectly situated among their sacred mountains; they knew where they had been created, how every rock had been made in mythic time, and the proper prayers and rituals for every mountain. The Navaho were almost as situated, but they had a more dynamic view; not for nothing was Changing Woman a particularly evocative deity. The Hispanics, staunch Catholics, had patron saints for their community churches, but no religious grounding in the land. The Mormons tied their lands to their religion by naming places for their own saints and holy places; St. George, Utah, is named not for the dragon-slayer but for an early Mormon pioneer, an exemplary member of the "Latter-Day Saints." Finally, the Texans had no religious or other ties to the land, and now and then were heard to complain about it and wish they could go home to Texas. (Indeed, several did.)

Language, of course, differed dramatically and basically, except for the Mormons and Texans (and even they spoke quite different dialects of English). At the time of the study, the Native groups had scarcely even begun to lose their languages. Today, alas, most young Zuñi and Navaho in that area do not speak their heritage languages, but many do. Music differed somewhat less vividly. Generic resemblances between Zuñi and Navaho are clear, as they are between Mormon and Texan. As with irrigation and agriculture, the Hispanic music turned out to be heavily Moorish in origin (see Robb 1980, though the full extent of Moorish influence has become known since that book). There was no environmental forcing of musical taste, and traditional musics go on. The Zuñi and Navaho have slowly gravitated toward rural Anglo-American musical styles, but they preserve their own heritage, too. Clothing and other public forms of cultural identification have converged on Anglo-American norms except during festal occasions.

Thus five cultures coexisted in the same environment. They did it to a great extent by having complementary ways of exploiting the environment. The three irrigated-farm traditions could have gotten in each other's way, but in practice, the Zuñi preferred to settle around springs and develop small plots; the Hispanics preferred mountain streams with a strong head of pressure for the irrigation ditches; and the Mormons preferred large alluvial areas where they could develop very extensive irrigation works. The Texans took over vast dry steppelands of little interest to the others. The Navaho ran sheep on areas ideal for that activity but essentially worthless waste for anything but a *churro* (New Mexican Spanish for a hardy local sheep).

Basically, these cultures adapted to the local area by preserving what they had already, making the best use of that, and adding to it by selectively adapting useful ideas from the prior stock of ideas of their neighbors. Not much new was developed, but some interesting syntheses were made, not least in cooking styles, and many stories and songs were composed.

Thus the values the Kluckhohn-Vogt teams studied turned out to be rather minor in effect and often in feedback with the ecological adaptations. Different attitudes to time made little real difference. Different attitudes toward space and toward family had much to do with making a living. Patriarchy mattered, affecting life and behavior, but the matrilineal Navaho did not seem massively helped, handicapped, or otherwise affected by being the odd society out in a sea of patriliny.

Of course, the most important conclusions of the study are:

1) People who live not only adjacent to each other but all mixed in with each other can have *extremely* different ecologies, and thus extremely different bodies of traditional knowledge.

2) All these different bodies of knowledge can be comparably successful at dealing with the environment.

3) This is especially true if one looks at what the people *want,* rather than at some arbitrary measure of development. The Mormons may make more money than the Navaho, the Texans more than the Hispanics, but all five societies agreed that a close family is more important than wealth. All five valued good simple food and regarded their homes and the beautiful landscape as beyond all price. These they had, and shared.

4) On the other hand, no one way was perfect (if it had been, it would probably have displaced the others). All were hard on the environment. Stock-raising

(Texan, Navaho, or otherwise) was particularly costly, producing small benefits for large damage to grasslands. Irrigated farming had its costs, too, in soil damage, timber loss, and erosion. For what it is worth, the Hispanics seem (from later detailed studies, e.g., Devon Peña, work in progress) to have the system that supports the most people over the longest time, partly because it integrated livestock, irrigation, and dry farming without going too heavily into any one. If this is true, it speaks well for the long mix of cultures and peoples that made the Hispanic background, but we do not really know yet. The story is not over.

Ironically, when culture change finally came to the region and eroded the five cultures, it was not through superior success or through superior environmental adaptation. It was through superior control of media. Urban Anglo-American culture, in its popular TV variant, is devastating all five of the cultures in question, though all five remain stoutly resistant and are not giving up the ghost easily. It would be impossible to imagine a culture worse adapted to central New Mexico than TV America, with its water-wasting lawns, its industrial agriculture developed for Iowa soils and topography, and its diabetes-producing diet. Its fantastic waste of energy and raw materials is leading to global warming, which is rapidly desertifying New Mexico. Its lack of community and of any way of maintaining community is destroying that virtue in the five cultures and thus destroying their future in that demanding environment. Its adulation of urban values and ideals is problematic for people who needed their tough, independent rural spirit to survive.

In every way, it is the exact opposite of what is needed by small, tight communities that based their lives on extremely thrifty and fine-tuned use of exceedingly limited resources. But the human animal is so constituted that he or she finds it impossible not to imitate the lifestyle of whatever reference group is held to be the prestigious and "appropriate" one. In the end, this bit of biology—apparently all too genetically determined—is winning and is a factor (along with global warming, urbanization, profit-taking, racism, and other problems) in making a desert of New Mexico.

NOTE

1 The inevitable questions of intellectual property rights and copyright for designs is particularly vexed in Australia, where designs may be thousands of years old and widely shared by cultural groups. An insight of major world importance emerges from this. As Howard Morphy, a major expert on Aboriginal art, puts it:

> Under Indigenous Law[s] rights in art are distributed in accordance with more general descent-based rights in land and sacra. This is because paintings, song and dance are part of a society's ancestral inheritance. The exercising of rights involves

a complex intersection of group and individual rights.... Within a community, permission to produce a painting is usually implicit. (Morphy 2000b:686)

But individuals must be properly initiated and otherwise grounded in order to use many
(if not most) designs. Clearly individual creations now fall under copyright, but traditional
design motifs have only recently been seen as needing copyright protection. This came after
massive appropriation of designs by the white world—and sometimes even by unentitled
Aborigines! Seeing traditional art motifs as part of indigenous land, landscape, and religion is clearly a step forward, because it is much closer to Aboriginal views on the subject.

This must be seen against a background of exploitation and callous treatment. The
Australian Aboriginals suffered the usual effects of European conquest in a culturally different land: massacre, local genocide, enslavement, "culturocide" (deliberate attempts to
destroy the local culture), reduction to poverty and marginal circumstances, and so on.

Some 50,000 children were stolen from parents and placed in orphanages, foster homes,
missions, and so on. This had the expectable psychological effects, especially because physical and sexual abuse are inevitably common in such situations. The unedifying story has
been told repeatedly and need not be addressed here (see, e.g., Attwood and Marks 1999;
Elder 2003; Kleinert and Neale 2000; Moses 2004); certain recent attempts to whitewash
the past have been thoroughly refuted (Manne 2003). Surprisingly, white English children
often fared no better. Tens of thousands were transported—often from orphanages, but often
actually stolen from their parents—and used as child labor and sex slaves in Australia in the
twentieth century (Bryant 2009). It seems that more than racism was affecting Indigenous
children; they may take cold comfort from knowing that countless white children suffered
similar trauma, though without the culturocidal overtones.

Aboriginal is being replaced by *Indigenous* in many general contexts as of this writing,
but the two terms coexist, and the art is usually referred to as Aboriginal. Possibly terms
will shift back and forth over the years (cf. *American Indian* and *Native American*). I therefore
use both terms herein.

PART II

AREAS: PARTICULAR CULTURES

CHAPTER FOUR

The Yucatec Maya

KNOWLEDGE

Yucatec Maya swidden farming requires not only the knowledge of plants and animals noted previously, but a detailed knowledge of soil types, ground and landscape features, climate and weather, and stars (which set the calendar). It requires an encyclopedic knowledge of the whole process of selecting a field, clearing it, burning the slash, planting, weeding, managing growing crops, harvesting, and storing. Maya farmers have to be able to assess regrowing vegetation to see when a field is ready for reuse; some fields require more than fifty years fallowing, some only four or five, depending on soil. They have to know what weeds to spare (many are useful), which ones to chop back but leave alive, and which ones to kill. They created vast areas of forest garden, ranging from totally planted orchards to huge areas of intensively managed wild trees (Anderson 2003; Ford and Nigh 2009). Whole books have been filled with Maya knowledge of farming (e.g., Terán and Rasmussen 1993).

The people I know are the original "Maya," the people who actually call themselves and their language *Maayah*. The word has been generalized to cover some thirty related languages, but the speakers of those languages had other names for themselves. If they knew the *Maayah,* it was the Yucatec and their neighbors that they were talking about. The following account is synthesized from my field work (see Anderson 2003, 2005; Anderson and Medina Tzuc 2005; Barrera Marín et al. 1976; Barrera Vásquez 1963, 1965, 1980, 1981; Barrera Vásquez (ed.) 1980; Blair and Vermont Salas 1965; Hanks 1990; see also Hervik 1999; Restall 1997, 1998).[1]

The Yucatec Maya, the other Native American group I know fairly well, are less well covered, but a great deal of their environmental ethical teachings are recorded in their own works (e.g., Balam 1992; Llanes Pasos 1993) and those of anthropological observers (e.g., Anderson 2005b; Faust 1998). Other Maya groups have also been studied, with use of Indigenous texts and materials (e.g., Atran et al. 2002; Atran et al. 2004; Hofling 1991; Lenkersdorf 1996), and Estuardo Secaira was good enough to send me a superb recent study he has done of the Maya groups of Guatemala (Secaira 2000). It deserves wider circulation.

The Yucatec Maya language divides knowledge into several types. The basic vocabulary is as follows:

Oojel to know (Spanish *saber*).

Oojel ool to know by heart; *ool* means "heart." *Cha'an ool* is a rare or obsolete synonym.

K'aaj, k'aajal to recognize, be familiar with (Spanish *conocer*)

K'aajool, k'aajal ool to "recognize by heart" (Spanish *reconocer*): to recognize easily and automatically. The separation between *ool* and *k'aaj* is so similar to the Spanish distinction of *saber* and *conocer* that one suspects some influence, but the words are ancient. (Many languages worldwide make this distinction; in addition to French and other Romance languages, we have Thai *ru* or *saap* "know" vs *rujak* "be acquainted with, recognize.")

K'aajoolal (or just *k'aajool*), knowledge; that which is known.

U'ub- to hear; standardly used to mean "understand what one said," implying just to catch it or get it, as opposed to *na'at,* which refers to a deeper level of understanding.

Na'at to understand.

The cognate word to *na'at* in Tzotzil Maya is *na'* and has been the subject of an important study by Zambrano and Greenfield (2004). They find that it is used as the equivalent of "know" as well as "understand," but focally it means that one knows how to do something. It is a word so closely related to practice and action that, when asking if someone wants a soda, one says *"Mi xana'*

Photo on Facing Page: Yucatec Maya: careful cultivation—crop-orchard interplanting. Photograph by E. N. Anderson.

yuch'el rasqu?"—literally, "do you know the drinking of soda?" (Zambrano and Greenfield 2004:256). A better translation would probably be "Do you wish to experience a soda?" but the point is made: *na'* means, focally, to *do* something on the basis of knowledge of it. This keys us into the difference between Tzotzil knowing and Spanish or English knowing: Tzotzil know by watching and then doing (as do many other Native Americans; see Goulet 1998, Sharp 2001), whereas Spanish and English children and adults today know by hearing lectures or by book-learning. It seems fairly likely that a culture that sees knowledge as practice would not make a fundamental or basic distinction between magic, science, and religion. The distinction would far more likely be between embodied knowledge or *habitus* and knowledge known only from others' stories. Such distinctions are made in some Native American languages.

Ook ool religion, belief; to believe; secret. *Ool,* once again, is "heart." The root meaning of the actual verbal stem, *ook,* is unclear; it is hard to imagine it is related to *ok* "hit," let alone *ok* "foot." (Yucatec has short words and limited phonology and, therefore, many homonyms.) Yucatec do not usually use this term. When talking about Christianity, they generally speak Spanish. In Maya, they are more apt to talk about supernatural beings (*ik'* "winds," *aluux* "elves," *yum* "lords," etc.) and about particular ceremonies, such as the *cha'ch'aak* "praying for rain" and *loh* "ceremonies for asking for blessings or thanking the spirits for them." People speak of a *loh* to ask the *yum il k'aax* "lords of the forest" to protect their fields.

The Yucatec Maya have used Spanish words cognate with the English ones for 500 years now and have assimilated the European worldview. However, the ancient Maya belief system was like the Native Northwest Coast one. In it, the opposition is between public knowledge and secret healing and shamanic knowledge, not between secular and religious. In Mayan Spanish the usual word for *magic* is not *mágica* (though that Spanish word is known) but *secretos,* "secrets." This indicates that what matters is not a distinction between science and magic but a distinction between exoteric and esoteric. This we know to have been a critical distinction for the ancient Maya. (On the other hand, native Spanish speakers in Mexico tend to use *secretos* this way, too.)

A fascinating characteristic of the Yucatec Maya is their meticulous care and concern with place, space, direction, and location. The language is rich in words for these matters, including *deictics* (words like *here* and *there*). The great linguist and fluent Yucatec speaker William Hanks studied this for twenty years, eventually producing a 600-page book that *summarizes* Maya discourse on space and direction (Hanks 1990).

From a quite different viewpoint, Wendy Ashmore and others have painstakingly studied and partially re-created Classic Maya construction of space in their great cities (Ashmore 2005; cf. Gottdiener 1997 on the general issue of how societies produce and construct urban space). The great Maya cities are models of planning. Palenque, for instance, is a symphony in stone—so exquisitely planned and so perfectly fitted into its site that people have been moved to tears by its beauty, even in ruins. Its architects had a comprehensive urban vision second to none in the world (Stuart and Stuart 2008). Water management was excellent technically, too (Scarborough 2003, 2009).

The Maya of the Classic Period (200–800 AD) may have overused their environmental resources, leading in part to the famous "collapse" of the eight through the tenth centuries (Diamond 2005). Copan, for instance, shows signs of environmental overuse. But the situation is evidently complex. Drought in the tenth century was certainly a part of it, probably a very large part (Gill 2000; Hodell 2011). Lake and stalactite data show considerable drought in the 800–1000 period, especially around 830 and 928, when the reduction in rainfall was as high as 40 percent. By far the major reduction was in the summer rain, making maize farming difficult to impossible during those years.

Most authors who actually know the Maya now stress multiple factors (Aimers 2011; Webster 2002). War and ecological decline were evidently locally important, and other, currently untestable factors like crop and human diseases have been proposed (Webster 2002). Arthur Demarest (2004) has highlighted the effects of war on some areas long before either ecological "overshoot" or drought were visible factors. Particularly telling is the fact that the western lowlands collapsed in the 700s, well before the droughts. Piedras Negras's last inscription dates from 795, Palenque's from 799 (and the great Central Mexican cities had declined around the same time or only slightly earlier). Evidence for warfare is clear there, but not evidence for any ecological decline. It would be hard to imagine even the worst drought or ecological overshoot destroying Palenque. That city is situated in a fertile, well-watered area and is strategically near the Usumacinta-Grijalva Delta, in those days possibly the most biologically productive spot on the North American continent.

Kitty Emery (2010) has shown that animal abundance did not change much during the collapse in the Petexbatun area. The Maya kept right on hunting deer and other animals. In contrast to some other areas, the deer continued to browse from forest and brush, rather than switching to robbing gardens for maize. (This can be told from the bone chemistry.) The collapse there, evidently, did not eliminate forests and animals the way it apparently did in some areas.

Moreover, only the central lowlands (including the areas where I work) actually "collapsed." Maya civilization went right on in the north—the core Yucatec area—and south. This fits the drought theory well, and so does the timing for the most central sites, like Tikal, whose last inscription dates from 869. The central lowland region is more vulnerable, the north has more permanent water sources (sinkholes known as *cenotes*), and the south has more rain. The

Maya, then as now, had a skill-intensive system, pouring highly skilled labor on the land and managing it well, but they presumably learned this through trial and error; there is evidence of early learning-the-hard-way in extensive silting up and degradation of wetlands in the earliest civilized periods (Scarborough 2009). But the fact that most of the Yucatec heartland was not much affected by the collapse shows that the Yucatec had, by and large, learned good management by 800 or 900 CE. The collapse was largely confined to areas speaking Cholan and closely neighboring Yucatec areas, which makes one wonder if something about classic Cholan culture made for special susceptibility.

The Maya, now and probably in the past, have an amazing knowledge of plants and animals. A recent compendium lists 2,166 species of plants used and (almost all) named by the Maya (Arellano R. et al. 2003). This appears to be a record for any small-scale local society. Several others have been added to the list since that book came out. I recorded more than 1,300 plant names for almost as many species, including no fewer than 350 used medicinally, in central Quintana Roo alone. Knowledge of habitats, of animal behavior, of agriculture, of forest ecology, and of all other matters of wood and field craft is correspondingly incredibly high.

Having lived with Yucatec for several periods totaling a year and a half, I am acutely aware of these matters. They are extremely careful to specify exactly where and in what direction everything is, how it occupies space, and everything about its location. Their religion and folk culture are heavily based on having everything arranged and oriented exactly. (The same is true of other Maya groups; see, e.g., Vogt 1993.) They were often impatient with my hopeless inability to get oriented—though I have fairly high spatial skills for a ts'uul (foreigner). Working with them in forest and field taught me how desperately important these skills are. Knowing exactly where you are, where a jaguar is, where water is, where the path to the village is, and so on are obvious matters of life and death.

The Yucatec have no concept of "nature" as opposed to a human-influenced realm. The idea of a nonhuman wild nature does not exist. (As emphasized by Eugene Hunn in a comment, and confirmed by my own observation, highland Maya have a more clear distinction between the sown and the unsown, but they still do not see the latter as "wilderness" in the English sense; cf. Lenkersdorf 1999.) The whole Yucatan Peninsula is one vast managed landscape. The Maya have been farming it and managing its lush, rich forests for thousands of years. They also grow vast amounts of trees in orchards, gardens, and rural settings, like the Southeast Asians (see Chapter 7), and in fact, the two regions have exchanged many trees and other crops.

There is not an inch of the Yucatan Peninsula that has not been cultivated at some point. Ruined cities and towns from the Classic Maya period are scattered thickly throughout. Older farmers can provide a cultivation history for every acre of land for miles around their towns. Thus, there is no word for *wild* or *wilderness* in Maya. The opposition the Maya use is between the village (*kaah*, "community"), the fields (*kool*), and the forest (*k'aax*). Tame animals are *alakbil*, "[human]-reared things," in opposition to *ba'alche'*, "things of the trees." The latter are wild in the sense that they are not tame, but they are not wild in the sense that they live in a wilderness; they are managed by hunting and other activities as part of a managed landscape. In general, Maya referring to any area or thing remote from settlement talk about it with those words: *k'aax* or *che'* ("tree"). A contrast of "urban" and "rural" now exists, but cities are Hispanic territory, alien to most *hach Maayah* ("real Maya").

There is a quite different word, *taalkii* (perhaps from *taal*, "to touch"), that means *natural* as in "natural to a person or a family" or "it's natural for kids to be kids."

Almost all Maya are bilingual now and use *natura* and *naturaleza* in more or less the Spanish sense. However, from endless discussions on the matter with my Maya friends, I believe that the more traditional ones use it more or less as a translation of *k'aax* (and perhaps *taalkii*).

Natura refers to flowers, trees, wildlife, the unfarmed landscape. It certainly does not have the implications it has in standard Spanish, of a dangerous, unpleasant place that is "wild" in the bad sense. The Hispanic Mexican worldview has changed dramatically since I began working in Mexico a third of a century ago; today, the Hispanic-Mexican view is more like the Maya one. *Naturaleza* is a beautiful world of flowers and birds, not a dark brooding world. Even the writings of individuals show the change. The great Mexican writer and scholar Fernando Benitez wrote luridly of the alien and menacing rainforest in 1956 (Benitez 1986), but later became a leading environmentalist.

Less traditional younger Maya use *naturaleza* in the Spanish sense, but retain it as a Spanish concept—not taking it into their basic psychic framework. Maya also routinely use *monte* "woods, forest" and *arboles* "trees" with the connotations of the Maya words, not the Spanish ones.

The contrast of village and forest is found all over indigenous Mexico. The Yaqui at the extreme opposite corner of the country oppose village to the *sea ania,* the "flower world" (translated into Spanish as *monte*). It is very much like the Maya (Evers and Molina 1987; Painter 1986). The flower world is not alien; in fact, it is the place for hunting, gathering edible and medicinal herbs, meditating, and, often, fighting. It is about as important to the humans as the village is. It is the realm of animals, whereas the village is the proper home for humans, but humans and animals and their worlds need to interact. The Huichol have more or less the same opposition. The Nahuatl seem to have done the same. Their worldview is now heavily Hispanicized, but reading between the lines of early Spanish Colonial compilations (especially Ruiz de Alarcón 1982 and Sahagun 1950–1982) one sees a worldview like the Yaqui one. A beautiful world of greenery, flowers, and mountains surrounds the settlements and is as important for life as the village community.

"Hill" or "mountain" is *wiits.* Mountains are remote, untamed, and lush. *Wiitsil*—"people of the hills"—has sometimes had a meaning similar to "hill-billies" in English. Mountains were sacred in the old Maya world and still are sacred in the highlands. Each community has its own (see Pitarch 2010). Very dramatic is Huitepec, just outside San Cristobal de las Casas, Mexico; all around is heavily populated and overused, often eroded to bare rock, but the sacred Huitepec maintains its magnificent forests (personal observation). "Huitepec" is Maya *wiits* plus Aztec *tepec,* which means the same thing. (People love such redundancies. Torpenhow Hill in northern England is "hill hill hill hill"—in pre-Celtic, British Celtic, Danish, and English, respectively.) Supposedly, the animal spirits for the whole region live within this peak. The higher peaks of Guatemala are also still sacred. The high pyramids that dominate Yucatan's flat landscape were artificial sacred mountains. Ancient Maya art shows the "flower mountain," with its caves and lush vegetation (Taube 2004). The flower mountain is a feature of all ancient Mexican cosmology and is in fact a local form of the sacred mountain cult found throughout Eurasia and the Americas.

A Maya not exposed to contemporary environmentalism would not normally say *in yakuntik le baalche'oobo* ("I love the things of the trees"—"things of the trees" is about as close as one can get in Maya to "nature"). Maya do love many wild plants and animals, and do say so; my coworker Felix Medina Tzuc recently said to me, *"me encanta la selva, me encantan las arboles"* ("the forest enchants me, the trees enchant me"; Medina Tzuc, personal communication, 2005). The Maya understand a holistic world, including humans and nonhumans. They represent it religiously, via the various gods of forests, fields, animals, and so on. Their emotional response to it is intense, quiet, often loving, and impossible to verbalize. (I know it from sharing thousands of hours, over many years, in the forests and fields with many close friends.) Basically, there is a deep, intense, pervasive involvement. However, for many Maya, *love* is quite an inappropriate word; they do not say they "love nature" as they do say they love their homes, spouses, children. They do, however, love their gardens and fields, and often love particular plants and flowers.

Involvement with the living environment is perhaps wider and deeper than love. The nonhuman world means food, shelter, security, familiarity, and indeed life itself. Years or decades of intense interaction have colored experience. A Maya farmer is not only mentally influenced, but physically shaped, by his or her patterns of work. Knowledge of the environment is truly embodied (cf. Mauss 1979).

COSMOVISION

Modern Maya cosmovision is a fusion of Spanish Christian religion with Maya cosmology. The latter dominated actual practice on the ground until recently and still does for many older rural people. From Christianity comes monotheism; God is named *Dios*—the Spanish word is normally used. Jesus is often called by the name of the ancient maize god (*k'ichkelem yum,* "handsome lord") and has the same general attributes; actually, the maize god has simply continued to be worshiped under the new name. The old idea that the gods created humans from corn dough and then animated it by shedding their blood on it is still somewhat remembered, though it is fading fast. It survives in the Maya word *masewal* for ordinary Maya people; this is borrowed from Nahuatl *macehualli,* meaning, roughly, "those for whom the gods sacrificed themselves."

The everyday world is dominated by the rain gods (*chaak*), lords of the field and forest (*yum il kool, yum il k'aax,* and other *yum*), lords of game and animals (such as *Siip* the deer god), cardinal directions personified as deities, elves (*aluxo'ob*), shadowy chthonic lords (*bataboob*), and a vast range of other mysterious beings collectively called "winds" (*ik'*). Many of the *ik'* are evil, causing sickness or bad fate in humans and other life-forms. *Yum il k'aax* is *dueño(s) del monte,* "owners of the woods," in Spanish, and that Spanish term has been used very widely all over Mesoamerica for these and similar Presences. In fact, the idea that the wild and the animals are protected by their own guardians is almost universal in one form or another in North America.

Christian saints are more shadowy, lying behind this group or being equated with some members of it. Fusions of Christianity and Maya religion include the talking crosses worshiped in Quintana Roo (now largely confined to the west-central part). These have been worshiped since the Caste War of 1846 and almost surely have older antecedents. Witches and other malevolent beings also indicate fusion of beliefs. The Maya goddess Ixtabay has fused with the evil witch-woman of Spanish and Moorish legend to produce the *xtabay,* a much-feared shade taking the form of a beautiful woman who lures men to their deaths. She is associated with wells (as in Spain and Morocco) and ceiba trees (as Ixtabay had been).

Direct management of weather, forest, field, disease, and so on is strictly in the hands of the Maya supernaturals, now believed to be delegated by God for the purpose.

Respect even applies to stones. Among the related K'iche' Maya of Guatemala, the men must not touch the metates that women use to grind corn, for such mixing of gendered tools "shows the stone no respect" (Searcy 2011:93). The Yucatec rarely use metates now, but respect ancient Maya stonework and have a due respect for the rocky hills of their homeland.

This worldview seems to have been astonishingly consistent and general until recently, judging from ethnographic materials. Today, however, central Quintana Roo reveals everything from thoroughly traditional views to a Catholicism self-consciously "purified" of all Maya elements. One of the communities I study told their circuit-riding priest not to come back when he tried to wean them from traditional faith to "purified" Catholicism; they now hold *ch'a chaak* (rain-prayer ceremonies) and *loh* in the town church. There are also evangelical Protestant Christianity (several forms), Mormonism, Seventh-Day Adventism, and even various forms of revived Mayan "paganism."

Fortunately, the attitudes toward the environment survive all these various changes. Faith in at least some of the powers of the wild continues, along with belief in evil winds and witchcraft, among all but the most radical Protestants. Much more important, though, even the latter see that God is on the side of what their American equivalents call "creation care." It is not necessary to believe literally in the *yum il k'aax* to see that God wants forest protection and proves it by sending environmental problems to people who cause wanton damage.

This is a valuable and probably general point. The precise formulation of a cosmology is not a necessary condition for conservation ideology. On the other hand, experience and community responsibility, and *some* sort of ideology making them meaningful, are necessary. What erodes good management in Yucatan is not so much new religions (though they may have some effect) as urbanization. Both reorientation toward a machine-and-pavement civilization and exposure to strongly antinature norms are deadly. On the other hand, Mexican environmentalism has grown dramatically in recent decades, and the Maya are picking up rapidly on it and making the obvious linkages.

ETHICS

I have described Maya environmental ethics in great detail elsewhere, and also the wider and more general system of extreme knowledge, efficiency, and care in which the morals are embedded (Anderson 1996, 2003, 2005b; Anderson and Medina Tzuc 2005; see also Faust 1998; Fedick 1996, Gomez-Pompa et al. 2003; Martinez Reyes 2004; Terán and Rasmussen 1993). The nearby and closely related Itzaj Maya share more or less the same system, and an excellent literature on them explores this (Atran et al. 2004; Atran et al. 2002, comparing both cultures; Hofling 1991; Schwartz 1990).

The basics are very simple. In fact, the whole strategy of Maya teaching is to have simple principles but highly sophisticated, knowledge-intensive practice. Experience informs the user. This is a thought-provoking way to operate. The success of the Maya system indicates that simpler basic rules and much greater education of citizens may be the best way for the world's future.

The general Native North American rules apply. Taking more game or wild plant life than is immediately necessary for one's family and immediate neighbors is forbidden. The spirits, especially the guardians of the game and the forest, enforce this by sending bad luck. This can even include death, typically by a forest accident of some kind, sometimes by mysterious illness. A long and relatively expensive ceremony (the *loh ts'on)* is necessary to renew the luck of the gun after it has killed a few animals (an excellent account of this and other Maya environmental sanctions is found in Martinez-Reyes 2004, hopefully soon to be published in book form).

We are particularly fortunate in having a wonderful collection of stories told by an elderly Quintana Roo Maya hunter, showing how conservation was taught through personal stories involving the protector spirits of the game (Llanes Pasos 1993). Especially interesting is Eleuterio Llanes Pasos's account of the "leaf-litter turkey," a giant wild turkey that protects game birds and punishes those who overhunt. (Alas, the leaf-litter turkey has been inadequate; turkeys are especially severely overhunted in the peninsula.)

Damaging communal resources and public goods in general is not done; in fact, individuals are expected to protect public resources. Conservation and sustainable management are universal in forestry, field-making, and field maintenance. Cutting firebreaks around fields, or otherwise making sure fires do not spread, is one general rule. Usually this was unnecessary in wet Quintana Roo, but it was done at need. My friend Don Felix Medina Tzuc would cut small firebreaks around valuable tree seedlings he found in the forest and would clear old trails that had been neglected.

Wild trees of value are carefully preserved and thus increase and come to dominate the forest (see, e.g., Ford and Nigh 2009; Mathews 2009). Fruit trees and thatch-supplying palms were especially carefully preserved. Other trees were often coppiced to supply future shoots for firewood and the like. Large trees could be ringbarked but left standing; burned, they developed holes, which then became nests for bees, useful birds, and other valued wildlife. Indirect management for wildlife was consciously done (see also Greenberg 1992), for example by careful management of milpa regrowth and by protecting plants known to be important wildlife food.

Bees are important to the economy, and thus it is not surprising that they are treated with great respect (see Anderson and Medina Tzuc 2005), but even mosquitoes receive care; Betty Faust (1998) describes being told not to slap mosquitoes biting her arm. I have seen a mother make her children eat butterflies they had killed (Anderson 1996). Killing is for food only. My friend Antonio Chel was losing valuable orchard trees to leafcutter ants, but would not destroy the nests because the ants deserved to live, too. Maya friends picking up ants to show me would not only put them back down alive, but they would make sure they put them down pointing in the direction they had been going.

Many stories tell of the bad fate of people who overhunted, and many modern Maya tell stories of being warned by spirits. My friend Don Jacinto tells of having all the animals in the forest gather silently round him when he killed too many pacas at one time. He was terrified, but they silently warned him and let him go. He never hunted again. The Itzaj Maya, a branch of the Yucatec living in Guatemala, have the same conservation ethics, and some wonderful stories have been recorded from them (Hofling 1991:136–166; see also Atran 1993, Atran et al. 1999).

Morality is enforced by precept and example within the community. Elders and peers teach, model, and enforce through positive and negative comments—more or less as such people do everywhere. The difference is that the Maya never let up. They have, or recently had, high standards for community responsibility, including (but far from limited to) resource care, and they enforce these through community pressure. In my experience, this pressure is much more often of the positive kind: modeling, encouraging, talking about exemplary people, telling folktales, praising particularly good behavior, and so on. This may be unusual, because Chunhuhub is a generally very "positive," friendly, supportive place relative to many Maya communities I know. However, other descriptions (e.g., Martinez Reyes 2004) seem to indicate broad similarities elsewhere.

Maya ethical discourse remains to be studied in detail (though there is a large literature touching on it; see, e.g., Redfield and Villa Rojas 1934; Villa Rojas 1945). It is heavily informed by Christianity today, but still maintains a distinction from Hispanic Mexican morality and discourse thereon. Maya put a high value on peace, quiet, order, tranquility, and responsibility. Being a good member of the community—peaceful, nondisruptive, helpful, and above all responsible—is particularly valued. Care for the forest and animals is within this obligation. The plants and animals have rights and value of their own, and supernatural beings take care of them and sanction irresponsible users, but consideration for others in the human community is also important. One wants to preserve resources useful to all. Conversely, the whole local community may get together to hunt a jaguar that is killing their sheep, as happened in one village when I was there in 2001 (the jaguar got away).

Teaching through ceremonies is common (as superbly described for girls' education by Maas Colli 1983). Seeing a *loh* or similar ceremony for the environmentally protective spirits is a major educational experience. It brings a community together and reinforces their solidarity, specifically in regard to environmental conservation. All observers of the traditional Maya community have emphasized this (see esp. Redfield and Villa Rojas 1934; Villa Rojas 1945).

Song, poetry, and folktales are part of the pool. Many stories are simply Spanish folktales recycled, but traditional Maya stories represent environmental interaction, management, and conservation (Andrade and Collí 1990;

M. Redfield 1935, e.g., p. 24 on caring for dogs; see Hofling 1991, esp. pp. 136–166, for the Itzaj). A common story all over Mexico describes a man and his dog who overhunted game or killed for pleasure; they were captured, taken into the mountain (the home of the gods), and severely reprimanded by spirit beings. The dog died or was kept in the mountain. The man was released to tell others. Versions of this story are widespread in Maya cultures (see, e.g., Hofling 1991:136–153).

Songs and ritual texts show a tremendous love of flowers, plants, and animals (Barrera Vásquez 1963, 1965, 1980, 1981, 1986). Particularly valuable are early sources: materials written down in Spanish letters but obviously reflecting pre-Columbian material. The *Rituals of the Bacabs* is an amazing document, a collection of magical curing spells used ceremonially to deal with madness as well as more conventional medical problems such as scorpion stings (Arzápalo Marín 1987). It mentions jays, flycatchers, doves, jaguars, crocodiles, lizards, and many other animals, apparently magical ones, as well as many medicinal plants. The Songs of Dzitbalche' (Barrera Vásquez 1980) mention many kinds of flowers, certainly beautiful ones but probably also of ceremonial and religious value. The many "books of Chilam Balam" (Barrera Vásquez and Rendon 1989) also mention many plants and some animals. None of these texts mentions conservation per se, but the extremely high involvement with and valuation of animals and plants is obvious. The Books of Chilam Balam stress supernatural punishment for sin, including general civic irresponsibility.

Modern Maya visual arts are rather few and do not have a vital central role in representing the environment and human-environment interaction. The beautiful embroidery or cross-stitch on Maya dresses is usually floral, but these designs are ultimately Renaissance Spanish in origin, though some Maya have taken to embroidering local plants and birds.

The result is that the Maya forest survives—overused and scrubby in areas of high and long-established population, but still in superb shape in more thinly inhabited regions. Yucatec Maya can be harsh judges of people—especially outsiders—who misuse, overuse, or destroy natural resources (Anderson 2005b; Haenn 2005). Nora Haenn and I both found that outsiders moving to Yucatec Maya communities often adopt their relatively conservationist attitudes and behavior. On the other hand, communities vary, and some are not nearly as conservation-oriented as the ones I know in Quintana Roo (Faust 1998; see also the range revealed by the various papers in Faust et al. 2004).

Moreover, even within traditional rural communities like Chunhuhub, there is the expectable range of variation. Some people are modernizers who care little for the old ways, whether conservationist or not. Others are simply selfish (and their neighbors say so—frequently—so the problem is often soon corrected). Others simply have different priorities, or fail to look to the future. I describe above the general attitude that is not only a clear consensus among older farmers, but is the self-conscious line heard in community meetings, dealings with outsiders, and other public contexts. It is broadly shared throughout central Quintana Roo and neighboring Yucatán and Campeche states. However, few totally agree on it, and a few reject it outright. In some other communities, many reject it. I have been in communities—ones more exposed to outside pressures and domination than the ones I study—where the public has simply given up. One is not to expect uniformity in a highly individualistic society, which Maya society most certainly is, in spite of considerable homogeneity in lifestyle and public discourse.

That said, it is necessary and important to stress two things: first, there is a definite preponderance of opinion on the side of good management of resources, at least field and forest ones; and, second, there is virtually no (I believe in Chunhuhub literally *no*) support for the common old-fashioned Hispanic Mexican opinion that the forest, the milpas, and the wild animals must go because they are evil and backward and must be replaced by a purely human-created landscape.

Game has declined everywhere, but some communities have major problems with poaching, whereas others have relatively little (Anderson and Medina Tzuc 2005). Acculturation to Hispanic-Mexican norms is a major factor here, but I have observed that certain members of communities displaced for conservation are often serious offenders. Some in those communities support the conservation restrictions, but others become embittered. Ruled off their own commons, their sense of responsibility turns to one of wounded entitlement, and they treat everything as literally "fair game" (Martinez-Reyes 2004 also finds this). Thus does preservationism become counterproductive—as it has been in so many other cases around the world.

The sad truth is that even the best traditional practice is inadequate in densely populated circumstances, and the best practice is eroding with the progressive decline of traditional rural life.

However, outside influences today are often environmentalist or conservationist and, increasingly often, are based on awareness of the traditional Maya values on environmental management. More and more agencies are realizing that it is far better to work with such enlightened local values, instead of declaring a reserve and locking the local people out of it. The Si'an Ka'an reserve in Quintana Roo was set up on lockout principles but has changed progressively away from that (see, again, Martinez-Reyes 2004). The huge Calakmul reserve in Campeche was set up with much more awareness of the need to involve local people. This has been far from totally successful (Haenn 2005), but has not been a total failure, and points the way to better practice (see also Anderson 2005b; Anderson and Medina Tzuc 2005).

All this leads to a great deal of back-and-forth activity in the forests. The groups I work with remain skeptical of state-level forest management, though it has worked very well in neighboring communities. Nora Haenn continues her wonderful, nuanced work on this (Haenn 2011). The Zapotec Indigenous people face similar problems with a similarly strong conservation ideology, and their struggles have been chronicled in truly superb accounts by Andrew Mathews (2008, 2009, 2011)—essential reading for anyone interested in the politics of saving forests in Mexico or indeed anywhere.

Basically, the ethic stems from the need for extreme efficiency and for substituting extremely detailed and precise knowledge for physical capital. Maya agriculture is the opposite extreme from contemporary Californian agribusiness. It is intended to be as efficient as possible—a necessity in a land of poor soil, unreliable climate, frequent hurricanes, and other problems. It maximizes knowledge and minimizes material throughput. California agribusiness is adapted to a land of lavishly available, high-quality soil and a sparse, mostly nonlocal workforce. It maximizes material throughput and fixed capital, but minimizes efficiency and local knowledge. This attitude toward farming is spreading like wildfire in Mexico, and reaching even Quintana Roo. Maya conservation values are thus at a crossroads, and everything depends on whether the wider world supports them or undercuts them.

COMPARISONS: OTHER MAYA VISIONS

Presumably the spectacular and brilliant creations of the Classic Maya had some environmental functions, as well as many other functions, but we have little real clue to what these may have been. Sacred trees like ceiba and cacao are amply portrayed, and high valuation of water is shown by the frequency of water birds and water plants, but this is hardly helpful knowledge. City planning was excellent, with cities often being fitted into sites in ways that were both aesthetically superb and environmentally sophisticated. Drainage was managed to ensure water supplies, major buildings were kept off good farmland when possible, and buildings were carefully fitted into hill slopes. (This is largely my own conclusion from walking extensively through dozens of sites, but see, e.g., Andrews 1975; Ashmore 2005; Stuart and Stuart 2008; many other valuable sources exist.)

Surviving Classic Maya writings are largely unhelpful. Those we have are calendric or political, like public-monument writings everywhere in the world. Only four small books have survived. They are long post-Classic, and treat calendric matters. We must await the (highly improbable) discovery of a Classic Maya environmental management textbook.

On the other hand, extremely valuable comparative material comes from other Maya groups. The classic, best-known, most important work is the *Popul Vuh* (*Popul Wuh*), the origin myth of the Quiché Maya of highland Guatemala. The survival of this text is one of those cliffhangers that historians love. It was written down by anonymous Quiché after the Conquest (perhaps around 1560), when they had learned to write their language in Spanish letters. It was then copied, apparently out of sheer interest, by a Spanish clergyman, Francisco Ximenez, in the early eighteenth century. It survived in obscure manuscript form until discovered in Guatemala and copied by Carl Scherzer in the 1850s. Ximenez's manuscript was then lost, and all we have now is a copy of a copy (Christenson 2007:40).

Fortunately, it seems, by comparison with all other Maya literature, to be a reliable one. It reflects known myths in a thoroughly Maya literary style. The key episodes from the main part—the myth of the Hero Twins and the successive creations of the world—are shown on countless Classic Period monuments, vessels, and other art works. Particularly common is their slaying by blowguns the evil bird Seven Macaw (see Christenson 2007:94 ff.). The myths of the monster-slaying Hero Twins and the multiple creations are known in various forms all over North America. In the Maya versions, the early creations were imperfect and were destroyed because people sinned, especially by refusing to answer or honor the creator gods. Sometimes their own domestic animals and utensils turned on them (Christenson 2007:87). Maize is, of course, critically important, and appears in the final, successful creation, with animals bringing the various (symbolic) colors of maize (Christenson 2007:193 ff.). Since then, true people eat maize; foreigners eat wheat.

Christenson, in a footnote to his translation of the *Popul Vuh,* notes: "When I first began working as an ethnographer in Quiché communities, I found it curious that when I struck up a conversation in the Quiché language with someone I didn't know, that person would sometimes interrupt me in mid-sentence to ask what I ate, specifically if I ate tortillas or bread. When I affirmed that I ate what they ate, including tortillas, they would nod as if that explained a great deal. After a number of such experiences I asked a friend why people were curious about what I ate. He replied, 'I've never heard of anyone that isn't Maya that can speak our language. I wondered if it was because you ate maize from here. If so then you have the flesh of the ancestors in your flesh and therefore can speak what they spoke" (Christenson 2007:197). His friends added that the maize has to be sacrificed—ground and cooked—to be food, and wheat must also, thus showing the need for sacrifice in the world (Christenson 2007:295).

More recently, enormous amounts of data on the environmental knowledge and thought of the Tzotzil and Tzeltal Maya of highland Chiapas have been brought to light. The Harvard-Stanford-Chicago project to study these groups, organized by Evon Vogt (1993), produced the best data set available for any small-scale society in the world. The project officially terminated around 1980, but the participants and their students kept right on going, and today dozens of investigators flock to the area annually. (I, too, studied under Vogt and later under Brent Berlin, one of the project's graduates, and I, too, have done some slight research in highland Chiapas.) In addition to Vogt's project, Mexican investigators devoted a great deal of attention to these groups, who preserve many ancient traditions.

Vogt's dream was that the Chiapas Maya were relatively unchanged survivors of the ancient Maya world; this proved untrue, but the reality is even more interesting. They have been able to adapt creatively to an incredibly trying history and economy and do so through creative use—not mindless preservation—of their traditions.

In any case, the most interesting data for my purpose here is the enormous mass of folk literature recorded from the Tzotzil and Tzeltal by Gary Gossen (2002), Robert Laughlin (1996), and others, and from the Tojolabal by Carlos Lenkersdorf (1996, 1999). Lenkersdorf describes very well the close interpenetration of human and nonhuman realms, which is similar to that in Yucatec cosmovision, or for that matter in other Native North American groups. He thinks the structure of the language is a cause. Maya languages are ergative, focusing on verb-object (more accurately verb-patient) relationships rather than on subject-verb relationships as in Indo-European languages. Thus, the Maya direct their attention to actions and their results, not to the subject/actor. I am not convinced that this causes anything, if only because other rural traditional peoples with ordinary subject-verb languages have the same idea, but the point is still a thoughtful one. At the very least, the ergative bias of Maya fits perfectly with their cultural views.

The highland Maya, like other Mexican indigenous peoples, believe humans have animal companion souls. Among the Tzotzil these are called ch'ulel and tend to reside at the tip of the tongue in the human, but as animal spirits they reside in the sacred mountains of the Chiapas highlands, where they are kept by the Earth Lords, more or less as livestock are kept in stables. (There are similar, but not identical, ideas among the Tzeltal [Pitarch 2010] and Tojolabal [Lenkersdorf 1999].) Noble people have jaguars and cougars as animal companions, ordinary people have coyotes and similar animals, and low vile people have weasels, skunks, and rats. The introduced Eurasian rats are thought to be the souls of outlaw soldiers from the Mexican Revolution (Gossen 2002:943 ff.).

As elsewhere, the maize god has been assimilated with Jesus, and also with the Sun. Creation stories that are clearly pre-Columbian in origin have the solar Jesus creating food for humanity by slicing a piece from his thigh. It is maize and becomes the maize we all grow and eat (Gossen 2002 gives many versions of this story). This obviously relates to the Nahuatl and Yucatec story given previously, and is probably a modern form of it. The hummingbird was once the tobacco gourd of the solar Jesus and therefore has a soul and needs protection (Gossen 2002:97–99). Sweet potatoes come from the milk of the Virgin Mary;

one cannot help wondering if this is a transfer from a pre-Columbian goddess. Another story that must go far back is one of a man who married the daughter of an Earth Lord; he hit her, bloodying her nose; she wiped her nose on a corncob, thus creating red ears of corn and making them somewhat sacred thereafter (Gossen 2002:365). Of course she promptly left him, rescued by her father via a thunderstorm, and this is told as a cautionary tale to young men.

More specifically conservation-oriented stories seem rarer than in Yucatec narratives. People who hunted and ate game on Motozintla Mountain became coyotes (Gossen 2002:845–855), but there is no special explanation of this. Evidently a taboo was violated, but nobody seems to know quite what. The Tzotzil, however, see the woods as threatening, as opposed to the safe world of houses and fields (Gossen 2002:1057). Could this be a borrowing from the Spanish?

It is, however, clear from all the recorded folk literature that the Earth Lords guard their domain and their charges, and that humans who use the earth and its resources unwisely or wastefully are sure to suffer. The deer are the Earth Lords' horses, the rabbits their burros, helping with loads (Gossen 2002:1057). The rattlesnake warns them of trouble. Thus all these animals are under the Earth Lords' protection and cannot be lightly killed. Indeed, bagging any game animal requires prayers to the Earth Lords, "begging for forgiveness and understanding for taking a creature from their domain" (Gossen 2002:1058); this is, of course, the universal North American Native belief, once again.

NOTE

1 "Yucatec" is a Spanish barbarism, and should never be dignified by a pseudo-Indigenous spelling ("Yukatek"). It originated when Columbus, on first seeing the peninsula, stopped a canoe-load of Maya and asked, "What's the name of that land over there?" The man looked blank, and someone helpfully said, "He didn't understand what you said"—*ma' u yu'ub' ka t'aan i.* Columbus took the accented syllables (missing the *b*, which is slurred over in ordinary speech), and there we are. Maya never use it as a self-name; they use it (in the Spanish form *yucateco/a*) to mean anyone from the Yucatan Peninsula.

CHAPTER FIVE

Medieval Ireland

A LITERARY ENVIRONMENT

Medieval Irish literature provides a unique view of an environmental vision very different from anything found today. This vision runs through its epics, long stories and sequences of stories, lyric poetry, religious literature, and place-name accounts. These last are interesting because a proper toponymy includes the stories behind the names. These were called *dinnsenchas* and often involved quite long myths tracing place names to divine intervention. They reveal an intense involvement with, and extreme concern for, places and landscapes, often going back to religious associations of particular places.

For obvious reasons, this chapter must be very different from the others. We have no ethnographic access to medieval Ireland. We depend entirely on textual sources and on archaeology. By far the most useful are the literary sources, because these reflect with an almost unique degree of thoughtfulness and seriousness on people-in-nature. This chapter, then, will confine itself to bringing out literary materials. There is not, so far, sufficient wider evidence to allow us to create the full cosmological and moral story from these materials. Of course, this means we have no clue to how good environmental management was in the early medieval period. We can only recall that the home of modern conservation is the Celtic-Germanic "fringe" of Europe. There is every reason to believe these modern attitudes toward landscape have a long history, but I cannot read it yet from the data.

The sources examined here date from around the ninth century (sometimes earlier) to the thirteenth or fourteenth (Jackson 1935). The stories they relate are often centuries older. Many of these stories cluster around the time of St. Patrick, in the fifth century CE. Others go back far earlier, to misty, dateless epic times. There is no way of knowing how faithfully the medieval sources reproduce the writings of that distant past, but in at least a few cases archaic linguistic usage implies that material from as early as the seventh century is being used.

Obviously, some mix of ancient and medieval worldviews occurred. We have no way of factoring out ancient perceptions from later ones; the two, or rather the whole log of changing perceptions over the centuries, are inextricably mixed. Nothing can be done about this, and all one can do is report on what turns out to be an astonishingly consistent, clear, defined, and uniform worldview. Its broad similarities with traditional worldviews all across Eurasia may indicate that it is ancient, though we have it in medieval form. The direct medieval influences appear to be in large part from other Celtic societies, or sometimes from the Anglo-Saxon and Norse world with its rather similar views of nature and humanity. Poetry very similar to the Irish is known from early Wales, and in tiny fragments or late versions from other Celtic societies, as well as neighboring societies like the Anglo-Saxons.

The very different Mediterranean view was well known from Latin sources; formal education came through the Catholic Church and was thus in Latin. The main effect of this Latin input on classic Irish literature seems to have been to make our scribes and storytellers highly conscious of the fact that they had a distinctive worldview, very different indeed from others', and worthy of preservation. The Latin view saw nature as something frightening and hostile, to be tamed or eliminated, and saw the city as the place of all good. Even the romantic pastoralism of Ovid and other classical authors involved distancing of the urban poet from the pretty but alien rural landscape. This pastoral literature influenced the fusion literature that developed when Celtic epics met Romance conventions, especially on the medieval French lays and tales (by Marie de France, Chretien de Troyes, and others) derived from Celtic traditions. All these authors, from Ovid to the Celts to the later minnesingers, not only loved nature and described it passionately; they equated love for nature and love for

Photo on Previous Page: Skara Brae, Neolithic village on the west coast of Scotland. Photograph by E. N. Anderson.

women, and often merged the two, as in Ovid's many tales of women pursued by gods and turning into trees. There is little of this in the poems considered herein, but, moving into other Celtic literatures, consider the stories of Tristan and Ysolt, with their conscious and detailed counterpointing of the greenwood and meadow as both setting and metaphor for the loves of the couple.

The medieval Scandinavian and Germanic eddas and epics were part of the same general movement to retell the old stories for sophisticated courts. This literature is fascinating in its own right, but is well described elsewhere and is not really relevant for my purpose here. However, one recalls that it includes many stories of spirit journeys, shape-changing, animal companions, and other themes that clearly go back to shamanistic roots. It served as a bridge from those roots to modern fantasy writing.

Our sources were written down by anonymous scribes and have usually been recopied since. Many come to us from sixteenth or seventeenth century manuscripts, often in the possession of old Irish families. Most were written in medieval Irish Gaelic, which is close in spelling, but not in pronunciation, to modern Irish. (Irish, like English, has been very conservative in spelling. Irish spelling rules are also, to put it mildly, unique. It is impossible for anyone without a thorough knowledge of the language to sound out a word even approximately.) A few were written in Latin, and these are often particularly interesting. They show the level and type of interaction with Latin literary traditions.

Three sources stand out as particularly important for our purposes. First is the nearest thing the Irish have to a national epic, the *Tain Bo Cuailnge* ("the cattle raid of Cooley," pronounced approximately "tan bo cooley"; Kinsella 1969). It records conflicts involving the kingdom of Ulster in some undefined past, considered to be vaguely close to the time of Christ. The hero, Cuchulainn, is a classic mythic superman; he and the heroes of our next source remain major inspirations for the heroes of fantasy literature today. The story takes off from a cattle raid, but the plot quickly becomes so involved and so fantastic that it defies summary; fortunately we need look only at its background assumptions.

The second source is the *Acallam na Senórach*, "Tales of the Elders" (Dooley and Roe 1999). Surviving versions appear to have been put together around the twelfth century. This weaves some of the countless folktales about the mythic superhero Finn MacCool into a coherent narrative. St. Patrick comes to Ireland and meets a band of ancient, giant, spear-armed men. These are Ceílte and his few followers, the last of the *fianna*, Finn MacCool's wandering warrior band. They tower over Patrick, yet he is not intimidated and proceeds to convert them, driving legions of devils out of them in the process. Ceílte tells the saint the stories of the old times. St. Patrick, being a proper Irish leader, is a willing listener. Many of the stories are in the above-mentioned toponymic form: St. Patrick, on his missionary wanderings, asks how each place got its name, and

Ceílte tells him the fianna stories that explain this. In spite of the inevitable loose-jointed quality that this gives to the text, it remains a powerful, unified, and emotionally gripping narrative. The anonymous writer cast it as the contrast of two worlds, one beautiful, wonderful, harsh, and doomed, the other calm, peaceful, hopeful, and triumphant. He (the writer was certainly male) saw the full glory of the old, but recognized it was fatally trapped in a cycle of war and merciless raid that only Christianity could resolve. As a result, much of the narrative is heartbreaking. The grief of individuals over battle deaths and war losses is magnified, consciously and with brilliance, into a lament for an entire world lost. Yet the narrative keeps resolving back into hope; the old had to die, the new will be better.

The third is perhaps the most interesting of all medieval Celtic manuscripts: *Suibhne geilt,* "Sweeney mad." (It has been frequently translated; the scholarly edition is by O'Keeffe, 1913; there is a beautiful modern translation by Seamus Heaney, 1983.) It turns on the same theme, the loss of the ancient world in the face of Christianity. It is a more militantly Christian work, however. The stoutly pagan King Sweeney seizes the psalm-book of St. Rowan, an early missionary, and throws it into the lake. For this he is cursed with madness and remains in an altered state until finally taken in by the gentler St. Moling. (This counterpoint of vindictive and gentle saints is found elsewhere in medieval Irish stories.) Even there, he remains wild, until an accidental missile cast by a swineherd—the lowest of the low—fells him. He dies, finally redeemed and at peace, in the saint's arms.

Most of the account consists of Sweeney's adventures and songs during his madness. The equation of madness with pagandom does not stop the writer from portraying Sweeney sympathetically. More to the point, Sweeney's "madness" is unmistakably not insanity at all, but rather a "pagan" spiritual discipline very much like shamanism. Sweeney does not rave, fear incoherent visions, or otherwise act schizophrenic or mentally ill. Instead, he flies or leaps lightly over treetops, he changes shape, he talks with birds, he lives on cold water and watercress, he sings to tree spirits, and he calls on the powers of nature to pity him. In all these ways he acts as Eurasian shamans classically do (Eliade 1964; Humphrey 1996). The book can be rather precisely dated, on linguistic grounds, to the mid to late twelfth century, though it survived only in manuscripts. from the seventeenth (Murphy 2007:227).

In the course of his madness, Sweeney sings some of the most agonizingly beautiful nature poems in all world literature. (They do not translate well, because much of the beauty is in the rhyme and alliteration. Many a phrase that puzzles the English-language reader by its irrelevance to the rest of the verse turns out to fit the sound-system of the medieval Gaelic too perfectly to be sacrificed for mere consistency of meaning. Celtic bards regarded consistency as dispensable when a good rhyme is at hand. See Jackson 1935.)

From these and from many short lyrics, scattered stories, and other materials, we can reconstruct something of the old Irish view of people in environments.

The first and most striking perception is a total lack of separation of "people" from "nature." People live with deer, salmon, trees, wolves, waters, mountains, and birds, sometimes talking with them, often interacting as social equals in a single social sphere. Sometimes they even change into them. Sweeney's total absorption in the realm of trees and birds is admittedly extreme, but the same sort of incorporation is clear in the other texts. People eat deer, wolves eat deer and people, birds foretell the future, people care for birds.

WILD IRELAND

The actual backdrop for the stories, as revealed by archaeology, is a world that was far wilder than the "civilized" Celtic world of Caesar's Gaul (on which see Green 1996; Green [ed.] 1995; Webster 1995; for Ireland, see Flanagan 1998 and Harbison 1994, for the earliest part of our period; O'Croinin 1995 for the later parts). The old Irish lived by herding, fishing, hunting, gathering, and grain agriculture. One gathers the last was as much for beer as for anything else. Fields were small. Wealth was cattle, herded in great numbers in natural meadows or artificial clearings. Swine abounded, but seem to have largely gotten their own living from mast: "root hog or die." People lived in tiny huts or in great wooden halls—capacious but roughly built, easily burned or disassembled, easily rebuilt. Much of Ireland was covered by huge, dense, dark oak woodland. This was the original "derry down" later immortalized in folksong: Irish *deiri dun,* "dark oak wood." None of it survives except one tiny old-growth stand of oaks in the far southwest. People as well as swine lived on acorns and hazelnuts much of the time.

On the other hand, the extreme simplicity and rusticity of stereotypic portrayals of early medieval Ireland do not fit with what we see in the texts: rich monasteries, powerful manors, great feasts, ornate chariots. Some of the difference is due to the fact that the texts were actually written down much later, but it is also true that the image of a barbaric herding culture in the early Christian centuries has clearly been somewhat exaggerated.

Laurence Flanagan, in his prehistory of Ireland, defines archaeology as "the story of Man's attempts to keep the wolf from the door by means of better doors and better wolf-traps" (1998:3). He adds: "[T]he fact that humankind itself is unpredictable is the quintessential stumbling-block for archaeologists. We have to assume that the people whose dwelling-places, artefacts, lives even, we are dealing with were rational, integrated, sane, and sensible human beings. Then we look around at our own contemporaries and wonder how this belief can possibly be sustained" (1998:5).

Ireland lacked the sophisticated, intensive grain-based agriculture of Celtic Gaul (on which see Reynolds 1995) and had no need of the carefully managed woodlots that the Continental Celts had to maintain to provide timbers for great feast-halls (Reynolds 1995:194–202). Ireland had its sacred groves, but they were not closely and carefully managed. Ireland stayed forested until the English conquerors in the sixteenth and seventeenth centuries deliberately deforested it for military reasons (Anderson ms 1; Kiernan 2007). The Tudor campaigns of the mid-sixteenth century, the Nine Years' War that led to the Flight of the Earls in 1607, and the Cromwellian campaigns in the mid-seventeenth century completely deforested the island; there were not only no forests, but no groves or woodlands. The moors and heaths now beloved of Irish nostalgians were a result of the deforestation process, not usually a natural feature of the landscape.

Agriculture graded into management of wild food resources. One can probably assume that, for instance, wild hazelnuts were coppiced to make them grow better (as was done in historic times). Unfortunately, we have no idea of how the nature poetry might have fed into management strategies. Archaeology and history provide little help, partly because there was not much dramatic change of the landscape, partly because the ravages of time and harsh climate have erased the evidence for what there was.

Social organization is misrepresented by modern translations of *ri*, "chief," as "king." The overtranslation is due to its cognation with Latin *rex* as well as the institutional development of *ri* into true kingship in the early middle ages. The *ri*'s society in the time of the epics was a typical "chiefdom" in the sense of Julian Steward (1955). He was the head of a leading descent group. He led followers in raids and wars, but had little other real authority. Dozens of these petty *ri* competed in a land with only about half a million inhabitants. There were a few powerful leaders of whole districts, but as many as 150 *ri* may have existed at one time (Byrne 2001). Each held his or her position—there were women leaders—on sufferance; if he or she failed to bring in booty and distribute it lavishly to warriors, they drifted off to form their own bands or to follow some other, more lavish chief.

A chief had to keep running to stay in the same place. No war, no booty; no booty, no lavish generosity; no generosity, no followers; no followers, certain ruin at the hands of a more generous rival. Succession was often not by designated heirship, but by tanistry; after a chief's death, the followers picked a successor from among his heirs. This inevitably led to fighting among or over rival candidates, leading Shakespeare to call it "bloody tanistry." All this was the merciless driver of the endless cycle of war and raid, and this was what Christianity—bringing with it more formal legal and state institutions—could eventually end. Before it did, Christian missionaries tended to live as hermits or in tiny monastic communities. They often lived by hunting and gathering and a little gardening. For a long time, before modern states emerged, they modeled a totally different lifestyle: one committed to peace and simplicity. Christian poems from this world reflect—quite strikingly, and rather surprisingly—the full pre-Christian devotion to what we would now call nature.

A good *ri* or a devout saint could bring about fertility and productiveness in the land; the praise-poem that follows is not an isolated instance. Nut trees bore better, soil yielded more grain, animals reproduced more successfully, if the land was well regulated. Part of this is common sense: people work harder and their products are safer under such circumstances. But there was also a belief, universal in early Indo-European societies and found in one or another form almost worldwide, that the chief or king actually influences the natural fertility of the land. This was a powerful driver to the sort of deep, caring involvement in nature that we observe in the poetry.

Bards—the word is Celtic—made a good living singing the heroism and generosity of their chiefs. They, too, stayed only as long as the generosity lasted. The fate of a less-than-lavish chief is clear from the fact that every Irish school-child still learns a medieval taunt by one less-than-well-served bard:

> I hear
> he won't give horses for poems.
> He gives what his style allows:
> cows.
>
> (Kinsella 1989:40)

As early as the eleventh century, it was already a textbook example—literally—of scathing poetry (Murphy 2007:215). Nothing is known of this king's subsequent fate, but one has the uncomfortable feeling that he did not long survive. The bard's next employer probably took care of that.

One can find almost the same institution today in West Africa, where local leaders go in healthy fear of the *griots,* professional singers who can praise or devastate. Today, they sometimes have international audiences. We have progressed since old Irish times; with modern media, a stingy leader can be infamous overnight on three or four continents.

The chief's other followers would include at least one blacksmith, to make tools and weapons; many warriors; and a large, but not very large, number of ordinary people, to farm, herd, bake, brew, weave, fish, chop wood, build halls, and otherwise keep the system viable. The staple economy did not permit either dense populations or much in the way of specialized fine crafts. Superb gold jewelry and other fine craft items are known, but were rare before medieval times, and were certainly not made in ordinary chiefdoms. A few trading towns, like Dublin (largely a Viking foundation), arose, as contact with the outside world increased, and quality goods were made in such places or in other specialized centers of trade. Rare fairs provided distribution. The spectacular Irish art represented by the Book of Kells and countless fine metal items came late in our period, with the rise of true states, but it was based on design elements that flourished in the ancient times.

Strong individualism—the idea that individuals are unique, fully life-sized, and important just from being who they are—runs through all this literature. One may wonder if there is any connection between the Celtic attitude toward nature and the strong individualism seen in Celtic literature. The epics mentioned previously, and the Celtic ballads most famously preserved in Scotland, show an uncompromising focus on individuals—heroes, madmen, tragic lovers, religious figures, or ordinary people, often alone against the world or against enemies. People are never the faceless masses they often are in other literatures (and, most extremely, in modern movies, where mass murders occur routinely and without remark). Admittedly, the same could be said of epics and ballads everywhere. But Celtic individualism seems extreme even in comparison with other such literature. Modern individualism, worldwide, is very much a product of ancient Greece and of the Celtic and Germanic fringe. However, without much further research on the actual wellsprings of modern individualism, and still more on the relationship thereof to nature views, one can only speculate on the possibility of linkages between views of nature and views of persons.

RELIGION

Religious life in pre-Christian Ireland is notably obscure. The situation is not helped by the obsession of historians with "Druids" (Rees and Rees 1995). These were a sort of priesthood among the Gauls of France and neighboring areas; they are briefly and badly described by Caesar and Tacitus, who projected Roman ideas of proper priesthood on Celts whose institutions were quite un-Roman. The British Celts and the Irish had some sort of druids—the name does occur in the medieval texts—but the Irish ones (at least) were more individual and free, less like an organized priesthood, than anything described by the Roman writers. Nothing in any Irish poems, religious texts, or other contemporary material describes anything like an organized Druidic priesthood (except for some late texts influenced by reading Caesar and Tacitus). What we have instead are references to inspired individuals who prophesy, generate gnomic poems of mysterious significance, and see hidden things. The poems imply that these were ordinary individuals with special gifts, not specialized religious practitioners. Many were poets—bards. Others had healing powers, but we have no knowledge of specialized doctors; healers were simply individuals who had that gift. They might be kings, bards, or ordinary commoners. Other individuals, otherwise undistinguished, might be able to drink incredible quantities, or kill with every stroke, or hear things from miles off. (A glorious medieval parody of stories about such gifted individuals is found in Jackson 1971:202–204.)

In early times, the inspired bards, healers, and even chiefs with magical powers were very similar to the shamans of eastern Eurasia and northwestern Native America (see, e.g., Aldhouse-Green and Aldhouse-Green 2005). One obvious similarity of great importance is that the early Irish believed song had real power and that specially gifted singers could accomplish almost anything through proper songs. Some such power songs were spells and incantations; some were inspired individual creations. Below we shall consider the king and poet Sweeney, called "mad" in the late text about him, but clearly in a shaman-like state rather than an insane one. He could foretell the future. He and another "madman" meet at one point in the story and sing their futures to each other, then go their way.

Finn MacCool in youth had to cook the Salmon of Wisdom for his elders; burning his thumb on the fish, he stuck it in his mouth, and thus got some of the knowledge the elders were supposed to get. He thus could prophesy and see things at distance. Exceptional knowledge or skill of any sort was seen as deeply valuable gifts from the spirit world, as it was in other shamanic cultures.

One Irish romantic (a redundant phrase, surely) has likened this world of transformation, shape and identity shifting, and "multi-faceted reality" to "modern physics, where ghostly interlacings are inferred at the sub-atomic level" (Dames 1992). Apparently the early Irish and other traditional peoples had a more accurate view of the cosmos than did the Enlightenment sages who thought they could reduce it to a few simple, clear rules.

Another altered mind-state was the battle-frenzy of warriors, which was similar to (indeed, probably the same institution as) the idea of *berserk* (lit. "bear shirt") in Scandinavia. Battle-frenzy involved a physical transformation. Cuchulainn's was the most extreme. Warriors (not all of whom were male) used grease to make their hair stand up in spikes, because this was considered terrifying. Supposedly a bushel of apples dumped over Cuchulainn's head would never hit the ground; the apples would all be caught on the spikes.

Yet another religious belief that reminds us of shamanism is the *geis* or *geasa,* the prohibition. Any warrior or leader of note knew of certain things that would magically bring him misfortune. He, or she, knew the end was at hand when a situation arose that forced him or her to violate a geis.

The fairy-folk or *Sí,* later so important as supernatural beings in Ireland, seem not to have been supernatural in early texts. They are described matter of factly as ordinary people who fight with, intermarry with, and trade with the Irish. They were described in terms relating to gods, but also described more matter of factly as a previous wave of migrants into Ireland (the Celts clearly preserved memories of their own immigrant status, having come quite late, somewhere in the 1000–500 BC range.) The *sí* had some magical powers, but so did almost every Irish individual of note or station. It seems likely that the euhemerist school of British folklorists was right: the fairy-folk were originally a different ethnic group, probably the megalith-builders, who shared Ireland with the Celts until they were assimilated. Significantly, the *sí* lived in megalithic tomb mounds; possibly this shows the Celts understood that these mounds were indeed the abodes of the dead of earlier times. The transfer from "abode of the dead" to "actual living places of those now dead" would have been easy.

Animal transformation and shape-shifting were universal and important. In the Irish version of the widespread "swan maiden" tale, the swan maiden is a shape-shifting daughter of a *sí* chief, and she marries the hero (Oisin, who is part supernatural himself) in a perfectly conventional way—but only after both she and Oisin have taken swan form for a while (Jackson 1971:93–97; see Snyder 1979). Being able to turn oneself into a swan may seem a mark of supernatural status today, but in old Eurasia, shifting into bird form was a property of shamans and even some ordinary people. Anybody could do it, if they had the right songs. Bird-skin costumes were used all over ancient Europe for magical and shaman-like pursuits (Aldhouse-Green and Aldhouse-Green 2005). Other animal/human transformers included werewolves and were-seals. Were-seals abounded and did until well into the twentieth (if not twenty-first) century, as the legend of Scattery Island and the ballad of the great silkie (seal) of Sule Skerry remind us.

Magical animals abounded. Especially common were the ones most necessary in everyday life: pigs, dogs, deer, and seals. They were often red, or white, or—most magical of all—white with red ears (as in the Welsh Mabinogion). There is a ballad known all over Europe in which a jilted lover kills herself, and her ghost then appears to her betrayer in a dream, thus magically killing him; in one British Isles version he reports, "I dreamed my bower was full of red swine, My bride-bed full of blood" ("The Ballad of Margaret and William" as sung by A. L. Lloyd).

On the other hand, we have no evidence for the specific features of the Eurasian shamanic cult, such as the ability of animals to take human form and found human lineages. Ireland also lacked the mirrors, self-hypnosis, drum dancing, spirit horses, and other features that characterize classic shamanism (Eliade 1964). Ireland partook of an older and wider-flung form of the basic belief system. In eastern Eurasia and in Native North America, the realms were even less separated; animals became humans, humans married animals, animal species were incorporated into social groups along with people, and the world was kin. Ancient Ireland saw no separation between "man" and "nature," but not a complete union either.

Sources are silent on much of the old belief system, no doubt because it was "pagan." We have the names of gods, including the Daghdae, a high god who frequently acted like an ordinary human. Other gods seem typical of Celtic societies everywhere and thus related to Roman and Greek deities. Apparently the Eurasia-wide belief in a skyworld and an underworld were present, but we know little of their structure. The *sí* could access the underworld through their dwellings, often the tomb-barrows of the pre-Celtic peoples.

It seems possible that many of the beliefs of old Ireland were absorbed from these earlier cultures (whether or not they were the original *sí*). Archaeology reveals that the Celts absorbed earlier peoples. The Gaelic language itself has a number of unusual features that seem to imply influence from their languages. Barry Cunliffe (2001) pointed out that the Atlantic fringe of Europe had shared ways and adaptations, many of which long predated the Celts and long outlasted them. This makes it possible that Irish traditions include ancient beliefs that are far older and wider-flung than the specifically Irish Celtic material.

Christianity did not eliminate the Irish love of wild beings. St. Ciaran of Saighir in the sixth century had a wolf, a badger, and a fox, who helped him with his everyday work. When the fox stole Ciaran's shoes, the other two animals caught him and brought him back. The saint imposed due penance, and the fox returned to good behavior (Farmer 2003:107). Saints with pets, revered trees, loyal birds, and other spirit powers abounded. Dozens occur in the astonishing collection of folkloric "saints' lives" preserved in the medieval *Book of Lismore* (Stokes 1890). Continental saints, with the stunning exception of Francis of Assisi and his group, virtually never engaged in such things. (However, the thirteenth-century French Saint Guinefort was a dog; his tomb is still revered, in an area where the pre-Christian Celts had ritually buried canines; see Schmitt 1983). In fact, other saints were more apt to cut down sacred groves just to spite the pagans, as St. Boniface did in Germany in the early eighth century (Farmer 2003:66)—a scene I have seen portrayed in sculpture on an early medieval church in Lyon.

DIRECT KNOWLEDGE OF NATURE

All this is necessary prelude to consideration of human interaction with the nonhuman world. The economy was a simple, direct one. In the absence of a sophisticated monetized economy with complex divisions of labor, or of much urban life, people lived by working directly with animals and plants, waters and soils. They faced nature in all its moods; the poems are as matter of fact about the unbearable difficulties of winter as they are about the peaceful bounty of summer. They had to draw on every conceivable resource, and thus they had to know a great deal about everything in their environment: how to catch fish, what trees could be used for what purpose, what insects might offer something, what to make of the flight of birds.

One of the most famous songs from Sweeney's madness lists the trees of Ireland. It is closely related to a song about the values for firewood. They give essentially the same list of trees in almost exactly the same order (O'Faoláin 1968:61–63). The firewood song was widespread and used to teach young people about woods. A version from Wales (but in English) survived into the twentieth century (Yeldham 2007:121–122). The extreme importance of firewood, and of knowing which woods burn best, is now forgotten by many city people, but many older rural people are still aware of it. Sweeney's song mentions seventeen species (not all trees); the firewood songs mention sixteen and fourteen, respectively.

Many of these trees were sacred in pre-Christian Ireland, and the religious aura carried over into Christian times (see, e.g., Delahunty 2007). Most venerated was the oak. Oak groves were sacred, as they were all across the Celtic world; as far as Anatolia, the Galatians—Celtic migrants—established their center at a place they called Drunemeton, "Sacred Oak Grove" (Byrne 2001:27). The Irish Gaelic *nemed* or *fidnemed* "sacred grove" is cognate with *nemeton*.

Evergreens—holly, ivy (possibly not native), yew—were venerated for their power to withstand winter. The yew was especially venerated, being both evergreen and productive of extremely hard, tough, serviceable wood. It has now declined from early abundance (it profited from early clearing) to eventual restriction to churchyard and ornamental plantings, partly because its foliage is poisonous, and thus a danger to cattle (Delanhunty 2007). It was often planted in the medieval period on castle grounds, to serve as a bow source. Many of these yews survive. Ash, the preferred source for spears, was also carefully managed.

Hawthorn (whitethorn) was notably holy and retained a major religious and cultural presence into modern times in Celtic and English folk beliefs. The apple tree was extremely important and visible in poetry and even provided the Celtic place name Avalon (*avallon,* place of apples). The hazel is not recorded as having much religious significance, but it almost certainly did have, judging from the reverential way it is mentioned in the poems. Its value as a food source got it frequent mention, and it was regarded as a model of loveliness. All the above except the whitethorn were listed as highest-class trees in an eighth century law code, and huge fines were levied for damaging them if they were owned (Kelly 1999). Second-class trees included, besides the whitethorn, the willow, elm, alder, rowan, and other important but not vitally important trees. A third class listed rare and fairly useless trees.

Christianity was unkind to sacred trees. In France, missionaries made a point of cutting them. Irish missionaries were gentler, but later English invaders cut down the groves not only to chase out resistance fighters, but also to hurt the Irish psychologically (Anderson ms 1; Kiernan 2007). The traumatic English invasions in the sixteenth and seventeenth centuries, which reduced Ireland to a wretched and burned-over colony of England, essentially deforested the island. We therefore know less than we might about exactly what these trees signified and how they were involved in worship and ritual. Nevertheless, tree lore survives in Ireland, including many of the ancient beliefs about hazel, oak, apple, and others (MacCoitir 2003).

Herbs attracted less attention. Watercress, wild garlic, and wild cresses were prized foods. Poets appreciated flowers, but less in early texts than in later ones; the flower cult seems to have spread up from the Mediterranean world in later medieval times. Grass was valued food for livestock, and meadows were a relief from the endless dark forests. The forested landscape had few herbs and flowers to show, and trees naturally attracted most of the attention of the poets.

All the major animals feature in poetry. Domestic ones, especially cattle, are the most important, but deer, foxes, and wolves are about equally significant poetically. Dogs are sometimes symbols of contempt, but hunting hounds—necessary for life, because deer were vital to the economy—were loved, well-treated, and respected. (Cuchulainn got his name from killing the monster dog of the tribe's blacksmith Chulainn; he had to promise to fill the guardian role himself, thus becoming the "dog"—*cu*—of Chulainn.) Badgers, seals, otters, and other smaller animals appear frequently in the texts. Bees made honey, the only sweetener and the source of mead; bees also seem to have had some of the religious significance they had in mainland Europe, judging from their abundance in religious poetry. (Modern Irish and Scottish folklore stresses animals greatly, but is more like modern European animal lore in general, valuing some, devaluing others, and preserving much of the Celtic vision but far from all of it; see Low 2007.)

One striking parallel with the Northwest Coast is the importance of salmon (recall Finn's adventure, above). One myth of a hero's birth tells that his mother first bore a pure-white lamb, then a flawless silver salmon, then the hero himself (Byrne 2001:98; history does not relate how the woman felt about this). Pairing the hallmark symbol of Christianity with the salmon indicates strongly that the salmon had extremely high significance in the old pagan system. A heroine reuniting with her lover almost died of joy; as the story puts it, "It was little but that the salmon of her life fled through her mouth with joy" (Joyce 1907:200).

The loud, beautiful cries of cranes and their strong high flight made them power beings, too, frequently mentioned in poetry. Herons, blackbirds, and other birds are also featured. Flight was so important in mystic and shaman-like activities that birds associated themselves with "madmen" (i.e., shamans or the equivalent), magic-workers, poets, and other people in altered states. Birds tell people of the future and otherwise make themselves useful as omens. Humans take bird form, or in "madness" act like birds. The human soul is sometimes birdlike. Evidently, birds were extremely important in pre-Christian religion; spiritual and magical involvement of people and birds was exceptionally close.

In later times, and presumably in early ones, the wren was the king of birds, because his song is so powerful that it can be heard clearly above the roaring of the horrific winter storms (Lawrence 1997; see also Armstrong 1958). The same species is a major power animal to the Native peoples of the northern Northwest Coast of North America, too, and for the same reason (personal research, Haida Gwaii). The wise and mournful-voiced ravens had a significance rather similar to that they hold on the Northwest Coast of America, also. These coastal cultures also shared a fascination with wolves, eagles, and other predators, but so does every culture within the ranges of those animals. Apples and berries had a special place on both coasts, but this again seems a logical correlate of their economic value. Still, the parallels between northwest Eurasia and northwest America are thought-provoking. The biota are broadly similar, the societies were both warlike chiefdoms, where feasting and generosity attracted followers and power, and the cultures of both areas were based on special knowledge, often realized through song. Even some myths—the Swan Maiden story is the clearest example (Snyder 1979)—repeated themselves all the way from Ireland to Canada.

Seagulls are sometimes mentioned and had a major place in closely related Welsh nature poetry. More important to the late medieval Welsh, but not to earlier Celts, was the nightingale, which migrated up from southern Europe, both literally and in its figurative role as a symbol of song and love. The nightingale thoroughly deserves its reputation as a singer. (I really have never heard anything like it.) It is also quite tame. Thus it often occupied the secret bowers where lovers trysted in the warm parts of the year. The old Greek and Latin poets had already made the obvious connection, and indeed made it a cliché, but the medieval Celtic poets gave the image new life. The medieval Welsh poet Dafydd ap Gwilym, who specialized in boasting of his conquests of other men's girlfriends, seems almost physically incapable of keeping nightingales out of his poems about this dubious activity. However, the nightingale, and that other Mediterranean cultural icon, the rose, are singularly absent from the oldest Celtic poetry.

Thus, although the actual religious content of animal and plant lore has thinned considerably by the time our sources are recorded, the poetry shows intense, clear-sighted involvement in the nonhuman world. People are emotionally involved with animals and plants and landscapes as deeply as they are with other humans. Places are familiar, and each has its story, often a heartbreaking one. People communicate with powers of the wild. Christian hermits seem perfectly happy with the company of foxes, birds, and even wild swine. Everything seems washed in magical water that makes it clearer, more brilliant, more vivid, and more intensely beautiful than it is for us today. The sheer loveliness of the scenes breaks men's hearts and makes women weep, especially if the scene is bound up with their lives, as in the stories that make up the *Acallan na Senorach.* Again, the "other" Northwest Coast provides insights; there, such tales were not just diversion, but were vitally important social narratives connecting people socially and spiritually to their lands (Cruikshank 1998, 2005).

Michael Dames (1992), ever the true Irish author in that his scholarship is as romantically imaginative as his phrases are inspired, says that the wonderfully and wildly exaggerated Irish stories, "though absurd in detail, are rational in overall effect, in that they integrate human hopes and defeats into a much bigger drama. In this they differ from a modern rationalism, which is so rational in detail, yet unreasonable to the point of madness in its broader consequences. They were involved with war *in* Nature, as distinct from war *on* Nature. For all our skill in measuring, we are now frequently surprised by 'unforeseen side-effects,' whereas in antiquity there *were* no side-effects, since everything was presumed to be interconnected" (Dames 1992:161; there were surely many unforeseen interconnections, however).

THE TEXTS

A strange, seemingly meaningless, encounter that captures as much of the Celtic mind as any I know is found in a legend of the eleventh century. Three brothers are voyaging on the sea:

"Another beautiful shining island appeared to them. Bright grass was there, with spangling of purple-headed flowers; many birds and ever-lovely bees singing a song from the heads of those flowers. A grave gray-headed man was playing a harp in the island. He was singing a wonderful song, the sweetest of the songs of the world. They greeted each other, and the old man told them to go away." (Jackson 1971:162). This has it all: the beautiful flowery land, the birds, the bees, the song—and the strange unexplained banishment of ordinary humanity from this ancient paradise.

Also famously revealing much in short compass is a bit of doggerel (it rhymes in Gaelic) that an anonymous medieval monk wrote on the margin of a Christian text he was copying, a bit after 900 AD:

> A wall of woodland overlooks me.
> A blackbird sings me a song (no lie!).
> Above my book, with its lines laid out,
> the birds in their music sing to me.

> The cuckoo sings clear in lovely voice
> in his grey cloak from a busy fort.
> I swear it now, but God is good!
> It is lovely writing out in the wood.

> (Kinsella 1989:30)

Among the great and extended texts, few are more revealing than a dialogue between *ri* Guaire, a brilliant and powerful ruler of the seventh century, and his brother Marbán, who had taken up the hermit's life. This pairing is a significant one; Christianity and kingship were so linked that a king would often have a leading churchman for a brother, and not infrequently the *ri* was a church leader himself. This pattern reminds us of the tendency for American Northwest Coast chiefs to have brothers who were shamans—thus consolidating power in both human and nonhuman realms. Surely the ancient Irish had had such a pattern before Christianity came. Hermit or no, Marbán was powerful enough to own a valuable white boar (Byrne 2001:243) and no doubt other property. This is a very early poem, probably 9th century. Only the verses that stress nature are quoted here from a very long poem. Alas, translation cannot catch the torrent of alliteration, end-rhyme, internal rhyme, partial rhyme, and other word-music that make this poem striking even by medieval Irish standards.

Guaire asks Marbán:

> Hermit Marbán, why do you not sleep upon a bed? More often would you sleep out of doors, with your head, where the tonsure ends, upon the grounds of a fir-grove (Byrne 2001:240).

The translation continues from Jackson (1971:68–70).

> I have a hut in the wood, none knows it but my Lord; an ash tree this side, a hazel on the other, a great tree on a mound encloses it.
> 　Two heathery door-posts for support, and a lintel of honeysuckle; around its close the wood sheds its nuts upon fat swine.
> 　The size of my hut, small yet not small, a place of familiar paths; the she-bird in its dress of blackbird colour sings a melodious strain from its gable.
> 　The stags of Druim Rolach leap out of its stream of trim meadows....
> 　A tree of apples of great bounty, ... a seemly crop from small-nutted branching green hazels, in clusters like a fist.
> 　Excellent fresh springs—a cup of water, splendid to drink—they gush forth abundantly; yew berries, bird-cherries....
> 　Tame swine lie down around it, goats, young pigs, wild swine, tall deer, does, a badger's brood....

Fruits of rowan black sloes of the dark blackthorn; foods of whorts, spare berries....

Beer with herbs, a patch of strawberries, delicious abundance; haws, yew berries, kernels of nuts.

A cup of mead from the goodly hazel-bush, quickly served; brown acorns, manes of briar, with fine blackberries.

In summer with its pleasant, abundant mantle, with good-tasting savour, there are pignuts, wild marjoram, the cresses of the stream—green purity!

The songs of the bright-breasted ring-doves, a beloved movement, the carol the thrush, pleasant and familiar above my house.

Swarms of bees, beetles, soft music of the world, a gentle humming; wild geese, barnacle geese, shortly before All Hallows, music of the dark torrent.

A nimble singer, the combative brown wren from the hazel bough, woodpeckers with their pied hoods in a vast host.

Fair white birds come, cranes, seagulls, the sea sings to them, no mournful music; brown fowl out of the red heather....

A beautiful pine makes music to me, it is not hired; through Christ, I fare no worse at any time than you do....

Note the fondness for bird song, especially the wren, and even the humming of insects here.

Moving downward in time, arguably the most powerful poem in the *Acallan na Senorach* is Creide's lament for her lover Cael, who drowned just after she pledged herself to him. The anonymous author makes her lament a focus of his book, and a lament for the whole lost society of old Ireland. Ceílte buries Creide and her lover together, just as he later buried his whole world through conversion to Christianity and through recording his tales for a Christian future. Just as Creide uses her animals as sharers and parts of her own grief, so Ceílte uses her story to tell his own grief for his lost world. In turn, the anonymous author of the *Acallan* uses Ceílte's persona to make his own lament for the past. Such nesting of voices is typical of longer Celtic literature.

> The harbour roars out
> over the fierce flow of Rin Dá Bharc.
> The hero from Loch Dá Chonn drowned;
> the wave mourns it against the shore.
>
> The heron is crying
> in the marsh of Druim Dá Thrén.
> She cannot guard her young:
> the two-colored fox is stalking them.

Mournful is the whistle
of the thrush on Druim Caín.
And no less mournful is the call
of the blackbird on Leitir Laíg.

Mournful the music
of the stag on Druim Dáa Léis:
The doe of Druim Silenn is dead
and the great stag roars at her loss.

My grief
that hero dead, who lay with me,
that woman's son from Doire Dá Dos
with a cross set at his head.

My grief that Cael
is fixed by my side in death,
that a wave has drowned his pale flank.
His great beauty drove me wild.

Mournful is the roar
the ebbing wave makes on the strand.
It has drowned a fine and noble man.
My grief Cael ever went near it.

Mournful the sound
the wave makes on the northern shore,
rough about the lovely rock,
lamenting Cael who is gone.

And mournful the fall
of the wave on the southern shore.
As for myself, my time is over,
my face the worse, for all to see.

There is unnatural music
in the heavy wave of Tulach Léis:
It is telling its boastful tale
and all my wealth is as nothing.

Since Crimthann's son was drowned
I will have no other love.
Many leaders fell at his hand
but his shield on the day of need was silent.

"And the girl stretched out beside Cael and died of grief. The two of them were buried together in one grave. I myself," said Caílte, "had the stone set up over them where they lie...." (translated by Thomas Kinsella 1989: 79–80).

The place names, meaningless to the modern reader, would have been richly evocative to the medieval Irish audience—a major part of the symbolism. Creide's comment on her face is not self-indulgence; a ravaged face was a mark of spiritual anguish in early Ireland. The poem is in an unusual meter that effectively captures the sound of a woman lamenting. Of course it is a highly sophisticated poem that must have taken days of skilled poetic work—not a spontaneous lament (Murphy 2007:148).

The tale of mad Sweeney, in the form currently known, is from the late twelfth century, but parts of it are apparently much older. King Sweeney (or Suibhne) lived in the seventh century, and this fantastic tale had apparently crystallized around him by the ninth.

Here is Sweeney's song of the trees:

> The bushy leafy oak tree
> is highest in the wood,
> the forking shoots of hazel
> hide sweet hazel-nuts.
>
> The alder is my darling,
> all thornless in the gap,
> some milk of human kindness
> coursing in its sap.
>
> The blackthorn is a jaggy creel
> stippled with dark sloes;
> green watercress in thatch on wells
> where the drinking blackbird goes.
>
> Sweetest of the leafy stalks,
> the vetches strew the pathway;
> the oyster-grass is my delight
> and the wild strawberry.
>
> Low-set clumps of apple trees
> drum down fruit when shaken;

scarlet berries clot like blood
on mountain rowan.

Briars curl in sideways,
arch a stickle back,
draw blood and curl up innocent
to sneak the next attack.

The yew tree in each churchyard
wraps night in its dark hood.
Ivy is a shadowy
genius of the wood.

Holly rears its windbreak,
a door in winter's face;
life-blood on a spear-shaft
darkens the grain of ash.

Birch tree, smooth and blessed,
delicious to the breeze,
high twigs plait and crown it
the queen of trees.

The aspen pales
and whispers, hesitates:
a thousand frightened scuts
race in its leaves....

(Translated by Seamus Heaney, 1983:32–34)

More revealing of attitudes, though, is Sweeney's song on finally settling in peace, knowing he was near death. Recalling his "madness," he again goes beyond self-regard to imply the passing of the whole lost world in the face of Christian peace, and here the anonymous poet breaks out of his Christian shell and gives us an anguished lament worthy of Ceílte. Seamus Heaney's translation captures some of the stark, driving rhythm and ragged, erratic rhyming of the original:

There was a time when I preferred
the turtle-dove's soft jubilation
as it flitted round a pool
to the murmur of conversation.

There was a time when I preferred
the mountain grouse crying at dawn
to the voice and closeness
of a beautiful woman.

There was a time when I preferred
wolf-packs yelping and howling
to the sheepish voice of a cleric
bleating out plainsong.

You are welcome to pledge healths
and carouse in your drinking dens;
I will dip and steal water
from a well with my open palm.

You are welcome to that cloistered hush
of your students' conversation;
I will study the pure chant
of hounds baying in Glen Bolcain.

You are welcome to your salt meat
and fresh meat in feasting-houses;
I will live content elsewhere
on tufts of green watercress.

(Heaney 1983:72–73)

Kenneth Jackson memorably translates the last two verses:

"Though you think sweet, yonder in your church, the gentle talk of your students, sweeter I think the splendid talking the wolves make in Glenn mBolcáin.

"Though you like the fat and meat which are eaten in the drinking-halls, I like better to eat a head of clean water-cress in a place without sorrow …" (Jackson 1971:255). The "wolves" are actually "hounds" in the text, as translated by Heaney, but wolves were almost certainly intended. They were regularly called "wild hounds"; Irish lore and literature often refer to wild animals as God's livestock. Glenn mBolcain was Sweeney's refuge—his wild, lonely, but safe home in his madness.

Here is a totally unrelated poem—a bardic effort in praise of a chief. Like countless other chiefs in praise-poetry worldwide, this chief is so magical and so divinely favored that his presence increases the fertility of his lands, and the bard is eager to provide lush exaggeration accordingly—no doubt for a very large reward. Note also that the bard sticks in a political spike at the end, advocating peace at a time when war was idealized:

> [O]wing to our chieftain every bright-branched hazel has become red, and the fruits of the pleasant bending sloe-bushes have grown jet black.
>
> In his time the cattle are like part of the [mythic] Cattle-Tribute; nuts are the hue of coppery gold for the descendant of gentle Mugh; the fruit-flowers in their fresh white tresses have sweetened the cool streams of the tree-blessed shore; green corn grows from the earth close up to the mighty woods, and the bright hazel branches are filled with sap.
>
> At evening, the flowers of the fair-plaited hazel have cooled the sunny earth, the home of stranger birds; drops of honey and of dew, like dark tears, will keep the fringe of the thin-grassed wood bent down; the saplings around the Boyle are bowed with nuts because the slow soft eye of the descendant of Bron looks down on them.
>
> Nuts dropping into the white-foamed murmuring Boyle will fall down beside the great trees with twisted boles; the flower of every tree of them, like dark purple, is empurpled for the race of great muirchertach.
>
> A shower of honey upon slim-formed saplings in the fresh bowed forks of the golden graceful wood—this is but another boon from his holding of the peace—and the slow cows with their full udders from the lands of the plain of great Tuam ...
> (Jackson 1971:236)

Unique in world literature is the lament of Muireadhach Albanach Ó Dálaigh for his wife. Open expression of passionate erotic love is rare in funeral songs, but rarer still—and extremely moving—in a lament for a wife of twenty years who has borne eleven children. What concerns us here, however, is his brilliant and extended metaphorization of his wife as a hazel tree. This, like the above poem, indicates more religious veneration of the hazel than other records attest. It is also a superb example of classic Irish poetry at its best. The complex patterns of rhyme, alliteration, and other devices are brilliantly managed to maintain an intensely tragic sound. Again, this sadly disappears in translation.

> Last night my soul departed,
>   a pure body, most dear, in the grave,
> her stately smooth bosom taken
>   from me in a linen sheet,
>
> a lovely pale blossom plucked
>   from a limp downcurving stem,
> my heart's darling bowed low,
>   heavy branch of yonder house.

I am alone tonight, O God.
  It is a crooked, bad world you see.
Lovely the weight of the young flank
  I had here last night, my King.

That bed there, my grief,
  The lively covers where we swam
—I have seen a fine lively body
  and waved hair in your midst, my bed!

One of a gentle countenance
  Lay and shared my pillow.
Only the hazel bloom is like
  her womanly dark sweet shade.

Maol Mheadha of the dark brows,
  my vessel of mead, by my side,
my heart, the shade who has left me,
  a precious flower, planted and bowed.

My body is mine no longer.
  It has fallen to her share:
a body in two pieces
  since she left, fair, lovely and gentle

—one foot of mine, one flank
  (her visage like the whitethorn;
nothing hers but it was mine):
  one eye of mine, one hand;

half my body, a youthful blaze
  (I am handled harshly, O King,
and I feel faint as I speak it)
  and half of my very soul.

My first love her great slow gaze;
  curved, ivory white her breast;
nor did her body, her dear side,
  belong to another before me.

Twenty years we were as one
  and sweeter our speech each year.
Eleven babies she bore me
  —great slender-fingered fresh branch.

I am, but I do not live,
   since my round hazel-nut has fallen.
Since my dear love has left me
   the dark world is empty and bare.

From the day the smooth shaft was sunk
   for my house I have not heard
that a guest has laid a spell
   on her youthful brown dark hair.

Do not hinder me, you people.
   What crime to hear my grief.
Bare ruin has entered my home
   and the bright brown blaze is out.

The King of Hosts and Highways
   took her away in His wrath.
Little those branched locks sinned,
   to die on her husband, young and fresh.

That soft hand I cherished,
   King of the graves and bells,
that hand never forsworn
   —my pain it is not beneath my head!

(T. Kinsella 1989:95–97)

Finally, a modern love song (again, the rhyme and rhythm are lost in English) is too perfect to miss:

She's the white flower of the blackberry, she's the sweet flower of the raspberry, she's the best herb in excellence for the sight of the eyes.
She's my pulse, she's my secret, she's the scented flower of the apple, she's summer in the cold time between Christmas and Easter.

(anonymous folk song, tr. Kenneth Jackson, 1971:110)

LITERATURE AND WORLDVIEW

In contrast to truly shamanic societies, old Irish society was not fused totally with the other-than-human world. Animals were not people, though they might show human traits, and though humans might take animal form. Gods were humanoid, not animal powers. In other words, it is meaningful to talk of a "nature," separate from "culture," in a way that is not appropriate for the American Northwest or for native Siberia. Chief Guaire chose people; his brother Marbán's choice of nature was a clear and conscious one that involved cutting ties with ordinary society.

Irish writers showed an involvement with nature that goes far beyond the patronizing "pastoralism" of the ancient Mediterranean or the self-conscious romanticism of Europe since 1800. These latter two poetic traditions assume, and depend on, an extreme contrast between the sophisticated urban observer and the wild landscape. The wild is fascinating precisely because it is so daunting and unfamiliar.

The Irish poets saw birds, trees, bees, and landscapes in clear and intensely brilliant light. Everything is sharp, beautiful, and distinct, as in the illumination following a storm. Even more significant is the recurrent use of birds, trees, and landscapes as personae for the singers. The poet *is* the heron, the deer, the river. This trope occurs in poetry worldwide, but I know of no other poetry that so systematically, repeatedly, and powerfully uses it. There is nothing between the poet and the natural world—no barriers of "civilization" or rhetoric or class. The poet sees without barriers.

This vision of the world survived, progressively attenuated, in the writings of their descendants. Christians would hardly abandon it just because of its identification with pagandom; they simply took it over, as we can see in Marbán's matchless poem above.

All this is directly ancestral to one major strand in modern ecological and environmental thought. Irish and Scottish love for and involvement in the natural world provided a very disproportionate amount of environmental thought, from scientists like Hutton, to plant explorers like David Douglas. Scottish and Irish conservationists have had a particular version of loving the natural world, a version characterized by deep personal involvement in it and sometimes by distancing from ordinary human society.

It is no surprise that Irish, Scots, and American descendants thereof created so much of the modern conservation literature, from the writings of John Muir and Sally Carrighar to the poetry of William Butler Yeats, Robert Graves, and Robinson Jeffers. Michael Dames (our Irish romantic) holds that we have no time to wait for rational self-interest to teach us; "Ireland is in a position to offer its mythic, flame-filled peat to a world in need of sacred meaning" (Dames 1992:19).

CHAPTER SIX

China

Obviously, China's interactions with the environment cannot be summarized in anything less than an encyclopedia, so this chapter must limit itself to a few topics. Many scholars have published extensively on the more pragmatic aspects of China's traditional environmental management (see esp. Elvin 2004; Elvin and Liu 1998; Marks 1998, 2009, 2012; McNeill 1998). Religion and ethics in relation to environmental management have also received much attention in recent years, and are well covered (Callicott and Ames 1989; Girardot et al. 2001; Tucker and Berthrong 1998; Tucker and Williams 1997; Waldau and Patton 2007). I have contributed somewhat to these literatures (Anderson 1988, 1996, 2001, 2007, 2012; Anderson and Anderson 1973; Anderson and Raphals 2007; Buell et al. 2010) and do not need to repeat myself in much detail.

I will begin with general observations on Chinese representation of knowledge, especially environmental knowledge, and then focus on environmental management. I then turn to aesthetic interaction with the environment and the representation of environment in aesthetic terms. This is an area of considerable recent scholarship (much of it summarized in, and extended by, Elvin 2004).

NATURE: IDEOLOGY AND BEHAVIOR

"There was a time when the trees were luxuriant on the Ox Mountain. As it is on the outskirts of a great metropolis, the trees are constantly lopped by axes. Is it any wonder that they are no longer fine? With the respite they get in the day and in the night, and the moistening by the rain and dew, there is certainly no lack of new shoots, coming out, but then the cattle and sheep come to graze upon the mountain. That is why it is as bald as it is. People, seeing only its baldness, tend to think that it never had any trees. But can this possibly be the nature of a mountain? Can what is in man be completely lacking in moral inclinations? A man's letting go of his true heart is like the case of the trees and the axes." (Mencius, tr. D. C. Lau, 1971:164–165; the word translated *man* actually means *person*—Mencius is referring to all genders).

China's philosophy, cosmology, and views of morality and nature were set in the late Warring States period and have lasted surprisingly well. In the following section, I will describe the concepts of cosmos, morality, and knowledge as they were outlined at that time and during the Han Dynasty and make some notes on continuities. Of course the last two or three centuries have seen vast changes in all aspects of Chinese thought, but I am not concerned with those in the present book; I am dealing with principles of environmental management that persisted, mutatis mutandis, over centuries.

A critical word is *jiao*, "teachings." This refers to an organized body of philosophic or religious knowledge that stems from a canonical book or books. It is sometimes translated "religion," but organized philosophic traditions are *jiao* whereas unorganized religion—like the Chinese folk cult—is not. Organized knowledge is *xue*.

Everything came together in the cosmology on which landscape management was based. This begins with *qi*, literally "breath" or "gas," more generally the subtle forces that are the dynamic shapers and movers behind the static landscape of mountains and plains. Currents of qi run through the landscape, just as they do in the human body. Stagnant qi is pathological, but pooling qi can be beneficial, bringing good influences together at particular points.

Qi can be relatively *yang* or *yin*. (In an alternate view, there are different qis: yang qis and yin qis. My consultants in Hong Kong were never very clear as to whether qi is all one or a cover-term for many separate forces.) This introduces

Photo on Facing Page: Hong Kong, 1966. Cultivating, with traditional village and fengshui wood in background. Note the scarecrow. This area is all high-rise apartments today. Photograph by E. N. Anderson.

us to a fascinating take on gendered discourse. China may be the only traditional culture in which "male" and "female" are considered more or less accidents of a more basic set of forces, rather than basic aspects of the universe. Males are 2/3 yang in balance of forces, females 2/3 yin. (This is, in fact, the ratio of androsterone hormones to estriol hormones in males and females, respectively, showing that the Chinese had a very good sense of reality.)

The terms *yang* and *yin* originally referred to the sunny and shady sides of a hill. This is clear from the characters. *Yang* is a word for *sun,* and the character for yang force is the old character for sunlight written with an additional radical meaning *hill.* Similarly, yin force is the radical *hill* next to the word *shadow.* So the root meanings are the sun shining over a hill, and the shadow of it on the side away from the sun, respectively. In terms of qi, this means that yang qi is the energy that is seen in bright, dry, warm, golden-red influences, and yin qi is the energy of shady, moist, cool, dark influences. Males are thought to be more active and outgoing, whereas women not only live within the house (supposedly) but have dark moist wombs, hence the gendered use of the terms.

The *Huainanzi,* a text from around 130 BCE (Liu 2010), has conservation advice: the most evil people of earlier historic times came to disaster because they "ripped open pregnant animals and killed young ones, . . . overturned nests and broke eggs" (p. 268), set fires, piled up earthworks indiscriminately, dug and channeled and pounded and otherwise made public works (p. 269), and ruined good farmland. These passages begin a long chapter (Chapter 8) that is virtually a hymn to conservation and wise use. One long section begins: "Generally speaking, disorder arises from profligate indolence" (p. 280). Three pages of examples of wasteful conspicuous consumption follow, covering every sort of environmental damage for luxury display. One interesting section concerns use of whole forests to make charcoal for smelting metals:

> In order to melt bronze and iron . . .
> The mountains are denuded of towering trees;
> The forests are stripped of cudrania and catalpa trees;
> tree trunks are baked to make charcoal;
> grass is burned to make ash,
> [so that] open fields and grasslands are white and bare . . . (p. 282)

And so on at considerable further length (see also Wagner 2008:228 on this passage). By contrast, the good people who prospered:

> when hunting they did not wipe out herds;
> They did not catch fawns or baby animals,
> they did not drain marshes to get fish;
> They did not burn forests to capture [animals] (p. 331).

They did not chop small trees, kill pregnant animals, take fish under a foot long, or kill pigs less than a year old (p. 331). In general, they were careful not to overhunt or deforest.

These of the old kings is very similar to practices advocated in the *Li Ji,* a similar text that purports to give the rules of governing of the much earlier Zhou Dynasty, but is actually only a bit earlier than the *Huainanzi.*

One early king did not want people to catch small fish, and the people refrained out of respect for him (p. 472).

VIEWING LANDSCAPES

As in other civilizations, we have only the elite view throughout most of history, but a lively folk society always existed. Even in earliest times, glimpses of it got through the class filter. Among other reasons, China has always had what might be considered a culturally penetrable class system. Studying folk songs in Hong Kong in 1965 through 1966, I was somewhat surprised to find semiliterate folk-singers reciting classic Tang poems, and village sign painters writing classical couplets in calligraphy for pasting on farmworkers' houses. Conversely, from the Book of Songs (ca. 500 BCE) to Feng Menglong (1574–1646), Chinese elites have loved to collect folk songs, sometimes adapting them, sometimes not. Feng recorded one that I heard in Hong Kong from illiterate sailors 400 years later (translated as "A Boat Trip," Barnstone and Ping 2005:319). Stories from history were widely known, and people who had never been near a school knew the more common quotes from Confucius and Mencius.

There was constant back-and-forth motion between classes. The hard separation between classic and folk that Europe knew in the nineteenth and early twentieth centuries was unknown in China (see, e.g., Johnson et al. 1985). Sometimes the route was of the highest level: temples and temple priests became the poor family's art museum and classical music and poetry hall. Sometimes the route was of a socially lower order: prostitutes sang classical songs to entertain elite clients and then sang them again for the less elite. Meanwhile, elite clients, including the aforementioned Feng, often learned the prostitutes' far more earthy verses.

Nowhere was this clearer than in landscape attitudes. Chinese classical poets worked with and learned from farmers, fishermen, and woodsmen. The latter learned countless classical poems, which spread widely through the social fabric. Temples were notable here. Thus, when I describe attitudes largely from elite materials, the reader should not conclude that these attitudes are not widely typical. They were shared, not perfectly but always appreciably, at all levels.

What was shared is a view of people-in-nature of a sort almost unknown in the Western world. Even when Westerners can get beyond their usual "people vs. nature" view and see nature as having some positive qualities, they usually keep it at arm's length. Those who make a living from it, if they do not seek to "subdue" or "conquer" it, see it largely as "resources" (though many small farmers and ranchers still have emotional and deep ties to the land). Those who enjoy it most tend to be urbanites who leave their sheltered houses only on vacation trips.

Chinese, by contrast, whether elite or working-class, had a view of nature that included intense bonding. Daoist mysticism involves direct confrontation and interaction with reality, dropping the barriers of conventional categorization, cultural learning, ordinary social experience, and anything else that can lock the mind into particular patterns. The ideal is to see nature (and people) with no intervening prejudice or blinders. This leads to incredibly intense experience, especially of anything dramatic or beautiful, but also with anything familiar and worthy of attention. Daoist mystics and poets felt this most strongly—and Buddhists, too, after Daoism influenced Buddhism substantially in the early middle ages—but even ordinary workers and farmers felt it, as I can testify from years of experience with ordinary farmers and fisherfolk.

This leads to nature poetry that is unequaled outside East Asia. There is nothing at all comparable in the West, outside of early Celtic poetry and a few recent authors like Robinson Jeffers and Gary Snyder (the latter of whom was strongly and directly influenced by Chinese poetry, some of which he has translated). Great Western poets, from Homer to Rilke and Wallace Stevens, tended to use nature as a backdrop.

The Chinese poets often write about human relationships with similar intensity. Here, of course, Western poets are their equals. The contrast is striking: Chinese tend to see human relationships in a natural context and feel the same intensity toward persons and landscapes

Ultimately, the human animal naturally loves mate, family, and home. People everywhere love the landscape they grew in. The Chinese, and following them other East Asians, build on this to create a single intensity of affect toward all three. Western philosophy tends to decouple landscape from the mix. (Some Greek philosophers claimed to be so influenced by Stoic philosophy that they ignored even family, as did some extreme Buddhists in China. One wonders.) Emmanuel Levinas's concept of the infinitely important Other (Levinas 1969) perfectly describes Chinese relationships with the whole landscape, just as it describes Native Americans' relationships with animals and trees.

LANDSCAPE PAINTING

Guo Xi's famous essay on landscape painting (Kuo 1935; Chinese orig. late eleventh century) gives directions on the techniques of painting, but, above all, counsels staying in a landscape till one really feels it. A great landscape differs from a good one in that it has *qi*.

Most of the serious painting and sculpture in old China was in temples. Perhaps the most basic tenet in folk religion was keeping gods and ancestors happy and comfortable—*si fuk* in the Cantonese I learned in the field. So fine art was absolutely necessary in temples and any formal locations. In this climate, with art a sacramental way of capturing spirit and achieving unity with godhead, landscape art meant much more than it did in the Western world. A painted landscape, like a garden or a bonsai tree (Stein 1990), captures the spirit of the land and brings it into one's home.

There are countless folktales about this. I have picked up several in my travels. According to one, a painter stopped for one night at an inn. He got some bamboos and planted them outside his room. Someone asked, "Why are you planting bamboos when you are staying here only one night?" He turned to the bamboos and said, "What is the use of talking to such a person?"

Another tells of a painting contest where all the hot-shot artists of the area competed to see who could be most realistic. The usual feats emerged: the birds flew down to peck at the painted grapes, and so forth. Then a scruffy old man in a shabby Daoist robe appeared out of nowhere. With a few quick strokes, he painted a crane on the wall. He got on its back and it flew away with him.

Another, more believable but no less charming, was one I learned in a hotel in west China. I had noticed that many Chinese hotel lobbies had a big painting of a pine behind the reception desk, with "Welcoming Guests Pine" written on the picture. Obviously there was a story here. I learned that there was once an artist so poor that he could not afford a servant, but so dedicated to his work that he often missed knocks on the door. Wishing to give his visitors the best of welcome, he thus painted a huge and beautiful pine, labeled it "Welcoming Guests Pine," and hung it in the entrance hall. Hotels picked up the idea and have kept the tradition ever since.

Landscape paintings are called "mountain and water pictures" in China, and that is what they are. A painting of flat ground was unthinkable, though some riverscapes minimize the peaks. China's mountains are dramatic. After years of talking about "wildly exaggerated" crags and peaks in Chinese landscapes, Western critics were dumbfounded when photographs of China's more remote ranges began to appear in the last few decades. The painters did not exaggerate more than any other painters do—not that they ignored chances for a bit of artistic license, but they did not need to invent fantastic scenery.

The vast majority of landscapes thus show dramatic mountains and crags, with streams, waterfalls, and sometimes rivers. Almost always there are trees, ranging from dense forests to scraggly isolated trees on cliffs. These paintings "reflect the painter's belief in an ordering principle inherent in nature" (Kuhn

2009:171); it is a dynamic, shifting, flowing principle—the Dao of Laozi—rather than "order" in the Western sense. Hence the love for flowing waters, moving clouds, shifting scenes, flying birds. Instead of point perspective, the perspective of the paintings (especially the long scrolls) is in planes, tracking the way the eye shifts its focus. Moreover, the perspective on large paintings shifts, to match the viewer's eye as he or she looks over the painting. It is as if the viewer were actually journeying through the scene.

Landscape art goes back to very early times (see Sullivan 1962, 1980, 2008). Representations of mountains with crags and trees appear on religious art in the Han Dynasty. The large mountain-and-water pictures familiar today apparently have an origin between Han and Tang, traditionally with Gu Kaizhi (344–406). We probably have no surviving Tang landscapes, though scenic backdrops for religious themes survive on religious paintings from late Tang in Central Asia. We have copies of more central, elite pictures. Like European artists, Chinese artists trained by copying the masters. Often, these copies were not mere training pieces but serious reinterpretations of classic views. Of course these involved changes from the original, so we have a rather imperfect idea of Tang art.

Fortunately, originals survive in some numbers from Song (960–1279) and later. By Song, the paintings were known as "mountains and water pictures," and did indeed show those things. The typical Chinese landscape shows huge, dramatic peaks and crags, with waterfalls or rapid streams, and often a river or lake in the foreground. Sometimes only mountains in mist, or only vast spreading waters, are shown. Mountains almost always have trees, usually scattered and dramatic, sometimes in dense forests. (For a particularly fine and sizable collection of Chinese art, see Ho 1992.)

Landscape paintings almost always involve some human presence. The mountains and water dominate, but there will usually be a house, a few boats, or a temple, and almost always a human observer. Most often, this is a scholar, often followed by a serving-boy lugging a musical instrument or a set of painting equipment.

However, the Western idea that Chinese landscape paintings always show elite scholars is wrong. (The scholarly literature does not claim it; I have heard it stated informally, more or less as urban folklore.) Sometimes the figure is a fisherman, who may be a scholar out for some fun but is often a professional fisher. Fishermen and firewood gatherers are intensely evocative figures in China (and even more in Korea). They depend on wild nature and its productions and thus have a special relationship with the world. They are always poor, but always have the most beautiful and evocative scenery around them. Often, they are shown happily discussing the relative merits of their lifestyles.

I know from experience that actual Chinese fishermen did indeed delight in the scenery around them. Because of this, poets and artists often fished themselves and wrote or painted themselves into the occupation.

The wider context of all this involves a deep experience of landscape: Chinese nature mysticism. This goes back to shamanic and similar spiritual roots. Ancient China had a form of shamanism much like that of the neighboring Tungus peoples, who gave us the word: *shaman* has been known in China at least since the twelfth century, when the Tungusic Qin Dynasty ruled northern China. The Chinese word is quite different, *wu,* but it may just possibly be an Indo-European loan, cognate with Persian *magus;* Victor Mair has defended this view (Mair 2005). The Cantonese pronunciation is *mou,* and this and other forms allow us to reconstruct something like *mag* or *mwag.* In any case, many early poems, as well as surviving practices of minority peoples like the Yao (Mian), prove that full-scale shamanism, with trance-journeys to the land of gods and dead, was common in old China. The word *wu* now applies to spirit mediums who go into trance and become possessed by gods.

Mountains were the domain of hermits, meditators, and seekers for longevity and spiritual power. This evidently goes back to something very much like the Native North Americans' quests for spiritual power. A cult of sacred mountains exists throughout Eastern Asia. In China, five mountains representing the four directions and the center were particularly revered, and the Kunlun Mountains in the far west were considered a spiritual realm.

Thus, a mountain painting, especially of a sacred mountain, had some magical power. This is clearer in Korea, where the Diamond Mountains (now in North Korea) were the sacred range and heart of the nation. Diamond Mountain paintings are a whole genre (Zozayong 1975), and painters got incredibly creative, often downright surrealistic, in painting visionary landscapes with crags as spirit-beings. These paintings actually had magical power; they evoked the power of the mountains. Again as in Native America, the aesthetic power of a painting was assumed to show its actual power. To the extent it was aesthetically effective, a Diamond Mountain picture averted evil, brought good, and generally made the world better for the owner.

Koreans also painted grapevines with ink made from grape juice; the grape's sinuous twining made it a "plant dragon," and the paintings would have spiritual power accordingly. Paintings of tigers, dogs, longevity symbols, and other virtuous beings had similar magical power. Even scholars' equipment was painted; such portrayals inspired young scholars and created a proper ambiance.

Educated and uneducated Chinese in old Hong Kong certainly believed in the real-world power of painted gods and spirits, so sacred mountain pictures must have had some effect. On the other hand, Confucius's disdain for worrying about ghosts and spirits was also well known, and (to paraphrase Freud on cigars) sometimes a landscape is just a landscape.

Among the common trees were not only the bamboo but also pines and flowering apricots. These three species are the "three friends" of many a painting;

they all endure winter, and they can stand for the three religions of China. The Confucian pine stands tall and straight against all storms, the Buddhist bamboo (bamboos are commoner toward India) bends down but never breaks, and the apricot shows a wild Daoist spirit by flowering in midwinter, with zany indifference to circumstances. (The flowering apricot or *mei, Prunus mume,* is routinely mistranslated "plum" in English literary works. The plum is *li* in Chinese.)

Such paintings can grade into "flower and bird pictures," another genre of environmental interest. One thing the paintings show is a steady decline of trees and wildlife. The later the dynasty, the barer the landscapes. The faithfully painted trees and birds of earlier art are replaced by abstracted or "copybook" trees and birds in later work; the artists did not have so many real ones to use as models. Early paintings of birds were as accurate as scientific illustrations. (See, for instance, the beautiful tenth-century painting reproduced by Dieter Kuhn in *The Age of Confucian Rule,* 2009:172.) Over time, accurate paintings of birds give way to stylized ones. After 1700, and especially in urban popular art, the birds become more often generic; China's birds were too depleted to provide ready models, at least of the larger species. Moreover, the birds that were realistically portrayed were those that can be found in small urban gardens (sparrows, wagtails). The eagles and cranes of early art disappeared or become generic, clearly not done from life. (This is my own observation; I have not done a formal analysis, but I have seen hundreds of originals and thousands of book illustrations.)

The question is: Did these landscape paintings sell conservation? They were not obviously or directly bent to that purpose. They were not used for some Chinese equivalent of Sierra Club calendars. On the other hand, they enormously reinforced the Chinese idealization of mountain and rural landscapes, the ideal of escape into such landscapes, the ideal of at least having a beautiful and rich garden if one could not get to the mountains, and the ideal of maintaining temples and temple lands in beautiful environments with natural groves and flowers. They eliminated any lingering desire to pave over everything wild-looking just to get rid of it.

The paintings were not conservation propaganda. They were, instead, part of a whole complex of expressive forms that maintained deep personal involvement with the landscape. This landscape was not a wilderness in the Western sense; it was managed and used. But it was left as rich, natural, and productive as possible.

In America today we are used to dealing with hard straight lines that separate trackless wilderness areas (the few, tiny plots that exist) from hi-tech farming, parking lots, and urbanization. Intermediate landscapes—well-managed forests, small farms, hunting preserves—were common even in my youth, but are less common now. The Chinese maintained most of their land in an intermediate state: heavily used and cropped, but with its richness, diversity, and beauty intact to varying degrees. In the north and near cities, nature barely hung on, but in the "mountains and waters" elsewhere, the human presence ranged from pervasive but nondestructive to vanishingly small. The landscape art was part of a whole conscious worldview that maintained this.

LANDSCAPE POETRY

> Seventy, and still planting trees....
> Don't laugh at me, my friends.
> I know I'm going to die.
> I also know I'm not dead yet.
> (Yuan Mei, tr. J. P. Seaton, 1997:92)

Landscape poetry developed along with painting, but we know of much earlier forms of it. China's oldest poetry is the *Book of Songs,* supposedly compiled by Confucius around 500 BCE (see Karlgren 1950). These are 305 old folksongs, court songs, and lineage ancestry chants. Most of them have the true folksong characteristic of being extremely short and sparse but extremely evocative, resonant on many levels; thus they are easy to memorize but never boring. They have continued to delight us for 2,500 years. Confucius selected ones that, to him, displayed proper morality: loyalty, probity, courage, respect, reverence. Our interest in them here is in the attitude toward nature that they reveal.

Confucius himself noted that they teach the names of animals and plants, and this is of interest today, because it gives us an extremely rich record of ancient Chinese ethnobiology (E. N. Anderson 1991). Like many folksongs worldwide, they record a high level of knowledge of nature: the folksongs mention caterpillars turning into moths, parasitic wasps preying on larvae, sagebrush getting moisture by absorbing it from mist, and various kinds of plant associations and communities. They certainly imply, but do not state, a conservationist and sustainable-management approach.

Shi—not just the *Book of Songs,* but all Chinese lyric poems—are *songs,* not poems in the European sense of the word. *Shi* were sung or chanted in traditional times and even within my memory. They were not just "read" in an ordinary voice, as Westerners read poetry. When a man in a painting is alone in the wilderness with his mouth open, he is singing *shi.* He may even sing them to a musical instrument he is playing. In Chinese, the *shi* follow complex rhyme schemes and tone contours that are quite strikingly beautiful and effective when sung (see below, Vietnam). Alas, over time, classical Chinese pronunciation got decoupled from ordinary speech, so the rhymes and tones became archaic and poorly understood, leading to eventual decline of the medium into word games—just as Latin poetry declined in the Western world. Other lyric poem forms in Chinese were also sung, and in fact a poem's only title may be "To the Tune of" some popular song. Western translators and readers often ignore this and come to believe that Chinese poems were the prosy, wordy pieces we see in translation.

Many of the lyrics in the *Book of Songs* follow a very distinctive pattern: quatrains (usually with four words to the line) in which the first two lines give a natural image, the second two provide a parallel human emotional condition. The second and fourth lines rhyme. (The following are my translations.)

The famous first song begins:

> Kuan, kuan, ospreys
> On the river island;
> The fine and lovely girl
> Is the lord's good mate.
>> (My translation. There are several more parallel
>> verses. Ospreys really do call *kuan*.)

Beginning of song 129:

> Reeds and rushes deep green,
> White dew becomes frost;
> The one I call "my man"
> Is near the stream.

This type is very characteristic of East Asian poetry, surviving today not only in China but in Malay *pantun* verses and many other languages (see Chapter 7, Southeast Asia). Everywhere, the themes of loyalty to a prince and love for a mate are typical, and are mixed; the latter is often taken to be a metaphor for the former. Many Euro-American folksongs have very similar form and content, which begs for explanation, but no evidence of derivation from Asia has been discovered.

The next major event in Chinese landscape poetry is the *Chu Ci*, the Songs of Chu (Hawkes 1959; Waley 1955; *ci* are long chants, as opposed to *shi*, short lyric songs). Chu was a southern state that was at least partly Thai-speaking, and the Chu songs are culturally different from the *Shi Jing*. The Chu Ci are long, elaborate, rich in images and—again—plant names, and often exuberantly religious. They range from laments at ill treatment (complete with attacks on the mis-treaters) to visionary shamanic songs. Supposedly at least some of them were composed by Qu Yuan, a poet of the fourth century BCE who was slandered and driven to suicide by drowning himself in a river. (There is no evidence he existed; the whole thing may be a legend, and the poems are too stylistically diverse to be written by one individual.)

Qu's cult thereafter co-opted a local ritual for the dragon lord of the river: food, and sometimes young maidens, were thrown to the dragon. Today, special food—tamales made with sticky rice and wrapped in lotus leaves—is thrown to Qu Yuan's spirit. One of the songs involves ritual coupling of a shamanic human figure with a goddess on a mountaintop and introduces the metaphoric parallel of "clouds and rain" and sexual intercourse. "Clouds and rain" remained the standard euphemism from then on.

These remained an aberration in Chinese poetry. *Fu*—long rhyme-prose pieces—maintained some of their exuberance in later court contexts. *Fu* are pedantic and stilted, as far as could be imagined from the wild shamanic visions of the Chu Ci. There are, however, exceptions, with striking descriptions of nature; a wonderful poem on monkeys and other animals, by Ruan Ji (210–263; see Holzman 1976:56–57), is really a biting satire on the court, but to succeed as satire it has to be lively animal poetry. Ruan had to be careful to hide his frequent and scathing criticisms of his government under a cloak of metaphor. The period was a bloody one, and he came from a royal family of a former kingdom. He eventually got too near the edge and was indeed executed.

The *shi* tradition presumably continued unbroken, but we have little evidence until Han and not much nature poetry until even later. However, nature poetry and the image of the hermit out in the wild was established by the end of Han or shortly after; it owed everything to the ideals of Zhuang Zi and other early Daoists. One Ying Qu (190–252), a wide-ranging writer and litterateur, had a good deal to do with the stereotype of the recluse living by choice in poverty and simplicity (Lin 2009). There is no evidence that he did any such thing, however, and the trope seems simply to have been a stock persona for him and later poets.

This changed dramatically with the great and highly focused writings of Tao Yuanming (known as Tao Qian; 365–427 CE). He ran a small farm in the brush country of rural North China. He briefly served in government, and one of his poems from that time mentions servants doing the farmwork. However, he swiftly tired of bureaucracy, threw up his job, and retired to the farm. After that the money was scarce, and we never hear of servants again. He was happy with his millet, mallow greens, and chrysanthemum tea. He stayed drunk as much as possible, but this was a free good; he made beer from the millet (apparently not always leaving much for food) or scrounged it from the neighbors, evidently in exchange for songs. (Remember these were songs, not "poems." I like to think that he was a superb singer.) He was one of the greatest, if not *the* greatest, among the poets of the simple rural life, and his effect on East Asian culture cannot be exaggerated. He owes more than we once realized to earlier poets like Ying Qu (Lin 2009), but he was still a true original.

He influenced practically every garden today, by popularizing the chrysanthemum. In his time—and still, in its wild weedy form—it was and is a scruffy roadside weed, with tiny yellow flowers, brewed for cooling tea (it contains an anti-fever chemical). He moved from drinking the tea to praising the plant for its humble, neglected, ever-present, underfoot beauty and healing. Every chrysanthemum in your garden, or any other garden, owes its presence to this one man's passion. He would, however, be saddened and depressed at what we have done—turning his symbol of humble beauty into just another showy, overblown flower.

> I built my hut among people's dwellings,
> Yet lack horse coach sounds.
> You ask how can this be?
> My heart is distanced from the world.
> I pick chrysanthemums under the east fence,
> I look away to the south mountain:
> Mountain air freshens with evening,
> Flying birds together come home.
> In this lie thoughts of truth;
> I want to speak Can't remember words.
>   (my translation)

I have preserved Tao's telegraphic, ambiguous speech, especially in the famous or infamous last line (literally "Want speak Can't remember words"), which really deserves to be known in English in all its difficulty. On the one hand, he cannot find the right word, but on a deeper level he is so lost in the experience that he literally cannot remember human speech at all, and on yet another level we are all in there with him. The ambiguity is thoroughly intentional and brilliantly managed. The omission of any pronoun leaves us wondering whether he or all of us are forgetting speech; leaving out pronouns is normal for classical Chinese, but by no means obligatory—note the "you" in line three (it is in the Chinese). The first part of the fourth line literally says simply "heart far," but *far* is a verb here and must be overtranslated accordingly.

Tao's other most famous piece has major importance for Chinese landscape history: it is his one known piece of prose, "Peach Flower Stream." This is a short story of a fisherman who sails through a cave and finds himself in a beautiful, tranquil area of peach orchards. The people tell him they fled war and disorder centuries earlier, and had been living at peace there. When he leaves to go home, they tell him, "there is no need to mention this to others." But eventually he tells the governor, and an expedition is sent out. They miss the stream and get lost. After that someone else tries, once, "but nothing came of it. Since then no one has tried to find the crossing." Again, we are left wondering whether the fisherman's trip was real, a dream, or a shamanic journey to a spirit land. Rather few people have picked up on the bitter realism of the last line: real or visionary, no one cares about beauty and peace any more. More often noted is the powerful sexual reference: peaches and peach flowers are the standard symbol of female sexuality in China, and the image of going through a wet cave into peach flowers has a significance that no one in old China would miss.

The effects of Tao's work on Chinese experience and management of nature cannot be overstated. *Every* educated Chinese in the old days could quote at least some of this material, and indeed most educated Koreans and Japanese could, too. No one after Tao could really ignore the spiritual side of nature and rural living, let alone the aesthetic side.

The next major landmark was both a poet and a prose writer. Xie Lingyun (385–433) was the antithesis of Tao. Xie was a rich, overbearing landlord who drove his servant workforce mercilessly in creating gardens and parks. But he was also a sensitive and emotional travel writer. He created that entire genre of travel literature in East Asia (Frodsham 1967). His poetry was self-consciously styled, ornate, allusive, and literary, and he has thus traditionally been considered less "natural"—*ziran*—than Tao. Of course Tao worked just as hard to sound like a farmer and was a creative and hard-working poet rather than a peasant, so the term *natural* has complex meanings here. In a fascinating pair of studies, Wendy Swartz (2008, 2010) has examined views over time of these two poets. She points out that the degree to which critics hold Tao to be "more natural" has more to do with devotion to an image of rusticity than to actual spontaneity of the poets, both of whom were self-conscious literary craftsmen.

The great watershed of East Asian culture, the Tang Dynasty, lasted from 621 to 907 CE. Its glory days were shorter, from the late 600s to the late 800s. Tang poets specialized in short poems. The goal was to capture an extremely compact, multiply evocative image, especially in poems called "cut-shorts": four-line poems with five syllables to the line in the original Chinese.

One famous fishing poem has been the subject of literally millions of paintings:

> Thousand peaks Flying birds gone
> Ten thousand paths Human footprints lost.
> Lone boat Bamboo-cloaked old man
> Solitary fishing Cold river snow.
> (Liu Zongyuan, eighth century; my translation.)

The two different words for *alone* in the last two lines are famously striking. The ambiguity in the last line is (again) deliberate. "Lost" rather undertranslates a character that implies that the fisherman is disappearing—merging into the falling snow. Liu both empathizes with the fisherman—forced by poverty to work under circumstances that have driven everyone else home—and identifies with him: the fisherman becomes Liu in a spiritual snow-world of Buddhist meditative isolation.

The very highest point was in the middle 700s. Tang rule brought China to new heights of wealth and power. A rebellion in 756, however, almost destroyed it. The emperor was thrown out; the rebellion was suppressed, but the crown prince took over the throne. The greatest poets suffered along with everyone else. Du Fu, generally considered China's greatest poet of all time, wrote his deepest and more heartbreaking poems after losing his position, his wealth, and his home in the rebellion. He and his family wandered in desperate straits; one of his children died of hunger.

Tang rallied, but was never quite the same. The late Tang poets took refuge in exoticism or faced the new world with stern morality. Han Yu brought a return to strict Confucianism after centuries of Buddhist and Daoist speculation and ritual. This, too, had incalculable effects. Desperately needed at the time, this correction of increasingly other-worldly attitudes started a steady rise of a Confucianism that later became increasingly narrow and puritanical, leading ultimately to Singapore today—chewing gum and rock music outlawed—and, yes, this actually does trace back directly to Han Yu. It traces much more obviously to Zhu Xi in the thirteenth century, but he claimed—rather unfairly, if you dislike puritanism—that he was following Han Yu.

Han himself was a much more pleasant and poetic soul. One bit of nature writing reveals it: he was exiled from court for some particularly sharp (and valuable) criticism of the emperor and sent down to govern Chaozhou, a remote and backward area. Here the local folk assumed that because he was an imperial government authority, he could order off a local crocodile that was threatening people. So he wrote an edict, and of course used the crocodile as an exceedingly transparent image for his enemies at court, laying into them with all due formal ferocity (translated in Giles 1923:128–130). The result is one of the funniest edicts in history, and one suspects it had a good deal to do with getting him recalled to court.

A final Tang influence was Han Shan. The name (no relation to Han Yu) means "Cold Mountain," and refers to an anonymous Buddhist hermit who hid out on that mountain near the Yangzi Delta and meditated there for the rest of his life. He left a large store of poetry scattered around. This was later collected by other Buddhists on the mountain. Much of the material is clearly not by him; style, references to current events, and other indications show it accumulated over a century or so. But a core of the best poems seems to be by one hand. They reveal a totally uncompromising loner and nature-lover, perfectly happy in the wilderness, rarely concerned with people except insofar as they can face the physical, mental, and spiritual difficulties of coming to him on Cold Mountain.

Han Shan anchors one extreme end not only of Chinese tradition, but of world tradition; not one Western poet has ever been so far into the wild and so remote from fellow humans. Unlike Tao Yuanming, who may have been introverted but did live "in a zone of human habitation," Han Shan was an almost total loner in an almost totally wild landscape. Arthur Waley (1961) has done some of the best translations, and so has Gary Snyder, but the major translation effort has been by "Red Pine" (Red Pine [William Porter] 2000), a Buddhist who has actually sought out Cold Mountain itself and meditated there.

Here are two poems:

Faint, faint, Cold Mountain road,
Thick, thick, streamside growth.
Chirp, chirp—always those birds
Silent, silent—never any men.
Sighing, sighing wind in my face,
Flurries and eddies of snow cover my body.
Day after day, never see sun,
Year after year, never know spring.

If you want an image of life and death,
Look to ice and water.
Water cools, turns to ice,
Ice melts, turns back to water.
Whatever dies must be reborn,
What emerges in birth must then die.
Ice and water do each other no harm;
Life and death are both beautiful.
(my translations)

Less well known is Jing Yun, but he provides tremendous insight into Tang attitudes toward landscape painting (of which more anon):

This time I think
I got it: one pine real
As the real.

Think about it:
Search in memory, is it
Real, or not?

> Guess I'll have to go
> Back up the mountain ...
> South past Stonebridge,
> The third one on the right....
>> (Jing Yun, late ninth century, tr. Jerome P. Seaton;
>> Seaton and Maloney 1994:76)

This Buddhist painter would have been more interested in getting the *qi* of the pine than its actual shape, but early Chinese painters also worked at biological accuracy.

From the Yuan, we have a poem by a painter. The great Buddhist artist, poet, and chef Ni Zan thus metaphorized a favorite bird:

> Where is the woodpecker?
> Far in the high trees.
> Fragile, he works so hard;
> All day I hear his sound.
> He works so the woods will flourish,
> No worms gnawing trees away.
> Woe to the crowds of humans—
> Never a heart like this bird's.
>> Ni Zan (a great Yuan Dynasty artist and writer; my translation)

I think this must have inspired a much more famous, but (sadly) anonymous, Korean poem:

> What kind of bug has
> Eaten away the great pine-trees?
> Where is the long-billed woodpecker?
> Where has he gone now?
> When I hear the trees crashing down on the bleak mountain,
> I can hardly contain my sorrow.
>> (Anonymous, tr. Kim, 1994:190)

In both poems, the worms and insects are likened to evil courtiers. This is not just symbolism; the worms have the same irresponsible, destructive mind and the same damaging *qi*. Such organic homology is *ganying* (lit. "resemblance," but implying a deep reason for the resemblance) in Chinese.

In Ming, poetry somewhat declined, but prose writing soared. My favorite quote about appreciating nature is truly deathless:

"When someone in antiquity who was gripped by an obsession for flowers heard speak of a rare blossom, even if it were in a deep valley or in steep mountains, he would not be afraid of stumbling and would go to it. Even in the freezing cold and the blazing heat, even if his skin were cracked and peeling or caked with mud and sweat, he would be oblivious. When a flower was about to bloom, he would move his pillow and mat and sleep alongside it to observe how the flower would go from budding to blooming to fading. Only after it lay withered on the ground would he take his leave.… This is what is called a genuine love of flowers" (Zeitlin 1991:3).

The landscape poetry that was so fresh and graphic in early dynasties became increasingly formulaic after Tang. By late Ming and Qing it had become little more than a word game. Literary classical Chinese was always a bit artificial. It developed from court records—basically stenography—and thus was telegraphic, omitting many function words and other redundancies. By Qing, it had become as far from spoken Chinese as court Latin is from Spanish. Rules of tone, rhyme, and meter that made perfect sense in Tang no longer had anything to do with the spoken language. Images froze into a narrow stock. The same old orioles, willows, mei flowers, and dashing horses were recycled endlessly.

The best insight into this almost mindless process is found, as usual, in the great eighteenth-century novel *The Story of the Stone* (Cao and Gao 1973–1986). That novel's teenage protagonists engage in many poetry meets and contests, but the poems are purely stock and artificial. Real feelings are described, but in a language so formal and repetitive that it is mind-numbing. The author, Cao Xueqin, did a brilliant and ironic job of capturing the artificiality and also making the poems suit their writers: the heroes are insouciantly stylish, the heroines perfect but self-pitying, and the hero's long-suffering but stable wife-to-be talented but matter of fact. There were, however, some inspired and original poets even then, including women (see Idema and Grant 2004).

Music, too, echoed the natural world. In this case, echoes were, once again, resonance. The sounds called up the feelings and moods evoked by the natural world. Many classic Chinese tunes evoke natural phenomena and have titles like "Snow in Sunny Spring," "Rain and Clouds Over the Rivers Xiao and Xiang," and "Wild Geese Descending on Level Sands." Connoisseurs conjure up the scenes in mind when these pieces are played.

COMPARISON

Japan and Korea formed something of an extension of Chinese values, adding their own religious views. Both have indigenous animistic and nature-revering traditions: shamanism in Korea, Shinto in Japan. Both adopted Buddhism and

Confucianism enthusiastically and paid great attention to the life-preserving and conservationist views of those faiths. It is clearly and specifically due to this that they are the only nonwestern countries to reforest successfully—to restore vast areas of rich, lush, diverse forests.

Japan was left with very little forest at the end of the civil wars of the sixteenth century; the Tokugawa shogunate aggressively reforested, with the result that Japan was 90 percent covered with productive, diverse forests by 1900 (Totman 1989; cf. Diamond 2005). Japan also conserved local fisheries (their high-seas behavior is another matter). Community management, again owing a great deal to the Tokugawa regime, enforced sustainable use (Ruddle and Akimichi 1984). In the case of both forests and fish, the Tokugawas wanted and needed the products and thus leaned hard on communities to maintain so they could deliver. Until recently, the Japanese protected cattle and other large livestock, eating very little red meat. Japanese gardens are, of course, world famous; gardens, temple plantings, and other aesthetic plantings are extensive enough to be a significant part of landscape cover.

Issa, slightly later, could be as original:

> Akikaze ya!
> Hyoro-hyoro kama
> No kageboshi

> The autumn wind!
> It shakes
> the mountain's shadow
> > Issa (1763–1828); my translation, based on Lewis
> > MacKenzie's (1957, p. 2)

The effect of moving air masses makes the shadow seem to tremble. The autumn wind, one of the most overworked clichés in Japanese, is suddenly turned to a Buddhist comment on the frailty of power and greatness.

KOREAN:

> Red-necked mountain pheasant over there,
> Duck hawk perched on the branch,
> White egrets watching for the fish
> In the watered paddy field out in front,
> If you were not around my grass roof
> It wouldn't be easy for me to pass the days.
> > Anonymous, tr. Jaihiun Kim (1994:190)

Fish in the pond in my front yard,
Who caught you and stocked you here?
How come you left the deep blue of the north
Sea to come and stay here?
Once in, you cannot get out;
Now I see we are in the same boat.

                    Anonymous, tr. Kim (1994:191; *ganying* again)

A FINAL QUESTION

Clearly, folk religion and cosmology really did save a great deal, especially through temple groves and lands and the odd institution of feng shui.

One question in all this, however, is: Did this elite fondness for the natural environment actually influence resource management?

One would like to answer "yes," and to say that the leaders of society thus instructed the masses. In China, as in the West from Plato on down, the intellectuals' assumption often is that the Great Minds lead and the people follow. However, the ordinary Chinese have a different idea, expressed in the sayings, "Heaven is high and the emperor is far away" and—in the *Book of Songs*—"we plant in spring and harvest in fall; what does the emperor have to do with us?" Moreover, anthropologists are aware that elites and intellectuals are, if anything, even more the products of their culture than are the ordinary farmers. The latter must take account of immediate environmental realities that the former can ignore. And certainly China's good management—its sacred groves, rice fields, orchards, and marshes—were creations of the ordinary people, whereas its disasters—vast reclamation projects, forced transplantation of people to frontiers, and so on—were often elite-organized government projects.

The question has been posed most clearly by Helen Dunstan (1998), in an important article on official thinking about the environment (mainly in the Qing Dynasty). Dunstan finds that many officials were deeply concerned about the environment, but their Confucian fixation on humanity and its needs kept them from having a full, comprehensive ecological view. (Apparently none of them had the old Daoist-Buddhist vision.) They thus worked hard to protect forests, waterways, and other rural amenities, but from a rather "blindered" anthropocentric view, usually without a deep view of "nature's services." Some simply saw nature as something to get rid of, to make room for people. Some, however, had a quite modern view. They were aware, for instance, that deforestation causes erosion and siltation as well as loss of timber, wildlife, and other forest amenities. Dunstan is less than impressed with their vision, comparing them unfavorably with modern environmentalists. This is, however, a somewhat unfair comparison. If one compares the officials she quotes with modern officials and development agents, especially in China, the former are astonishingly enlightened and aware—far more so than most of their modern counterparts.

One searches, therefore, for credible links from elite poetry and landscape art to the actual farms and groves. Fortunately, these are not hard to find (Santangelo 1998). A point amazingly little known outside China is the enormous degree to which elite and popular culture interpenetrated and mutually influenced each other (see, e.g., Anderson 2007; Johnson et al. 1985). In my research in rural Hong Kong in 1965–1966, I found landscape and other paintings in every temple and in many ordinary offices and businesses. These ranged from classical-style to rather popular in feeling. This is a very old tradition, going back at least to Tang and Song (see, e.g., Kuhn 2009:168). Almost everyone knew at least the key quotes from Confucius and Mencius (just as almost everyone in America in my youth knew at least some quotes from the Bible). The Ox Mountain story quoted above was quite widely known. Dunstan makes this point about her officials. We have evidence from earlier periods that more Buddhist-Daoist officials, including the poet Su Dongpo, were highly conscious of conservation and managed it well.

Gardens and garden art were another point of contact (see detailed discussion in Santangelo 1998). Everyone aspired to having a garden, and those who could not could at least have potted plants, often including the dwarfed trees that the Japanese know as *bonsai*. These, as we have seen, began as meditation subjects, to allow scholars in urban streets to imagine remote mountain scenery and thus to experience the entire cosmos in miniature (Stein 1990). Of course gardens were larger and thus more effective at doing this, and their role in miniaturizing the cosmos for home contemplation was widely known and recognized. The ultimate proof of elite poetic influence was the universality of chrysanthemums—one poet's love creating a whole floral culture.

Thus, from the elite to the folk came a view of the ideal landscape. It was one of trees, bushes, flowers, rocks, and birds. It had fields and buildings incorporated into a broadly natural landscape. It paid full respect to living things of all sorts. It recognized a spiritual dimension in the landscape: the natural world was a shifting, living flow of qi and other forces. The more literal saw it as inhabited by gods, spirits, dragons, unicorns, and other supernatural beings. It deserved contemplation, with due awe and reverence. Harmony and peace with nature were imperative.

From the folk to the elite came a view of the landscape as necessarily protected and managed, through groves, dykes, canals, orchards, fields, and ponds. It had to be maintained in the healthiest and most diverse possible way, but this involved hard and constant work.

This created a tension, one of those productive contradictions that makes people think and innovate: nature must be respected, life can be sustained only through going with nature, but controlling nature takes effort. The resolution was that going with the Dao requires finding that Dao and then putting the necessary conditions into play. Water delivers goodness, but only when properly channeled. Management is needed, but bad water management is worse than none. Trees had to be pruned, watered, and tended, but only insofar as it actually helped them flourish; overmanaging was as bad as neglect. Obviously, finding the exact way to do this was not easy.

As usual, the great Chinese novel *The Story of the Stone* (Cao and Gao 1972–1986) is a perfect source for finding out how this played on the ground. The Jia protagonists were a rich landlord family, managing estates and constantly talking to their farm supervisors and gardeners. Some of the Jia were "poor relations," much closer to the soil. The Jia gardens were so famous that scholars preserved bits and pieces of the actual gardens that Cao Xueqin used as his models, so we know what eighteenth-century gardens were like, and they were not only beautiful but environmentally sound. In short, there was simply no way to isolate the high elite from the realities of soil, water, and growing things. Today's urban elites, living by resource throughput and totally isolated from and unaware of both agriculture and nature, were simply not possible in old China. On the other hand, the Jia were less careful about their farming, willing to let estate overseers do the work, and they had a low opinion of farmers and farming (Zhou 2013).

Even the extreme anti-civilization attitudes of the early Daoists or of Han Shan had some influence. Large areas of China were preserved for temple complexes and meditative retreats. The ideal models or templates of this system were rather generally known and accepted. Elite meditation on nature was far from the reality of village hunters, fishers, woodcutters, and tillers of the soil, but there were many ways to bridge the gap. Both elites and rural workers recognized that everyone depended on a harmonious, sustainable management system.

On the other hand, there was no way to impose a real conservation ethic on the rural folk. They had to make a living, and that often involved using desperate measures. Also, the demands of the elite were not in harmony with their landscape ideals. They consumed far too much game, forest products, medicinal herbs and animals, and other wild goods. Whole mountainsides were deforested to provide not only utility goods but also paper and ink for books, kiln fuel for exquisite porcelains, and charcoal for sophisticated metallurgy. Thus, ironically, the very poetry and art that sustained the landscape led to consuming it. The very medicine that emphasized harmony with the natural order led to destroying it, through overuse of wild medicinals.

This, however, can be overstated. Wild medicinals, for instance, were not used in the massive and destructive way they are today. Many studies show they were harvested conservatively and often with sustained-yield measures firmly in place.

I agree with Nicholas Menzies (1994 and personal communication, 2013) that most of the damage to the environment in premodern China was done during periods of dynastic weakness, decline, and breakdown. Corruption and war were the worst wreckers. As long as "great peace" reigned, the farmers and rural folk managed their lands very well indeed. The elite influenced this only slightly, but the influence was real and possibly even critical. Their influence was a mixed bag: poetry and art for good, overconsumption and overuse for ill.

PART III

Broader Regions

CHAPTER SEVEN

Southeast Asia

THE REGION

Southeast Asia had, until quite recently, the best record of any region in the world of supporting large, dense populations for thousands of years without ruining the environmental system. As of 1900, Southeast Asian countries had dense populations, living well and comfortably when they could avoid war and imperialism. Yet it was 90 percent forested, with the richest and most biodiverse forests in the world outside of Amazonia. Even more impressive, it still had the full complement of megafauna: elephants, rhinos, bears, tigers, clouded leopards, orangutans, wild cattle, rare and exotic deer. The Vietnamese saola, an extremely rare, local, and sensitive antelope, survives today in spite of Vietnam's dense population.

In a brief but brilliant article, Chan Yuk Wah (Chan 2011) turned a tiny question about food into a deconstruction of "Southeast Asia" as a region, pointing out that foodways—as well as language, political ideas, and much else—tend to link parts of Southeast Asia with parts of China, and indeed that Southeast Asia is a region of convenience rather than a cultural bloc. In spite of general influences from China and India, it is not unified by history and culture the way Europe or Latin America are. However, Southeast Asia does have considerable unity, shown in dress, food, housing styles, folk religion, borrowed folktales and linguistic usages, and, above all, it its agricultural and environmental management system. This demonstrates variants of a single basic pattern dependent on wet rice in lowlands, hill rice on slopes, extensive tree cropping, and mixed plantings in dooryard gardens.

Java and Bali in particular have sustainably supported populations as dense as an American suburb for centuries. They fed themselves and preserved virtually all natural biodiversity, until the fascist Suharto government devastated Indonesia. Even the small hill societies of Southeast Asia, such as the Akha (Wang 2008, 2013), have done a superior job at sustainably supporting dense populations.

The most dramatic proof of the genuine superiority of their system has been the devastation of nature brought about by Westernization in the last sixty years. This might have been excusable if it had benefited the people, but in fact it did not. With the important exception of medical care, the vast majority of Southeast Asians are little or no better off than they were in 1950. (The three clear exceptions—Thailand, Malaysia, and Singapore—are special cases. Thailand did not suffer the full social and economic devastations of colonialism. Malaysia and Singapore were developed intensively by the British. Singapore is a largely Chinese city-state, not a full-scale country with a huge rural sector.) Health is better today, but economically people are poorer than ever. Almost all the benefits of Westernization have gone to a small elite. The paper gains of the rest—the majority of the population—are offset by their loss of the free goods, from firewood and food to herbal medicines, fish and game that they formerly got from the environment.

The main direct reason for traditional success was a system based on wet rice, forest management, and upland mixed cropping. This system was integrated in such ways that people were virtually forced to use the maximum number of resources with maximal efficiency. Depleting one resource to increase supply of another was impractical, partly because the most "downstream" crop—the paddy rice—was the staple food. Devastating upstream areas was not practical. One could always get more food by driving the rice system harder and harder (Geertz 1963), but overusing the headwaters meant catastrophic erosion that would wipe out the rice fields.

Photo on Facing page: Veneration of a street tree, Hue, Vietnam. Photograph by E. N. Anderson.

Rice farming is easily intensified, and rice-growing systems tend to use entire environments. It is easy to combine intensive rice-growing with agroforestry, orchards, vegetable gardening, intensive root-cropping, and other diversified small-scale high-yield enterprises. Under such circumstances, it makes sense to teach respect for and preservation of all life.

Significantly, the rice regions show few of the "decline and fall" scenarios so prominent in the West and in parts of the pre-Columbian New World (notably the Classic Maya central lowlands). Angkor fell and stayed down, but only because the Thai conquered its last flowerings and established regional domination. The Cham civilization of South Vietnam similarly lost out to the Vietnamese. Otherwise, cyclic declines of dynasties merely meant a new dynasty taking over (see, e.g., Lieberman 2003). The profound, centuries-long depression that affected Europe and north China in the Dark Ages was unparalleled in the rice-growing southeast.

Cultural influences are varied, with great local differences. Foreign ideologies have been important for millennia, with India influencing the western regions, China the northeast and east, and both more indirectly influential deep into Indonesia. Classic Southeast Asian trade (see Reid 1988, 1994; Dove 2011) carried small amounts of diverse commodities not only over short distances, but even over long distances. Southeast Asia and Indonesia had a huge trade with India and China by 2,000 years ago.

On the other hand, the hill societies have managed to remain outside the close control and cultural dominance of the lowlands (Scott 2009), and they are often the very best managers. (See again Wang 2008.)

Another major material reason for good environmental stewardship was that the other major component of the agricultural system was tree cropping (on this and its relation to rice, see Klee 1980). Over much of Southeast Asia, coconuts were the second most important calorie source after rice. Bananas (technically a giant herb, not a "tree," but managed as tree crops) were probably native to New Guinea; at least some species were. Banana-coconut intercropping locally produced as many calories per acre as rice agriculture. Bananas swept across Southeast Asia as superior hybrids were developed in the quite distant past. Durians, jackfruit, breadfruit, and several other trees produced enough food to be major calorie sources; breadfruit and pandanus became staples in many Pacific islands. Even the toddy palm became a staple in some areas (Fox 1977); its sweet sap produced a sugar (similar to maple sugar) that was the staple food on some islands. Mangoes, tamarind, canarium nuts, and dozens of other tree species were important. After 1500, more and more new plants came from the New World, including rubber, now a major commercial crop.

Tree cropping has countless advantages (Smith 1950). It takes very little fertilizer. It does not involve plowing or otherwise disturbing the soil; in fact, it inhibits erosion. Many of the trees (including tamarind and the very common horseradish tree, *Moringa*) fix nitrogen and thus fertilize the soil and can therefore grow in sterile beach sand and other difficult sites. There are trees for every ecological niche, including sites with such acid and metal-rich water that they are toxic to almost everything. Rubber loves nothing more than the horribly tough and infertile laterite of Southeast Asia's granite terrains and thus complemented food crops rather than competing with them. Unfortunately, a more recent introduction—oil palm—competes directly with almost everything, from forest to rice, and oil palm cultivation is rapidly destroying Southeast Asia's ecology. The future is bleak.

The greatest advantage of all, however, is that trees allow even densely inhabited spaces to yield food and fuel. The trees fill the air space over the houses. In 1970 and 1971, when I worked in Southeast Asia, one could barely see villages or even most cities from the air. The buildings were hidden by dense canopies of coconut, mango, rambutan, and other trees. The roots spread under the houses, which were generally built on stilts (piles), off the ground; the space under the floors was used for storage and drying. It was certainly the most efficient use of space and the most efficient way to produce food that I have ever seen.

Trees can be grown in layers, reproducing the layered look of a tropical rainforest. Three layers are common; typically this involves tall emergents (coconut, durian); a canopy layer below that (mango, rambutan, mangosteen, citrus, and many others); and a short tree layer still lower (papaya, guava, and so on). In edge situations, where sun reaches all the way down, perennials (pineapple, fruit bushes) can be grown under those, and annual vegetables still lower, for a five-layered system. I have seen this in many places.

The major disadvantage of trees is that if they die it takes several years to replace them. This has led to a steady reduction in coconuts, worldwide, as diseases spread through the monocrop stands of coconuts that have developed on beaches and shores all around the tropical coasts of the world. An annual crop struck by plague can be replaced in a year, but coconuts take about fifteen years to come to full fruit. Other trees, fortunately, grow in less time.

Overall, Southeast Asia's production and management strategies were similar everywhere. Yet the grand ideologies of the nations could not have been more different. (On history, and the issue of similarities and differences in Southeast Asia, see Lieberman 2003; Scott 2009.) Muslim, Theravada Buddhist, "pagan," and in recent decades Christian polities have flourished, and Vietnam had a unique mix of Confucianism and Mahayana Buddhism. The languages, too, were diverse, including hundreds of languages representing at least six distinct phyla. Kinship systems varied from matrilineal to patrilineal to cognatic. Some "optative" systems in Indonesia were unique in the world in allowing an individual to pick how he or she wanted to be grouped—with father's kin, mother's kin, both, or some mix.

The Southeast Asian management system, from the practical (rice farming) to the spiritual (a basic animism), crosscuts religion, as well as class, rural/urban divides, and other obvious splits. In it, people are intensely responsible for each other, for the community, and for preserving a livable environment for the community over time. Thus, people work to establish a lifestyle of simplicity (but not puritanism), low-impact, sustainability, recycling, and people-in-nature.

All this suggests that our model is right: economic and ecological adjustments are prior, and Marx was broadly right in seeing ideology and consciousness as following from co-work within these. However, Weber was still more correct, in seeing it as basically a feedback process, in which beliefs and representations constantly influence the production process as well as the other way around. It seems likely that Southeast Asia would have developed a conservationist ideology in any case, given the realities of rice farming. But people have to be motivated, and that requires something beyond economics: some institution that compels emotional solidarity.

Some cultures—the Akha, Karen, and Balinese, for example—manage resources better than others. This derives (wholly or partially) from the need to manage it integrally, using all resources and depending on maintaining themselves in a fairly steady state. Key to conservation is using as many different resources as possible and then becoming more intensive and efficient in utilization over time. This automatically leads to managing for sustainability, because one must maintain the system to have the whole range of goods. The feedback is that ideology then keeps people managing for a wide range of goods. Once again, recent Westernization proves this point: idealizing monocrop agriculture has come in as a new concept, leading to catastrophic ecological collapse over millions of acres as rice, opium, oil palm, and sugarcane take over from mixed plantings and forests.

It is also clear that rapid population increase over the last fifty years has led to many formerly sustainable systems becoming unsustainable and, indeed, seriously problematic. However, this has been exaggerated (Pinkaew 2001). Technological and agricultural change seems more important in many cases than population growth per se. The combined effects of population and local change are utterly trivial in comparison to the devastation brought about by modern industrial monocrop agriculture. The damage blamed on swiddening was actually done in most cases by modern logging and monocropping (see, e.g., Conklin 1957; Dove 1983, 1985, 2011; Dove et al. 2005; Geddes 1976; Peluso 1992; Pinkaew 2001; Spencer 1966; Yos 2008; compare also the case of Latin America, where damage sometimes blamed on swidden is done mainly by large-scale cattle operations; Painter and Durham 1995 and personal research). Even export-crop agriculture is environmentally sustainable and successful if done by traditional smallholders. Local smallholder rubber planters, for instance, not only conserve the landscape in spite of planting a great deal of rice and rubber, they actually outdo the plantations at producing rubber successfully, especially under harsh environmental or economic conditions (Dove 2011; I can amply confirm this from my own research).

An amazing triumph of anonymous small farmers was the conquest of the Burma delta in the late nineteenth century. Once the British pacified the area and provided minimal infrastructure, peasants rushed in and turned it into one vast rice bowl in a generation, in spite of tigers, poisonous snakes, and other problems (Adas 1974).

The Southeast Asian pattern of intensive, nondamaging agriculture fades out rapidly in eastern Indonesia. It grades there into the world of New Guinea (Irian Jaya and Papua-New Guinea), with less conservation ideology. Even here, however, scholars report strongly environmental consciousness and values even without a "conservation" idea (Kirsch 2006; Rappaport 1984; Sillitoe 2010; West 2006).

MANAGEMENT

The environmental management system is complex and diverse. Ideology or technoeconomic path dependence worked together to create a stable, sustainable system. (What follows is largely from my own research [see Anderson 1993a, 1993b] and that of my students, notably Richard Lando [1979, 1983], Lynn Thomas [1977, 1985, and personal communication], and Jianhua "Ayoe" Wang [2013]. I have experience in most of the Southeast Asian countries, including a year of field work in Malaysia, Singapore, and Indonesia in 1970–1971, plus very wide reading, a good deal of which was in Chinese and Bahasa Indonesia. I have cited only the latest or most comprehensive sources consulted. Some general surveys include Fox and Ledgerwood 1999 for Cambodia; Geertz 1963, Indonesia; Hanks 1972, Thailand; Klee 1980; Lansing 1987, 1991, 2006, Bali; Roumasset 1976; Spencer 1966.)

Wet rice is the staple food. In traditional times—and today, in many areas—it provided 90 percent of calories for the vast majority of the people. Under traditional Southeast Asian conditions, paddy rice produced about 2,500 pounds of grain per acre per crop, with two or three crops per year being typical where water supply permitted—thus, 5,000 to 7,500 pounds per year. Some areas were much less fortunate; much of Cambodia has infertile soils and only seasonal water, producing about 1,500 pounds/year (personal observation).

The great virtue and deadly trap of wet rice, as Clifford Geertz (1963) memorably pointed out, is that it can be intensified almost indefinitely. More labor, more fertilizer, more working and leveling of the soil, more careful control of water depth, and more pest control will always pay off at the margin—at least a tiny bit. For subsistence cultivators, it is always worth doing a little bit more. Thus, in a fairly free or community-level polity, people can get very prosperous. In a top-down repressive system, however, rice agriculture can get more and more intensive, while the rulers take all the marginal product. This is, in Geertz's terms, *agricultural involution*. It occurred largely under colonial authorities, who exploited the peasants while encouraging them to work the system harder and harder. (Geertz has been accused of "blaming the victim," but he spends dozens of pages proving the fault lay with the rulers.) The workers get steadily poorer, but can always feed another mouth by increasing field production. The same occurred in south China (Huang 1990, and personal research).

Today, with modern inputs and plant breeding, rice can produce 15,000 pounds per acre per crop, and the end is not here yet. This, once again, has allowed the free to prosper (as in Thailand) and the less free to survive by ever more involution. Geertz was describing Java under colonial exploitation; independence changed nothing. Java continues to feed more and more people by growing just a little bit more, and poverty continues as ever.

The dryland systems of the West could not do this under premodern conditions, and the West was generally saved from involution by this. Today, even wheat can intensify to incredible levels of production, but that is a new development, permitted by modern science. The maize-root crop systems of tropical America could intensify and involute, but not to the extent of wet rice.

Root crops and others were once more important than now, and today the New World crops maize and manioc have taken over large areas, but rice still dominates everywhere. The maize and manioc allowed more involution in Southeast Asia, because they allow labor to be poured into drier and poorer lands, inadequate for rice (Geertz 1963).

Wet rice demands level fields. Thus, in hill and mountain areas, however, rice was usually "dry," that is to say, rain-fed. This is much less productive. Paddy rice under traditional conditions produced about 2,500 pounds per acre per crop, with two to three crops possible per year. Dry rice produces about 300 to 500 pounds per acre per crop, with only one crop a year (see, e.g., Spencer 1966). Many mountains are thus terraced to allow wet-rice production, especially in areas like Yunnan and Sichuan in China and Luzon, Bali, and Java in island Southeast Asia. But terracing is a lot of work, and a good typhoon can wreck a whole system. Thus the usual rule in the uplands is dry rice.

A pound of rice will feed a person for a day, but only if other foods are eaten to provide nutrients. Labor increases the food requirements proportionately, so the requirement for a farmer working in the field is closer to two pounds.

The range of crops is incredible. Dozens of fruit tree species are grown, including not only the Old World tropical species but almost all the New World species. Even obscure local ones have made their way to Asia. Hundreds of species are grown as vegetables and herbs. Southeast Asia is home to most of the world's spices, and these are grown in quantities great enough to provide significant benefits to nutrition and health.

Rice is usually grown as a monocrop, but in both wet-rice and dry-rice communities; other crops are grown in mixed plantings that recapitulate the tropical forest (Geertz 1963).

Dry rice is raised in swidden systems: the forest is cut and burned, rice is planted for two years, and the field is partially abandoned. However, almost invariably, people have planted longer-yielding species like manioc, yams, and fruit trees. These go on giving as the forest regrows. After anywhere from ten to fifty years, the forest is recut, and the cycle begins again. Traditionally, very steep and otherwise hostile country was rarely cropped, with about 50 percent of upcountry Southeast Asia being left to old-growth forest. Today, extreme population pressure and poverty force people to cultivate almost everywhere.

A vast range of local variations of this general system exists, but need not concern us here. The point is that this system depended on extremely intensive cultivation, high levels of skill, maintenance of great biodiversity, and above all on management by local communities. The irrigation systems for wet rice, coordination of burning cycles for dry, development and protection of orchards, and maintenance of harvestable game and wild herbs depended on comprehensive control, coordination, and cooperation at the community level. Usually, bonds of kinship held the community together, and it is no accident that Southeast Asia has some of the most elaborate, complex, and highly organized kinship systems in the world. Everywhere, kinship is used to organize agriculture, especially wet-rice production (Hanks 1972; Lando 1979).

Religion may be diverse, but local religious beliefs and practices provide more unity. Local spirits are extremely important everywhere, with tree spirits particularly so. Local goddesses of rice and cultivation are crucial. Kinship rituals and ancestor worship maintain the all-important kin groups and communities. All these beliefs are similar throughout the region, down to details of how to divide up the ritually slaughtered buffalo for kin group feasts (Lando 1979; Wang 2013). Marriage patterns and other links between kin groups integrate communities and local regions.

This developed in feedback with a world of small farmers and close, tight village communities. The small farmers were usually independent owner-operators, not serfs. Though they were taxpayers and subjects of autocratic local states, they could manage their lives, farms, and villages as they saw fit. They produced for markets, taxes, and local imposts, not as forced slave labor. They, therefore, had every incentive to intensify and diversify. The more they produced, and the more varied it all was, the more they could earn and the more security they had against failure of one crop.

Southeast Asia's rulers often did not care about the people one way or another, except to tax them. Because taxes rely on a successful economy, the rulers were not about to ruin the environment or the community system.

The situation was different in some of the old feudal states. They had local but harsh slavery (Scott 2009). Large landed estates worked by slave labor, however, did not flourish and did not maintain themselves. They could not really compete with the small farmers. They existed as patronage, but did not last over the long term.

James C. Scott (2009), writing on Southeast Asia, has argued that wet-rice agriculture serves states and state interests, whereas shifting cultivation (mostly dry-grown rice) serves the "anarchist" world of the hill peoples. This is only relatively true. Shifting cultivation is indeed almost impossible to control, or to milk for large revenues per village, but so is wet rice under premodern hill conditions. Many of the freest and most independent peoples grew wet rice. Wet-rice regions can be effectively monitored, integrated, organized, and managed as units, but this can serve the interests of independent hill peoples just as much as it can serve the states. Wet-rice systems support large, strong populations who can successfully resist state takeover for centuries. Tibeto-Burman peoples like the Hani (including Sani, Akha, and others), Apa Tani, Na, and Moso stand as examples. So do the Batak and Toraja peoples of Indonesia. Scott maintains that the terrace-building mountain peoples of Luzon (or at least some of them) were refugees from settled state lands.

Scott is correct in stating that shifting cultivation makes independence almost inevitable; no states were based on it in Southeast Asia, and few even managed to integrate strictly shifting cultivators into their polities. (This was *not* true in other parts of the world, incidentally.)

Scott idealizes the free world of the uplanders. It was highly diverse. There were small states like the Shan states and old Laos and Chiangmai; there were tribes that went in and out of statehood (Leach 1954; Ayoe Wang, unpublished research). There were tribes that were independent but rather meek, staying free largely because of their rough habitat. Finally, there were a few groups that fit Scott's idea: fiercely proud and independent, and quite ready to stay that way by indomitable military efforts. Such groups included the Nosu of west China (Lin 1961; Winnington 1962), who routinely took Chinese as slaves. Even more "wild" (in colonial terms) were the Wa of the Burma-China border, and the Batak peoples of Sumatera (Lando 1979). The Nosu and Chinese Wa were virtually independent of the Chinese state until the late 1950s. The Wa of Burma are *still* free of effective central control. Philippine's Luzon and Mindanao highlanders and Malaysia's Iban also stayed independent until recently by indomitable fighting.

Wet rice allows people to build up dense populations and feed large defense forces. These are as apt to be anti-state as supportive of states, and, indeed, the

Luzon peoples were far from the only wet-rice groups to flee to the mountains to hold out. China throughout its entire history had a terrible time conquering and holding wet-rice lands in the south and southeast. The hill peoples of south China were at least as troublesome as the Central Asian nomads, though less visible.

Scott introduces the idea of "escape crops" (Scott 2009:199 ff.), crops that can be grown in remote mountain areas without fancy technology or investment in land management and field development ("landesque capital"). Such crops are buckwheat (the Nosu staple), millets, dry-rice varieties, and so on. New World crops proved a godsend to escapers: maize, manioc, and, in some areas, sweet potatoes allowed high production on steep slopes and terrible soils.

IDEOLOGY

Ideology and ecology interacted to maintain all this, of course. One advantage is a heritage of Buddhism, Hinduism, and other highly environment-friendly religions. Another was a basis in a much older "animistic" tradition of belief in spirits of trees, rocks, and other landscape features. (The large mounds of mud erected by mud-lobsters were worshiped in one village where I lived.) Naturally, Scott has seized on animism as yet another driver of anarchism. These faiths teach responsibility for the wide-flung community—human and trans-human. It also has a local culture that favors working with nature rather than destroying nature in hopes that something good will emerge.

It seems no accident that Hindu ahimsa (nonviolence to all life), Buddhist compassion to all beings, Jain protection of all living things, and Southeast Asian reverence for nature all started in the rice-growing belt that stretches from north-central India around to south China. Early Hindu sources speak of rice as a staple, and Hinduism and Buddhism both use rice in most of their ceremonial offerings. *Hinduism* is a British imperial neologism, but it is a good short term for a whole cluster of influences that affected Southeast Asia, especially from about 400 to 1000 CE. With it came Buddhism and Jainism. The combined belief system involved taking life as little as possible, protecting animals and plants, and revering natural kinds. The ideology of local spirits and Hindu-Buddhist respect for all life is perfectly suited to this intensive, diverse, community-level production.

The economic system based on wide-flung and sustainable use took over, so that religion ceased being a criterion (if it ever had been). The Southeast Asian management systems survived the coming of Islam and Christianity. Muslim and Christian areas I studied in 1970–1971 were as successful as Buddhist and animist ones at maximizing yields while minimizing environmental damage. Islam, though not specifically teaching nonviolence toward animals, at least forms a powerful solidary bond for community and a force for rational management of resources. The Southeast Asian traditional forms of Islam that I knew and studied in Malaysia and Sumatera in 1970–1971 were environmentally and ecologically sensitive.

Religion still matters in some areas: the Hindu-Buddhists of Bali (Lansing 1991, 2006), the animist groups, and the smaller local Christian groups and Muslim sects have resisted much better than the mainstream social groups, including Javanese and urban Malays (cf. Dove 2011; Li 2007).

Buddhism teaches care for all beings and has been a great source of support for saving trees. It teaches reverence for life, though it teaches neither conservation per se nor love of nature per se. In fact, it teaches that one should *not* have such attachments to evanescent things. However, it has merged everywhere with local spirit cults, including tree veneration. This has led to preserving sacred trees and groves, a technique recently elevated to enormous scales in Thailand, where the king and the Buddhist religious communities designated vast areas of forests sacred to protect them from rampant logging (Darlington 2013; Yos 2008:108–109). Myanmar has now adopted the technique, and the Burmese Buddhist clergy and laity is moving rapidly to save trees and other living beings (Chong 2012).

Even the Islamic areas have these heritages. Most of them also had a liberal form of Islam, tolerant of local custom (*adat*) and strongly promoting pro-social values. These latter included considerate care for personal and community resources. Thrift in one's own life and thoughtfulness about other peoples' livelihoods was enjoined. In my research in Malaysia and Indonesia, I encountered individuals, sects, and movements that were actively pro-environment. Their influence on local culture was more visible a generation ago, before extremist, hostile Islam was propagated from Saudi Arabia.

Southeast Asian cultures often possess an explicitly conservationist ideology. Among settled wet-rice civilizations, the Balinese have a religion that involves water management for optimal ecological performance (Lansing 1987, 1991, 2006), and their Hindu-Buddhist traditions involve respect for life and care for living things. The Thai and their neighbors also have complex religious rituals associated with irrigation and rice (Hamilton 2003; Yos 2003, esp. pp. 171 ff., 195 ff.). These beliefs are quite different from those of North America and of the modern environmental movement, but they actually work better in terms of performance; they have protected a fragile environment for centuries under conditions of dense population and heavy use.

Widespread is an idea that the forest is the domain of spirits, the rice fields and villages are the domain of humans. The Thai traditionally believed the *pa* "forest" was a wild, disordered, uncontrolled space that was the realm of spirits, as opposed to the orderly, controlled, managed world of paddies, orchards, and towns, though hermits and monks found in the forest a proper habitat (Pinkaew

2001; see esp. pp. 66–68). However, they conserved watershed forests, utility forests, and sacred forests (Yos 2003:35). This attitude was replaced in the twentieth century by a view that reclassified *thammachat* (a concept roughly equivalent to "nature"—the wonderful big world out there) as *sappayakon thammachat* "natural resources," mere commodities (Pinkaew 2001:13). The spirits lost ground in a literal Weberian disenchantment. This led to a change from letting forests be, to be cropped on long cycles, to active logging, and then to massive interference with local peoples because of greatly exaggerated claims that they damaged the forest by shifting cultivation.

The Karen, hill people living in the border zone between Thailand and Burma, have a similar system (Pinkaew 2001, esp. pp. 144–151). They love and protect forests, seeing them as sacred and valuable. They are aware of, and sensitive to, wildlife and watershed protection values. They protect forests where streams join (Yos 2008:104), presumably for the same reason the Chinese do: to protect the watercourse and water supply. They have a complex typology of forests. This includes a distinction between male forests (warmer, taller, often drier) and female ones (moister, nearer water, shady, with rich soil and many animals; Pinkaew 2001:148, 200). This is recognizably similar to, and surely related to, the Chinese distinction of *yang* and *yin*. My analysis of satellite photographs on Google Maps shows that Karen areas of Thailand stand out for their largely intact forests.

Most impressive of all, perhaps, is a practice reported for one group (the Pwo Karen): They "periodically thank the forest for the bounty that it provides them by turning over to the forest and forest animals an entire swidden, compete with standing crops" (Dove 2011:277, summarizing ethnography of J. Jorgenson).

The Karen and Akha also have elaborate and precise classifications of regrowing swiddens (Wang 2013; Yos 2008:102); like the Maya, they know every stage and manage it for production. Watershed forests and ridgetop forests have protective spirits. The Karen are learning from the Thai to protect forests by Buddhist ordination (Yos 2003:55). Often, trees are planted and grow to be useful forest additions—a practice found all over Asia. Another Karen practice with widespread analogues is placing the umbilicus of a newborn baby in a tree in a special forest. The forest is then saved for the child; it protects him or her spiritually, and cutting it could kill the child (Yos 2003, 2008:104). (The practice of putting the umbilicus or placenta in, or burying it under, a growing tree—usually revered thereafter—is known from Asia to Europe to Native California; I have even encountered it among modern Euro-Americans.)

The Hmong, though among the less good at preserving forests, have a rather similar rule to the Northwest Coast Native Americans' rules in regard to hunting: "Every hunter must kill animals only to meet his subsistence needs. Whosoever hunts too much game will be turned into the same animal in the next life and will be hunted" (Yos 2003:12, 39). The Thai Lue have a similar ideology, protecting forests as sacred and as the proper realm for spirits, but also because of their benefits for watershed protection and nontimber plant and animal resources (Yos 2003, 2008).

The Akha, mid-level dwellers in the mountains where Yunnan meets Southeast Asian countries (Wang 2007, 2008, 2013; Lewis 2002; Sturgeon 2005; Yos 2003), have a similar view. They formerly had a small kingdom (Jadae) but later a more local government of religious leaders and chiefs (Wang 2013). The Akha are probably typical of long-settled hill peoples in having a complex belief in spirits that guard and protect trees, wildlife, and forests, and that avenge themselves on humans who damage that half of the world. They hold that humans and spirits (*nae,* cognate with Burman *nat*) divided up the world in the beginning, with the spirits getting the forests and the humans getting the fields.

The Akha see the forests as beautiful and lovable, unlike the Thai, but also see the forests as spirits' rather than humans' realm, and therefore daunting. Night is also the spirits' property, so people try not to be out late. The Akha divided their landscape into five: villages, sacred sites, protected forests, other forests, and arable land (Wang 2013). The village is surrounded by a *puchang,* a grove where the local guardian spirit dwells. Another type of sacred and protected land is the *lawbim,* the cemetery. Certain trees are sacred, notably the large banyan-type figs, as elsewhere in south and east Asia. In the protected but not sacred forests, one can collect but not log; these are largely watershed-protective forests. Protecting figs and other large trees naturally leads to saving large tracts of forest.

Arable land is owned by the *yawsang* spirits, which must be asked permission for use and then offered sacrifices—a practice strikingly similar to the Maya reverence for the spirits of the fields and forests. Sacred and protected animals include lorises, hornbills, certain wild geese, rhinos, pangolins, eagles, crows, peacocks, wildcats, wild buffaloes, and others (Wang 2008:13, 2013). Water sources, and caves into which streams vanish, are sacred. Areas where animals drink or bathe, or where they get salt, are protected. All are domains of the *nae,* and misfortune would occur to anyone ruining them. Landslides are caused by dragons (as in Chinese belief) and thus are protected ground. *Daw* rules—taboos enforced by spirits—protect pregnant and mating animals and enforce respect and taking no more than necessary. No one may take more than nine large animals in a year. Rattan, a commercial product, is carefully managed. Folklore and epics speak somewhat of this, though more often concern human affairs; on the other hand, they deal with animals' spirits, powers, and sentience (Lewis 2002; Wang 2008). Recent changes have led to loss of belief and consequent reduction in spirit groves to tiny remnants (Wang 2013). This has been blamed locally for floods and droughts; some are aware that the link is real but is due to scientific causes instead of (or as well as) spirits.

Several other Yunnan groups have similar ideas, and have conserved their forests extremely well until recent times (Pei 2010). Indeed, Yunnan may have been even more successful than other Southeast Asian areas that supported large, dense populations over thousands of years with almost no major damage to the ecology. This conservationist attitude extends to neighboring Tibet, which has a completely different ecology but had the same value on preserving it until Communist takeover (Huber 1999; Salick et al. 2005; Studley 2010).

Modern life has not been easy on this protected landscape; missionaries oppose spirits, and the Chinese Communist government cut down the groves and forced or encouraged planting commercial rubber instead.

Some hill peoples have a reputation as "eaters of the forest." This is often mere blaming poor people for deforestation actually caused by the state and by large-scale interests (Dove 2011; Pinkaew 2001). However, there are some genuine problems. Some rapidly expanding mountain peoples, largely forced out of China by military and political troubles, have devastated large areas, in marked contrast to the long-settled hill peoples of the region. Pinkaew studied the long-established, broadly "conservationist" Karen of west Thailand; satellite photographs there show magnificent forest with few clearings in this area. However, on satellite images and in the field, I have seen far more devastated zones not far to the northwest, where newer groups with much less local attachment have come in. Pioneer fringes in east Indonesia have also had major problems.

ARTS REPRESENTING IDEOLOGY

The Art of Rice (Hamilton 2003) shows how elaborate the representation systems are. Rituals for the rice goddess are everywhere. Out of consideration for her, the rice is cut with small reaping knives, which leads to almost no harvest loss, and also preserves the straw intact; it is a major resource. Also, the best and most beautiful ears of rice are the ones where she has nested for the coming year, so they are selected and saved for seed. The obvious selective advantages of this practice are widely known and are believed to prove the goddess's favor. I suspect this belief survives even where modern genetics is known. It has persisted in spite of snobbish dismissal by introduced religions and modern science. Why should one particular bunch of rice have the best genes? If it was not deliberate choice by the beautiful young girl who hovers on misty moonlit nights over the crop, what could have singled that bunch out?

Specific rituals for her are diverse. In one community, at the beginning of the harvest season, a white stone representing her is thrown into the river, and young men dive for it (Hamilton 2003). The Freudian implications of this have not escaped the local people. Some Karen select a youth to make seven planting holes and a maiden to plant rice seeds in them, as the beginning of the rice planting season. A ceremony is performed over these. The rice maiden then descends from the "Elephant star"—a star (alas, not identified in text) where she dwells—and gives fertility to the whole field (Yos 2003:146).

As elsewhere in the world, breakdown of community, loss of local spirit beliefs, and agricultural and rural degradation and deterioration have all come in the last few decades. They mutually exacerbate each other in a vicious cycle.

Southeast Asia has a landscape art rather similar to, and heavily derivative of, the art of India and China, but more important may be the sheer significance of fine art goods in Southeast Asian culture. Especially noteworthy are textiles. A single textile might take years to produce. This is one region of the world where textiles, not painting or sculpture, is the most pervasive visual art. This is recognized by the Malay saying on poverty: "Even though ten ships come, the dogs have no loincloths but their tails." The ships are understood to be carrying fine imported fabrics.

The emphasis on quality rather than quantity, and on beauty made from ordinary materials rather than expensive mass-produced junk, fits perfectly with Southeast Asia's cultural patterns of conservation and wise use. The contrast with America's ugly and wasteful status displays (McMansions, yachts...) could not be stronger.

Southeast Asia does not have a special literary or philosophical tradition of love of nature per se. On the other hand, the Buddhist teaching stories, such as the widespread "Jataka tales" of the Buddha's former births, involve respect for all beings and compassion toward them. This is not just nonviolence. It involves an injunction to be proactively caring. This has animated wildlife and tree conservation through the region.

A far older tradition involves use of vivid natural images as parallels for human love and other social matters. Universal from China to Indonesia is a characteristic quatrain form drawing an explicit metaphoric connection, and typically sung in courtship or in boy-girl dance parties:

> Hendak gugor, gugor-lah nangka
> Jangan menimpa si-dahan pauh.
> Hendak tidor, tidor-lah mata,
> Jangan di-kenang orang yang jauh.

> Then fall, fall, jackfruit,
> Just don't fall on the delicate pauh tree.
> Then sleep, sleep, eyes,
> Just don't think of the one far away.
> (Hamilton 1959:13, my translation)

I have chosen this example partly for the beauty of the sounds of the Bahasa Malaysia original, which are fortunately quite accessible to a non-Bahasa-speaking reader; the letters are pronounced as in Italian. Note those four consecutive internal rhymes in the last line. Similar songs—same rhythm, same type of imagery—are found from ancient China to modern Indonesia. (In fact, something like them is worldwide—my Appalachian mountain forebears and my Maya friends have the same kind of courting verses! Truly, human minds do run in the same channels.)

In Vietnam this tradition served as a foundation on which to build a great structure of Chinese and Chinese-style poetry, often involving more explicit—and largely Buddhist-derived—love and protection of nature. The folk tradition is more indigenous and more directly concerned with managing the environment and motivating people to do so.

THE MODERN WORLD COMES

Comparison of Southeast Asia and Europe shows the incredible persistence of systems that tightly integrate economic and technological forms, social institutions, and ideological beliefs. These self-maintaining systems take on a life of their own. Development becomes "path dependent" and the resource production system is a "lock-in." Imagine trying to change the American farming system to the Southeast Asian one. Changing the Southeast Asian one to the plantation-monocrop model has been a very long, slow, painful process, involving incredible social injustice and cruelty as well as the total destruction of nature and environment in the affected parts of the region.

The real contrast seems to be that, compared with wheat-cattle farming, rice agriculture is easier to intensify and rice farmers are harder to rule. Thus the regimes cannot so easily impose estate agriculture. In Southeast Asia they tried hard, but proved too weak to make it stick. In China, they tried and succeeded, but the economic and political problems were overwhelming. Chinese emperors from the beginning onward generally favored small intensive farming, which made them supportive of the wet-rice world, in spite of their frequent complaints about the difficulty of controlling it.

The fact that there is not some mysterious superiority to the Asian psyche is shown by the speed with which the very worst of the West was imposed in colonial and postcolonial times. All it took was a government strong enough to force uneconomic behavior on the people. Colonial regimes were frankly racist; postcolonial ones have their own systems of patronage. The term *crony capitalism* was coined in and for Southeast Asia.

Where left to themselves, Southeast Asians responded to the Western world by incorporating its crops and animals into their own agriculture. Maize, manioc, chocolate, rubber, turkeys, and every other worthwhile New World domesticate were integrated into the system.

Southeast Asian farmers remain desperately poor, and Anglo-American ones are rich, but this is politics, not ecology, at work. There are enough rich Asians and poor Americans to prove that many times over.

Thus it is clear, as in other cases, that the real key is community management versus either individual or remote top-down management. Community solidarity is maintained by both institutional ties (here, largely kin) and collective representations. Without those it fails.

This is particularly true in rice agriculture, which requires intensive labor—a vast workforce, or expensive and complex machinery, or both. Wheat is the other extreme, producing heavily with very little labor or fertilizer, and therefore an ideal crop for extensive (as opposed to intensive) agriculture on individual farms.

Tragically, Southeast Asia's superb management systems are dying fast. Colonial regimes and repression devastated them (see, e.g., Geertz 1963; Li 2007). The Western strategy came in with colonialism, but has really flourished—rather ironically—since "independence" (note scare quotes). Westernized agriculture in the region has generally destroyed forests, mangroves, prairies, marshes, traditional cultivation, and indeed everything except whatever monocrop was wanted by world trade: rubber, sugar, coffee, palm oil, and so on. It has generally been as wasteful as possible in using and processing these, and meanwhile has destroyed local environments and ruined local cultures (Adas 1974; Dove 2011; Geertz 1963; Li 2007; Peluso 1992; Tsing 2005). It is surely no accident that so many of the best studies of the destructive effects of modernization come from this region. The ideology, propagated by colonial administrators and developers, outran the economics. People converted from a stable, successful system to an unstable, dubious one on the basis of promises and status emulation. Some have prospered; most have not.

Religion has lost some of its protective value. When modernization brought catastrophe in the form of total environmental destruction for monocrop agriculture or mining, Buddhists, Confucians, Christians, and Muslims all got swept up in the process. New and deeply problematic forms of Islam and Christianity invaded; they teach intolerance of anyone outside the narrowest confines of the faith and indifference to the environment, in very sharp contrast to older forms of Islam and Christianity in the region. (This comes largely from personal research; it is inadequately reported in the literature, much of which is by people who had minimal contact with earlier local forms of Islam and who often compound ignorance by wrongly thinking that modern Salafism and Wahhabism are "traditional" or "fundamentalist" Islam, instead of new movements pushing the bounds of orthodoxy. See also Wang 2013, on Christianity; compare the new, environmentally callous movements he records with, for example, the more sensitive Christianity of the Philippines.)

In Thailand, for example, forests survive and flourish in swidden areas, but the lowlands are deforested for wet rice. Modernity makes things worse; comparing my photographs in 1970 with observations and satellite photographs in 2010, I found that mangroves gave way to shrimp farms, orchards to factories, sacred trees to wider roads, and everything to urban sprawl—which has run far beyond urban areas, especially as factories move away from pollution control. Even the intensively cultivated areas have been stripped of trees.

In the Thai highlands, minorities suffer. The Karen faced conflict and dispossession by Thai foresters who blamed their swiddening (Pinkaew 2001; Yos 2008). This led to almost surrealist levels of cluelessness when Thailand's forestry department restricted Karen cultivation and yet planted pine trees, which—as the Karen correctly recognized—are less conducive to biodiversity and more prone to fire (Yos 2008; my wife and I are personally familiar with the area in question and can vouch for the accuracy here). The resulting burns will dwarf swidden burning into insignificance. One might also mention that Thailand's great forest product was teak, now gone because of overcutting. Yet teak is a fire-follower, not an old-growth forest tree. Its former abundance was clearly due to swiddening. In Laos, I have observed dozens of small groves of teak grown deliberately by local farmers on old swidden fields. By contrast, Thailand's foresters until recently planted not only pine but the even more fire-prone and useless eucalyptus—the favorite tree of incompetent foresters everywhere. It grows fast and looks impressive, but the species grown outside Australia usually have no wildlife or timber value and little value even as firewood.

The sorry history of oil palm—recently a favorite fat for uses ranging from margarine to biodiesel—is the extreme example. Vast oil-palm monocrop plantations now cover much of lowland Malaysia and Indonesia. Local farmers have lost their lands or seen their lands ruined. Processing waste—most of the actual palm fruit—has destroyed the fish in many rivers and streams. American and European food processing firms have profited enormously. A few local businessmen and plantation owners have profited a bit. All other locals have lost out, often being completely ruined.

Between plantation agriculture, predatory and destructive logging, military actions, and other interferences, the incredibly rich forests of the region (especially Malaysia and Indonesia) are gone forever, to the enormous loss of all future generations. Not only is the benefit/cost ratio poor; the benefits have largely been captured outside the region. Typically, local people were displaced, or at best alienated from the (few) income streams generated. This led to devastating poverty for the many, while small numbers of outsiders gathered the profits—and this is spite of the clearly superior regimes of production of the locals.

Increasingly, protected areas face a phenomenon I have seen among the Maya: Local people who were excellent managers of the land were forced off to "protect" the forests. The people are then forced into poaching. Having lost all real ties to the land, they destroy it instead of conserving it. Hoang Cam (2007) provides an excellent study of this process in Vietnam. Alternatively, the outsiders, from local elites to colonial masters, take over the land and ruin it for their own profits (Dove 2011; again as in rural Mexico).

The majority of the population is as poor as ever, but without the local subsistence resources that once gave them simple but beautiful and satisfactory lives. A system that could have taught the world has instead been ruined for a handful of palm oil.

Geertz summed all this up in a classic line, even more true today than when he wrote it fifty years ago:

"The real tragedy ... is not that the peasantry suffered. It suffered much worse elsewhere, and, if one surveys the miseries of the submerged classes ... generally, it may even seem to have gotten off relatively lightly. The tragedy is that it suffered for nothing" (Geertz 1963:143).

CHAPTER EIGHT

The Western World

> What we call Man's power over Nature turns out to be a power exercised
> by some men over other men with Nature as its instrument
> *(C. S. Lewis; quoted by Peter Coates*
> *1998:46 from Lewis's The Abolition of Man,*
> *Oxford University Press, 1944, p. 28)*

THE ANCIENT NEAR EAST

Obviously, a chapter cannot possibly chronicle the whole history of Western
attitudes toward nature. Nor is there a need to; the job has been done by Clarence Glacken (1967) and Peter Coates (1998). I will confine myself to discussing a particular tension that they missed, between two worldviews, and how
that and the Western agricultural system played out in producing our modern
environmental situation.

Northern Europe, and probably all of Europe, had in ancient times a variant of
the Old Northern view. We know this from the wide occurrence of classic folktales
associated with that view: the swan maiden and Orpheus stories, stories of animals
transforming into humans and vice versa, near-identical tales of floods and giants,
and countless more. The trickster fox is widespread in Old Northern realms, grading
into the trickster raccoon-dog of Japan and the trickster coyote of North America.

A very different view, widely dominant in the world today, later began to develop within the urbanized Near East and Mediterranean, long after civilization began there. It sees the human world as sharply separate from the natural. The natural world is hostile, inimical, and unpleasant. The job of humans is to conquer nature and impose a fully artificial environment. The city is idealized; the agricultural countryside is picturesque but backward; the wilderness is horrific. Much of this attitude is summarized in the word *civilization*, from Latin *civitas*, "city."

The civilized lands that turned against the old nature-worshiping view comprised the *oikumene* of the Greeks. This was the urban-civilized world they knew, centering of course on Greece, and stretching from Persia and Egypt to Spain and Italy. North of this, the Old Northern ideals continued.

The fearful, oppositional view of nature appears from humanity's earliest texts, those of ancient Mesopotamia (Herren 2002). Anthropomorphic gods help humanity, slaying evil nonhuman deities like the chthonic dragon Tiamat. Yet even the anthropomorphic gods are often savage and vengeful (for this and what follows, see also Dalley 1989; Fontenrose 1981; Jacobsen 1987; Kovacs 1985; Wolstein and Kramer 1983).

The earlier generation among these scholars often contrasted this fear of nature with the ancient Egyptian view of nature as benign. This is overdrawn and oversimplistic, but there is something to it; the fear of storms, floods, and wild animals is stronger in Mesopotamian writings, whereas Egypt, with its animal gods and divine sun and sky, seems much more positive about the nonhuman world. One can assume that ancient Egypt, an African society with animal powers and gods and dependence on the natural Nile flood, was much more pro-environment. Egypt's extensive literature, however, reflects a Mesopotamian-style world of cities, towns, and small gardens. Pharaohs are shown hunting in reed beds, but otherwise wild nature barely exists. Egypt consisted (and still consists) of an extremely fertile, and totally cultivated, valley complex, surrounded by uninhabitable and barely traversable deserts. The wild was therefore not a place one could inhabit, let alone love. Later desert communities of monks depended on food from the settlements and viewed their life in the desert as penance and suffering, not return to idyllic nature.

The most ancient substrate of Mesopotamian myth seems close to the Old Northern view. In addition to Tiamat, there are several deities that seem like

Old Northern spirit beings. The hunter-shepherd Dumuzi, who is transformed into animals and then winds up in the underworld with the dead, seems an Old Northern spirit-traveler related to Orpheus. If true, this would prove what seems fairly clear in any case: the nature-fearing urban mythology and management system developed with cities and high culture.

This latter worldview developed in an area where settled urbanites traded with rough hill tribes, often trading grain for animal products, and this trade was religiously represented (Kramer 1955). Cities are idealized, the loci of all things good. The countryside is rough and uncouth; the mountain wilderness is literally beyond the pale—the fences that protect human property.

At least some of the hostility to wilderness was evidently due to fear of such hill men. The thoughtful Native American biologist Ray Pierotti has suggested that dependence on domestic animals may have been a factor: people learned to dominate, rule, and control animals rather than living with autonomous and uncontrolled wildlife (Pierotti 2011). At least as important was the exceedingly narrow base of species on which the ancient Near East depended. Plant staples were wheat and barley. These, plus chickpeas, lentils, dates, and a few minor items, were about all the early Mesopotamians and Egyptians had by way of crops. They had flax for cloth and sesame for oil; the word *sesame* goes back to Sumerian. Domestic animals were limited to dog, sheep, goat, cow, and pig. (Donkey, horse, and chicken, as well as crops like rye, oats, fruit trees, and olives, came later, but still in quite early times in the Near East. On Mesopotamian agriculture, see Potts 1997.) The hills were relatively nonproductive.

None of these crops yields heavily per acre, especially under ancient Near Eastern conditions (500 kg/ha was a good yield), and the highly intensive agriculture of East Asia was not possible. Irrigation on rich soil allowed fairly impressive yields, and barley would grow fairly well even on the worst soils, but extensive fields of rather low-yielding grains were the rule. Animals grazed thin, dry upland pastures, and often wintered on fallow fields, creating a mutual dependence between migrant herders and settled farmers.

This set the stage for a dependence on an extremely narrow species base, with crops typically grown in large monocrop fields. This is still characteristic of the Western world, the world whose agriculture is derived from the ancient Near East. Today, most of the world's food is provided by the three great staples of the three great agricultural realms: the wheat of west Eurasia, the rice of east Eurasia, and the maize of the New World. With South American potatoes and manioc and African millets and sorghum, these provide almost all the world's starch calories. This dependence on a few crops and domestic animals can encourage a negative attitude toward nature, which must be destroyed to create monocrop fields. More surely, the dependence on a wide subsistence base, including wild resources, lies behind good environmental management, from

Native America to Southeast Asia to Japan. Most of East Asia depends on rice, but it has always been grown through intensive cultivation in small fields, and it can dominate only in irrigated valleys. Moreover, it is not rich in vitamins or minerals. Because of these factors, it is always grown in complementarity with a vast range of other crops. In contrast, wheat and barley can take over whole countrysides, and cattle and sheep can occupy any land too rough for those crops and can provide most other needed nutrients.

The stage was also set for vast monocrop plantations owned by absentee elite landlords and worked by landless, impoverished labor forces. Agricultural estates in ancient Sumer and Egypt were often owned by temples or by ruling elite individuals. The extremely fertile alluvial fields and the extensive wheat-barley agriculture allowed this, indeed made it a likely outcome. Temple fields were worked by slaves or landless workers. The estate-owning elites, priestly or secular, had the power in society. One assumes that then as now the small farmers were numerous and productive, but their political power was almost nil compared with that of the great landlords. The pattern had been set, and it exists to this day in the Western and Westernized world.

In the *Epic of Gilgamesh* (Kovacs 1985; cf. Herren 2002), the hero is idealized as the perfect civilized man. His companion Enkidu is the archetypal wild man, equivalent to Bigfoot or the Yeti. Enkidu is a protector of the wild animals. He is hairy, uncouth, lustful, and so easily corrupted by alcohol that he is caught and tamed by beer left out for him. Enkidu is at his worst when he first confronts civilization. In the wild, he at least was innocent of alcohol and other urban temptations. This stereotype of civilization corrupting the "savage" and turning him to drink is still with us. Gilgamesh saves Enkidu and humanizes him. The two slay inhuman chthonic monsters and tame the wilderness. One monster they slay is Humbaba, the guardian of the cedars of Lebanon; is this a symbolic slaying of old conservation ideas? It certainly symbolizes the progressive cutting of the cedar forests, now reduced to a few scattered trees.

Wild men like Enkidu are part of folklore everywhere in the world, but only the Near East, and, later, Europe, made them important in myth. Later, the founders of social theory, more influenced by Mediterranean classical traditions than by reality, foolishly believed the stereotype of Natural Man as an uncouth loner. Hobbes's "warre of each against all" and Locke's original state of humanity stem from this stereotype, not from any reality. So does Freud's "Id." Roger Bartra (1994) provides a superb history of this idea. Through the influence of this urban tradition on the classical civilizations, it became part of the Western intellectual tradition, a major component of Western thought to this day.

Valuing individuals simply for being human is foreign to this tradition. Urbane heroes like Gilgamesh stand out against a faceless mass of ordinary people: slaves, commoners, urban masses. They can be killed with utter indifference.

From Gilgamesh to Roman circuses to Nietzsche to Hollywood, Western writers and audiences have adulated superheroes and reduced the rest to faceless masses that can die in thousands without anyone caring. The contrast between this and the Old Northern view is conspicuous (in spite of exceptions on both sides); in Old Northern stories, each individual has at least some value; victims and conquered enemies are often treated sympathetically.

This view probably matured in the Near East as the land became entirely tamed. Cities and cultivation spread wherever possible, and the desert wastes were either intensively grazed or feared as wild and evil. Mesopotamia obliterated most of its natural landscape early. The city-states were surrounded by a totally artificial environment of croplands, date orchards, and regular irrigation canals.

With civilization came a need for storage and distribution. Temples were probably instrumental in this—such is the traditional view, but inevitably the revisionists have gotten at it, and we are not as sure as we once were (Herren 2002; Potts 1997). In any case, the temples were part of the ruling system. The latter oversaw large estates, specialized in producing grain for the cities. Other official agencies oversaw gathering of grain, storing it, and dispersing it. Milk was increasingly processed into hard cheese, presumably invented at some point in this process for the express purpose of making dairy products storable. Perishable foods were not a part of this picture and thus were peripheralized.

Presumably even before cities, there had been a focus on storable foods. But with urbanization came the dependence of a huge population, including essentially all the elite, on foods that were gathered, stored, and distributed relatively far from their places of production. Five thousand years of intensification of this dynamic have brought us to America today, with its billionaire absentee landlords drawing more billions of dollars in direct and indirect subsidies for the production of "commodity crops"—staple grains, cotton, sugar, soybeans—and lack of support for other crops or for mixed farming (Imhoff 2012).

Probably the little-known societies of Anatolia were fonder of nature, at least judging from surviving art. Early sites from Göbekli Tepe (Mann 2011) to Çatal Hüyük (Hodder 2004) show animal figures, but these tend to be menacing ones, making inferences difficult. Cybele, the west Anatolian mother goddess, was a protector of animals (Fontenrose 1981:216), but she was also a terrifying figure, demanding castration of her priests. Thus Mesopotamia was surrounded by societies more aware of human embeddedness in nature, but with ideologies little known because of limited evidence.

The Bible shows a progression. The earliest books, including the Jewish laws listed in Leviticus and Deuteronomy, show strong reverence for nature and protection of trees, crops, and animals (Tirosh-Samuelson 2002). However, a conflicted attitude is reflected in the first two books of Genesis, which give two quite different accounts of the creation. In the former, God tells humans (both sexes, created and enjoined together) to "subdue" the earth and "have dominion" over the animals (Genesis 1:28). In the second, God tells Adam (not Eve) to take care of the garden of Eden, "to dress it and to keep it" (Genesis 2:15), but to avoid certain fruit; thus man (*sic*) is the Lord's steward, *not* the owner or dominator, and has to take care of it for the Lord. He does not have free license to use everything as he sees fit and gets humanity in serious trouble when he disobeys.

Traditionally the differences were ascribed to the period when the Israelites were divided into two kingdoms, Israel on the north and Judah on the south. The "domination" view was supposed to be Judah's origin myth; modern scholars tend to ascribe it to later priestly authors during or after the Babylonian Captivity (Hillel 2006). The "stewardship" view was Israel's, and probably the older and more traditional view, dominant before—and in most places after—the two-kingdom period.

In any case, it is the view that animates the Bible in general. From the earliest sections (notably the rules in Leviticus for taking care of livestock) to the latest (Jesus on grapevine management), the Bible is solidly for stewardship and against abuse (Borowski 1998; Hessel and Reuther 2000; Hillel 2006; Tirosh-Samuelson 2002). There is never any question: the earth is the Lord's, and humanity is a steward, not an owner. Yet, also, "domination" is frequently mentioned. Judah's view, apparently more "priestly" and thus more influenced by late Babylonian civilization, never lost out entirely.

The conflict between Judah's and Israel's rules has been with the Western world ever since. Judah was less enlightened about nature, but by our modern standards more enlightened about women—Adam and Eve were created together. Israel was the reverse; it is from Israel's version that we get Adam's earlier creation, Eve's later manufacture from a spare rib bone, and Eve's weakness in the face of temptation.

Moreover, the early books of the Hebrew Bible contain no fewer than forty references to cutting down sacred groves or trees. These were the groves, trees, or poles of the Canaanite fertility goddess (or goddesses), Asherah (Hadley 2000). Yahweh himself once had a companion Asherah. Asherah became anathema quite early, as the Israelites moved toward monotheism. Thus an antipathy to sacred groves entered the Judeo-Christian tradition and has resurfaced many times since, especially when Christianity expanded at the expense of tree-worshiping pagan religions in Europe and more recently in Africa and Asia. Trees are almost always described in very favorable terms in the Bible, but sacred groves and idols of wood are not.

Yahweh in those days had plenty of company; the Hebrew Bible continues to refer to divinity in the plural—*Elohim,* "gods"—throughout the first books. He was the main god of the Israelites, in rivalry and frequent war with other gods.

He became *the* God only quite late. King Solomon, persuaded by his foreign wives (women again!), worshiped "Milcom the abomination of the Amonites" and other "abominations"—that is to say, rival gods (1 Kings 11).

This is said not just to qualify what would otherwise be the sort of bland overgeneralizations about worldview that makes anthropologists grit their teeth. ("Western civilization has always held … " "Capitalism thinks that … ") Quite the opposite. The whole dynamic of Western environmental thought has been *caused* by these conflicting views. They are most sharply put in the Bible, but they are also seen in the endless tension between the Old Northern view and the ancient Near Eastern view, throughout European history. They are also seen in the tension between African roots and borrowed Mesopotamian ideas in ancient Egypt. Strongly environment-conscious and strongly antienvironmental views both became established by the time of Jesus and have remained in dialogue since. We are drawing on two quite different traditions here, and, if Mesopotamian literature and the better-known cases of Greece and Rome are any guides (see below), these traditions are ancient and widespread ones.

Awareness of this tension of views caused people to create nature poetry, conservation, and environmentalism. They were forced to think about the issue. They were confronted with extreme antienvironmental and anticonservation positions.

East and Southeast Asia, always the counterfoil to the West, never had to confront extreme antienvironmental positions. This is, I believe, why they never developed local conservationist movements as such, until the west brought them antienvironmentalism and then environmentalism. A general background in Hindu and Buddhist religions and local spirit cults did the job adequately. In China, traditional management was far from perfect, and the same dialogues between transforming and protecting took place, but the amplitude was far less; the wrenching change from explicit "harmony and balance" (*heping*) in all things, including ecological management, to Mao's "struggle against nature" was late and extremely dramatic. In Japan, the change from superb fisheries management in the Tokugawa period (Ruddle and Akimichi 1984) to cold, systematic fishing out of tuna and whales has been almost as dramatic a change, though less public.

The later books of the Bible, and especially the New Testament, are more human-centered than the early books. The New Testament has enough references to crops and husbandry to suggest that the old sense of protection was maintained, but the Gospels and Epistles are almost totally devoid of any references to nature. There are a few key lines, however, especially the injunction to the angels in the Book of Revelation: "Hurt not the earth, neither the sea, nor the trees" until the final end of the world (Revelation 7:2). The message is for humans as well as angels. Yet humans are still sharply separated from nature. In later Christian thinking, this position became far more extreme: Humans (or at least Christians of one's own sect) need total unqualified love, but nature is of no concern at all.

The Near East developed a strong ideology of care for domestic species but not for wild ones. The Mesopotamian texts and the Bible teach care for livestock and attention to crops (Hessel and Reuther 2000), but do not detail any care for wild resources, though some management of forests must be assumed. Nomads care for grass resources, but I do not recall a passage in the Bible or the Mesopotamian literature that counsels caring for wild resources other than major trees for lumber and grass for grazing. The Psalms and the Song of Solomon are full of exquisitely beautiful nature imagery, but the Psalms, Prophets, and many other books are also full of horror at lions, storms, deserts, and other natural problems. One gets the strong sense of a people deeply moved by the beauty of nature, but scared of its stronger manifestations, helpless before them (except through the Lord's protection), and basically wishing that all were cultivated and settled. Nothing is worse than "a waste."

When the Lord wishes to do His worst to a people, He makes their home a wasteland. Thus Isaiah: "For it is the day of the Lord's vengeance ... Zion ... shall lie waste ... the cormorant and the bittern shall possess it; the owl also and the raven shall dwell in it ... " (Isaiah 34:8–11). Similarly, Jeremiah says that the man who knows not God "shall be like the heath in the desert, and shall not see when good cometh; but shall inhabit the parched places in the wilderness, in a sad land and not inhabited." But he who trusts in the Lord "shall be as a tree planted by the waters, and that spreadeth out her roots by the river, and shall not see when heat cometh, but her leaf shall be green; and shall not be careful in the year of drought, neither shall cease from yielding fruit" (Jeremiah 17:6–8).

These verses show a thorough knowledge of irrigation. Bad irrigation leads to salination; foolish misuse of water has made the land a salt marsh, home of the cormorant and bittern ("bittern" in English is related to "bittern" for concentrated salt brine). The Lord punishes stupid environmental misuse, which becomes a perfect symbol for faithlessness, here as in many biblical passages.

Yet, in extremely dramatic contrast to this, the Bible includes some of the greatest nature poetry in the world. The 104th Psalm is perhaps the finest:

"Bless the Lord, O my soul. O Lord my God, thou art very great; thou are clothed with honour and majesty,

Who coverest thyself with light as with a garment; who stretchest out the heavens like a curtain:

Who layeth the beams of his chambers in the waters; who maketh the clouds his chariot; who walketh upon the wings of the wind ...

The high hills are a refuge for the wild goats; and the rocks for the conies [rock hyraxes]....

The young lions roar after their prey, and seek their meat from God.

The sun ariseth, they gather themselves together, and lay them down in their dens...."

The attention to the lowly hyrax (an unclean animal to the Israelites), and the sympathetic portrayal of God's care for lions, are particularly noteworthy, but the whole poem is a masterpiece of composition, and its exalted view of nature has never been surpassed in any world literature. Yet it is not alone; other psalms, such as the 23rd, approach it in awareness of nature and equal it in sensitivity, and Isaiah cold move from lamenting waste to seeing a paradise in which—admittedly unnaturally—the lion would lie down with the lamb. Other Near Eastern poetry has similar passages; Akhenaten's hymns to the sun are quite similar to Psalm 104.

These visions have colored perceptions of nature ever since. One can, for instance, see these psalms in the Romantic movement's nature poetry and art in the nineteenth century. Still, negative attitudes toward the wild have, for better or worse, remained the view in most of the Christian West. They are displayed today by the many antienvironmentalists, often militantly "Christian," who say conservationists "prefer bugs to people."

AGRARIAN EMPIRES

Over the long run, the choices that seemed reasonable and even necessary in the ancient Near Eastern river valleys and dry uplands cast a long shadow over the world. Economies based on plow agriculture are notably unfriendly to natural landscapes. The plow scars the soil (though early ones did so far less than later models). Intensive animal-rearing is needed to provide protein and also traction for the plow and other implements. The wheat-barley-cattle-sheep system, in particular, spread from the ancient Near East to Europe, and through central Asia to north China and north India. Everywhere, it brings wide destruction of nature and a history of large slave-worked estates. Such estates proved too unprofitable to retain in most of Asia, but they flourished in medieval Islam and in Europe. They finally took off beyond all measure in the New World. The wheat-cattle-plow system also correlates with the world's worst repression of women, which occurs in precisely those lands where that system has been longest established, but this may be correlation without causation. Certainly the plow itself is innocent; plow agriculture accompanies matrilineal societies with real female power in much of the rice-dependent parts of Asia. It is the whole Near Eastern plow-agriculture system that is problematic.

Latifundia flourished on such cultivation, and extensive cultivation and especially extensive herding thus became prestigious. Small-scale mixed farming was almost impossible in the great river valleys. The pressure to have huge grain-farming estates was too great. There was little space for small farming.

The latter flourished in the hilly regions outside the river valleys, as in Canaan and Israel. But it was always the recourse of the politically and economically weak. Thus, though generally much more intensive, it was devalued. It persisted, however, providing a way for more ecologically sensitive and sensible attitudes to prevail locally.

Bruce Lerro (2000) has pointed out a number of effects of the rise of kingdoms and then of empires. First, international trade and commerce skyrocketed in importance, especially in the Levant and Mesopotamia. This led to coined money, internationally recognized weights and measures, the alphabet (created by Phoenician sea-traders), mathematics, and a host of other highly analytic things. This in turn created a "hyperabstract" way of reasoning: trade elites and others involved in a highly rationalized, statistics-ridden economy learned to break the world down into commodities and measurements. The rise of formal logic, rational science, and rigid classification systems could not be far behind and was developed in such states as Athens—a polity based on sea trade. The same thing happened in China, with the central, well-to-do, trade-based states playing the Athenian role, and the rough frontier states acting like Sparta and Persia. However, China differs from the West in that neither religion nor philosophy ever cut nature off or developed a religious concept of "dominion" and exploitation.

Even in the old agrarian empires, the new economic world (math and all) distanced people from nature, reduced nature worship, and led to the rise of high gods—a quite literal rise, for they went off to the sky, increasingly banished from the immanent world of springs, mountains, and fields. Religion came to be more and more a matter of individuals dealing with a remote transcendent Deity, rather than societies dealing with fellow people who happened to be deer or oak trees or springs. (On this and what follows, see Bellah 2011.)

Of course the transition was slow, with the mercantile elites leading and the up-country peasants following—thousands of years later! Max Weber chronicled the end-point of the process in *The Protestant Ethic and the "Spirit" of Capitalism* (2002). This system spread to Europe and eventually affected even northwest Europe, by making a very few crops all-important. Northwest Europeans, for all their love of nature, have historically displayed "demonstrated preference" (economists' jargon for actually paying good money) for few crops beyond grain, meat, alcohol, and fuel crops, and later for cotton, sugar, tea, and other plantation products.

Mythology tracked all this. The gods are absorbed into a single high God, increasingly remote from humanity. He spoke directly to Moses, inspired later prophets, then became more and more distant—appearing again only in the form of Jesus (in Christianity) or in a final vocal message to Muhammad (in

Islam). He no longer talks to us, at least not publicly as of old. He leaves us cut off from both him and nature. Our elites are urbanites who rule from cities. We master the world by technology, destroying nature in the process. During the Roman Empire, the urban plan was projected on the countryside, through neatly gridded irrigation works, neatly row-planted orchards, and neatly terraced hillsides. This is with us today.

In short, the vices of modern Euro-American agriculture are not new and are not the result of some vast vague philosophy. They are not caused by capitalism, however much they have been exacerbated by it in the last few centuries. They are the result of practices that made good sense in the hierarchic, riverine world that was Western civilization 4,000 years ago. They came to provide a classic example of a "lock-in": an economic and technological fix, and its ideological representation, that becomes so dominant that everything else is premised on it.

Alfred Crosby (1986) described "ecological imperialism" in the Old World conquest and settlement of the New World, but something similar happened— though more slowly—as Near Eastern plants and animals took over Europe. Wheat, barley, sheep, goats, and the rest of the Near Eastern domesticates conquered the continent. Only cattle and swine were native to both regions. No significant crops were domesticated in Europe.

Near Eastern views of the world came to Europe not only with religious writings, but with all the science and agronomy that flowed in a vast stream from east to west throughout prehistory and history. These various views, in their turn, faced in Europe the people-in-nature, environmentally sensitive Old Northern views. We have much evidence of environmental overexploitation associated with cities even in ancient Greece, and from Imperial Rome onward the destructive, antinature view has dominated in much or most of urban Europe. The pro-nature view, supported by common experience of the need to manage and conserve, survived in rural areas everywhere, but flourished largely on the fringes, especially the Celtic and Germanic northwest and the Finnish and Balto-Slavic northeast, where the Old Northern view persisted.

Clarence Glacken, in his magistral summary of Western civilization's attitudes toward nature (1967), does not clearly separate these different worldviews. I see them as quite distinct, each with its own history. However, the two form a constantly braiding and rebraiding channel in Western history. Glacken is concerned not with pro- or antinature views, but with the ideas of nature as God's creation, as purposeful, as planned, and as influenced by people; he traces especially the steady rise of recognition that humans were altering the earth. In this, the two worldviews were united.

ANCIENT GREECE

The ancient Greeks apparently came into Greece from the north, bringing with them an Old Northern type of view. Proving the latter is their enormous range and variety of hunter stories in which the hunter, or huntress, or both, is transformed into an animal, star constellation, or natural feature; for Joseph Fontenrose (1981:253), "the hunter mediates between the savage and the civilized man." In my interpretation, the hunter in Greek myths mediates between the ancient nature-revering Old Northern worldview and the newer Western core antinature ideas coming from the Near East. Moreover, hunters and especially hunt goddesses such as Artemis (Marinatos 2000) are typically celibate (though sometimes far from so). The virginity of Artemis appears to be a function of progressive distancing of civilized Greeks from open sexuality, seen as wild or barbaric. With Fontenrose again, there may be "memories of hunting tabus" on sex (Fontenrose 1981:255); tabooing sex before hunting is virtually universal in the Old Northern world.

Shamanism, or something like it, existed in ancient Greece (Dodds 1951). The Orpheus story and other shamanistic elements have been considered specifically Thracian or Scythian (McEvilley 2002:105), apparently on no other grounds than that we know the Scythians had shamans. Surely, foundational myths would not have been borrowed late from "barbarians." There is every reason to believe they go back to, and before, the very roots of Indo-European culture. Either way, the magic musician who charms animals and can sing his way into the land of the dead is the absolute prototype of the shaman (cf. Humphrey 1996).

Another bit of Greek culture, which I take to be Old Northern, but which may be a later development, is individualism; I think Greek and Celtic individualism are both from a common root. Others think individualism evolved via heroes and hero-tales into the fully developed form seen only late in Greek, and, separately, Celtic cultures (Lerro 2000). The two views are not entirely mutually exclusive, because by any standards it is quite a journey from the raucous (and clearly ancient) autarky of myth and epic heroes to the self-conscious, philosophically constructed, politically socialized individualism of classical Athens.

Star tales—the myths that gave us astrology and constellations—are a mix of Mesopotamian originals, Old Northern myths, and Greek rationalism (cf. Thompson 1955-1958). Many beings transformed into stars. Gods also routinely transformed themselves into other natural forms; Zeus became a swan, a shower of gold, a bull, and various other commodities to get at women he wanted. Gods also transformed nymphs and mortals, often into trees or stones (Ovid 2000).

A classic Old Northern story recounts the pursuit by the great dog Lailaps of the savage Teumessian Fox (Fontenrose 1981; Ovid 2000:187–188); nothing could escape Lailaps, and nothing could catch the fox, so after a rousing chase the gods turned them into stone to avoid an impossible situation. This sort of animal tale, its paradox, and its ending in stone, are all standard in Old Northern myths. Indeed, such myths may be the source of Greek philosophy's love of paradoxes and contradictions.

Tribes of ancestral Greek invaders from the north, speaking a variety of dialects or closely related languages, quickly settled Greece and neighboring coasts and islands. There they met all manner of Mediterranean and Near Eastern views. They learned especially from the high civilizations of Babylon and Egypt, as Herodotus recorded (and possibly overstated). The assimilation was gradual and led to a spread of views, all held by someone, all mixed with each other, and many inconsistent. An individual (Plato, for one; Glacken 1967:121) might be able to advocate forest conservation on one hand, and idealize taming the wild on the other.

Greek agriculture ranged from small mixed farming to fairly substantial slave-worked estates. Most of the actual food seem to have come from the former. Factual accounts and idealized, poetic ones agree that the typical case was a small family growing grain, olives, figs, vines (for wine), a few animals (mostly sheep), a few onions and cabbages, and a few herbs and other assorted items.

The small mixed farm apparently owes its long career in the Western world to the logic of production; we know it from ancient Canaan, Greece, and Rome. It has generally dominated demographically but has been subjugated politically by the elite owners of great estates. Of course there was a continuum between tiny peasant holdings and the great estates of the rich. Intermediate-sized farms existed, such as the farm described by Xenophon in *Oikonomikos*. This work gave us the word *economics*, now far removed from Xenophon's usage of it. It is, in fact, the oldest known agricultural manual. It takes the form of a Socratic dialogue, with a farmer teaching Socrates by Socratic questioning (Xenophon 1990). Xenophon was obviously a successful and knowledgeable estate manager, and the dialogue is well worth reading, if only to see how sophisticated Greek farmers were. We know of earlier and fuller agricultural manuals, now lost.

The ancient Greeks were in a tension zone, and they knew it—idealizing nature, criticizing deforestation, but also idealizing the city and the intensively managed farm. The Greeks only slowly and imperfectly adopted the new Near Eastern view. The Greeks retained the classic swan-maiden and Orpheus myths, trance-speaking oracles, and other evidences of a shamanic past. As settled peoples, at first they celebrated the countryside. Homer and Hesiod sang of a rural world of beautiful and beloved fields and woods and of gods and spiritual forces inspiring this landscape.

Like the northern Europeans and the more distant Asian peoples, to say nothing of many Native American societies, the ancient Greeks worshiped tree spirits. They had a vast number of sacred groves (*alse,* sing. *alsos;* Bonnechere 2007). These fitted into a complex spiritual landscape that also held sacred springs, hills, rocks, and other features. Noteworthy among spirits were the oak-dwelling dryads (*drys* "oak"; cf. Celtic *drus*). This led to conservation (see poems in Jay 1981, and Jay 2006 for the general vision).

Few others poetized the oak so well, but the classic English folksong chorus "hey, derry, derry, down" began life as Celtic *hei deiri, deiri dun,* "oh the dark oak grove." The Celts, too, worshiped oaks.

The shamanistic stories make up a very old stratum of tales, probably much older than the Mesopotamian-sounding stories of human deities like Zeus, Aphrodite, and their outrageous kin. The tension between the views was quite clear to them and came out in such things as the conflicted view of Artemis. A fascinating mix of Old Northern and later urban views occurs in her story. She was, anciently, a protectress of the game, similar to the keepers of the game or lords of animals that Native Americans still respect. Artemis has been incorporated into the later myth cycles—but as a harsh, cruel, sexually frigid being, literally throwing would-be lovers to the dogs. Spirits of the animals are more or less friendly and protective in most of the world. Only late Mediterranean belief made Artemis, and her counterparts like Cybele, cruel.

Another Old Northern figure who suffered in translation was the animal trickster figure, who lies behind Pan, the goat-horned, goat-footed god who sends "panics" to scare people away from his haunts. (Humans, and other mammals, have an instinctive fear of dead-air spaces where they can hear the wind all around but cannot feel it on them. This fear evolved in animals that had to smell predators coming to keep themselves safe. Humans may well have the instinct, and certainly have long observed it in livestock. It is one origin of the idea of "panic.") Pan fell to being a mere figure of fun and then fell further to become the Christian Devil—with some help from his Celtic equivalent, the horned god Cernunnos. This is where old Satan got his horns, hooves, and tail. The iconic relationships of horned gods in ancient Europe remains controversial, but Pan was quite explicitly equated with the Devil by early Christian writers.

Theocritus in the third century BC perfected the genre of poetic idylls about nature, but he was an urbanite, writing in Alexandria of an impossibly romanticized Greek landscape that he may have remembered but did not describe from immediate experience. He writes of oak groves, quaint shepherds, and artless shepherdesses, not of the desert and delta landscapes he actually knew. His romanticizing of nature is nature-at-a-distance—a faraway ideal. This attitude begat Marie Antoinette's shepherdess costumes and Watteau's idealized paintings; these French urbanites read Theocritus, as well as countless lesser imitators. Later landscape painting and poetry was duly influenced. Modern urbanite environmentalism often shows his influence.

Thus Greece became culturally rather removed from nature. The long Greek debate over the human place in the world is with us today, and all sides in the environmental conflicts of our time can appeal to one or another Greek analog. Recent deforestation (McNeill 1992) has accelerated a process of slow ecological decline in Greece itself. This, however, has been exaggerated. Some accounts see Greece as having once been covered with lush forests. This is obviously wrong. The hot, dry lowlands and foothills can never have supported much more than brush and grass, and many montane areas, including the stereotypically idyllic Vale of Arcady, are too stony to have supported anything very lush.

Classic modes of thought varied from fascination with nature—as in Aristotle's writings—to a deep philosophical devaluing of nature. Even Aristotle concluded that all nature was made simply for human use, a standard position then and since (Glacken 1967:48). It will be remembered that Aristotle also found slavery reasonable, because many people were naturally slavish (Aristotle 2013); I suspect that C. S. Lewis's quote at the head of this chapter may have been written with Aristotle (among others) in mind.

This set the stage for later thought. As Juliet Clutton-Brock, leading expert on animal domestication, puts it: "Aristotle, who was born 384 BCE, believed that everything in nature had a purpose, and this purpose was for the benefit of mankind. . . . For more than 2,000 years, from writings that are even earlier than those of Aristotle . . . it was usual throughout the Western world to believe that the universe had been created in a 'Scale of Nature' or a 'Great Chain of Being' with 'man' at its pinnacle. The widespread view that the world is divided into the 'human,' which is inherently unnatural, and the 'animal,' which is natural, is the cultural inheritance from this historical premise and from the belief that humans are created in the image of God and have an everlasting soul, while animals are without souls" (Clutton-Brock 2012:1). Of course this later belief came after Aristotle, with the rise of Christianity, and especially after Descartes, as will appear below. The idea that humans are outside of and better than nature also gathered momentum with time. It was to fuse with the idea that "things of the flesh" are "evil," and thus that the natural or animal-like side of humanity—from sex to strong emotion, even love—is evil.

Pierre Hadot (2006) has described the ways that *physis*, "nature," changed meanings. At first it seems to have referred to the active, causal force or forces in things, and to their coming into being. It evolved into what we know as "nature." Early on, Heraclitus made a cryptic remark, roughly meaning that "nature loves to hide herself." This was variously interpreted over time, as Hadot shows.

At first, philosophers saw this as a charge to find out the facts. Aristotle was the climactic figure in this enterprise, starting a stunning scientific agenda. The epicureans, stoics, and cynics all had relatively pro-nature views, though their ideas of *physis* were quite different (Karabatzaki 2002).

They also agreed that there was a single God, in Aristotle's view a First Cause. The gods of myth were either subjects of this infinite, abstract divinity or were pure fairy tale. Philosophy gave the educated Greeks a firm monotheism—just as folklore gave the medieval Christians a firm polytheism, with their virgins and saints and sacred trees and multiple apparitions. The textbook lines between monotheism and polytheism have little to do with reality. In both paganism and Christianity, monotheism was the religion of the elite and polytheism the religion of the folk, until long after the end of the ancient world.

ANCIENT ROME

Like the Greeks, the Romans began as tree-worshipers with sacred groves, shamanic stories, and other evidences of some Old Northern background. Their very origin story is perilously close to shamanic animal transformation and totemic worship of animal ancestors: the founders of Rome were "suckled" by a she-wolf. One suspects that in the original version they were actually her cubs. A sculpture of her survives, still displayed on the Capitoline Hill after some 2,500 years; it is as powerfully and brilliantly evocative of the wild and of the animal powers as anything in world art (see the excellent book by Presicce, 2000).

The Romans chose an urban, and later an imperial, world, but, like the Greeks, they had a rather conflicted view.

Long after Romulus and Remus, Lucretius, the great poet of natural history, lamented the decline of woods and wilds—but he also celebrated their replacement by culture (Coates 1998:27; Lucretius 1928, orig. first century BC). He gave a wonderful account of what we would now call cultural evolution, from the club-wielding "savage" (*silvaticus,* "forest person") to the modern city. He saw the savage as an isolated loner at war with all (Lucretius 1928:406–409). The "savage" in the writings of Thomas Hobbes and John Locke owes everything to Lucretius (and other classic writers) and nothing to reality, though Hobbes and Locke could have found good accounts of real hunter-gatherers if they had cared to search. For Lucretius, the savage lived a poor, bare life but at least did not have to deal with war, dangerous sea trading voyages, and civilized crimes and punishment. Above all, he did not have organized religion inflicted on him; Lucretius, an Epicurean, believed the gods were remote and indifferent to humans, and that religious worship was a foolish waste. Still, Lucretius preferred the civilized world—war, religion, and all. Forests were a realm of beauty and wonder, but were the true realm of "savagery."

The Romans developed the word *natura* in its modern meaning, based on the Greek *physis.* The root is *nasci-* "be born," and *natura* originally meant an animal's birth canal (Kwiatkowska 2002:87). Of course, they also gave us the word and concept of *civilization.* Over time, Romans saw Rome as the best of all places; other cities as superior to the country; and human-dominated, highly managed estates as superior to wild nature. The Romans loved their country estates and even the carefully preserved and managed forests they had there, as we know from the acute and sensible agricultural writings of Cato, and the later, more extensive ones of Varro (1935) and Columella (1941–1955).

The love of nature was not lost, however. Roman art is full of gardens, woods, wild beasts, birds, and fruit trees. Anyone viewing the surviving mosaics of Roman North Africa can be overwhelmed by the love, awareness, and incredibly close and accurate observation of nature that they show. Roman poetry, especially from the earlier poets, shows a similar consciousness.

Virgil's poetry, especially the *Georgics* (a versified farm manual), is filled with love for nature and the flourishing, burgeoning biotic world. Virgil deserves special consideration, because his two rural poems shaped European attitudes for two millennia. Educated people knew them, often by heart, and their role in forming attitudes cannot be overstated. Raised in a small farming village in what had been Gaulish lands shortly before, Virgil knew whereof he spoke. He may very well have been influenced by Celtic attitudes to the land. His book of *Eclogues* (Virgil 1999) is a beautifully simple riff on Theocritus but without the snobbism; quite the opposite, Virgil actually protests landowner injustice to poor tenants (Book 9), an advocacy almost unheard of in Roman literature. The *Georgics* (Virgil 2006) is lusher and farther from the soil, interweaving myth and current politics with flowery (and beautiful) poetic advice on farming to his famous patron Maecenas. Of course, Maecenas had no plans to do farm work himself; he presumably had a country estate. Virgil's knowledge is heavily based on earlier manuals, but the poem is full of startling images that imply real love of the countryside.

There is, however, no love of wilderness, wild things, or untamed nature; Virgil describes in shuddery terms the wilder parts of the earth and the savages who dwell there, "clothed in the tawny furs of beasts" (Virgil 1999, Book 3, line 383). They are reduced to using homemade ferment and sour mountain-ash fruits to make a dismal imitation of wine (Book 3, line 380; his "sour" opinion of beer). Then as now, nothing could be worse to an Italian than being without good wine, a point confirmed by the way grape-growing and winemaking are featured not only in the *Georgics* but in all the agricultural writings of the ancients.

The Romans did at least preserve ancient conservation ideals based on reverence for trees, springs, and other natural objects. Virgil's slightly younger contemporary, Ovid (Publius Ovidius Naso), versified in *Metamorphoses* many of the old Greek stories in which profaners of nature are punished by the gods. Nymphs often change into trees, and they or their divine lords often punish those who chop the same. In Arthur Golding's inimitable translation of 1567, for instance, we hear of Erisychthon,

... a person that despysed all his lyfe
The powre of Gods, and never did voucsauf them sacrifyse.
He also is reported to have hewen in wicked wyse
The grove of Ceres, and to fell her holy woods which ay
Had undiminisht and unhackt continewed to that day
(Ovid 2000:217)

Naturally, he gets his comeuppance. Ceres sends the spirit of Famine (the description of whom is too long to quote, but is quite graphic) to make him unable to assimilate food, and he spends eternity starving—clear evidence that the Greeks and Romans knew the ecological results of deforestation. One wishes the ancient Israelites and later Christians who cut down sacred groves had gotten the message.

This tale is followed in Ovid by several other stories with conservation effect. Ovid also retailed here and in other works wonderful descriptions of the Golden Age of hunting-gathering. His tales are Greek, not Roman, but they show the Romans could care, and indeed the Romans had plenty of their own conservationist stories. The Roman belief in tree nymphs was strong enough to influence grammar; even trees with masculine-sounding names like *quercus* "oak" and *pinus* "pine" take feminine adjectives. This has been charmingly preserved in modern scientific Latin, giving us, for instance, *Quercus durata* "leatherleaf oak" and *Pinus ponderosa* "ponderosa (ponderous) pine."

In Ovid we meet, not for the first time in ancient literature and certainly not for the last, the correlation of love for nature and love for women. Ovid is the best example of it in Western literature, for three reasons: first, his enormous influence on subsequent literature; second, his famous (or infamous) focus on love; third, his merging of love for women and love for trees. This last is downright shamanic; he is retelling the ancient Greek transformation stories that go right back to Old Northern "roots." When Apollo chased Daphne, "even as when the gredie Grewnde [greyhound] doth course the sielie [silly] hare," she prays to escape and is turned into the laurel tree:

This piteous prayer scarsly sed: hir sinewes waxed starke,
And therewithall about hir breast did grow a tender barke.
Hir haire was turned into leaves, hir armes in boughes did growe,
Hir feete that were ere while so swift, now rooted were as slowe.

Apollo does what he can:

Well (quoth Apollo) though my Feere [mate] and spouse thou can not bee,
Assuredly from this tyme forth yet shalt thou be my tree.
(Ovid 2000:21–22)

Which is why the laurel is to this day the crown of victors. Ovid tries to bring all the major Greek transformation stories together in this book, and many involve this change of girl to plant; Syrinx becomes a reed, hence the word's use for pipes and windpipes.

Other poets, such as Horace and Catullus, sang the beauties of nature and of women in the same breath. By the end of the Roman Empire, it was a cliché. The rose, most beautiful of flowers, and the song of the nightingale, finest of singers, became established as the proper symbols of erotic passion. The rose and nightingale were to last in erotic poetry throughout the Western world, up to the present day. They were shared with Persian poetry, and, eventually, via Persia, with Muslim poetry as far as India. The facts that the rose resembles the vulva and that the nightingale sings in courtship did not escape the learned. In fact, the courting aspect of the nightingale's song was considerably exaggerated, because it sings to hold territory, defy and out-sing rivals, make friends with its neighbors, and bond with its family as much as for courting. And the reason the nightingale sings in rosebushes is not love of roses—let alone setting its breast on a thorn because suffering is necessary to great music. The real reason is the protection the thorns provide for a bird making itself conspicuous by singing. Any old thornbush will do.

Prose writers like Tacitus could be highly aware of the virtues of conservation, and the uses of religion in protecting rivers, sacred groves, fields, and other amenities (Glacken 1967:135), but Tacitus knew the Celtic and Germanic cultures with their Old Northern views. Centuries after them, late-Imperial Latin poetry could sometimes reach heights of beauty in describing nature, but largely in the Celtic and Germanic fringes. The fifth-century poet Ausonius wrote passionate Latin verse about his Moselle River country.

But all these writers still saw the city as the true home of the good. The conflicted worldviews we briefly noted among the Greeks came to a head in the writings of Virgil, Lucretius, Ovid, and other classical writers. They were evidently well aware of the tension. Like the Greeks, they often harked back to a Golden Age of hunting and gathering, and a decline through pastoral life into the squalid world of today. But they never for a moment thought of going back to the Golden Age in practice.

The Roman love of cities, and of plantation agriculture based on a few crops, contrasts dramatically with the love and even worship of nature and trees in northern Europe. Caesar (in *De Bello Gallico*) and others (e.g., Tacitus in *Germania*) endlessly discussed and emphasized the contrast between the collectivist, urban-oriented Romans and the individualist, countryside-oriented Celts and Germans. The Romans continued to pay reverence to trees, springs, and other natural phenomena (see, e.g., Haberman 2013), but the educated, urban Romans who actually ran the empire saw such things as childish superstition.

They worshiped abstract deist concepts (as Lucretius and Pliny did), or paid dutiful reverence to Jove and the pantheon, but their hearts were in their worship of the Divine Emperor and of the gods of wealth (including Pluto, whose name gives us "plutocracy"). Ovid may have immortalized the old shamanic tales, but he was writing pleasant tales for bored urbanites, not powerful chants for believers in the elder gods.

Rome supported itself to a great extent from vast *latifundia* owned by patricians and worked by slaves or other servile landless laborers. The patricians would visit their estates and sometimes even live there, but their real life was in the city, where they served as politicians and governors. Slaves were of very little account. St. Augustine notes without much surprise or outrage that "more is often given for a horse than for a slave, for a jewel than for a maid" (quoted in Adams 2002:80). Augustine had broken with the extreme antinature ideas we shall examine below and developed a more forgiving and enlightened attitude.

There were many small mixed owner-operated farms—indeed, these possibly dominated actual production—but these were very low on the status hierarchy (on all these matters Gibbon [1995, orig. 1776–1788] remains a great source).

Three major farming manuals survive from Roman times. Cato the Censor (1935) wrote a number of notes and short essays in the second century BC, and these were compiled (and rather mixed up) at some point. In the mid-first century BC, Varro (1935) wrote a largely literary compilation. Finally, Columella (first century AD; Columella 1941–1955) wrote a really serious and major work reviewing all aspects of farming.

They all describe a similar estate: a large, diverse, slave-worked property, based on grain, olives, and wine, with supplemental orchards, kitchen gardens, willow thickets for crafts (basketry etc.), a woodlot, and an oak grove for mast for swine. It is commercial, selling the olive oil, wine, and various minor crops and craft products in town markets, and using a good deal of technology and other purchased inputs of some degree of sophistication. Varro also speaks of extensive commercial cattle-herding, which he seems to realize is not ideal for producing food or maintaining the soil (see, e.g., 1935:309). Details of calculating the business end of the estate are supplied.

All is patterned after Xenophon, but is far from his simplicity and personal touch. Commercial agriculture based on a very few commodities is the rule here. Nature is excluded. Most of the lands under estates had been thoroughly cultivated for hundreds or thousands of years by this time; Europe was substantially cleared and farmed by 5000 BCE. But in North Africa, where Roman colonization moved aggressively into fairly wild lands, we see a more dramatic picture of imposing strict urban order and rationalized commercial agriculture on what had been a fairly wild landscape. (This could be notably successful. In Dougga, Tunisia, I have seen Roman houses, reroofed by modern squatters but otherwise unrepaired, providing better housing than recently built houses in the town! I have traveled in and observed the old Roman landscape fairly extensively in Morocco and Tunisia. The landscape was often more tamed and rationalized then than now.)

These manuals (especially Columella's) show a depressing tendency to increase yields by whipping slaves harder rather than by applying science. But they do include a great deal of science, in the sense of sophisticated, complex agricultural techniques based on close observation and test. They also modeled the "improving squire," a type that never died out, and that flourished exceedingly in England and elsewhere from the Renaissance onward. The "Agricultural Revolution" that coincided with the "Industrial Revolution" in England was only the final flowering of a major movement that goes back to the enlightened estate managers of the late Middle Ages and through them to Rome. One should note that China, medieval Islam, and other areas had their own improving squires, agricultural manuals, and enlightened estate managers; the type is probably worldwide.

Cato was raised on a small farm, though he wound up landlord of huge slave-worked estates; his manual speaks of both. Columella, writing the most comprehensive of the farming manuals, is definitely writing for rich absentee landlords employing mass slave labor. His manual includes a whole book (a rather amazing mix of sound science and preposterous magic) on treating horses and cattle, but almost nothing on taking care of slaves, who were far less worthy of consideration. What little he says on that subject is, basically, that the owner should make sure the overseer is not merciful and should whip the slaves for any offense. Note that this implies the owner is absent and has left it all to an overseer, likely a slave himself. Cato and Varro also assume an overseer is actually running the farm on the ground.

Conservation of the wild is conspicuously absent from these manuals. Varro talks at length about catching wild songbirds in massive quantities for sale (Varro 1935:438 ff.), a practice still the bane of Italian woods. Ovid's pretty conceits were viewed as ancient Greek lore, rather than living traditions to emulate. On the other hand, careful management of diversified woodlands and careful soil and grassland management are recommended in enormous detail and on the whole could be taken from a modern organic farming book. The infamous erosion of soil in classical Italy seems likely to have been a product of the decline of empire rather than of the empire at its height, just as in the Tarascan Empire of Mexico erosion tracked social collapse and depopulation rather than population increase and intensive farming (Fisher 2005, 2009).

The giant estates—*latifundia*—began to develop on a serious scale in the 200s BC, partly because constant wars took many peasants away from home for long periods, allowing the rich to capture the land. Serious latifundization—the word has entered English—occurred in the following century as rising population, rising wealth, and rising numbers of elites had the all too familiar effect of increasing the gap between wealth and poverty and the power of the rich to take over what the poor might have had (Turchin and Zefedov 2009:190–192). There is disagreement about the extent of this in the early period. My cautious sense is that latifundia and the slave economy were not so extensive in the Roman Republic (a common "revisionist" position), but grew out of control after the empire began. Small mixed farms, *minifundia*, continued to dominate demographically and lose out politically, as they were fated to do for most of history. The progression is clear, whether one looks at the agricultural manuals, the poetry, or the treatment of wild resources: Rome began well, but attitudes toward nature hardened as latifundia grew and the city of Rome became the center of the universe.

The large slave estate is only one (though the most widespread and typical) case of elite Roman land management. The Romans had smaller, better managed estates and many small yeoman farms. The huge estates comprised land management by people who wanted quick returns at minimal expense and had no long-term stake in the land.

China in Roman Empire times was almost as dedicated to slave-worked estates as Rome was. But the Chinese saw the problem and more or less fixed it. China became increasingly a world of small farms. These were, until fairly modern times, far more productive than the Western world's. When the West did finally surpass China, it was due to social reforms as well as to economics.

The vast monocropped estates of Mesopotamian temples and Greek and Egyptian rulers anticipate the plantation; but it seems to have been left to the Romans to completely rationalize the system based on vast, orderly monocrop fields, worked by servile landless labor, using technology instead of human skill, and eliminating not only nature but also the diverse cropping system of the small farm. Italy was never converted—Italy is still a refuge for small farms growing a quite incredible range of crops. But the rest of the world learned. The vast oil palm plantations of Malaysia and Indonesia, as insane nutritionally and economically as they are ecologically, testify to the power of the Roman vision. The Romans locked in not only a farming method and organization system, but a whole concept of "growth" and "development" based on it. Over time, an accounting system arose that counts such things as "growth"—counting anything that transforms and destroys nature, but not counting nature's services.

As the Roman world grew more and more urban and developed, people came to see all good things as centered in the larger cities. The country was uncouth. *Pagan*, like *boor* and *yokel*, was a slur term that originally meant "country person." Christians used it against their opponents to brand the latter as backward.

A final note is that Roman interest in nature seems to have been limited to the useful. Science did not flourish. The young learned their science from Greek tutors, who were actual slaves. Lucretius and a few others cared about nature, but more typical was Pliny the Elder (see Pliny 2004), who invented the phrase "natural history." His book is a collection of statements without much organization, system, or analysis. Pliny disbelieved in some things (such as werewolves and Persian magic) but generally cared little whether a statement was myth, traveler's tale, or truth; he had no concept of fact-checking. For 1,500 years, he remained the great basic source for stories of dog-headed men, tribes with faces on their chests, 300-foot-long eels, lions that spared pleading women, and many other tall tales repeated endlessly in popular and learned books. Some, such as elephants' fear of mice, are still established in folklore.

He is, however, useful and reliable as a source on Rome of his time. He was sharp enough to see the irony of cutting down a fig tree in the center of Rome to keep it from interfering with a statue of Sylvanus, the god of forests (Coates 1998:31; Pliny 2004:201) though this may be a folktale. At least the Romans had the good taste to make a sacrifice before doing this. He also was a stout monotheist: "God is the complete embodiment of sense, sight, hearing, soul mind and of himself. To believe in ... an infinite number of deities ... plumbs an even greater depth of foolishness" than to try to comprehend God's infinity (Pliny 2004:12). Though Pliny lived within the Christian era, he was uninfluenced by, and probably unaware of, Christian monotheism; his beliefs are taken squarely from the Greek philosophers, many of whom were monotheist long before Christianity.

The Romans exterminated the European lion, the North African elephants and hartebeests, and even the silphium plant, a medicinal herb (Koerper and Kolls 1999). The Roman circuses exterminated large animals over thousands of square miles, solely for the amusement of seeing them killed. Thousands of animals a day might be killed for pleasure (cf. Coates 1998:37–38). Hunting, woodcutting, and plant gathering were practiced with few or no limits and with no visible concern over exhaustion. Unlike the Greeks and the later western Europeans, the Romans rarely (if ever) mentioned things like deforestation or depleted fisheries. We see here—squarely and exactly located—the origins of our current destructive attitudes toward natural resources. Mesopotamia and Greece had seen transforming nature as necessary; imperial Rome saw it as downright desirable and fun, even without economic reason.

THE RISE OF DUALISM AND THE HATRED OF NATURE

The Hellenistic world—the Greek world during the dominance of Rome—was at first a great age of science (Glacken 1967), but its relative stagnation after Rome turned imperial, and the decline of the Roman Empire itself, apparently led—rather unsurprisingly—to wide adoption of Neo-Platonic and other anti-worldly attitudes (see historians from Edward Gibbon 1995 to Peter Green 1990).

Increasingly, nature was seen as merely a gross material world that is a bad expression of higher ideals. This attitude developed within Zoroastrianism, Platonism (starting with Plato himself), Gnosticism, Manicheanism, and other Near Eastern religions. Plato's own idealism was not nearly so antinature. It is likely that much more of this philosophy came from Eastern dualism than from Plato. At least since Gibbon, it is usually considered to stem from "Iranian dualism"—the Zoroastrian and Mazdaist view that drew extreme contrasts between Good and Evil. Good formerly was identified with the realms of the gods—heaven or spirit; Evil with the fleshly world. The soul was regarded as part of the eternal unchanging Ideal, as opposed to the world—the latter variously seen as illusion, or disgustingly contaminated, or outright evil. (On all these matters see McEvilley 2002, who makes detailed comparisons with Indian thought).

This led to a great deal of asceticism and self-mortification. Some of this goes back to the "prophets" of old, who were wild and remote characters living in poverty and hard conditions. A rash of local cults developed in Hellenistic times. Little is known of these cults. They seem to have no roots in Mesopotamian religions. Glacken cites scholars who think they came with the rise of the huge cities that developed in the Mediterranean after 300 BC (Glacken 1967:25).

Neo-Platonists took to extremes Plato's preference for changeless Ideas over changeable material reality. The neo-Platonists viewed nature and the physical world as a dismal veil over ideals or over the Good (McEvilley 2002:586; Remes 2008). They viewed spirit as better than and antithetical to flesh; reason as similarly superior to emotion; and, in general, men as more spiritual and reasonable than, and thus superior to, women. Neo-Platonists ranged from seeing material things as merely the least good to seeing them as downright evil, as the Gnostics did. Neo-Platonism and Gnosticism profoundly influenced early Christianity and, later, Islam. Neo-Platonism in particular, through the Greek and Arab connections to modern philosophy and science, influenced all Western thought (see, e.g., Coates 1998:32 ff.; Remes 2008:197–207).

In early Christianity, a competitive mortification of the flesh entered the picture. As in some earlier Levantine cults, people competed to see who could be the most saintly by living in the most public discomfort. Edward Gibbon tells the stories in *The Decline and Fall of the Roman Empire* (1995 [1776–1788]): "stylite" monks who competed to see who could live on the smallest and highest-raised platform, and so on. One of this type—St. David the Dendrite—at least served trees by living perched in an almond tree for three years; he is portrayed in a beautiful fresco on the Chora Church in Istanbul (personal observation). Christian divines wore hair shirts or chains and spikes and stood meditating for hours in the "cross" position. They avoided the baths. This unedifying spirituality Gibbon called "enthusiasm"; we would now call it "fanaticism." Kant condemned it in a memorable passage: "The more useless such self-castigations are and the less they are designed for the general moral improvement ... the holier they seem to be; just because they are of no use whatsoever in the world and yet cost painful effort they seem to be directly [*sic*] solely to the attestation of devotion to God" (Kant 1960:157). Kant's position has been reinvented as the "costly signaling" theory deployed by evolutionary biologists to explain such behaviors in courtship and in religion (Atran 2002).

Hatred of the flesh and the natural world, entering from the Near East, fused with Imperial Roman love of cities and farms and the idea that humanity's goal was to turn wilderness into the most thoroughly artificial thing possible. These two antinature attitudes, originally quite separate and unrelated, fused in the Roman Empire. They were logically consistent with each other and fit the Imperial Roman obsession with dominance, control, and naked power. Tragically, they became part of the general worldview in the Mediterranean oikoumene, spread with it, and have now gone worldwide.

These attitudes entered Christianity quite early. They were lacking in the earliest church. Jesus himself was more concerned with solidly material matters such as healing the sick and feeding the hungry. However, anti-flesh attitudes were already visible in Paul. (Actually, these passages may very well have been created by a later writer using Paul's name; Borg and Crossan 2009.) They became prevalent in the second and third centuries. The orthodox Origen and Tertullian and the heretical Marcion were alike notable for promoting them. They and other church fathers were the parties who imported it to Christianity and launched that faith on its dualistic course.

This attitude is clearly related to the antinature, plantation-managing, urban-idealizing elite attitudes of Rome and Syria, and probably of Persia. Extreme dualism appears to be an alienated, dour version of that view that was held by priests and holy men, as opposed to senators and large landlords. One can imagine an elite, educated man surviving on a priest's low salary, and subject to the same bitterness that animates many academics today.

Christianity owes its endless problems with puritanism, anti-woman sentiments, and extreme asceticism to this cluster of late-Classical cults and philosophies. Early Christians were not philosophers, and their adoption of this antinature view shows the view was general at the time. Glacken (1967:162–163) traces it to Christian meditations on original sin and the resulting corruption of the flesh and the world, but it clearly predates Christianity. Glacken notes that it has no real excuse in Scripture, which maintains the earth is the Lord's and therefore cannot be evil. The attitude arose as Christians became otherworldly, oriented to heaven (Glacken 1967:163, 181). Christian authors could even maintain that the evils exist specifically to turn our minds away from the world (Glacken 1967:197).

The world-hating view seems to have risen and crystallized during the long night when Christianity was suppressed by the Roman Empire and was a faith of celibacy, self-denial, poverty, and constant fear. Science seemed a vain luxury. Knowledge of God alone mattered; knowledge of this world was imperfect and idle (Glacken 1967:183). The result was a sour, anti-"flesh" ideology that is still very much with us in Christianity and has often spread into Judaism and Islam.

The extremes that this attitude reached at that time would be unbelievable today if not soberly attested by the best authorities. "St. Anselm, writing at the beginning of the twelfth century, maintained that things were harmful in proportion to the number of senses which they delighted, and therefore rated it dangerous to sit in a garden where there are roses," as well as other flowers, songs, lovely fruits, and the rest (Clark 1979:3). Nature-hating puritanism almost to this level still existed in my childhood and surfaces today in the more extreme antienvironmentalism of media personalities like Rush Limbaugh—who links it with his championing of junk food above healthy eating. Apparently being healthy is too fleshly a concern. The "holy anorexics" of the Middle Ages would have understood (Bell 1985).

Possibly the most influential two-page article in the history of environmentalism was Lynn White's classic "The Historical Roots of Our Ecologic Crisis" (1967). White argued that Christianity, especially its contrast of "things of the spirit" (good) with fleshly and natural things (bad), was the reason, or at least the major reason, for the world ecological problem. Subsequent scholarship has cast the blame rather earlier, as we have seen. But the hatred of nature that got into early Christianity from dualist philosophies certainly deserves a huge share of blame. Christians have misquoted the Bible to turn "dominion" into a sanction for ruin; White quotes an all too large and representative selection. However, Christianity was never united behind this attitude, and White himself saw hope in the tradition of St. Francis (see below).

The link between sexual repression, oppressing women, and disliking the natural environment has been frequently made, especially by ecofeminists. Linking of women with "nature" is part of this dour ideology, not a given fact of life, and ecofeminists who buy into it are doing themselves no favor. This view is one source of the correlation between Western agriculture and repressive gender relations.

More generally, bullying people naturally leads to bullying landscapes, and vice versa. One is reminded of James Scott's findings on how states manage people (Scott 1998, 2009). Scottian ideas of legibility and statism certainly explain some of the adulation of grid-patterned cities and plantations and the hatred of wild nature.

Throughout the Dark Ages and into the Middle Ages, there is little awareness or interest in nature visible in south European (including Byzantine) literature. Latifundia were developing into ranches and plantations. Most people lived in poverty, many in slavery. For much of this period, the world was declining economically, culturally, and in every other way. Only slowly (largely after 1000) did people realize that a new and beautiful world was being born from the ruins of the old.

The lands culturally shaped by Rome are still identifiable today by the relative lack of interest in nature, biology, and natural history. Compare the natural history museums of Spain or Italy with those of England or Scandinavia. You can find good science museums in Paris and Madrid, but outside of them there is little indeed. Barcelona, for instance, has some of the best and most sophisticated art and architectural museums in the world, but its natural history museum is an ancient, dusty little place with century-old labeling. Most Spanish cities have none at all.

Christianity also had to contend with "pagans" who had sacred groves, sacred boundary stones, oracle shrines, and other survivors of more environmentalist spiritualities. The Christians thus began a savage campaign against sacred groves, especially when Christianity reached the lands where Celtic and Germanic religions were still strong and still based in these plantings (Anderson ms. 1; Glacken 1967:310). Many saints achieved fame by cutting the groves down. I have seen in Lyon, above a medieval church door, a carving of a saint cutting a sacred tree such that it falls on the local druids. Possibly not the high point of Christian charity. Similarly, Charlemagne's victory over the Saxons climaxed with cutting down their sacred tree. All this confirmed Christians in their Mediterranean attitudes of love for cities and the spirit, hate for the countryside and the flesh (or wood). Nature was there to be dominated, overcome, and ruled, and people who worshiped it were in for an even more brutal and dictatorial fate (see Coates 1998, esp. p. 52). As the Christian writer C. S. Lewis later put it, "what we call Man's power over Nature turns out to be a power exercised by some men over other men with Nature as its instrument" (quoted by Coates 1998:46 from Lewis's *The Abolition of Man,* Oxford University Press, 1944, p. 28).

Nature, for the early Christians, was a source of parables and metaphors. The countless editions of the "Physiologus," and other animal fable books, tell stories that have little relation to reality but much to Christian dogma. The pelican, for instance, kills its young, then beats its breast in sorrow until blood runs, which revives them. The Christian parallel is obvious. The biological reality is that pelican young are lax and immobile until the parents return with food in their crops. The parents then pump their bills up and down (as if beating their breasts) to make themselves bring up the food for the young to eat. (Religious environmentalist Luis Gutierrez recently created the wonderful religious-environmentalist website and journal, *Mother Pelican,* from this symbol.) Animal tales such as this lie behind heraldry, with its complex symbolism (Rosenberg 1939), and behind the incredibly complex bird, flower, and tree symbolism of Renaissance art (Friedman 1980).

The orthodox church saw the flesh as sinful and only the transcendent world of God and Heaven as worthwhile. But at least it saw the world as God's creation and humans as redeemable. It had limited patience with the true dualist idea—the idea that Satan made and controlled this world. That idea survived by being absorbed into Christianity as a heretical undercurrent (Runciman 1955).

A strong form of the evil-flesh theory surfaced among the Bogomils, the Cathars, and the Puritans. Rebecca West described the dualist faith (as it was among the Bogomils) in a memorable sentence: "The whole of modern history could be deduced from the popularity of this heresy in Western Europe: its inner sourness, its preference for hate over love and war over peace, its courage about dying, its cowardice about living" (West 1941:173). Writing at the beginning of World War II, she was thinking of it as ancestral to fascism, which, in part, it was. (There are more positive takes on the Cathars [O'Shea 2002], and we know a good deal about their ecology [Le Roy Ladurie 1978], but they certainly propagated this anti-world gospel.)

Calvinism did not go so far as to see the world as Satan's, but it certainly sees the world as evil and the flesh as sinful, and so does its Catholic reflex, Jansenism, and much of American evangelical Christianity. We see the full belief that this is Satan's world revived by some factions of the Christian right, in our own time.

These sects have given us a worldview too conformable with the antienvironmentalism of the latifundia. Some sects go even farther and hold that our duty is to destroy nature, even if we produce nothing of value in the process. This view has profoundly colored modern "development" ideas. Secular or even atheist developers and economists spout a view of nature derived from the dourest fundamentalists.

However, where other authors have seen the West's environmental problems as caused by Christianity or as being due to economic organization, I follow Max Weber (2002) in seeing religion and economy as interlocking institutions, each with its own life, but each feeding back on the other. Demonstrably, the anti-flesh views—orthodox or dualist—are not part of capitalism, industrialism, or anything similar. They are evidently related to extensive wheat-barley-livestock farming and its connection with the rise of the state, the spread of tyranny (in the classic Greek sense), and the rise of estate slavery. This did not really require dualism, but it made it likely. The endless wars and power-jockeying of Mesopotamia and the Mediterranean did the rest. It was in the most downtrodden and war-ridden parts of the east Mediterranean that world-hating, nature-hating ideologies arose and spread.

The worst of these ideas, the ones that prevail in international development today, are visible from space, in the form of the neat squares of soybeans that are replacing fantastically diversified natural and agricultural landscapes all over Latin America today. The very worst of the associated ideas is not an ecological one, but a human one: the idea that agriculture should be managed by huge, politically powerful interests, the work being done by servile landless laborers—serfs, slaves, subminimum-wage hirelings. Communism has proved to us that commissars and "the state" are no better than absentee landlords. We recall C. S. Lewis's point here. Second is the always-awful idea of "man vs. nature." Flipping this around, "saving nature" by driving indigenous people off their lands and locking up the territory, is no improvement. Third is the idea that we can depend on a few strains of a few crops and sacrifice biodiversity. Fourth is the idea that these crops are best grown in vast areas of monocrop that are maintained by chemical fertilizers and pesticides, with no attention to soil type, water, natural cover, or anything else natural.

ISLAM AS POTENTIAL ALTERNATIVE

The Middle East has been an ecological problem area for almost the full five millennia of its civilization. Devastation of natural environments has led to massive salinization, soil erosion, desertification, overhunting of game, and general ruin of the natural resource base. The region survives today by exporting oil and is overdrawing its water resources ever more dangerously. One fears for the future when oil and water run out. Islam is a religion of good management (Foltz et al. 2003), but it has had little headway against a momentum already unstoppable when Islam appeared in the seventh century AD.

When anthropologist Carleton Coon asked Iranian rural people about deforestation (around 1950), they said sadly that they could not station a guard "behind every tree" (Coon 1958:7). This was no new problem. Both the Bible and the ancient Egyptian literature note extremely heavy exploitation of the forests of Lebanon. They and many other forests were cut to pieces long before the time of Christ.

However, and indeed partly because of these problems, Islam has very strongly emphasized "stewardship"—*khilāfa* in Arabic—instead of "dominion" (Foltz et al. 2003). The very word *Islam* means surrender to God's will, which rules out both acting like a lord of creation and wasting resources. The earth remains God's, and humans are merely allowed to use it for the common good (Foltz et al. 2003; see esp. excellent discussion in Llewellyn 2003 within that volume). Use for ill is absolutely prohibited. This precludes damaging the earth or wasting any resource. The Qur'an says: "Do not waste: verily He loves not the wasteful!" (Qur'an 6:141 and 7:31 as quoted in Llewellyn 2011:198).

Islamic rules and conservation ideas are particularly concerned with water, a very carefully regulated and administered resource, as befits a religion originating in the desert; animal, plant, and land resources must also be carefully managed for collective good (Foltz et al. 2003). Muslims are charged with being kind to animals and giving them freedom. Keeping birds in cages is theoretically forbidden, whereas kindness and charity to animals, even insects and the unclean dog, is rewarded (Foltz 2006; Haq 2003:148–150; Llewellyn 2011:230–235; Nurbakhsh 1989). Considerable experience in Islamic societies forces me to admit that practice sometimes runs well behind ideology, especially in the harsher parts of the Middle East. Sport hunting, for instance, is banned in Islam, but widely practiced to the point of nearly exterminating many species. This, however, is probably a relatively recent matter; see Haq (2003).

Islam, too, has its traces of dualism and flesh-hating, especially in the extreme forms of Islam found today in Saudi Arabia, Iran, and elsewhere. Perhaps these explain the gap between law and performance. Islam traditionally avoided neo-Platonic nature-hating and remains notably pro-environment (Foltz et al. 2003), but Islamic societies have often devastated the landscape. Several modern Islamic societies have claimed a return to "true" Islam, but in fact their thoroughly un-Islamic extremism is shown as much by their environmental profligacy and mismanagement as by their terrorist mass murders of innocent civilians—all these being explicitly outlawed by the Qur'an.

Muslims picked up devotion to cities as they conquered the Syrian towns in the first decades of Islam. Thousands of poems in classical Near Eastern literatures celebrate places, but, from my wide reading, almost all are about cities. The Arabs in their desert days, before Islam, wrote exquisite praises of the desert and the nomadic life, but the Arabs since then have praised Baghdad, Cordova, or Tunis.

However, in Malaysia and Indonesia, in Bangladesh, and other areas outside of the Middle East where I have actually observed Islamic life at the village level, gratuitous cruelty to animals is no worse than in reasonably decent societies elsewhere. In Malaysia and Indonesia, especially, the Southeast Asian tradition of caring for nature was very much alive when I was there nearly half a century ago, and animals were treated well. Mystical Sufi sects in particular teach and practice kindness.

Shari'a law clearly specifies that land is to be used for the good of people, but careful preservation is often involved. This is especially true of water sources; springs are sacrosanct. Many groves, hills, and other areas are sacred. The institution of *ḥimā* allows lock-down preservation for the common good (Foltz 2006:39–41; Llewellyn 2011). The most famous of these reserves were established by Muhammad to protect the sanctity of Mecca and Madina. In the vicinity of these holy cities, no vegetation can be cut and no wildlife killed (though urbanization has taken its toll). Thousands of these reserves exist, ranging from lock-down preservation of sacred precincts to collectively used grazing and foraging lands where vegetation is carefully managed. Some are reserved for flowers for honey production (Llewellyn 2011:215). These reserves and other grazing and forest lands were normally managed by villages or tribes.

Land and resource ownership is squarely placed on God, with the Caliph or, failing that, local ruler as steward in charge. As Alan Mikhail says of the Ottoman Empire: "From the perspective of both imperial subjects and the dynastic elite, no one—except perhaps God or his shadow on Earth, the sultan—owned nature in the way that a human owned a building or a sack of coffee. Plants, trees, and other natural resources—though often commodified, moved, and transferred—were not simple commodities like any other. These living things were, in some sense, everyone's and at the same time no one's" (Mikhail 2011:157). There is an apparent miswriting here: the "perhaps" should go *after* "God or . . . ," not before. There is *no* question in Islam and its Shari'a who really owns, controls, and ultimately disposes of the resources. Nothing is done without Him.

Early Islam, up into the thirteenth century, was strongly influenced by Aristotelianism, and most scholars adopted a highly scientific, rational worldview. This changed over time (for a number of reasons), but in its early centuries the Dar-al-Islam (realm of Islam) was the world center of '*ilm*, systematic empirical knowledge including science and scientific research. It led the world in most fields.

Of course, as in all religions, practice fell far short of rules, and overhunting, overcutting, abuse of animals, and pollution were noted in Islamic literature from early times; but at least they were noted to condemnation. Most reserves have disappeared or degraded—often recently, with the coming of "modernity." However, apparently many still function, in spite of the overwhelming tide of overgrazing, overhunting, and deforestation that history—especially in the last couple of centuries—has unleashed on the Islamic world. Thus, corporate management reduced, but did not eliminate, the "tragedy of the commons."

A person can lose a claim to land if the land goes neglected for years. It reverts to the Lord—public domain, de facto—and can be reclaimed. However, things like gathering medicinal herbs from the wild would qualify as use.

Arabic and Persian literature classically portrays the environment in idealistic terms, though during the high Islamic period from 700 to 1100 there was relatively little about nature or the wild in Near Eastern verse. Even so, Persian poetry in particular produced a great deal of flowers-and-nightingales poetry, especially after 1100, in close parallel to Europe; because exactly the same tropes figure largely in both Persian and European poems, linkages are obvious, but are too poorly documented to allow us to ascertain where they started.

In short, Islam is typically Abrahamic in its privileging of humanity and human concerns. In this it contrasts with the Eastern Asian religions. But

Islam is strongly devoted to stewardship for the common good, as opposed to the equivocal stances of the other Abrahamic religions, which have been all too tolerant of individuals ripping off the system for personal aggrandizement.

CARE FOR NATURE RESURGENT IN MEDIEVAL EUROPE

In Europe, too, a strong thread of "creation care" continued. The West never lost a sense not only of need for the wild but of love for it. That had to flourish as a dissident strain within Western thought. Cities and rural areas took a quite modern view of what was needed. Many environmental regulations were passed, to control pollution, overuse, and so on (Coates 1998:62; Glacken 1967:302–338); some were extremely enlightened by modern standards (e.g., Vincenti 2002).

Medieval Europeans were intensely aware of pollution and had quite modern attitudes about it, but generally did not know what to do about it. A famous Latin poem, known in several versions, is a debate between water and wine about which should be the proper drink for humanity. Water argues that wine drives people mad and makes them do foolish things, but wine wins (of course!) by describing graphically and at length the pollution of water:

> You absorb, by way of riddance,
> Bilge from privies drains, and middens,
> Many nameless filths as well,
> Nasty droppings, waste, offscourings,
> Poisonous drenches and outpourings
> More than I would care to tell
> (Whicher 1949:245; from "The Debate Between Water and Wine," pp. 238–247)

And so on, verse after verse! In the middle ages there was some action taken, but much more in the Renaissance, where stronger states could regulate tanners, butchers, and other major polluters. England later had plenty of "dark satanic mills" (as William Blake wrote), but as early as 1585 it had enough concern for pollution to ban the production of blue dye from woad within eight miles of a royal palace (Thick 2010:269); the process involves fermenting the woad, which stinks. However, this introduces a significant note of class. Only Queen Elizabeth and her courtiers avoided the stench, just as the elite avoided the pollution from Blake's satanic mills more than two centuries later. In England, environmental protection was for the upper classes; paying the price for it was for the lower classes.

Love and reverence for nature continued unabated in the East European, Celtic, and Germanic fringes. In the twelfth century, Hildegard of Bingen in Germany cared for herbs and animals and wrote an excellent medical herbal (as well as some beautiful sacred music). Ritual burial of dogs in the pagan Gaulish world metamorphosed into the cult of St. Guinefort, the dog who was worshiped as a saint from around 1200 well into the twentieth century (Schmidt 1983). His tomb is still known and revered near Châtillon-sur-Chalaronne, central France, where the local historical society calls itself the St. Guinefort Society. People continued to worship sacred wells, sacred hills, and even sacred trees. England had the thorn of Glastonbury, a mutant hawthorn that flowered in midwinter, miraculously close to Christmas.

Trying to drive moles out of their area, one community appealed to them to leave on their own, and promised "safe conduct … with an extra fourteen days grace being allowed for pregnant females and their young" (Holland 2002:ix). Such things, as well as trials and executions of animals that hurt their masters, have traditionally been taken by historians as proof of childishness and ignorance, but they are better seen as survivals of the Old Northern view of society as including animals and plants as well as humans.

Forest protection laws could get savage (Glacken 1967:328–338). Poachers could at least theoretically be blinded or castrated (Coates 1998:45). Admittedly, this says more about lords' attitudes toward peasants than about love for nature, but forest conservation and game protection, however selfishly and greedily intended, were extremely serious matters. People not only knew of the necessity, but were willing to use draconian means to enforce it. However, the classism persisted in England and tainted conservation there with a stain not yet rubbed out. It gave the "lower classes" a most unfortunate tendency to destroy when they had the chance; they had no share in conservation and saw it as elitist and irksome (Coates 1998:47; Thompson 1975). This attitude persists, and is visible in Northwest Coast loggers and miners today, and in many other working-class rural folk. It has merged with the antinature attitude from the ancient world.

The medieval literatures, especially the Celtic, are full of natural images (see chapter on Ireland). Celtic literature exploded onto the medieval European scene via the writings of Christine de Pisan, Marie de France, and others. They imported Celtic tales into French literature. Their many refined and elite followers and imitators brought more and more tales, complete with their beautiful and elaborate nature lore, into the major European languages. Intense and beautiful nature imagery entered the stories of the Holy Grail and other mystical religious lore. This brought into European literature a genuine nature mysticism, previously absent from the Western Christian tradition. Juxtaposing these authors with Hildegard of Bingen and others shows that women had a huge share in this development—a point noted by feminist ecologists.

Celtic poetry shows the equation of love for nature and love for women in a truly dramatic fashion. Evidently this had Celtic sources; it certainly did not wait for Ovid to be rediscovered. The climax comes in the various versions of the story of Tristan and Ysolt, where the passionate descriptions of the forest serve as counterpoint and emphasis for the passionate love of the protagonists—who met in the greenwood, and in some versions are saved by it.

Poets also rediscovered nature from the south. Troubadour and trouvère poetry, after 1100, said much about nightingales, roses, groves, and other stock nature images (see, e.g., Goldin 1973). Part of the immediate trigger for this development was Arabic culture working its way up from Moorish Spain and Sicily. However, the main ultimate sources of inspiration were Ovid and other classical Latin poets.

New Latin verses by the "Goliard" poets celebrated spring and flowers (Whicher 1949). These often combined Latin images with Celtic or Germanic ones. Other Celtic themes and poetics came from Galicia, the northwest part of the Iberian Peninsula, which had recently converted from a Celtic language to the strongly Celtic-influenced Romance language known as Galician. The region was a fertile source of troubadours and songs (Zenith 1995). Germanic awareness of nature entered at the same time but at the other end of Western Europe, via the poetry of the Minnesingers. Arabic literature, coming via Spain, also contributed to this development (though the actual amount and nature of the contribution remains controversial).

These literary movements met and fused in the great French and German epics of such writers as Chrétien de Troyes and Wolfram von Eschenbach. Both of these were prime sources for the equation of love, noble knighthood, and the greenwood. The usual tropes also spread into English literature, and in Welsh poetry Dafydd ap Gwilym worked them almost to death—including the ever-popular rose and nightingale, love's symbols from ancient Greece to medieval Wales and on to modern Turkey and Pakistan. (I assume Northeastern Europe was not without similar traditions, but I know little about them. Finnish folk poetry is heavily shamanistic and full of natural images [Dubois 1995]. Later Russian poetry and folklore are full of nature [cf. Caldwell 2011], but much of it is due to borrowed west European romanticism. Russians also had a strong frontier-subduing tradition that carried over into Communist attacks on nature and indifference to pollution.)

Nature was still terrifying, the wild forest was dangerous, the plagues and storms deadly and life threatening, but medieval people could still appreciate fully the beauty of flowers, woods, birds, and outdoor life (cf. Robinson and Westra 2002, passim). The love of nature was conscious, real, unfeigned, and thoroughly sophisticated. Nobles hawked and hunted, poets sang the beauties of the wildwood, peasants had flowers in their gardens.

The poetry was evidently related to the emerging views on nature that led to creation of hunting parks, elaborate gardens, and early anti-pollution rules. The high medieval period was a time of extreme self-consciousness about manners and status. Manners in even quite lowly houses of that latter time make ours today look boorish, as the many etiquette guides of the period show. The popular myth of the gorging, guzzling medievals, who cleaned their hands by letting the dogs lick them, is not entirely fiction, but it refers to the Dark Ages, a period long gone by 1200. The "civilizing mission" of post-medieval Europe is urban folklore.

Highly sophisticated agriculture, based on designing with nature, entered Europe from the Arab world, especially in Spain and Sicily. (I have observed and studied surviving and re-created farms and systems in these areas; see also Ibn Luyūn 1975; Maurici 2006; Remmers 1998; Watson 1983; there are many other sources. My historical notes below owe much to Slicher von Bath 1963.) Agricultural innovations from alfalfa to the horse-collar revolutionized farming.

All this led to a new relationship with the land. On the one hand, domination and exploitation were easier. On the other, working with nature and working with the whole resource base of the landscape was also easier—and a great deal more economically attractive than wrecking everything for small profits. Rob-ber barons may have viewed the land as something to rip off, but sounder heads constructed irrigation systems, managed groves and woodlots, and developed gardens. These all replaced wild nature, but by concentrating intensive man-agement on a few small areas, and by working with natural laws and materials, they still advanced what we would now consider an environmentalist cause. The worst problem for this agenda was that it was, in too many quarters, associated with the oft-hated "Moors" and "Saracens."

Another source of knowledge of and connection to nature was hunting. This had previously been a subsistence activity. Richard Almond, in *Medieval Hunting* (2003), provides a superb survey of medieval hunting and its enormous ethnobiological knowledge base. In the Middle Ages, it became an elite pastime and an art, and in some cases it actually became a mystical journey; hunter saints like St. Hubert recall masters of the game in shamanic religions and were indeed equated therewith by converted shamanistic peoples.

A truly amazing case of hunting-turned-science is *The Art of Falconry* of Frederick II of Hohenstaufen (Hohenstaufen 1943; see also Glacken 1967), an incredible compendium of thoroughly scientific observation, so accurate and detailed that it is still read and used by falconers and ornithologists. As usual, caring for nature goes with tolerance for people; crusades or no, Fred-erick dedicated the book to his fellow falconer the Sultan of Egypt. This book was not unique. It evidently drew on an enormous amount of folk and noble knowledge. We really have very little sense of the obviously vast folk wisdom of that underestimated time.

The early Muslim thinkers rehabilitated Aristotle and empirical research on the real world. In the late Middle Ages, this attitude spread to Europe and dramatically changed the latter. Albertus Magnus's great student St. Thomas Aquinas was instrumental in converting the Catholic world from Platonism to Aristotelianism. Stephen Gaukroger (2006) has argued at length that this, not the Renaissance, was the watershed, the time when the modern world began; the Renaissance followed fairly naturally once Aristotelian common sense was established. Mary Frances Wack says "[t]he twelfth century witnessed not just altered physical relations with the natural world, but the emergence of the *idea* of nature" (Wack 1990:31). Peter Coates (1998:63) thinks this went with a triumphalist or dominating attitude toward nature. (Recall that Aristotle held that nature was created for human use.) This claim is, however, only partially true. Science rediscovered the value of looking at real things and the priority of nature over hallowed text.

Religion did not escape this influence. St. Francis of Assisi in the thirteenth century forever changed the Western world's attitude toward animals, plants, and the sun. St. Francis is typically presented today as a simple soul in touch with nature. In fact he was a highly educated aristocrat in one of the most advanced, learned cities in Europe. His extremely self-conscious revaluing of the natural world was evidently part of the rediscovery of the Aristotelian view, as it was interpreted in Italy. Even St. Francis condemned attachment to the flesh and can sound downright dualist on occasion, but at least he loved God's creations.

A few centuries later, Raphael painted Plato pointing to the heavens, Aristotle to the earth; this was his unforgettable visual summary of the Renaissance view of the difference between the two philosophers. St. Francis had seen the same contrast earlier and followed the Aristotelian trend that was sweeping Italy in his time.

Franciscan monks kept the faith, to a surprising degree. In the old Franciscan seminary (now a museum) in Zacatecas, Mexico, is a portrait of the seminary director in the mid-eighteenth century; he poses with his pet rabbit, pet mockingbird, and several other tame creatures, perching on him and nestling in his sleeves. It is a deeply touching image, and it certainly shows that St. Francis's spirit lived on. Even today, many churches perform a blessing of the animals on St. Francis's day; farmers bring their livestock, and children bring their pets. Alas, in the end, St. Francis's impact on the Christian world was rather small. Catholicism was not transformed either by him or by the massive Celtic input via Grail epics. Instead, Roman Catholicism replaced Celtic Christianity, bringing Mediterranean disinterest in nature to previously Old Northern lands.

The result of all these currents of thought was an amazing diversity of behavior in the later Middle Ages. Among other things, this certainly proves that simple environmental determinism, ignoring ideology, does not give very thorough accounts of human ecology! The simple medieval agricultural system, very backward by Asian standards, was accompanied by an incredible ferment of environmental representations. Not only did Europe display a range from hatred of the flesh to reveling the beauty of nature, St. Francis's case shows that the same individuals could hold (or at least speak for) both attitudes at different times!

Monks felt it their religious duty to tame the wilds—even if it cost them; it was a mortification of the flesh rather than an economic enterprise. "[M]anual labor, once despised as the lot of slaves, became a [religious] guiding principle (Glacken 1967:303). Glacken goes on to quote many accounts of the amazing exploits of monks and monastic orders in taming the wilds and creating estates. Some have even seen the origins of modern capitalism in these, rather than in moneymaking activities (Collins 1998). Yet the monks often loved nature, especially where Celtic attitudes persisted. 'These monastic enclaves in the forest... apparently became asylums and refuges for wild beasts hunted by royalty; there is much legend concerning the friendship of monks for wild animals, including the deer and the wolf. In the life of St. Sequanus, wolves become laborers helping with the clearing and building" (Glacken 1967:310). Sequanus lived in Burgundy—a formerly Celtic and then Germanic area.

Of course, the secular world had to preserve forests for more crass reasons. The forests were the source of all sorts of raw materials, as well as food for pigs and humans. Modern accounts (e.g., Glacken 1967:320 ff.) stress the value of acorns for swine, but seem to miss completely the incredible importance of acorns, chestnuts, hazelnuts, beechnuts, and the rest for humans. Vast areas of Europe depended on nut crops in the Middle Ages, and not a few did so until modern times. This is abundantly attested by tales and folksongs. Many ballads describe the lord's daughter going to the greenwood to "pull the nut and sloe" (wild plum); they are not talking about mere fun.

Thus the ambivalent Western attitude toward forests continued, often dramatically so; confrontations between foresters and deforesters could be violent, especially as forest conservation became a self-conscious agenda with the rapid rise in population in the late Middle Ages (Glacken 1967:330). Charlemagne had already demonstrated a split personality, ordering both cutting forests for fields and saving forests for wood and forage (Glacken 1967:334). As population grew and put pressure on the hunting and gathering resource base, peasants had to deal with the lords taking over more and more rights to pasturage, mast for swine, and even firewood and estovers (stove fuel; Slicher von Bath 1963; Tuchman 1978). Further laws simply carry this forward—right up to our "multiple use policy" in America today.

One major reason for deforestation in old Europe was scorched-earth warfare. Eliminating sacred trees was not mere psychological war. Guerrillas and outlaws hid in and fed from forests. Serfs could escape there. Forests were not only safe space, they afforded all manner of commodities that a surreptitious economy could depend on. Ballads are the best evidence: Think of Robin Hood and many other ballad heroes with their poached deer.

The extreme case of deforestation happened as war occurred in Ireland. From the beginning, the English knew that the Irish relied heavily on their forests both economically and psychologically. They therefore cut the forests systematically, with major elimination campaigns in the Tudor and Cromwellian periods. By the time Ireland was finally crushed politically by the Tudors in 1607, there was little left. By the time Cromwell conquered and then lost Ireland for his dubious cause, there were *no* forests or groves in the entire island. Much of it degraded to moorland, which now seems romantic and nostalgic, but which is actually the effect of scorched-earth terror campaigns at their very worst. A few tiny groves have recovered in the far southwest and elsewhere.

Few, if any, other lands have been deforested solely by and for war, but many districts suffered similar fates, in Europe and elsewhere. Fortunately for forests but unfortunately for people, the usual result of war is depopulation, with forests benefiting. However, in Scotland and parts of northwest Europe as well as in Ireland, bogs and moors were the result of prolonged deforestation; they prevented forests from growing back. Similarly, in much of the Middle East, North Africa, and other drylands, both military and economic deforestation were common and led via desertification to permanent loss of soil and forests.

WHAT FOLLOWED

Fortunately for Western civilization, the world went right on drifting away from the older church and toward Aristotle. The Renaissance continued the rediscovery of nature. Petrarch (1304–1374), most important of those who rediscovered and revived Greek learning in western Europe, was also the first recorded European to climb a mountain and enjoy it—to the point that he felt guilty about such enjoyment of nature (Clark 1979:10), once again combining love and hate of fleshly delights in one person.

Science, natural history, love for nature, and nature poetry were all connected and all blossomed. The link between Natura and Eros was reaffirmed. Elizabethan poetry, for instance, frequently turns to love in the greenwood. This trope, as we have seen, goes back to the troubadours. John Dowland and Robert Herrick, among others, wrote songs urging their loved ones to come out to enjoy the May, and neither left any doubt what that meant. Herrick impatiently tells his lady that, already, "many a green-gown has been given"—that is, many a girl has gotten grass stains all over the back of her dress through rolling in the growing hay.

Experimental, inductive science as a self-conscious enterprise, distinguished from other types of knowing, arose in the sixteenth century. Presumably, its rise and enduring focus in the old Celtic-Germanic fringe countries (England, Scotland, France, Germany, the Netherlands) is no mere accident. It was largely an attempt to "know nature" or "know God's will as revealed in His creation." Because of this, it was highly nature-oriented and celebrated nature and natural kinds (Gaukroger 2006).

But the Renaissance was too little and too late to change all attitudes deeply. Puritanical, anti-natural, urban, and other antithetical currents were too strong and well established, especially in the Mediterranean world. Botany and natural science flourished there at first, especially in the sixteenth century, but dramatically declined after the religious wars of the seventeenth. Natural history and natural science became increasingly associated with the old Celtic-Germanic fringe.

Notoriously, René Descartes reached the extreme of separating humans from nature and putting humans far above. His famous philosophic grounding, "I think, therefore I am," in the *Discourse on Method* (Descartes 1999 [1637]:25), implied that one has to think to be a real person or self. Later in the book, he used language as the touchstone to separate humans from animals. Animals don't talk, but even human babies and extremely brain-damaged humans do (Descartes 1999 [1637]:41). Talking requires and implies reason, and for Descartes the lack of language implies the lack of reason. Animals are mere machines. A mechanical monkey would be indistinguishable from a real one (Descartes 1999:40). Animals seem to have feelings, but really cannot feel, being without reason (Descartes 1999:71–73). This belief caused infinite suffering when later scientists practiced vivisection at will under this justification. Modern research confirms the sharp separation of language from any nonhuman communication system, but shows that the higher social animals have extremely sophisticated and self-conscious communication and interaction systems and abilities—and of course can feel pain and emotion.

Descartes has often been blamed for separating Man the Rational from Nature the mechanical. In fact, many modern environmental writers (e.g., Willerslev 2007) seem to believe he single-handedly caused all the trouble with the environment that we now experience. Gregory Cajete, in an otherwise sensitive and aware account of Native American education, opposes the latter to "the rationalistic Newtonian-Cartesian paradigm" and believes that "[d]uring the Age of Enlightenment, Western culture broke with the ancient human 'participation mystique' ... [and] substituted a relationship based on objective scientific/rationalist thought" (Cajete 1994:82).

But Descartes was only following his Franco-Roman—and ultimately Platonic—intellectual tradition. He was also a Catholic, anxious to demonstrate that animals lacked souls. He has been accused of saying they lacked minds, but his word (when he was writing French instead of Latin) was *âmes*. And in his Latin tract on the subject, his whole discussion of animals comprises only three pages of a modest, somewhat messy essay. By itself, it was no game-changer. The idea that humans were rational and animals not so, that humans knew themselves (or could) and animals could not, stemmed from the Greeks and was general by Descartes' time. For instance, well before Descartes, one Anthony Stafford wrote in 1615 that God "made nothing since the beginning, which he thought worthy to participate of reason but man" (Stafford 1615:2). Stafford was an obscure popularizer of Greek philosophy rather than an original thinker himself and was hardly trying to innovate.

Also, before Descartes was writing, the French were cutting their own forests, civilizing the landscape, urbanizing it. The Spanish and Portuguese were carrying out their own civilizing missions in the New World, exterminating Native peoples and wild landscapes as fast and thoroughly as possible. The Jesuits in Canada were recoiling in horror from the forests and in shock from the "Indians" who ran in those forests "like wild beasts" (Blackburn 2000:50 ff.). The Jesuits also worked diligently to get the Indians to beat their children to discipline them, something the Indians strongly resisted; C. S. Lewis is right again. Yet the Jesuits had to admit that the Iroquois consoled their sick in such beautiful terms as this: "Do not be sad; if thou art sad, thou wilt become still worse; if thy sickness increases, thou wilt die. See what a beautiful country this is; love it; if thou lovest it, thou wilt take pleasure in it, if thou takest pleasure in it thou wilt become cheerful, and if thou art cheerful thou wilt recover" (Le Jeune, 1634, quoted by Eleanor Leacock in *Handbook of North American Indians,* vol. 6, p. 193). This treatment is quite typical Iroquois medicine.

In short, the "Cartesian" attitude toward nature and animals was there long before Descartes, and some perceptive Europeans already saw it was not what their converts or victims thought.

Others, however, continued it, because it fit so perfectly with their dehumanization of Africans, Native Americans, and others they wished to enslave, as well as with their attitudes toward nature. C. S. Lewis's principle again: animals were treated as slaves were. It surfaces today in such essays as Thomas Nagel's "What Is It Like to Be a Bat?" (1974). Nagel points out that we do not really know. The perfect answer to this was provided by James Uleman: "A colleague once asked me … if I knew what it was like to be a bat, referring to Nagel's (1974) famous essay … I said that I didn't even know what it was like to be me." (Uleman and Saribay 2012:337). This is the perfect sendup of Nagel's essay. Even if I were confident of my own understanding of myself, my wife would be the first to agree that I do not understand her. On the other hand, I can relate perfectly well, in general terms, to the western pipistrelle bats foraging in my garden as I write; they are delighted in their captures of gnats, hungry when they miss, scared when an owl comes out. Their simple but intense joys and fears are palpable.

Nagel's fantastically overdrawn contrast between "people" and "animals," "consciousness" and lack of it, is pure Descartes and is as pernicious as it is wrong.

In the seventeenth and eighteenth centuries, "dominion" rhetoric and behavior dramatically increased, along with autocratic centralization of government, but the stewardship ethic grew in reaction and—predictably—was often associated with the rapidly increasing reactions against autocracy.

Science was closely associated with religion; the scientists were more interested in proving Intelligent Design and understanding God's works than in denying divinity. Newton was an intensely religious man. Robert Boyle was a theologian for whom chemistry was merely one way of revealing God's will for the cosmos. When atheism arose, it arose from the philosophers (readers of Epicurus and other ancients) and the politicians; the scientists defended God. The "war of science and religion" did not come until the nineteenth century, with its thoroughly un-biblical revelations about life. Virulent anti-intellectualism has often been a part of Christianity, as seen in the old hymn:

> Other knowledge I disdain, 'tis naught but vanity;
> Christ, the lamb of God, was slain, He tasted death for me! ...
> Only Jesus will I know, and Jesus crucified.
> (Walker 1854:102)

But such attitudes did not dominate until the fundamentalist reaction after Darwin.

The rise of the "dominion" theme led not only to further deforestation and mining, but to a view that the world was made solely for human use. The rise and prevalence of this view, and its memorable savaging by Voltaire, Hume, and Kant, occupies much of Clarence Glacken's book (1967). Spinoza was one of the first to demolish it: "The attempt, however, to show that nature does nothing in vain (that is to say, nothing which is not profitable to man), seems to end in showing that nature, the gods, and man are alike mad" (quoted in Glacken 1967:378). But, of course, the belief is still very much alive, in the "intelligent design" theory that is at least as popular as Darwinian evolution, and also in the thoroughly unscientific economic theories that teach humans to do anything that brings quick profits, without thinking of the consequences.

On the other hand, Glacken (1967:689) points out that the old Argument by Design ("Intelligent Design") at least made people think the world was good. The eighteenth-century concept of Progress was based in the older alternative, the idea that the natural world is Satanic. It involved total assault on and devaluation of nature; everything was to be replaced by the tiny handful of crops that Europeans found profitable. The tens of millions of natural species were to be exterminated when possible, to be replaced by a miserable dozen cultigens.

From literally millions of possible examples, it may be sufficient to quote the first paragraph of Pierre Huard's and Maurice Durand's colonial (but sympathetic) book about Vietnamese culture:

"The life of the animal consists, simply, of adapting directly to its own environment that lets it find what it can. Humans are unique in that they rebel against the environment, inventing material and spiritual means to assure the persistence of their societies and the elimination of hostile nature. Thus are born civilization and culture" (Huard and Durand 1954:I; my translation). They go on to explain that the Vietnamese have gone far in this direction, but are notably less civilized than the French, who have done much better at subduing the environment and bending it to their will (see, e.g., pp. 63, 70–87). The measure of civilization is how much destruction has been wrought on the natural environment. Huard and Durand, though very sympathetic to the Vietnamese, were writing partly to justify the French colonial presence in Vietnam (yet again Lewis's point), and they never missed an opportunity to show how the French had brought progress and enlightenment to that tragic land. Ironically, their book was published just as the French were driven from Vietnam by the spectacularly successful military and political campaigns of the Vietnamese people. One hopes that the two Frenchmen reflected on the inadequacy of their colonial analysis. At least, we today can recognize that one need not be either French or antienvironment to succeed in this world.

The inevitable countercurrent included the rise of appreciation of views of nature (Glacken 1967:456) and subsequently of landscape art (see below). Naturalists like John Ray and John Evelyn, in the late seventeenth century, maintained the necessity of conservation and environmental protection. Evelyn provides an astonishing parallel to Mencius's famous story of Ox Mountain—naturally forested but turned into waste, first by the axe, then by cattle. It is so close that one wonders if Evelyn had read some version of Mencius's story in some returning missionary's account. Interestingly, Evelyn fails to draw the parallel with human behavior that was so beautifully clear to the Chinese author. At the same time, John Dryden coined the phrase "the noble savage"—a phrase that was never used by Rousseau (Ellingson 2001).

The Romantic movement and its dramatic revaluation of nature is too well known to need explication here, but does require mention. Even though it was most often an urban phenomenon that distanced "nature" and sometimes regarded it as fearsome, Romanticism was a dramatic reassertion of the old nature-loving side of European culture. It was, of course, the main source of our modern environmentalist attitudes, especially via the writings of Goethe, Wordsworth, Shelley, and especially Henry David Thoreau (Taylor 2010). Generalizations about the evil, destructive "West" generally forget the popularity of these Romantic authors and the incredibly long shadow their views cast on modern thought. Even the crassest "developers" advertise "view properties." An English socialist, Robert Blatchford, in the nineteenth century, called for radicals and workers to demand protection of nature and natural beauty (Coates 1998:160).

Scientists and environmentalists present a rational side of an attraction to nature that was somewhat equivocal among the Romantics. According to student notes (all we have, alas, of his teachings on nature), Maurice Merleau-Ponty commented that the German Romantics believed that "[r]eason is mistaken, and the rational human is conceived as what remains of a being that is now extinct, a being that would have lived in the golden age in contact with the potencies of Nature, a contact that we can no longer retrieve today except in a dream.... Heraclitus says that Nature is a child at play; it gives meaning, but in a manner of a child who is playing, and this meaning is never total" (Merleau-Ponty 2003:84).

THE ENDGAME: DOMINATION AND CARE IN THE LAST CENTURIES

Cold and dull psychological and economic lock-in blighted the hopeful visions of a world with some degree of harmony with nature. Throughout all these centuries, the latifundia system persisted in the Mediterranean. It took different forms in Christian and in Islamic societies. This is most clearly seen in Spain, where Christian and Muslim polities coexisted for eight centuries. The Moors' intensive agriculture was often on huge estates worked by servile labor. In the north, the Christians, confined to the less valuable land, developed extensive cattle-raising into the cattle ranching we know today. The leather-ware, hats, saddles, and other familiar Hollywood properties are all of Spanish origin, and some go back to late-Roman ancestors. They spread to Mexico and entered United States culture when Texas became independent of Mexico and then a part of the United States. The violence and feuding shown in Hollywood Westerns were also a legacy of that cultural realm.

Extensive cattle-raising, the bane of the Americas ever since the sixteenth century, thus developed in Spain in the middle ages. With the Reconquista, its identification with Christianity and the identification of intensive farming with the Muslims led to valuing extensive cattle-ranching over settled farming. This prestige hierarchy was transferred to the New World, where cattle ranches were idealized. Intensive farming was left to Indians. Native peoples and their small but meticulously cultivated farms still have a status far below extensive cattle-ranching in Mexico, Brazil, and elsewhere, and countless Native farmers have been displaced for vastly less productive animal herding (this is based to a considerable extent on my own research, but see, e.g., Melville 1997; Painter and Durham 1995).

However, specialized livestock raising is not usually highly damaging except on pioneer fringes or when it displaces settled farming for mere status reasons. Pastoralists generally know what the land can support and are able to move their animals around. History suggests (though there is no real proof) that the Spanish *mesta* (medieval cattle-ranching society) was not highly destructive except where it displaced local farmers for noneconomic reasons. It was destructive in the New World because New World fauna and flora had no evolved resistance to it, and because the Spanish succumbed to the pioneer effect. Established small-scale cattle-raisers in the New World have since become quite environmentally conscious in many cases (Hedrick 2007; Kaus 1992; Perramond 2010; Sheridan 1998). The problem comes when cattle are part of a large-scale grain-and-livestock system with giant landholdings and rich (usually absentee) landlords.

All this led to a truly pernicious ideological, economic, and technological complex. Varro and Columella were already warning their readers that inefficient, wasteful, badly planned agriculture is the typical result of absentee landlords and vast estates worked by slaves or other landless persons. No one has an incentive to do a good job. In fact, it is almost impossible for the parties to have any respect or affection for their enterprise. The landlord has his wealth and urban power. The slaves have nothing but resentment. By contrast, a small farmer is motivated both by economic need and by pride of ownership. Such a farmer normally develops a sense of unity with and responsibility for the land. As the English proverb has it: "The best dung for the land is the tread of the master's foot." Roman estates, and their Mediterranean and American descendants, had that too rarely.

It joins and fuses naturally with the dour, anti-flesh attitudes of dualism, Neo-Platonism and ascetic Christianity. One strongly suspects, in fact, that these arose from the landlord economy. The world's environment problems today are the product of this union: antinature ideology and a political economy that privileges and subsidizes vast estates worked by servile labor. Neither could exist nor maintain itself without the other. Again, we recall Max Weber and the feedback between economics and religion.

In the New World, pioneer attitudes led further to a hatred and scorn for everything native and a nostalgic idealization of the Old World and all its crops. Most of the New World was soon cleared for wheat, cattle, and other nonnative products. Maize, potatoes, and a few other crops proved too competitive to ignore, but the vast majority of the rich, productive, and ecologically successful agricultural and management systems of the Americas were sacrificed along with their Native American creators. Even things like tomatoes and green peppers were popularized in Europe—rather late—and had to be reintroduced to the New World (notably by Italian immigrants) to catch on north of Mexico.

An extreme form of antinature sentiment arose, due to pioneer-fringe phenomena. Settlers were primed to hate and fear the forests, beasts, and vast landscapes (to say nothing of the Native people). They often saw only material to destroy. The incredible hecatombs of game recorded by John James Audubon (1967 [1840–1844]) and other observers now stagger the imagination. Audubon soberly records seeing as many birds of some species destroyed in a day as there are members of those species left in the entire world now. The most heavily shot species are now extinct. Even then, there was some pushback; Audubon records some nascent conservation measures in older settlements such as Massachusetts.

Lawns, manicured fields, and other European features, all with European species, dominated. This was Alfred Crosby's "ecological imperialism" (Crosby 1986) with a vengeance. Isaac Weld, a European traveler, noted in 1799 that American pioneers "have an unconquerable aversion to trees ... they cut away all before them without mercy ... all share the same fate and are involved in the same havoc" (quoted in Morris 2010:509). An eighteenth-century New Englander cited by Clarence Glacken had this to say: "Take a View of a Swamp in its original Estate.... Its miry Bottom, and Harbour to Turtles, Toads, Efts [salamanders], Snakes, and other creeping Verm'n. The baleful Thickets of Branbles [*sic*], and the dreary Shades of larger Growth; the Dwelling Place of the Owl and the Bittern; a Portion of Foxes, and a Cage of every unclean and hateful bird" (Glacken 1967:692–693). After draining and cultivating, it became a glorious prospect of nonnative barley, flax, and so on. The idea is clear: almost everything native or natural in the New World is horrible and should be destroyed at all costs. This passage reads particularly ironically in this age when we realize how important wetlands are ecologically and what a dreadful mistake it was to drain them. Species from the Old World were introduced, meanwhile, with blithe indifference to their potential for disrupting local ecosystems; many Americans still cannot understand that invasive species can be a bad thing (Coates 2006), but they cost us tens of billions of dollars each year.

Fortunately, not everyone was such a fool. Glacken goes on to cite Benjamin Franklin's more enlightened and ecological views; Franklin pointed out that New Englanders had done away with blackbirds, only to have the crops decimated by insects the blackbirds had been eating.

Monocrop plantations developed in the sugar, rice, and cotton fields of the Americas. These were managed according to Roman traditions: landlords (though not usually absentee) owned slave-run plantations. These landlords, of course, held the political power in their home regions. Many were Latin-literate and quoted the Roman authors directly. Because the plantation owners also had disproportionate power in Congress, American farm policy has always favored huge monocrop enterprises over small or diversified farms, in spite of the Jeffersonian rhetoric. Farm policy today enormously subsidizes large-scale production and a few basic commodities—staple grains, soybeans, sugar, and of course cotton (Imhoff 2012). This has nothing to do with economic realities and everything to do with the political and social agendas established by the Roman senators and reestablished by the New World plantocracy in the eighteenth and nineteenth centuries. (On the plantation economy, see Beckford 1972; Mintz 1985.) Thousands of studies have shown that family farming and diversification pay better by every measure (see the classic review by Netting 1993; also Dove 2011), but power is power.

The concept spread to the newly opened cattle, wheat, and other landscapes of the west. By the twentieth century, the whole idea of a farm was changed: instead of a small diverse patch managed by a family, it became a vast spread, growing one crop, with no houses or trees in sight, managed by migrant crews. With the abolition of slavery, machines came to replace humans in the fields (cf. Hayami and Ruttan 1985). Communism enthusiastically adopted it, in a socialized form. Today, this strange and new image of "the farm" has gone worldwide and become the correct and proper way to manage the land, in spite of its pathological origin, uneconomic present (Netting 1993), and unsustainable future. In the United States, extreme bias in favor of such giant farms has led to heavy subsidizing of them and of their mass-produced commodity crops, at the expense of small farms (Anderson 2010; Bovard 1991; Imhoff 2012; Myers 1998). Agricultural policies under Eisenhower, Reagan, and the two Bushes, in particular, aggressively favored and supported large farms over small ones. The result has been inefficiency, waste, and pollution, as well as destruction of natural landscapes. Social and economic injustice have, of course, also proliferated. This obsession can verge on the insane; I have heard anecdotally that someone seriously proposed removing all African cultivators from the land and replacing them with a handful of American or Chinese farmers with full agribusiness machinery and chemicals.

In Mexico, Brazil, Honduras, and elsewhere, governments have routinely and systematically favored large-scale cattle ranching over all other rural activities, especially indigenous peoples' land uses (see, e.g., Painter and Durham 1995; Stonich 1993). World trade and economic organizations now follow this model, unthinkingly. It is enshrined in the plans of the World Bank and in those of rival bodies from far right to far left.

Cultural systems, once established, take on a life of their own; they become path-dependent. European unnaturalism is not the product of capitalism, still less of the giant corporations that now manage, propagate, and sell it. They maintain it against all economic sanity and force it on other countries, but they did not create it. They would not even profit from it, without the heavy subsidies. They find they must defend it through politics in a world of better alternatives (Anderson 2010).

This is the root of the entire modern economy of throughput maximization. It gave us the whole idea of massively transforming nature and maximizing resource use. It also established a policy of governments to subsidize the most powerful firms, almost invariably those that maximized profit in the short run by minimizing long-term concerns. Government has thus become a vast force for distorting economy in the most perverse direction.

American favoring of plantation agriculture and large-scale cattle ranching has inspired countless imitators. The political power of the elites led to its becoming heavily subsidized by governments. Costs are passed on to the general public, through pollution of water, loss of forests, and so on, rather than being internalized by the farmers. Large-scale monocrop cultivation thus appears, quite wrongly, to "pay." It is diligently promoted by the World Bank and other international bodies (Dichter 2003; Stiglitz 2003). The result has been destruction of resources, human and natural communities, and, above all, human lives. Colonial plantation agriculture left a legacy of hate and degradation that has surfaced in genocide and civil war from Haiti to Indonesia and from Rwanda to Sri Lanka. Postcolonial monocropping imposed by international bodies is now having the same effect worldwide.

This has cultural consequences. Materialism with concern for quantity rather than quality has been characteristic of all declining empires: declining Babylon, Hellenistic Greece, late Rome, late Qing, and today's America. A result is that getting people to care for the environment for aesthetic and spiritual reasons becomes more and more difficult.

It seems fairly clear that at *no* time was plantation and estate agriculture really economically rational (Netting 1993). Small intensive diversified farming, with stable viable communities, always pays better for everyone. Rulers use estates and subsidies to reward leading politicians, and then the estate sector has political power that it can use to obtain more subsidies and to get the army to eliminate dissident workers—a pattern visible from Spartacus's revolt down to modern Guatemala and Colombia.

On the other hand, at no time was this attitude completely prevalent. J. R. McNeill (1992) and A. T. Grove and Oliver Rackham (2001) have provided broad-scale overviews of good and bad land management around the Mediterranean, differing in focus. McNeill tells a straight, detailed, factual story of several cases ranging from best to worst. His best case is a Turkish mountain area, his worst, the burning rock deserts of Morocco where forests formerly grew (on which, see Mikesell 1961). I am familiar with both—but I can also point out that there are many rock deserts in Turkey and some splendid forests in Morocco. (On the latter, see Charco 1999, a great work that must be consulted by anyone interested in Mediterranean landscapes). Management regimes are (or once were) local in the Mediterranean, not national.

Grove and Rackham critiqued McNeill and defended Mediterranean management, presenting many best-case scenarios. I spent several months traveling through several Mediterranean countries ground-checking these works, visiting many of the areas they describe, and found that McNeill is the accurate one to read for the overall picture. However, Grove and Rackham record many genuinely good practices and are extremely thought-provoking. They show countless ways in which the ordinary peasants and small farmers and herders of the Mediterranean do a very good job with what they have. Still more impressive is a book-length study, Gaston Remmers's superb *Con Cojones y Maestría* (1998), of a Spanish village with incredibly successful management practices dating back to Moorish times. It could be a world model for social management of landscape.

Grove and Rackham, and to a lesser extent McNeill, tend to blame the all too visible trashing of the Mediterranean landscape on the devastating impact of "modern" agriculture and technology over the last 200 years. Though indeed the damage has gotten much worse in those centuries, the general point is contradicted by Mediterranean authors themselves. From the ancient Greeks on down, they regularly lamented deforestation and erosion and argued for better practice.

Ancient worldviews do persist and do matter. Even comparing Celtic-influenced northwest Spain with southern Spain, or north Italy with the Mezzogiorno, is quite enough to establish some differences that are hard to explain by simple recourse to recent history. And it certainly means something that although most Spanish words are derived from Latin, most Spanish tree names are Celtic, Basque, or Arabic (my count, drawing on Lapesa 1981).

On the other hand, recent histories matter, too. The northern areas of these countries have been less affected by landlordism and large-scale outside exploitation (see, e.g., Putnam 1993 for northern vs. southern Italy). This makes comparisons more difficult and *magna forte,* if one compares the British Isles or Scandinavia with the Mediterranean.

Inevitably, northwest European love of nature and Mediterranean distancing from it have never been separate. They invariably grade into each other. This is especially true in central and east Europe, from France to Russia, resulting in complex and often contradictory cultural practices. Russian authors ranged from real lovers of nature in a classic Old Northern tradition (Turgenev, Tolstoy, Chekhov, Gorky) to glorifiers of the machine, the city, and Progress (like Mayakovski and Leonov). A line in a 1929 school book from the USSR said "we must discover and conquer the country[side] in which we live" (Coates 1998:152). From such teachings came East Europe's pollution crisis and Mao's war on nature.

Even the Celtic and Germanic regions deforested most of the landscape, grazed cattle indiscriminately, and often hunted and fished beyond any sustainable level—often starting this even before Roman influence. But their consciousness of the environment and their love of the natural never seem to have flagged. Nature mysticism persisted well into the twentieth century in the form of charms and local beliefs (see Carmichael 1992).

People from these countries are, and always have been, heavily overrepresented in modern conservation, forestry, and environmental movements. Consider the endless attempts by northern Europeans to stop southern Europeans from hunting migrant songbirds for food (millions are killed annually). The northerners want to enjoy the songs next year; the southerners want to enjoy dining on *beccaficos*.

On the other hand, the Old Northern view surfaces in some astonishing places. The Greek-American chef Michael Psilakis remembers his father, a stern old-school Mediterranean head of family, introducing him (at 11) to butchering a lamb. Michael cried, and his father told him: "Why are you crying? . . . It is okay to be sad that the lamb is dead. Hold on to that sadness, because the taking of a life is never something to joke about. When you think about that lamb and what it gave up for us so that we could eat, you understand that we killed a living thing, and we must always respect and honor that animal by using everything it has to offer" (Psilakis 2009:140–141; the last is in reference to Michael's youthful squeamishness about organ meats, which he thus learned to eat). This is startlingly similar to Native American views and discourses on meat.

It would seem that modern conservation and environmentalism owe their existence to the tension between the two dramatically opposed worldviews: nature care and nature destruction. No such sharp contrast arose in China or southern Asia, and thus no specific "conservation" or "environmentalist" ideology per se, because there was no need. Sheer wanton destruction of nature on the scale of Roman circuses or nineteenth-century American buffalo hunts was simply unthinkable.

The nineteenth century was, notoriously, the climactic period for science as nature-mastering, but—partly in reaction—it was also the age that gave birth to conservation as a serious field of study. Modern environmentalists read with astonishment George Perkins Marsh's great book *Man and Nature* (2003 [1864]). One of the greatest works of nineteenth century science, it profoundly transformed thinking about forests, waters, sands, and indeed the whole earth's surface. Yet it is unequivocally committed to mastery and Progress, not preservation. Marsh forthrightly prefers tree plantations to natural forests and unquestioningly advocates draining wetlands. He wished not to stop human management of the world, but to substitute good management for bad management. His only sop to preservation is an awareness of the truth enshrined much later in the saying "Nature always bats last." He knew, for instance, that constraining rivers with levees was self-defeating if the river was allowed to aggrade its bed and eventually burst the banks.

The modern absorption with "nature" has been claimed as a product of the "Romantic movement." This is not the case. The Romantics did enormously increase interest and start the conservation idea seriously growing, but they always maintained a kind of personal distance, unlike the Medieval and Renaissance poets. The Romantics did manage to revitalize the age-old link between love for nature and love for one's sex partner. In the twentieth century, however, along with so much else connected with the environment, the link between these loves rapidly attenuated and finally broke. The great nature poetry of recent decades, from Robinson Jeffers to Gary Snyder, owes much more to older poetry—Celtic, biblical, Renaissance, Chinese, and other—than to the Romantics.

Romantics from the Celtic-Germanic fringe, including artists like Caspar David Friedrich (Hoffman 2000) and poets like Wordsworth, were powering up their local traditions, not starting something totally new. Romantics from Mediterranean Europe were notably indifferent to such concerns. Scientists from the northern fringe continued their interest in natural history and branched out to create forestry management (a German invention), agricultural science, and indeed most of modern biology—with major French input in this latter case. Except for notable Renaissance activity in Italy, the Mediterranean world has contributed relatively little to these agendas. (The contrast between northern and Mediterranean Europe still exists, has often been commented on, but has not to my knowledge been studied historically; it needs research.)

Throughout this time and space, love of wild nature has usually gone along with love of gardens and other tamed nature. The connection of love for nature with love for small diversified farming is explicit in Aldo Leopold (1949), for instance, and in most of his intellectual descendants today, such as Wendell Berry (see Taylor 2010). Rejection of the wild usually means rejection of even tamed nature, unless it is completely beaten down: the monocrop field, the clipped and pruned lawn and hedge, the overbred dog, useless for hunting or herding.

CODA: EUROPEAN LANDSCAPE PAINTING

Any book on representations of nature must come to terms with west Europe and its landscape art tradition. The glib generalizations about "idealization" and "bourgeois tastes" do not say much. Why do people idealize in a certain way?

In Europe, the Romans (and presumably the Greeks) had an enormous and robust tradition of portraying nature, gardens, fields, and animals. These survive in the murals of Pompeii, but especially in mosaics. The Dark Ages and obsessive Christian iconography—as well as iconoclasm, in the early medieval Byzantine Empire—destroyed this tradition. Paintings between about 500 and 1300 have no landscape backdrop, and representations of nature are extremely rare in any European art. Kenneth Clark emphasizes this by pointing out that the great painter Giotto in the early 1300s did not portray nature even in his paintings of the life and mission of St. Francis of Assisi (Clark 1979:9). The fourteenth century left us some tantalizingly well-done portrayals of nature, but nothing like a tradition.

However, there is at least one tiny indication that something major is lost. The Chora Church in Istanbul, dating from 1321, has a range of excellent land-scapes in both fresco and mosaic. They look, to my eye, enough like frescoes at Pompeii and mosaics in Roman North Africa to imply a continuous tradition (this is based on personal study of all the above). However, they are well past the Mongol invasions and their introduction of Chinese landscape art to the West, so they may not indicate continuity. I am aware of no comparable Byzantine work. (See illustrations, somewhat inadequate for the landscapes, in Dursun 2011 and Underwood 1966.) Moreover, the Pope's Palace at Avignon has a large number of spectacular wall paintings surviving from 1343; these show, in extremely accurate detail, many birds, plants, and animals (personal observa-tion; some can be seen figured in Magi 2010). Like the Chora paintings (but to a somewhat lesser extent), they are clearly continuous with Roman models. Most are hunting scenes, involving not only dogs hunting deer but even a ferret hunting rabbits. These paintings are as developed and accurate as most pre-1500 works and indicate a very vigorous but almost unknown tradition in the West as in the Greek East.

After that, art suddenly changed from sterile, hieratic iconography to vi-brant, living realism. This was clearly related to the above-noted rediscovery of Aristotle and the rise of attention to the natural world. The great cathedrals with their gargoyles and graffiti, and the coming of realistic manuscript illus-tration in Arab style, presaged the explosion of landscape and nature art in the fifteenth century (cf. Glacken 1967:245). Giotto and others developed natu-ralistic painting styles. More or less realistic landscape backgrounds appeared in Italian paintings around or shortly after 1400; the style was borrowed from Persian art, itself greatly affected by Chinese influence that had come with the Mongols (see Kadoi 2009).

The Mongol Empire introduced Chinese painting to the West, on a fairly large scale, after the conquest of Baghdad in 1248–1250. Art came especially through paintings and through scenes painted on Chinese export pottery. A vast industry of blue-and-white pottery developed under the Mongols and was to a great extent export-oriented (Buell 2009; Carswell 2000; Komaroff and Carboni 2002). Some of the best pieces made in China are now in the Topkapi Museum in Istanbul. Through this and other painted media, Chinese landscape art reached the Western world in massive quantities. Iran and then the rest of the Islamic world quickly began copying Chinese landscape styles. Significantly, China foregrounded the landscape, reducing humans to tiny figures admiring it. Iran in its medieval miniature paintings reversed this. Iranian painters made the landscape a stylized backdrop to human drama, pictorially and emotionally larger than life, in the foreground.

Particularly striking is an astonishingly modern and highly evolved miniature landscape by an anonymous artist painting around 1415 in a Book of Hours (that of Turin; Clark 1979:32–33). Though already unmistakably European in style, its use of water for the middle distance, hills for the horizon, trees for the right-hand height emphasis, small humans in the foreground, and many other traits link it equally unmistakably to Near Eastern derivatives of Chinese landscape art. At the same time, the "Très Riches Heures" of the Duke of Berry contains many magnificent landscapes, mostly backdrops for religious painting (Longnon et al. 1969).

By 1450, Italian painters were creating beautiful landscape backgrounds for their paintings of saints and sinners. Often the landscapes were identifiably local, but in Persianized Chinese style, as in Paolo Veronese's exquisite religious paintings, whose backgrounds show the scenery around Verona and Lake Garda; Joseph, Mary, and other holy figures appear in Italian Renaissance costume in the landscapes of the Veneto.

This standard Renaissance localization was not because of ignorance; the artists knew perfectly well what Near Easterners looked like. The idea was to personalize the biblical narratives and make them directly relevant to the viewers. Often, locally admired people were painted into the scenes as witnesses to the life of Christ, and locally hated ones were painted in as soldiers torturing him. In the Sistine Chapel, Michelangelo painted his meanest critic burning in hell with a serpent biting his scrotum. One wonders if the Catholic Church would accept such an image today.

Michelangelo supposedly deplored landscape (Clark 1979:54), but his contemporaries did magnificent landscape backdrops for their religious paintings, with heavy use of symbols and of mood-settings. Crucifixion scenes showed spare trees, cloudy skies, and falling flowers.

Leonardo's background for the *Mona Lisa* is rarely noted or appreciated, but it shows a strikingly realistic view over the river country of north Italy; Leonardo was ahead of his time as usual. From then on, the Chinese perspective based on planes of distance—the way the human eye focuses and thus actually sees the land—was, more and more, replaced by more contrived portrayal, notably vanishing-point perspective. Sometimes the old Sino-Iranian style was revived for religious paintings, in a bit of deliberate archaizing, as in Velasquez's paintings of old-time religious stories.

From the 1500s to the late nineteenth century, extremely realistic landscapes were the rule. The idea that the painting might show *nothing* but landscape—no foreground figure needed—appears around 1600. (The ancient

Roman murals often show gardens with no human figures; this seems completely unconnected with the new styles.) Thereafter the "landscape" became a genre of painting in its own right. If the Dutch did not invent the landscape, they certainly perfected it. While Rembrandt was making his name as a painter of portraits and religious figures, the Ruisdaels, Albert Cuyp, and others were creating huge and striking landscapes that portrayed the Netherlands so perfectly that they are still standards of excellence in the field. We now look at them for aesthetic pleasure, but social historians can actually get hard data from the paintings; they can count the mills in the cities, reconstruct the ecology of the marshes, and identify the fish sold in the markets.

Why did landscape paintings develop? Many have noted the association in time with the rise of merchants and trade. The spread from east to west under the Mongols was due to trade (including elaborately painted ceramics), not conquest. The landscape as rich backdrop for portraits, religious scenes, and town life emerged along with the dramatic increase of trade in the Italian states in the fifteenth century. The emergence of pure landscapes, without the dominant foreground figures, coincided with the emergence of modern capitalism and the wealth-based state in the Golden Age of the Netherlands (cf. Israel 1995; Slive 2005). Landscape art spread right along with capitalism to England, France, and onward.

It also spread through the old northern fringe. In spite of starting in Italy, landscape painting flourished most in the old Celtic, Germanic, and Slavic lands. The great trend-setting countries were the Low Countries, France, Germany, and the British Isles.

To some extent, landscape art was escapist amusement for rich burghers, or a view of their lands decked with resources that could make money. Many Dutch landscapes show profitable enterprises, and were commissioned for that purpose by their bourgeois owners.

However, there was also a genuine and rapidly growing love of nature. A painting of one's mill could be vulgar show, or it could be a fine painting that backgrounded the mill in a scene of rural opulence. A painting of one's ship in a wild beach scene, or of one's Brazilian farm, had to have artistic quality to be worth the bother.

All this accompanied the rise of science (notably biology), exploration, enterprise, travel, and interest in other lands and lifeways. In fact, the line between scientific illustration and art was notably absent. Technical illustrations in herbals merge insensibly into flower paintings. Records of mines merge into mountain landscapes. Starting with the long tradition of herbals, from Dioscorides onward, botanical and zoological illustration had a huge impact on knowledge of and appreciation for nature (Blunt and Raphael 1979). The great sixteenth-century herbals broke out of the medieval Dioscorides mold and quickly achieved major artistic success. Nineteenth-century painters like Redouté and Audubon brought this tradition to its height.

The developing landscape art has been accused of static, timeless portrayal, but actually the Dutch paintings are full of details that ground them historically. Ruins indicate a glorious antiquity, often juxtaposed with a humble peasantry in the foreground. The message—quite explicit in Dutch writings of the time—is that glory passes and crumbles to dust, but the humble world of ordinary hard-working people goes on. Other paintings show historic features, like Jacob van Ruisdael's romanticized views of Amsterdam's churches and of rural castles (Slive 2005). Stories about these buildings and sites were fresh news at the time, and any viewer would know them. Thus the paintings were grounded in a rich context of important events and discourses. Even a painting that shows nothing but old oak trees was often intended as a comment on time and growth.

Closely related to landscapes were still lifes, and these routinely showed transience, mortality, and decay—fading flowers, hourglasses, skulls, insects, and mice nibbling remnants of feasts, and other indications of time and mortality (Schneider 1992). Opposed to this melancholy school were paintings of the New World—some real landscapes, some idealized or symbolic representations (Honour 1975). These told of adventure, newness, and enterprise.

Modern claims that these paintings were "idealized" miss the graphic portrayal of poverty and exploitation in many of them. Socially critical references that were crystal-clear at the time are often cryptic now. Even the modern viewer can easily recognize that the Breughels's and Bosch's works, and many later Low Countries paintings, are outright social commentary (cf. Slive 1995). On a lowlier level, in the Prado hangs a Rubens painting of Emperor Maximilian riding proudly in a huge, ostentatious, absurdly overblown procession. Rubens focuses the viewer's eye on a royal spaniel pissing against a tree, right in center foreground. No one could possibly miss the message, and I am amazed that Rubens got away with it.

In fact, the role of dogs as message-carriers in such paintings was universal and deliberate. It reaches its apotheosis in a Paulus Potter painting in the Hermitage, St. Petersburg. Here stands a splendid but badly neglected old dog, chained and mangy. A vague distant cloud forms a halo around its head. All possible doubt as to the referent is removed by Potter's placing his signature on the name-board over the doghouse door (personal observation).

The charge of idealization sticks better for eighteenth-century landscapes, which tended to drift off into banal pictures of shepherdesses in dreamy pastoral settings. By the late eighteenth century this pattern was more than exhausted.

The English painter John Constable broke the pattern by going back to the Dutch, drawing on them for his incredibly dynamic, involving, passionate landscapes. "I never saw an ugly thing in my life," he said. "The sound of water escaping from mill-dams, willows, old rotten planks, slimy posts, and brickwork, I love such things" (Clark 1979:153). Though painting for the well-to-do, he portrayed the rural poor (as did a few other artists; Barrell 1980) at a time when most eighteenth-century pictures still focused on elite themes (Bermingham 1986). Painters tended to idealize the rural unfortunates, but at least showed them and often foregrounded them. Some painted them more because they were "picturesque" than because of pity, but others had genuine compassion (Klonk 1996:27). Incidentally, the "gypsies" referred to in Klonk's book are British "traveling folk," not Roma; the Roma had been expelled in the seventeenth century, and the paintings clearly show native British Isles travelers. In short, Constable realized that the whole environment is valuable and the people who live in and from it deserve full consideration as humans.

Constable was well grounded in the science of sight and perception (Klonk 1996), and made some significant technical innovations in the process. He painted at about the time that Goethe, Kant, and others were pointing out that people do not see what is there—still less can artists paint it. Painters obviously found this realization liberating (Klonk 1996:30–32).

The actual ways the eye and brain do this cocreating were not discovered until well into the twentieth century, but the general idea was well known. Descartes had said something similar (Hyman 2006), and even the Greeks had some concept of it. It turns out that the eye itself processes visual information; then the visual centers of the brain do more; finally, the higher centers of the brain finish the job of creating a visual experience. This is a true *representation*; Kant used that term for this internally constructed sensory experience. He realized that we do not "see reality"; our eyes and brain construct an internal reality that is shaped and corrected by external reality but is not a mere reflection of it. Optical illusions prove this. From Kant onward, more attention has been paid to collective, cultural or social, representations, and that leads us directly to the present book.

The point here is that this was a new way of looking at nature. It was far more involving. The viewer is there in the painting, living the experience of the landscape by being forced to construct it.

From this start, Constable learned to use a few dabs of paint to trick the viewer's eye into constructing a whole scene (Gombrich 1960). This trick has a history—the ancient Romans knew it, the Dutch developed it, the French continued it—but Constable went beyond received wisdom. (The Chinese had been doing this for centuries, but there is no evidence that Constable knew about them.) His perfection of the trick involves sophisticated use of human visual psychology.

Constable's contemporary, Turner, developed this to an incredible degree; Turner worked to see how little he could paint to make the viewer construct a whole scene. The Impressionists were to make a whole science out of it. The great authority Kenneth Clark (1979) regards such paintings as the height of naturalistic portrayal. Yet when you look closely at a Constable or Monet, you see brush strokes, not leaves or twigs. Distance and your active mind create the real image. John Hyman (2006) critiqued Gombrich's position, but Hyman is wrong even about Constable, to say nothing of Turner, Monet, and Van Gogh. A close scan of a Constable tree shows Gombrich is right; looked at from inches away, it resolves into a bunch of green daubs. You have to apply your own creative effort to make a tree out of it. You are then a sharer in creating the painting. It is more than Constable's effort; it is you and Constable in communication, cocreating. It is Levinas's "infinitely important Other."

Another type of challenge to canned shepherdesses came from Romanticism. Wild, stormy, mountainous, wind-whipped landscapes appeared, often without any human presence. Caspar David Friedrich vested these with an explicit religious and spiritual significance, placing crosses and other Christian symbols on his storm-wracked mountains (Hoffman 2000). Others, however, created more ordinary and less portentous landscapes, though often torn by storms and other elemental violence.

These often seem very distanced from the viewer. They portray Nature held at more than arm's length. It is grand, magnificent, awe-inspiring, and wonderful, but also foreign to humanity, often downright hostile in a cold, remote way. Part of the cause is the final alienation of people from nature, caused by the Industrial Revolution. Possibly related is the frequent nineteenth-century conception of God as an extremely grand, awe-inspiring, remote Being. This God is little involved with daily life and must be praised with hymns exalting Him but emphasizing His vast distance from the worshiper. (Compare hymns like "How Great Thou Art" with far more personal earlier hymns like "Amazing Grace" or later ones like "What a Friend We Have in Jesus.") This conception of God has everything to do with the social upheavals of the time, specifically the rise of vast impersonal industrial empires ruled by powerful but obscure bosses and entrepreneurs, lying behind the more visible but decreasingly powerful aristocracy.

Romanticism was quite explicitly a reaction against that grim and gray event, a desire to "build Jerusalem" among "England's dark satanic mills," as William Blake put it. The vast majority of the consumers of romantic art were making out like robber barons from the Industrial Revolution. Yet the art had a major lasting impact on Western views of the world.

Fatigue with storms and mystical visions soon set in. One direction for art was to move toward fusing some romantic methods with scientific illustration. John James Audubon in America and John Gould in England took zoological illustration into a whole new dimension, creating genuinely great art instead of mere diagrammatic textbook work. Audubon's incisive and well-crafted prose filled this out with an amazing mix of scientific rigor, personal narrative, and philosophic idealization of nature, though he came to the conservation idea only in later life (see Aububon 1967).

The most interesting and important pushback against overblown romanticism was done by a group of French artists who retired to the small and isolated village of Barbizon to get away from Paris. The Barbizon School—especially Theophile Gautier, Gustave Courbet, Albert Daubigny, and Jean-François Millet—had influences far beyond its own time and place. For instance, the Russian painter Ivan Shishkin (2008) portrayed his native land in impeccable Barbizon style (some are even straight covers, slightly Russianized, of specific Barbizon paintings by Courbet and others). I shall refer below to the movement's even more important Mexican aftershock.

By this time, painting directly from nature—"*plein air*" painting—had become well established. Painters worked outdoors, though often finishing their works in studios. This, of course, reinforces the new attitudes toward nature (see Cabanne 1998 for a superb history of *plein air* art). Pictures ranged up to huge and stunning—and even outrageously overdone—canvases like some of Courbet's (cf. Clark 1979:165) and Shishkin's, but they could just as often be extremely low-key, intimate, quietly beautiful paintings. Daubigny especially loved this approach and is consequently far too little regarded today. (Even Kenneth Clark didn't get it, finding him too "common"; Clark 1979:168.)

The economic correlate here is the most dismal phase of the Industrial Revolution, including its brutalization of rural life. The Barbizon painters reintroduced ordinary humanity and the human scale, banished by both the shepherdess-infested Classicists and the remote Romantics. Barbizon painters showed ordinary people in ordinary scenes. Some, notably Millet, went on to portray the horrors of the time in uncompromising paintings. The nobility of starving peasants came through strongly in Millet's paintings; the vileness of their exploiters was the unspoken but obvious end to that sentence. This is another case in which modern viewers usually miss the social commentary. Those peasants in Millet may look like mere idealized figures to us, but they carried a very explicit message to viewers of his own time (see Adams 1994).

The other Barbizon painters were usually less graphic, but the low-key beauty of Daubigny's fields and the dark and looming forests of Courbet make major points about nature and landscape. This was a new sort of art, advocating a people-in-nature and people-in-society view. The critics were well aware of this. Théophile Thoré, perhaps the leading art critic in France at the time, wrote that "there is ... nothing actual and real except for poetry and nature," and that such free goods far surpassed things of profit, which were "the ridiculous inventions of men" (Adams 1994:123). It is not mere coincidence that these painters and writers were contemporary with Henry David Thoreau and George Perkins Marsh.

Impressionism arose from the Barbizon school, whose painters anticipated much of the characteristic Impressionist style. Some of them, notably Daubigny, actively midwifed the new movement (Adams 1994). The Impressionist and Post-Impressionist movements, correlating with the golden age of capitalism in the late nineteenth and early twentieth centuries, radically changed landscape art. Insofar as landscape art survives in this postmodern world, it survives largely in the form that Monet and his contemporaries made it. Contrary to the stereotype of painting only for the elite, the Barbizon artists did some popular work such as book illustration—Daubigny illustrated a book of folk songs—and copies, images, and reproductions of their paintings were very widely sold for decades.

This radically transformative style was the final climax of the use of suggestive paint strokes to make the eye construct the scene for itself, thus making the viewer a cocreator with the artist. Monet became truly shamanic in his uncanny ability to make the viewer not only construct, but feel, smell, touch, and taste a scene. Obviously, a painting is going to be much more effective if the viewer has to do the real work herself; she can fill in the blanks as her experiences suggest. (The Surrealists later took this sort of visual science and physics to new heights, partly through overinterpreting the science; see Parkinson 2008.) Social commentary was generally backgrounded in this art—not always, but often enough to allow Clark (1979:179) to charge the school with too much attention to bourgeois amusements, too little to ideals and emotions. Of course he does not apply this charge to Van Gogh or the later works of Monet.

Later, celebrating the rise of Impressionism, the great poet and critic Stéphane Mallarmé wrote: "At that critical moment for the human race when nature desires to work for herself, she requires certain lovers of hers . . . to lose the restraint of education, to let hand and eye do what they will, and thus through them reveal herself . . . calm, naked, [constant]." (Adams 1994:210). This sort of personalization and idealization of nature was rare at the time and comes before Muir and John Burroughs wrote similar lines in America.

American artists never did much with landscapes, especially after the ambitious but rather maudlin work of the Hudson River School. From Thomas Moran to the debased derivatives in Currier and Ives prints, this calendar-type art celebrated a landscape viewed purely as something to use for money; they are paintings of elite farms, railroads, and standing timber. Even Moran's wild landscapes are painted from the viewpoint of an observer sizing up the place, not a human being deeply involved in it.

America's few later nineteenth-century landscape artists of note tended to be European immigrants. These were often more concerned with making money than with accurate art. For example, the most prominent immigrant, Albert Bierstadt (Robotham 1993), painted "Puget Sound" for an Eastern United States magnate who had economic interests in that area. Neither the magnate nor Bierstadt had seen Puget Sound. So Bierstadt painted a preposterously romanticized view of a lake in his native Switzerland, added a couple of dashed-off "Indian canoes," and satisfied both of them. (This painting now resides in the Seattle Art Museum, where I have spent hours with it.) Like many of Bierstadt's canvases, this one is at once stunning and laughable.

Still more sordid were the glorifications of slavery and post-slave plantations, with the inevitable portrayals of "Negroes" as childish and foolish (Vlach 2002). It is significant that America's first great African-American artist, Henry Tanner, avoided landscapes and eventually left America for France (Bruce 2002). Like Daubigny, Tanner seems sadly countercyclical relative to modern taste; though one of America's greatest artists, he is neglected today.

The same fate has affected America's few great nature artists, such as Abbot Thayer and Morris Graves. Local landscape art could be very good indeed, but, except in their work, rarely rose above the level of pleasant romanticization of familiar scenery (see Novak 1995). As to the twentieth century, just to mention some landscapes familiar to me, there are wonderful collections of local, often far too little known, paintings of California (Nash 1995; Shields 2006; Trenton and Gerdts 1990; Vincent 1990) and of Washington state (Harmon 2001). Most of the paintings are well done and even beautiful, but are mere romanticized views of pretty places. The best paintings in the Washington state tradition, however, are genuinely great art, making unique and distinctive comments on the scene and thus showing a serious psychological and personal involvement in it. Painters such as Morris Graves, Kenneth Callahan, and Gaylen Hansen lived the land and made painting it a personal revelation and transcendence.

Romanticization distances the viewer from the scene. Accurate portrayal can reveal a more deep concern, but need not. However, serious personal work on a powerful, compelling painting, one that forces the viewer's involvement, means that the artist not only is deeply involved in the landscape, but that he or she expects a large audience who is equally so.

One sidelight reveals much about this: the stunning success and unique fame of the great Mexican landscapist José Velasco (Altamirano Piolle 1993). He began as a biological illustrator and never lost a concern for scientific accuracy and detail. But he turned to studio art, made several trips to France in the late nineteenth century, and eventually developed a unique and powerful style. It was derived from the Barbizon tradition, with Impressionist input. His paintings of the wild and rugged landscapes of Mexico are as powerful, brilliant, unique, and compelling as any art in the world, and fortunately are appreciated in their homeland. He seems to have single-handedly made Mexicans not only love their landscape but realize that it had incredible grandeur and aesthetic potential. This shows why landscape art is worth detailed consideration in a work on environmental conservation.

Fondness for the pretty, plus the ease of doing bad Impressionist art, has made Impressionism the darling of the Sunday painter, and every local crafts fair reminds us that Impressionism is the most successful school in history in terms of numbers of followers. The gap between Monet and the neighborhood Sunday artist is large, but the legions of bad imitators reveal much about the psychology of viewing and appreciating nature.

Photography took over the job of recording beautiful scenes, and "modern art" drifted away from anything natural, into realms of abstraction. Even the more representational ends of the modern art spectrum returned to figures and still-life paintings, not to serious engagement with landscapes. Photography continues the great landscape tradition.

However, we are now seeing the revival of a very different sort of "land art" (Gooding and Furlong 2000). People now merge art into landscaping, earth modification, and sculpture on a large scale. This can get very striking indeed. Besides large-scale ditches and rock carvings, we have artists who throw out a rope and then plant flower along the sinuous path it lays on the ground (Hutchinson 2006; this may sound silly, but the book is a stunningly beautiful achievement). In these cases, the art does not portray the landscape. It *is* the landscape. It has fused with gardening, itself a fine art with ecological implications.

In all this, the reflection of wider political-economic currents is clear, as in the Dutch paintings of commerce and the Impressionist ones of steam engines. Was the Romantic era really an era of wild, unbridled emotions? No. Did the Impressionists really spend all their time at picnics or in quaint villages? No, and sometimes they were honest enough to show it: Monet's city scenes, Caillebotte's floor refinishers, Bonnard's interiors.

In the end, we can at least recall the attitude, attributed by Kenneth Clark to nineteenth-century critics, that "the inherent sanctity of nature had a purifying and uplifting effect on those who opened their hearts to her influence" (Clark 1979:230). The romantic nineteenth-century writers may have been more prone to state it, but the attitude is not new. It inspired medieval Books of Hours and Luca Signorelli's unbearably stark and painful backdrops to crucifixion scenes in the fifteenth century. It inspired Dutch landscapists to portray oak trees standing tall against the world in the seventeenth. It reached something of a final climax in Cézanne's rocks and pines in the twentieth. Cézanne's countless paintings of Mont Sainte Victoire turn it into a Sumeru, the Sacred Mountain at the Center of the Universe, around which all things revolve.

The final question is: in all this turning and twisting of representation, was conservation or resource management served?

The influence of romanticism on Thoreau and subsequent environmentalists is clear, but was largely through literature, not painting. Conversely, the association of Dutch painting with the rise of Dutch capitalism—as predatory and ruthless as any in history—has never been missed (see, e.g., Israel 1995). Patrons of the Barbizon school were such men as Emile and Isaac Pereire, the railroad and finance magnates (Adams 1994). (And the most wonderfully scented rose variety of all time was named Mme. Isaac Pereire.) Bierstadt painted his huge and overwrought landscapes for the very magnates who were destroying American nature as fast as they could. Monet, too, painted for the lords of pollution and destruction. Unlike Chinese landscape art, European landscape art does not seem to have a strong association with good management or with the propagation of a view of people resting lightly on the environment.

However, artists and scientific illustrators brought the details of natural beauty to a vast audience, increasing consciousness and concern. This contributed to saving nature, far more than has been realized or acknowledged.

On the other hand, one charge against studio art does not stick. Studio art has been widely regarded as strictly by and for the elite. This is not the case. In all the periods considered herein, for every "great" painting, there were thousands or even millions of knockoffs and minor works: etchings, prints, penny broadsides, student copies, Sunday-painter imitations, and in the last century and a half an infinity of photographic and other direct copies. No one who participated in national cultures remained totally isolated from the artistic currents of the time. In the Renaissance, every church had its copies of Raphael and Michelangelo. Dutch landscapes spawned a mass of cheap public prints.

Literacy, printing, and photography greatly increased the distribution of art among the masses, but did not start it and are not necessary for it. In Peru, I found that the "Cuzco school" of art, developed in the 1600s by an Italian teacher working with Quechua Indian painters, is still going strong, producing thousands of new paintings every year. These are sold cheaply on city street corners and curio shops. Anyone not desperately poor can buy a tolerable imitation of seventeenth-century art.

The delusion that landscape art (and art in general) was strictly for the elite is based on selective perception and selective preservation.

Wildlife art continues and has been a major channel—if not *the* major channel—for attracting supporters to the conservation cause. The Audubon Society, later joined by the Sierra Club, Ducks Unlimited, and other groups, has continued to lead.

260 ※ CHAPTER EIGHT

Photography has added itself to this agenda and become the major art form in the service of nature. From the beginning of landscape photography in the mid-nineteenth century, photographs have popularized conservation and preservation. In Barbara Novak's book *Nature and Culture: American Landscape and Painting, 1825–1875* (1995), for instance, one can see how nineteenth-century photographs revealed a stark, dramatic, noble landscape, while studio paintings continued to be banal and bathetic; the contrast is extremely striking. Ansel Adams, ardent Sierra Club member, represented the climax of the tradition. Close to half the calendars in the United States continue it. So do many conservation magazines and websites. They show nature or people-in-nature at their best. Conversely, photographs of massive clearcuts, gullying soil erosion, tropical deforestation, and industrial pollution have been more effective than scientific descriptions at mobilizing the public. Brilliant and innovative landscape photographers like Adams and like Galen Rowell have eclipsed landscape painters as publicists of the wild.

CHAPTER NINE

By Way of Conclusion

Thus, some societies, and some regions of the world, have saved their environments fairly well. Others have devastated theirs, and often without economic development to show for it. Some, like the Maya and many Southeast Asians, have preserved a rural unity, with forest, field, and garden worked into one sustainable system. Others, like many Mediterranean farmers, have managed farmlands well but not cared much for forests. Still others have found yet other accommodations. Some, like Indonesia, have changed from good management to devastation, without much benefit to the vast majority of the people.

The reasons for the differences involve a complex mixture of economics and ideology. Economic and ecological adjustments that began in small ways, often by sheer chance, become locked in. This gives us the "*longue durée*," which Fernand Braudel emphasized so much and so memorably. These locked-in management systems become ideologically represented. Often, other ideologies and representations invade from without, propagating through cultural solidarity or colonial power or military force or exigencies of trade.

Caring for Place: Ecology, Ideology, and Emotion in Traditional Landscape Management, by E.N. Anderson, 261–267. © 2014 Left Coast Press, Inc. All rights reserved.

Ideology by itself, without economic foundation, tends to be nothing but arid speculation, divorced from practice. On the other hand, contra the naive material or economic determinism popular in some quarters, ideology takes on an independent life. The clearest case in our survey is the opposition of pro-nature and antinature attitudes in the Western world, derived ultimately from hunting-gathering and plantation-agricultural traditions, respectively, but taking on a life of their own. They have formed a single braiding channel for thousands of years now, but are still visibly and sharply separate when one contrasts the ideals of the Sierra Club with the fiery antienvironmentalist rhetoric of Fox News commentators. A lifetime spent comparing these rhetorics with the moderate, accommodating views of traditional China has been instructive. Even more instructive has been watching the replacement of those reasonable (if often inadequate) Chinese views by the virulent "struggle against nature" ideology and practice of Chinese Communism. China remains the same country, with the same people, but with a totally different ideology—leading to a brief period of rapid but unsustainable growth that is now turning sharply toward inevitable decline.

We must therefore consider, to at least some extent, the constant feedback between material base and ideological construction. They compose one system. We have seen, for instance, how rice agriculture tends to encourage small mixed farming, but can be done as plantation monocrop if ideology and—consequently—economic organization is strongly enough biased that way. Conversely, stock-raising tends to be extensive and to occupy vast tracts of land, but intensive small-scale stock-raising is common in some areas around the world.

Religion has a mixed record for driving conservation ideology. In some societies it clearly works that way, notably in many of the smaller and more hunting-oriented Old Northern societies. In others it simply does not have that role at all, either because the societies do not practice conservation or because they encourage it by purely secular means. In societies with large, diverse, institutionalized religions—"world religions"—the particular sect is apt to matter more than the religion in general. Buddhism counsels protection for all beings, but even it is rather diverse in its success at carrying and teaching that message. At the other extreme is Christianity, with its split personality derived from the first two chapters of Genesis; some sects teach conservation, some teach domination in the most radical sense, and most take no firm position, leaving it up to the believers. The great project on religion and ecology organized by

Photo on Previous Page: Reunion Island, Indian Ocean. The Cirque de Mafate, where escaped slaves took refuge in the 19th century; their descendents still hold the area without allowing outsiders in (except doctors and nurses on muleback) and refuse electricity, roads, and electronics. They live by subsistence farming. The area is consequently among the best managed on any island in the world. Photography by E. N. Anderson.

Mary Beth Tucker and John Grim found major environmental and conservation teachings in all religions. But most religions have also accommodated large-scale environmental destruction. (The Jains, and to a lesser extent the Daoists and Theravada Buddhists, are apparent exceptions.) Some religions have sects that encourage bad practices.

It seems that in a world of religious diversity, including a great deal of fanaticism and extremism (which are generally associated with antienvironmental attitudes or behavior), we cannot expect deliverance by waiting for religions to take up Bron Taylor's "dark green religion" (2010). Research for the present book has convinced me that there is somewhat limited hope there. Fortunately, it has also convinced me that we do not need to wait for the conversion of all humanity to environmental religion.

Religion, throughout history and apparently prehistory, has engaged "hearts and minds" through arts—music, visual art, poetry, and even taste and scent, all integrated into ceremonies, rituals, and festivals. It is sufficient to cite Emile Durkheim's great work (1995/1912), but there are thousands of studies of this well-known fact. Looking across the world sample, it certainly appears clear (though needing further analysis) that societies propagate their resource management systems and ideals through arts—with or without religion. The Australian Aborigines, Durkheim's original subjects, teach their values to young people through rituals and daily arts. It is difficult indeed to imagine the Australians teaching their complex, difficult, and demanding knowledge and wisdom through the dry, long-winded methods of old-fashioned theology schools. Durkheim was right: "effervescence" is necessary to engage people in the "collective representations" of their religion, including—perhaps especially—its ecological dimensions. The same is clearly true of the Northwest Coast, the Pueblos of the American Southwest, the hill peoples of Southeast Asia, and many other groups around the world.

All those conservation measures began with a small, dedicated group, driven by love of nature and environment, persuading the majority to go along, by appealing to love of nature, shame over its ruin, and plain fear (especially in the cases of pollution control laws). The necessity is to make sure that people see long-term, wide interests and sacrifice some of their smaller-scale interests for the collectivity. No society can survive without this. Religion has generally carried that task, but too often by uniting people against the "heathen." Much more serious now is the failure of religion to construct the wider community, because now we *must* see that our community is the whole world and all creatures in it, not just humanity.

Religion does do this, especially in small-scale societies, and it works very well there. But in the world society of today, conservation NGO's do better. Even governments do better, by appealing to nationalism, patriotism, or simple personal responsibility. The common themes are simply making people realize we are all in this together and leading people to appreciate nature and if possible actively love it. Not all people will love it, but we have to convince the vast majority that we must at least be responsible about it. Anti-litter and park-preservation campaigns have worked. The Sierra Club and the Audubon Society have done better than the churches. Basically, we have to focus on the real message and appeal to every human emotion—overwhelmingly to the good emotions, though; appealing to hate and cowardice is a monopoly of the antienvironmentalists and should remain so.

American civil society, with its strong values on mutual aid and active responsibility and its sense that we are all equals and all in this together, is desperately needed now—but seems to be in decline. We desperately need more knowledge and better education, including civics. This was quite adequate for conservation through the twentieth century—with the many victories from national and state parks and forests through the migratory bird treaties to the Clean Air and Water Acts and the wilderness designations and Endangered Species Act. Today this is all threatened, by the political success of the giant primary-production firms and the loss of that civil culture with its grassroots values.

A strong sense of the "right" way to live and act, versus morally "wrong" and "irresponsible" ways, drove much or most of the conservation agenda in the twentieth century. So "civil religion," actually the secular, patriotic community spirit described by Lloyd Warner in *American Life: Dream and Reality* (1953), worked reasonably well. The problem now is reconstituting it—getting America back to being one country as opposed to fighting camps locked in a zero-sum or negative-sum game.

Arts have been separable from religion since time immemorial. In both China and the West, arts were substantially decoupled from religion centuries ago. The same has happened more recently, to varying degrees, in other societies. In Europe, we have seen how landscape art entered the great religious paintings of the late Middle Ages or early Renaissance, but spun off as a completely separate and almost totally secular art form in the Dutch art of the sixteenth century and remained a separate tradition. In spite of the best efforts of Caspar David Friedrich and a few others to return it to its religious base, it remained an almost purely secular form. Arguably the greatest master of landscape art, Claude Monet, sold his work for top franc to industrialists and bourgeoisie; he was a secular businessman, not a painter *ad maiorem Dei gloriam*. More to the point—because Monet was not painting in the service of conservation—the vast range of paintings and photographs that do encourage conservation, from Audubon to Ansel Adams and from nineteenth-century lithographs to modern Sierra Club books and calendars—are entirely secular.

Literature shows a much more radically secular evolution. Even the medieval texts were either openly secular (like the Provencal troubadours) or were religious only insofar as they told Grail stories and other tales with religious backgrounds. The inspiration of the great pagan and Islamic authors was recognized and often condemned by the churchmen. After about 1300, joyous celebration of themes taken from Theocritus, Ovid, and Virgil won the day. As with art, some have tried to return to religion. Among America's greatest poets of the environment, Robinson Jeffers taught a Hindu-like remote deism, and Gary Snyder is a devout Buddhist. But, overall, the general secular trend of literature in the West sweeps all before it.

China provides a comparison case, but a very different one. Landscape art in China was rarely explicitly conservationist and was usually secular. (Religion made some use of it, in temples and similar contexts.) However, it did express cosmological ideas and ideals that were basic to China's environmental management system, especially to the sustainable and environment-sparing parts of it. The art teaches harmony (*he* or *heping*) with nature, showing sages as tiny figures lost in meditation in vast mountain-and-water scenery. Arts fused with the most conservationist parts of the traditional worldview: feng shui, rural land management in general, Daoist and Buddhist religion, and just plain love of the wide world.

Chinese literature constantly recurs to ideals of small farms, remote lost paradises, and wild mountains. Much of China's best nature poetry is Buddhist, but most is not. Even music was pressed into service, as we have seen.

Modern secular society has decoupled environmental management, sustainability, and conservation from their original religious bases. They have become part of a wider morality that is shared worldwide by nature lovers and careful citizens, religious or not. The counter-value of using up resources and eliminating the natural are also shared worldwide, by religious and atheists, insofar as they find their hopes to lie with giant firms and "development"-oriented governments.

Where messages of creation care, sustainability, and conservation succeed, it is now generally because of secular art and science. The media report the grim forecasts of scientists, but these seem largely to scare people into passivity, if not downright paralysis. The survival and flourishing of nature depends more on wildlife programs, calendars, ecotourism, zoos, wild animal parks, and other secular (and often crassly money-making) forms.

Is this good for the future? One would like people to be creatures of reason, saving nature because they realize they cannot survive without it. However, people are creatures of emotion, and they notoriously discount the future at very steep rates. They will save from love, but not from rational long-term self-interest. No matter how much they may recognize the latter, it is never enough.

We are thus dependent on the great and unquestionably well-meaning artists like Ansel Adams and Galen Rowell, poets like Gary Snyder and any others who speak powerfully to the deepest human emotions. At present, we are relying too much on somewhat equivocal engagers of emotion, such as wild animal parks and ecotours. These can be excellent and well-managed, or they can be otherwise; conservation against itself is a major curse of our time (Brockington et al. 2008).

We are also perilously close to losing everything to the dominate-and-destroy ideology propagated by giant primary-production interests. Small farms and ranches still overwhelmingly dominate the world agrarian scene, and no one wants pollution, but the giant primary-production interests are calling the shots at high government levels everywhere and also among the high levels of the World Bank, International Monetary Fund, and similar agencies. There is dawning awareness in those quarters that an uninhabitable world is not really a good development goal, but they still finance big dams, monocrop agriculture, and unsustainable forestry projects.

Against this, the only clear hope is to advocate a few key points that are acceptable to any reasonable person of any religion or ideology. All world religions should be comfortable with those basics; the first two and the last are derived from teachings shared, to at least some degree, by all religions. The third I have taken largely from Judaism and Islam, which have explicit ideals of learning, but it is hardly alien to other faiths. Moreover, all four are points that anyone would conclude from using basic common sense or rational calculation.

Let me restate, then, the four points introduced at the beginning of this book:

We need to protect and preserve the environment—not through "preservation" as currently practiced, but through the sort of dynamic design-with-nature that characterized the best Southeast Asian and south Chinese systems. The goal is to find ways to support maximum welfare for minimum loss to the environment, through working for efficiency, sustainability, and simplicity. From all that has gone before, we learn that an absolute basic part of this agenda is to advance the beauty, fascination, and intrinsic value of "nature"—whatever that means—by any and every emotional and artistic means possible.

We need to refocus on learning and knowledge, and not just about the environment.

We have to accept nature and people. This does not mean accepting malaria, or genocide; it means basically accepting as much as possible of the real world, as it is, rather than working from prejudice, bias, denial, or destruction in hopes that something better will result. Prejudice against nature is bad enough, but far worse in the world today are the religious, ethnic, and ideological hatreds that are tearing our societies apart and making it impossible to work for a common goal. These hatreds benefit the wreckers of the environment, who routinely whip up hatreds so as to profit from the resulting disunity—including failure to regulate extractive interests (see Anderson 2010). Tolerance, valuing diversity, and solidarity must be major goals, and must be the core of any ideology if it is to have any value in conservation or anything else. The world simply cannot afford the current level of religious hatred, or of the callousness that leads us to ignore the poor, or of the economic bias that divides humanity into winners and victims.

Finally, we—not only all humans, but all ten million or so species of us—are stuck on one small planet, depending on each other.

REFERENCES

Abram, David. 1996. *The Spell of the Sensuous: Perception and Language in a More-than-Human World.* New York: Pantheon.

Abrutyn, Seth. 2009. *A General Theory of Institutional Autonomy.* Ph.D. dissertation, Dept. of Sociology, University of California, Riverside.

Acheson, James M. 1987. "The Lobster Fiefs Revisited: Economic and Ecological effects of Territoriality in Maine Lobster Fishing." In *The Question of the Commons,* Bonnie McCay and James Acheson, eds. Tucson: University of Arizona Press. Pp. 37–65.

———.2006. "Institutional Failure in Resource Management." *Annual Review of Anthropology* 35:117–134.

Adams, Madonna R. 2002. "Augustine and Love of the Environment." In *Thinking About the Environment: Our Debt to the Classical and Medieval Past,* Thomas M. Robinson and Laura Westra, eds. Lanham, MD: Lexington Books. Pp. 73–85.

Adams, Steven. 1994. *The Barbizon School and the Origins of Impressionism.* New York: Phaidon.

Adas, Michael. 1974. *The Burma Delta: Economic Development and Social Change on an Asian Rice Frontier, 1852–1941.* Madison: University of Wisconsin Press.

Agrawal, Arun. 2005a. "Environmentality: Community, Intimate Government, and the Making of Environmental Subjects in Kumaon, India." *Current Anthropology* 46:161–190.

Agrawal, Arun. 2005b. *Environmentality: Technologies of Government and the Making of Subjects.* Durham, NC: Duke University Press.

Aimers, James. 2011. "The Story of the Artefacts." *Nature* 479:44.

Alberts, Bruce. 2012a. "Failure of Skin-Deep Learning." *Science* 338:1263.

———. 2012b. "Trivializing Science Education." *Science* 335:263.

Aldhouse-Green, Miranda, and Stephen Aldhouse-Green. 2005. *The Quest for the Shaman: Shape-Shifters, Sorcerers and Spirit-Healers of Ancient Europe.* London: Thames and Hudson.

Almond, Richard. 2003. *Medieval Hunting.* Phoenix Mill, Thrupp, Stroud, Gloucestershire: Sutton Publishing.

Altamirano Piolle, María Elena. 1993. *Homenaje a José María Velasco (1840–1912).* Mexico City: Museo Nacional de Arte.

Anderson, Benedict. 1991. *Imagined Communities.* 2d ed. London: Verso.

Anderson, E. N. 1977. Comment on Marvin Harris' "Cultural Ecology of India's Sacred Cattle." *Current Anthropology* 18:3:552.

———. 1987. "A Malaysian Tragedy of the Commons." In *The Question of the Commons,* Bonnie McCay and James Acheson, eds. Tucson: University of Arizona Press. Pp. 327–343.

———. 1988. *The Food of China.* New Haven, CT: Yale University Press.

———. 1991. "Chinese Folk Classification of Food Plants." *Crossroads* 1:2:51–67.

———. 1993a. "Gardens in Tropical America and Tropical Asia." *Biotica n.e.* 1:81–102.

———. 1993b. "Southeast Asian Gardens: Nutrition, Cash and Ethnicity." *Biotica n.e.* 1:1–12.

———. ms. ca. 1995. Disenchantment and Deforestation.

———. 1996. *Ecologies of the Heart.* New York: Oxford University Press.

———. 2000. "Maya Knowledge and 'Science Wars.'" *Journal of Ethnobiology* 20:129–158.

———. 2001. "Flowering Apricot: Environmental Practice, Folk Religion, and Daoism." In *Daoism and Ecology: Ways Within Cosmic Landscape,* N. J. Girardot, James Miller, and Liu Xiaogan eds. Cambridge, MA: Harvard University, Center for the Study of World Religions, Harvard Divinity School. Pp. 157–184.

———. 2003. *Those Who Bring the Flowers: Maya Ethnobotany in Quintana Roo, Mexico.* With José Cauich Canul, Aurora Dzib, Salvador Flores Guido, Gerald Islebe, Felix Medina Tzuc, Odilón Sánchez Sánchez, and Pastor Valdez Chale. Chetumal, Quintana Roo: ECOSUR.

———. 2005a. *Everyone Eats.* New York: New York University Press.

———. 2005b. *Political Ecology in a Yucatec Maya Community.* Tucson: University of Arizona Press.

———. 2007. *Floating World Lost.* New Orleans, LA: University Press of the South.

———. 2010. *The Pursuit of Ecotopia: Lessons from Indigeonous and Traditional Societies for the Human Ecology of Our Modern World.* Santa Barbara, CA: Praeger (imprint of ABC-Clio).

———. 2011a. "California." Paper, California Indian Conference, 2010, Irvine, CA; revised 2011.

———. 2011b. "Yucatec Maya Botany and the 'Nature' of Science." *Journal of Ecological Anthropology* 14:67–73.

———. 2012. Environmental Ruin: The Drag on China's Future. Paper, California Sociological Association, annual conference, Riverside, CA.

———. ms 1. Disenchantment and Deforestation.

———. ms 2. Madagascar on My Mind.

Anderson, E. N., and Barbara A. Anderson. 2012. *Warning Signs of Genocide.* Lanham, MD: Lexington Books (division of Rowman and Littlefield).

Anderson, E. N., and Marja L. Anderson. 1973. *Mountains and Water: The Cultural Ecology of South Coastal China.* Taipei: Orient Cultural Service.

———. 1978. *Fishing in Troubled Waters.* Taipei: Orient Cultural Service.

Anderson, E. N., and Lisa Raphals. 2007. "Taoism and Animals." In *A Communion of Subjects: Animals in Religion, Science, and Ethics,* Paul Waldau and Kimberley Patton, . New York: Columbia University Press. Pp. 275–290.

Anderson, E. N., and Felix Medina Tzuc. 2005. *Animals and the Maya in Southeast Mexico.* Tucson: University of Arizona Press.

Anderson, E. N., Teik Aun Wong, and Lynn Thomas. 2000. "Good and Bad Persons: The Construction of Ethical Discourse in a Chinese Fishing Community." *Bulletin of the Institute of Ethnology, Academia Sinica,* 87:129–167.

Anderson, M. Kat. 2005. *Tending the Wild.* Berkeley: University of California Press.

Andrade, Manuel J., and Hilaria Maas Collí. 1990. *Cuentos Mayas Yucatecos.* 2 v. Mérida: Universidad Autónoma de Yucatán.

Andrews, George. 1975. *Maya Cities: Placemaking and Urbanization.* Norman: University of Oklahoma Press.

Arellano Rodríguez, J. Alberto, José Salvador Flores Guido, Juan Tun Garrido, and María Mercedes Cruz Bojórquez. 2003. *Nomenclatura, forma de vida, uso, manejo y distribución de las especies vegetales de la Península de Yucatán.* Mérida: Universidad Autónoma de Yucatán. Etnoflora Yucatanense no. 20.

Aristotle. 2013. *Aristotle's Politics.* Tr. Carnes Lord. 2d ed. Chicago: University of Chicago Press.

Armstrong, Edward. 1958. *The Folklore of Birds.* London: Collins.

Arnold, David F. 2008. *The Fisherman's Frontier: People and Salmon in Southeast Alaska.* Seattle: University of Washington Press.

Arzápalo Marín, Ramón. 1987. *El ritual de los bacabes.* Mexico City: Universidad Autónoma de México.

Ascher, William. 1999. *Why Governments Waste Natural Resources: Policy Failures in Developing Countries.* Baltimore, MD: Johns Hopkins University Press.

Ashmore, Wendy. 2005. "The Idea of a Maya Town." In *Structure and Meaning in Human Settlements,* Tony Atkin and Joseph Rykwert, eds. Philadelphia: University of Pennsylvania Museum. Pp. 35–54.

Aswani, Shankar, and Pam Weiant. 2004. "Scientific Evaluation in Women's Participatory Management: Monitoring Marine Invertebrate Refugia in the Solomon Islands." *Human Organization* 63:301–319.

Atleo, E. Richard (Umeek). 2004. *Tsawalk: A Nuu-chah-nulth Worldview.* Vancouver: University of British Columbia Press.

———.2011. *Principles of Tsawalk: An Indigenous Approach to Global Crisis.* Vancouver: University of British Columbia Press.

Atran, Scott. 1993. "Itza Maya Tropical Agroforestry." *Current Anthropology* 34:633–700.

———.2002. *In Gods We Trust.* New York: Oxford University Press.

Atran, Scott, and Douglas Medin. 2008. *The Native Mind and the Cultural Construction of Nature.* Cambridge: MIT Press.

Atran, Scott, Douglas Medin, Norbert Ross, Elizabeth Lynch, John Coley, Edilberto Ucan Ek', and Valentina Vapnarsky. 1999. "Folkecology and Commons Management in the Maya Lowlands." Proceedings of the National Academy of Sciences 96:7598–7603.

Atran, Scott, Douglas Medin, Norbert Ross, Elizabeth Lynch, Valentina Vapnarsky, Edilberto Ucan Ek', John Coley, Christopher Timura, and Michael Baran. 2002. "Folkecology, Cultural Epidemiology, and the Spirit of the Commons." *Current Anthropology* 43:421–450.

Atran, Scott, Lois Ximena, and Edilberto Ucan Ek'. 2004. *Plants of the Petén Itza' Maya.* Ann Arbor: University of Michigan, Museum of Anthropology, Memoir 38.

Attwoood, Bain, and Andrew Marks (eds.). 1999. *The Struggle for Aboriginal Rights: A Documentary History.* Crows Nest, NSW: Allen and Unwin. Imprint, Basic.

Audubon, John James. 1967 [1840–1844]. *The Birds of America.* New York: Dover.

Balam Pereira, Gilberto. 1992. *Cosmogonia y uso actual de las plantas medicinales de Yucatán.* Mérida: Universidad Autónoma de Yucatán.

Bamforth, Douglas. 2011. "Origin Stories, Archaeological Evidence, and Postclovis Paleoindian Bison Hunting on the Great Plains." *American Antiquity* 76:24–40.

Bandura, Albert. 1982. "Self-Efficacy Mechanism in Human Agency." *American Psychologist* 37:122–147.

———.1986. *Social Foundations of Thought and Action: A Social Cognitive Theory.* Englewood Cliffs, NJ: Prentice-Hall.

Bardon, Geoffrey, with James Bardon. 2004. *Papunya: A Place Made After the Story.* Carlton, Victoria: The Miegunyah Press, an Imprint of Melbourne Univ. Publishing Ltd.

Barnstone, Tony, and Chou Ping. 2005. *The Anchor Book of Chinese Poetry.* New York: Anchor Books (Random House).

Barrell, John. 1980. *The Dark Side of the Landscape: The Rural Poor in English Painting, 1730–1840.* New York: Cambridge University Press.

Barrera Marín, Alfredo, Alfredo Barrera Vásquez, and Rosa Maria Lopez Franco. 1976. *Nomenclatura Etnobotanica Maya.* INAH, Centro Regional del Sureste.

Barrera Vásquez, Alfredo. 1963. *Las fuentes para el estudio de la medicina nativa de Yucatán.* Mérida: Mérida: Universidad Autónoma de Yucatán, Revista, #27.

———.1965. *El libro de las cantares de Dzitbalché.* Mex: INAH.

———.1980. *El libro de los cantares de Dzitbalché.* (New ed.) Mérida: Ayuntamiento de Mérida.

———.1981. *Estudios Linguisticos.* 2 v. Mérida: Fondo editorial de Yucatán.

———.1986. *Lo ignoraba usted?* Mérida: Dante.

Barrera Vásquez, Alfredo (ed.). 1980. *Diccionario Maya Cordemex.* Merida: Cordemex.

Barrera Vásquez, Alfredo, and Silvia Rendon. 1989. *El libro de los libros de Chilam Balam.* Mérida: Dante.

Barrett, Scott. 2003. *Environment and Statecraft: The Strategy of Environmental Treaty-Making.* New York: Oxford University Press.

Bartra, Roger. 1994 *Wild Men in the Looking Glass: The Mythic Origins of European Otherness.* Ann Arbor, MI: University of Michigan Press.

Bates, Daniel G. 2005. *Human Adaptive Strategies: Ecology, Culture, and Politics.* 3ded. Boston, MA: Pearson Allyn and Bacon.

Beckerman, Stephen, Paul Valentine, and Elise Eller. 2002. "Conservation and Native Amazonians: Why Some Do and Some Don't." *Antropologica* 96:31–51.

Beckford, George L. 1972. *Persistent Poverty: Underdevelopment in Plantation Economies of the Third World.* New York: Oxford University Press.

Beinart, William, and Joann McGregor. 2003. *Social History and African Environments*. Oxford: James Currey in collaboration with Ohio University Press.

Bell, Rudolph. 1985. *Holy Anorexia*. Chicago: University of Chicago Press.

Bellah, Robert N. 2011. *Religion in Human Evolution: From the Paleolithic to the Axial Age*. Cambridge, MA: Harvard University Press.

Bellah, Robert, Richard Madsen, William Sullivan, and Ann Swidler. 1996. *Habits of the Heart: Individualism and Commitment in American Life*. 2d ed. Berkeley: University of California Press.

Bellant, Russ. 1990. *The Coors Connection*. Cambridge, MA: Political Research Associates. (Reprinted, Boston: South End Press, 1991.)

Benitez, Fernando. 1986. *Ki: El drama de un pueblo y una planta*. 2d ed. (orig. 1956). Mexico City: Fondo de Cultura Económica.

Benjamin, Roger (ed.). 2009. *Icons of the Desert: Early Aboriginal Paintings from Papunya*. Ithaca, NY: Herbert F. Johnson Museum of Art, Cornell University.

Bennett, John W. l976. *The Ecological Transition: Cultural Anthropology and Human Adaptation*. New York: Academic Press.

———.1982. *Of Time and the Enterprise: North American Family Farm Management in a Context of Resource Marginality*. Minneapolis: University of Minnesota Press.

———. 1992. *Human Ecology as Human Behavior*. New Brunswick, NJ: Transaction.

Berkes, Fikret. 2008. *Sacred Ecology: Traditional Ecological Knowledge and Resource Management*. 2d ed. Philadelphia, PA: Taylor and Francis.

Berkes, Fikret, Johan Colding, and Carl Folke. 2000. "Rediscovery of Traditional Ecological Knowledge as Adaptive Management." *Ecological Applications* 10:1251–1262.

Bermingham, Ann. 1986. *Landscape and Ideology: The English Rustic Tradition, 1740–1860*. Berkeley: University of California Press.

Bernal-García, María Elena. 2007. "The Dance of Time, the Procession of Space at Mexico-Tenochtitlan's Desert Garden." In *Sacred Gardens and Landscapes: Ritual and Agency*, Michel Conan, ed. Washington: Dumbarton Oaks. Pp. 69–112.

Bird, Douglas W., Rebecca Bliege Bird, and Brian F. Codding. 2009. "In Pursuit of Mobile Prey: Martu Hunting Strategies and Archaeofaunal Interpretation." *American Antiquity* 74:3–30.

Bird, Douglas W., Rebecca Bliege Bird, and Christopher H. Parker. 2005. "Aboriginal Burning Regimes and Hunting Strategies in Australia's Wesetern Desert." *Human Ecology* 33:443–464.

Blackburn, Carole. 2000. *Harvest of Souls: The Jesuit Mission and Colonialism in North Ameica, 1632–1650*. Quebec: McGill-Queen's University Press.

Blaikie, Piers, and Harold Brookfield. 1987. *Land Degradation and Society*. London: Methuen.

Blair, R., and R. Vermont Salas. 1965. *Spoken Yucatec Maya*. Mimeographed text, University of Chicago.

Bliege Bird, Rebecca. 2008. "Aboriginal Foraging: Firestick Farming and Ecosystem Dynamics in the Western Desert of Australia." Talk, Washington State Univ., Pullman, WA.

Blukis Onat, Astrida R. 2002. "Resource Cultivation on the Northwest Coast of North America." *Journal of Northwest Anthropology* 36:125–144.

Blunt, Wilfrid, and Sandra Raphael. 1979. *The Illustrated Herbal*. New York: Thames and Hudson.

Boehm, Christopher. 1999. *Hierarchy in the Forest*. Cambridge, MA: Harvard University Press.

Bonnechere, Pierre. 2007. "The Place of the Sacred Grove (*Alsos*) in the Mantic Rituals of Greece: The Example of the *Alsos* of Trophonios at Lebadeia (Boeotia)." In *Sacred Gardens and Landscapes: Ritual and Agency*, Michel Conan, ed. Washington, DC: Dumbarton Oaks. Pp. 17–42.

Borg, Marcus J., and John Dominic Crossan. 2009. *The First Paul: Reclaiming the Radical Visionary Behind the Church's Conservative Icon*. New York: HarperOne.

Borowski, Oded. 1998. *Every Living Thing: Daily Use of Animals in Ancient Israel*. Walnut Creek, CA: AltaMira.

Bourdieu, Pierre. 1977. *Outline of a Theory of Practice.* Tr. Richard Nice. New York: Cambridge University Press.

———. 1990. *The Logic of Practice.* Tr. Richard Nice. Stanford, CA: Stanford University Press.

Bovard, James. 1991. *The Farm Fiasco.* San Francisco: Institute of Contemporary Studies.

Boyce, Mary. 1979. *Zoroastrians.* London: Routledge Kegan Paul.

Brandt, Richard B. 1954. *Hopi Ethics: A Theoretical Analysis.* Chicago: University of Chicago Press.

Bray, David Barton, Leticia Merino-Pérez, Patricia Negreros-Castillo, Gerardo Segura-Warnholtz, Juan Manuel Torres-Rojo, and Henricus F. M. Vester. 2003. "Mexico's Community-Managed Forests as a Global Model for Sustainable Development." *Conservation Biology* 17:672–678.

Brockington, Dan, Rosaleen Duff, and Jim Igoe. 2008. *Nature Unbound: Conservation, Capitalism and the Future of Protected Areas.* London: Earthscan.

Bruce, Marcus. 2002. *Henry Ossawa Tanner: A Spiritual Biography.* New York: Crossroad Publishing.

Bryant, Nick. 2009. "Ordeal of Australia's Child Migrants." BBC News Online, Nov. 15.

Buckley, Thomas. 2002. *Standing Ground: Yurok Indian Spirituality, 1850–1990.* Berkeley: University of California Press.

Buell, Paul D. 2009. How Chinggis Qan Changed the World. Unpublished ms.

Buell, Paul D.; Eugene N. Anderson; Charles Perry. 2010. *A Soup for the Qan.* Leiden: Brill.

Buku-Larrngay Mulka Centre. 1999. *Saltwater: Yirrkala Bark Paintings of Sea Country.* Yirrkala, Northern Territory: Buku-Larrngay Mulka Centre and Jennifer Isaacs Publishing.

Bunker, Stephen G., and Paul S. Ciccantell. 2005. *Globalization and the Race for Resources.* Baltimore, MD: Johns Hopkins University Press.

Byrne, Francis J. 2001. *Irish Kings and High-Kings.* 2d ed. Dublin: Four Courts Press.

Cabanne, Pierre. 1998. *Les peintres de plein air.* Paris: Les Éditios de l'Amateur.

Cajete, Gregory. 1994. *Look to the Mountain: An Ecology of Indigenous Education.* Skyland, NC: Kivaki Press.

Caldwell, Melissa. 2011. *Dacha Idylls: Living Organically in Russia's Countryside.* Berkeley: University of California Press.

Callicott, J. Baird. 1994. *Earth's Insights: A Multicultural Survey of Ecological Ethics from the Mediterranean Basin to the Australian Outback.* Berkeley: University of California Press.

Callicott, J. Baird, and Roger T. Ames (eds.). 1989. *Nature in Asian Traditions of Thought.* Albany: SUNY Press.

Campbell, Joseph. 1983. *The Way of the Animal Powers.* New York: Alfred van der Marck.

Cao Xueqin (and Gao E., last vol.). 1973–1986. *The Story of the Stone.* 5 vols. Tr. David Hawkes (last vol. with John Minford). London: Penguin.

Capuder, Karen. 2013. Forked Tongues at Sequalitchew: A Critical Indigenist Anthropology of Place in Nisqually Territory. Thesis, Dept. of Anthropology, University of Washington.

Cardelús, Catherine, Margaret D. Lowman, and Almaheyu Wassie Eshete. 2012. "Uniting Church and Science for Conservation" [letter]. *Science* 335:932.

Carmichael, Alexander. 1992. *Carmina Gadelica.* [Orig. 1899.] Hudson, NY: Lindisfarne Press.

Carswell, John. 2000. *Blue and White: Chinese Porcelain Around the World.* Chicago, IL: Art Media Resources.

Caruana, Wally, and Nigel Lendon (eds.). 1997. *The Painters of the Wawilag Sisters Story 1937–1997.* Canberra: National Gallery of Australia.

Cato (Marcus Porcius Cato). 1935. "Marcus Cato on Agriculture." In *Cato and Varro,* Tr. William Davis Hooper, revised by Harrison Boyd Ash. Cambridge, MA: Harvard University Press, Loeb Classical Library. Pp. 1–157.

Chan Yuk Wah. 2011. *"Banh Cuon* and *Cheung Fan:* Searching for the Identity of the Steamed Rice-Flour Roll." In *Chinese Food and Foodways in Southeast Asia and Beyond,* Tan Chee-Beng, ed. Singapore: NUS Press. Pp. 1156–1174.

Chapple, Christopher (ed.). 2002. *Jainism and Ecology.* Cambridge, MA: Harvard University Press for the Center for the Study of World Religions, Harvard Divinity School.

Charco, Jesús. 1999. *El bosque mediterráneo en el norte de África.* Madrid: Agencia Española de Cooperación Internacional.

Chew, Sing. 2001. *World Ecological Degradation: Accumulation, Urbanization, and Deforestation.* Lanham, MD: AltaMira Press, Rowman and Littlefield Publishers.

———. 2006. "Dark Ages." In *Globalization and Global History,* Barry Gills and William Thompson eds. London: Routledge. Pp. 163–202.

Chong, Kwek. 2012. "Religiously Protecting Myanmar's Environment" [letter]. *Science* 337:1604–1605.

Christenson, Allen J. 2007. *Popol Vuj, The Sacred Book of the Maya.* Norman: University of Oklahoma Press.

Clark, Kenneth. 1979. *Landscape Into Art.* Rev. ed. New York: HarperCollins.

Clottes, Jean. 2008. *Cave Art.* London: Phaidon.

Clutton-Brock, Juliet. 2012. *Animals as Domesticates: A World View through History.* East Lansing: Michigan State University Press.

Coates, Peter A. 1998. *Nature: Western Attitudes Since Ancient Times.* London: Polity Press.

———. 2006. *American Perceptions of Immigrant and Invasive Species: Strangers on the Land.* Berkeley: University of California Press.

Cocks, M. L., and A. P. Dowd. 2008. "The Cultural Use of the Wild Olive Tree by the *amaXhosa* People in the Eastern Cape Province of South Africa." *Journal for the Study of Religion, Nature and Culture* 2:292–308.

Colding, Johan, and Carl Folke. 2001. "Social Taboos: 'Invisible' Systems of Local Resource Management and Biological Conservation." *Ecological Applications* 11:584–560.

Collins, Randall. 1998. *The Sociology of Philosophies.* Cambridge, MA: Harvard University Press.

Columella, Lucius Junius Moderatus. 1941–1955. *On Agriculture.* 3 v. Cambridge, MA: Harvard University Press (Loeb Classical Library).

Conan, Michel (ed.). 2007. *Sacred Gardens and Landscapes: Ritual and Agency.* Washington, DC: Dumbarton Oaks Research Library and Collection.

Conklin, Harold C. 1957. *Hanunoo Agriculture.* Rome: FAO.

Cook, Roger. 1974. *The Tree of Life: Image for the Cosmos.* New York: Avon.

Coon, Carleton S. 1958. *Caravan: The Story of the Middle East.* New York: Henry Holt.

Cozzo, David. 2012. "Revitalization of Traditional Cherokee Artisan Resouces." Paper, Society of Ethnobiology, annual conference, Denver, CO.

Crosby, Alfred 1986. *Ecological Imperialism: The Biological Expansion of Europe, 900–1900.* New York: Cambridge University Press.

Cruikshank, Julie. 1998. *The Social Life of Stories: Narrative and Knowledge in the Yukon Territory.* Lincoln: University of Nebraska Press.

———. 2005. *Do Glaciers Listen? Local Knowledge, Colonial Encounters, and Social Imagination.* Vancouver: University of British Columbia Press.

Cunliffe, Barry. 2001. *Facing the Ocean: The Atlantic and Its Peoples, 8000 BC–AD 1500.* Oxford: Oxford University Press.

Dalley, Stephanie. 1989. *Myths from Mesopotamia.* Oxford: Oxford University Press.

Damasio, Antonio. 1994. *Descartes' Error: Emotion, Reason, and the Human Brain.* New York: G. P. Putnam's Sons.

Dames, Michael. 1992. *Mythic Ireland.* London: Thames and Hudson.

Darlington, Susan. 2013. *The Ordination of a Tree: The Thai Buddhist Environmental Movement.* Albany: SUNY Press.

Delahunty, J. L. 2007. "The Ethnobotanical History and Holocene Extent of Yew (*Taxus baccata* L.) on the Irish Landscape." *Journal of Ethnobiology* 27:204–217.

Demarest, Arthur. 2004. *Ancient Maya: The Rise and Fall of a Rainforest Civilization.* Cambridge: Cambridge University Press.

Denevan, William M. 2001. *Cultivated Landscapes of Native Amazonia and the Andes*. New York: Oxford University Press.

Denham, Tim, Mark Donohue and Sara Booth. 2009. "Horticultural Experimentation in Northern Australia Reconsidered." *Antiquity* 83:634–648.

Descartes, René. 1999. *Discourse on Method and Related Writings*. Tr. Desmond M. Clarke (French orig., 1637). London: Penguin.

Deur, Douglas, and Nancy Turner (eds.). 2005. *Keeping It Living: Traditions of Plant Use and Cultivation on the Northwest Coast of North America*. Seattle: University of Washington Press; Vancouver: University of British Columbia Press.

Diamond, Jared. 2005. *Collapse: How Societies Choose to Fail or Succeed*. New York: Viking.

Dichter, Thomas W. 2003. *Despite Good Intentions: Why Development Assistance to the Third World Has Failed*. Amherst: University of Massachusetts Press.

Dilthey, Wilhelm. 1985. *Introduction to the Human Sciences*. Ed./Tr. Rudolf A. Makkreel and Frithjof Rodi. (German original ca 1880.) Princeton, NJ: Princeton University Press.

Dodds, E. R. 1951. *The Greeks and the Irrational*. Berkeley: University of California Press.

Dooley, Ann, and Harry Roe. 1999. *Tales of the Elders of Ireland: A New Translation of Acallam na Senórach*. Oxford: Oxford University Press.

Dove, Michael. 1983. "Theories of Swidden Agriculture and the Political Economy of Ignorance." *Agroforestry Systems* 1:85–99.

———. 1985. *Swidden Agriculture in Indonesia: The Subsistence Strategies of the Kalimantan Kantu'*. Hague, Netherlands: Mouton.

———. 1992. "The Dialectical History of 'Jungle' in Pakistan: An Examination of the Relationship Between Nature and Culture." *Journal of Anthropological Research* 48:231–256.

———. 2003. "Forest Discourses in South and Southeast Asia: A Comparison with Global Discourses." In *Nature in the Global South: Environmental Projects in South and Southeast Asia*, P. Greenough and A. Tsing, eds. Durham, NC: Duke University Press. Pp. 103–123.

———. 2004. "Anthropogenic Grasslands in Southeast Asia: Sociology of Knowledge and Implications for Agroforestry." *Agroforestry Systems* 61:423–435.

———. 2005. "Knowledge and Power in Pakistani Forestry: The Politics of Everyday Knowledge." In *Political Ecology Across Spaces, Scales, and Social Groups*. S. Paulson and L. Gezon, eds. New Brunswick, NJ: Rutgers University Press.

———. 2006. "Indigenous People and Environmental Politics." *Annual Review of Anthropology* 35:191–208.

———. 2011. *The Banana Tree at the Gate: A History of Marginal Peoples and Global Markets in Borneo*. New Haven, CT: Yale University Press.

Dove, Michael, Maria T. Campos, Andrew Salvador Mathews, Laura J. Meitzner Yoder, Anne Rademacher, Suk Bae Rhee, and Daniel Somers Smith. 2003. "The Global Mobilization of Environmental Concepts: Re-Thinking the Western/Non-western Divide. In *Nature Across Culture: Views of Nature and the Environment in Non-Western Culture*. Kluwer Academic Publishers. Pp. 19–46.

Dove, Michael, Percy Sajise, and Amity Doolittle (eds.). 2005. *Conserving Nature in Culture: Case Studies from Southeast Asia*. New Haven, CT: Yale University Southeast Asia Studies.

Dubois, Thomas. 1995. *Finnish Folk Poetry and the Kalevala*. New York: Garland.

Dunstan, Helen. 1998. "Official Thinking on Environmental Issues and the State's Environmental Roles in Eighteenth-Century China." In *Sediments of Time: Environment and Society in Chinese History*, Mark Elvin and Liu Ts'ui-Jung, eds. Cambridge: Cambridge University Press. Pp. 585–614.

Durkheim, Emile. 1995. *Elementary Forms of Religious Life*. Tr. Karen Fields. Fr. orig. 1912. New York: Free Press.

Dursun, A. Haluk. 2011. *Chora Museum*. Istanbul: Bilkent Kültür Girişimi.

Dyson-Hudson, Neville. 1966. Karimojong Politics. Oxford: Oxford University Press.

Eichenwald, Kurt. 2000. *The Informant*. New York: Broadway Books.

Eliade, Mircea. 1964. *Shamanism: Archaic Techniques of Ecstasy.* London: Routledge & Kegan Paul.

Elder, Bruce. 2003. *Blood on the Wattle: Massacres and Maltreatment of Aboriginal Australians Since 1788.* 3d ed. Sydney: New Holland.

Ellerman, David. 2005. *Helping People Help Themselves: From the World Bank to an Alternative Philosophy of Development Assistance.* Ann Arbor: University of Michigan Press.

Ellingson, Ter. 2001. *The Myth of the Noble Savage.* Berkeley: University of California Press.

Elster, Jon. 1983. *Explaining Technical Change.* Cambridge: Cambridge University Press.

———.2007. *Explaining Social Behavior: More Nuts and Bolts for the Social Sciences.* Cambridge: Cambridge University Press.

Elvin, Mark. 2004. *The Retreat of the Elephants: An Environmental History of China.* New Haven, CT: Yale University Press.

Elvin, Mark, and Liu Ts'ui-Jung (eds.). 1998. *Sediments of Time: Environment and Society in Chinese History.* Cambridge: Cambridge University Press.

Emery, Kitty. 2010. *Dietary, Environmental, and Societal Implications of Ancient Maya Animal Use in the Petexbatun: A Zooarchaeological Perspective on the Collapse.* Nashville, TN: Vanderbilt University Press. Vanderbilt Institute of Mesoamerican Archaeology Series, Vol. 5.

Engels, Frederick. 1966. *Anti-Duhring: Herr Eugen Duhring's Revolution in Science.* New York: International Publishers. (New printing. Orig. US ed. 1939. Orig. English ed. 1894.)

Escobar, Arturo. 2008. *Territories of Difference: Place, Movements, life, Redes.* Durham, NC: Duke University Press.

Evans, Nick, and Patrick McConvell. 1999. "The Enigma of Pama-Nyungan Expansion in Australia." In *Archaeology and Language II,* R. Blench and **M.** Spriggs, eds. London: Routledge. Pp. 174–191.

Evers, Larry, and Felipe S. Molina. 1987. *Yaqui Deer Songs.* Tucson: University of Arizona Press.

Fairhead, James, and Melissa Leach. 1996. *Misreading the African Landscape: Society and Ecology in the Forest-Savanna Mosaic.* African Studies Series, 90. Berkeley: University of California Press.

Farmer, David. 2003. *The Oxford Dictionary of Saints.* 5th ed. Oxford: Oxford University Press.

Faust, Betty B. 1998. *Mexican Rural Development and the Plumed Serpent.* Westport, CT: Greenwood.

Faust, Betty B., E. N. Anderson, and John Frazier (eds.). 2004. *Rights, Resources, Culture and Conservation in the Land of the Maya.* Westport, CT: Greenwood.

Fedick, Scott (ed.). 1996. *The Managed Mosaic: Ancient Maya Agriculture and Resource Use.* Salt Lake City: University of Utah Press.

Felger, Richard, and Mary Beth Felger. 1985. *People of the Desert and Sea: Ethnobotany of the Seri Indians.* Tucson: University of Arizona Press.

Fienup-Riordan, Ann. 1994. *Boundaries and Passages: Rule and Ritual in Yup'ik Eskimo Oral Tradition.* Norman, OK: University of Oklahoma Press.

———.2005. *Wise Words of theYup'ik People: We Talk to You because We Love You.* Lincoln, NE: University of Nebraska Press.

Firth, Raymond. 1959. *Social Change in Tikopia; Restudy of a Polynesian Community after a Generation.* London: George Allen and Unwin.

Fisher, Christopher T. 2005. "Demographic and Landscape Change in the Lake Pátzcuaro Basin, Mexico: Abandoning the Garden." *American Anthropologist* 107:87–95.

———.2009. "Abandoning the Garden: The Population/Land Degradation Fallacy as Applied to the Lake Pátzcuaro Basin in Mexico." In *The Archaeology of Environmental Change: Socionatural Legacies of Degradation,* Christopher T. Fisher, J. Brett Hill, and Gary M Feinman, eds. Tucson: University of Arizona Press. Pp. 209–231.

Flanagan, Laurence. 1998. *Ancient Ireland.* New York: St. Martin's Press.

Flood, Josephine. 1997. *Rock Art of the Dreamtime.* Sydney: Angus and Robertson (div. of HarperCollins).

————. 2004. *Archaeology of the Dreamtime*. Sydney: Angus and Robertson (div. of Harper-Collins). New ed.

Flora, Jan, Cornelia B. Flora, Florencia Campana, Mary García Bravo, and Edith Fernández-Baca. 2006. "Social Capital and Advocacy Coalitions: Examples of Environmental Issues from Ecuador." In *Development with Identity: Community, Culture and Sustainability in the Andes*, Robert E. Rhoades, ed. Wallingford, England: CABI. Pp. 287–297.

Foale, S., P. Simon, S. Januchowski, A. Wenger, and M. Macintyre. 2011. "Tenure and Taboos: Origins and Implications for Fisheries in the Pacific." *Fish and Fisheries* 12:357–369.

Foltz, Richard. 2006. *Animals in Islamic Tradition and Muslim Cultures*. Oxford: Oneworld.

Foltz, Richard, Frederick Denny, and Azizan Baharuddin. 2003. *Islam and Ecology*. Cambridge, MA: Harvard University Press for the Center for the Study of World Religions, Harvard Divinity School.

Fomin, E. S. D. 2008. "Royal Residences and Sacred Forests in Western Cameroon: The Intersection of Secular and Spiritual Authority." *Journal for the Study of Religion, Nature and Culture* 2:391–407.

Fontenrose, Joseph. 1981. *Orion: The Myth of the Hunter and the Huntress*. Berkeley: University of California Press. Classical Studies, Vol. 23.

Ford, Anabel, and Ronald Nigh. 2009. "Origins of the Maya Forest Garden: Maya Resource Management." *Journal of Ethnobiology* 29:213–236.

Ford, Jesse D., and Dennis Martinez (eds.). 2000. "Traditional Ecological Knowledge, Ecosystem Science, and Resource Management." *Ecological Applications* 10:5:1249–1340.

Foucault, Michel. 1997. *The Politics of Truth*. New York: Semiotext(e).

Fox, James J. l977. *Harvest of the Palm*. Cambridge, MA: Harvard University Press.

Fox, Jeff, and Judy Ledgerwood. 1999. "Dry-Season Flood-Recession Rice in the Mekong Delta: Two Thousand Years of Sustainable Agriculture?" *Asian Perspectives* 38:37–50.

Fratkin, Elliot. 2004. *Ariaal Pastoralists of Kenya*. 2d ed. Boston, MA: Allyn and Bacon.

Friedman, Herbert. 1980. *A Bestiary for Saint Jerome: Animal Symbolism in European Religious Art*. Washington, DC: Smithsonian Institution.

Frodsham, J. D. 1967. *The Murmuring Stream: The Life and Works of the Chinese Nature Poet Hsieh Ling-yun, Duke of K'ang-Lo*. Kuala Lumpur: University of Malaysia Press.

García-Zambrano, Ángel Julián. 2007. "Ancestral Rituals of Landscape Exploration and Appropriation Among Indigenous Communities in Early Colonial Mexico." In *Sacred Gardens and Landscapes: Ritual and Agency*, Michel Conan, ed. Washington: Dumbarton Oaks. Pp. 193–220.

Gaukroger, Stephen. 2006. *The Emergence of a Scientific Culture: Science and the Shaping of Modernity 1210–1685*. Oxford: Oxford University Press.

Geddes, W. R. 1976. *Migrants of the Mountains: The Cultural Ecology of the Blue Miao (Hmong Njua) of Thailand*. Oxford: Oxford University Press.

Geertz, Clifford. 1963. *Agricultural Involution*. Berkeley: University of California Press.

George, Earl Maquinna. 2003. *Living On the Edge: Nuu-Chah-Nulth History from an Ahousaht Chief's Perspective*. Winlaw, BC: Sono Nis Press.

Gibbon, Edward. 1995 [1776–1788]. *The Decline and Fall of the Roman Empire*. New York: Penguin.

Giddens, Anthony. 1984. *The Constitution of Society*. Berkeley: University of California Press.

Giles, Herbert. 1923. *Gems of Chinese Literature*. Shanghai: Kelly and Walsh.

Gill, Richardson. 2000. *The Great Maya Droughts*. Albuquerque: University of New Mexico Press.

Girardot, N. J., James Miller, and Liu Xiaogan (eds.). 2001. *Daoism and Ecology: Ways Within a Cosmic Landscape*. Cambridge, MA: Harvard University Press for the Center for the Study of World Religions, Harvard Divinity School.

Glacken, Clarence J. 1967. *Traces on the Rhodian Shore: Nature and Culture in Western Thought from Ancient Times to the End of the Eighteenth Century*. Berkeley: University of California Press.

Goffman, Erving. 1959. *The Presentation of the Self in Everyday Life.* Garden City, NY: Doubleday.

Goldin, Frederick. 1973. *Lyrics of the Troubadours and Trouveres.* Garden City: Doubleday Anchor.

Goldschmidt, Walter. 1969. *Kambuya's Cattle: The Legacy of an African Herdsman.* Berkeley: University of California Press.

Gombrich, E. H. 1960. *Art and Illusion.* New York: Pantheon.

———. 1979. *The Sense of Order.* Ithaca, NY: Cornell University Press.

Gómez-Pompa, Arturo. 1987. "On Maya Silviculture." *Mexican Studies/Estudios Mexicanos* 3:1:1–17.

Gómez-Pompa, Arturo, Michael Allen, Scott Fedick, and J. J. Jiménez-Osornio (eds.). 2003. *The Lowland Maya Area: Three Millennia at the Human-Wildland Interface.* New York: Haworth Press.

Gonzalez, Roberto. 2001. *Zapotec Science: Farming and Food in the Northern Sierra of Oaxaca.* Austin: University of Texas Press.

Gooding, Mel, and William Furlong. 2000. *Artists, Land, Nature.* New York: Abrams.

Goodman, Steven M., and Jonathan P. Bestead (eds.). 2003. *The Natural History of Madagascar.* Chicago: University of Chicago Press.

Goodstein, Eban. 1999. *The Trade-Off Myth: Fact and Fiction about Jobs and the Environment.* Washington, DC: Island Press.

Gossen, Gary. 2002. *Four Creations: An Epic Story of the Chiapas Mayas.* Norman: University of Oklahoma Press.

Gottdiener, Mark. 1997. *The Social Production of Urban Space.* Austin: University of Texas Press.

Gould, Richard A. 1969. *Yiwara: Foragers of the Australian Desert.* New York: Scribners.

Goulet, Jean-Guy A. 1998. *Ways of Knowing: Experience, Knowledge, and Power among the Dene Tha.* Lincoln: University of Nebraska Press.

Grau, Andrée. 2000. "Land Body, and Poetry: An Integrated Aesthetic among the Tiwi." In *The Oxford Companion to Aboriginal Art and Culture,* Sylvia Kleinert and Margo Neale, eds. South Melbourne: Oxford University Press. Pp. 356–361.

Gray, Sandra, Mary Sundal, Brandi Wiebusch, Michael A. Little, Paul W. Leslie, and Ivy L. Pike. 2003. "Cattle Raiding, Cultural Survival, and Adaptability of East African Pastoralists." *Current Anthropology* 44 suppl: S3–S30.

Green, Miranda. 1996. *Celtic Goddesses.* New York: George Braziller.

Green, Miranda (ed.). 1995. *The Celtic World.* London: Routledge.

Green, Peter. 1990. *Alexander to Actium: The Historical Evolution of the Hellenistic Age.* Berkeley: University of California Press.

Greenberg, Laurie S. 1992. "Garden Hunting Among the Yucatec Maya: A Coevolutionary History of Wildlife and Culture." *Etnoecologica* 1:1:23–33.

Gross, John. 1983. *The Oxford Book of Aphorisms.* Oxford: Oxford University Press.

Grove, A. T., and Oliver Rackham. 2001. *The Nature of the Mediterranean World.* New Haven, CT: Yale University Press.

Guha, Ramachandra. 1990. *The Unquiet Woods: Economic Change and Peasant Resistance in the Himalaya.* Berkeley: University of California Press.

———. 2000. *Environmentalism: A Global History.* New York: Longmans.

Guo Xi. 2005. "Advice on Landscape." Tr. John Hay, Victor H. Mair, Susan Bush, and Hsio-yen Shih. In *Hawai'i Reader in Traditional Chinese Culture,* Victor Mair, Nancy Steinhardt, and Paul R. Goldin, eds. Honolulu: University of Hawai'i Press. Pp. 380–387.

Haberman, David L. 2013. *People Trees: Worship of Trees in Northern India.* New York: Oxford University Press.

Hadley, Judith M. 2000. *The Cult of Asherah in Ancient Israel and Judah.* Cambridge: Cambridge University Press.

Hadot, Pierre. 2006. *The Veil of Isis.* Tr. Michael Chase. (Fr. orig. 2004.) Cambridge, MA: Harvard University Press.

Haenn, Nora. 2005. *Fields of Power, Forests of Discontent: Culture, Conservation, and the State in Mexico.* Tucson: University of Arizona Press.

———. 2011. "Who's Got the Money Now? Conservation-Development Meets the *Nueva Ruralidad* in Southern Mexico." In *Environmental Anthropology Today,* Helen Kopnina and Eleano Shoreham-Ouimet, eds. Abingdon, Oxford: Routledge. Pp. 215–233.

Hames, Raymond. 2007. "The Ecologically Noble Savage Debate." *Annual Review of Anthropology* 36:177–190.

Hamilton, A. W. 1959. *Malay Pantuns: Pantun Melayu.* Singapore: Eastern Universities Press.

Hamilton, Roy W. 2003. *The Art of Rice: Spirit and Sustenance in Asia.* Los Angeles: UCLA Fowler Museum of Cultural History.

Hanks, Lucien. 1972. *Rice and Man.* Chicago, IL: Aldine.

Hanks, William. 1990. *Referential Practice.* Chicago, IL: University of Chicago Press.

Han-shan. 2000. *The Collected Songs of Cold Mountain.* Tr. Red Pine (Bill Porter). Revised ed. Port Townsend, WA: Copper Canyon Press.

Haq, S. Nomanul. 2003. "Islam and Ecology: Toward Retrieval and Reconstruction." In *Islam and Ecology: A Bestowed Trust,* Richard C. Foltz, Frederick M. Denny, and Azizan Baharuddin, eds. Cambridge, MA: Harvard University Press for the Center for the Study of World Religions, Harvard Divinity School. Pp. 121–153.

Harbison, Peter. 1994. *Pre-Christian Ireland.* London: Thames and Hudson.

Hardin, Garrett. 1968. "The Tragedy of the Commons." *Science* 162:1243–1248.

———. 1991. "The Tragedy of the *Unmanaged* Commons: Population and the Disguises of Providence." In *Commons Without Tragedy,* Robert V. Andelson, ed. Savage, MD: Barnes and Noble. Pp. 162–185.

Harmon, Kitty. 2001. *The Pacific Northwest Landscape: A Painted History.* Seattle, WA: Sasquatch Books.

Harris, Judith Rich. 1998. *The Nurture Assumption: Why Children Turn Out the Way They Do.* New York: Free Press.

Harris, Marvin. 1966. "The Cultural Ecology of India's Sacred Cattle." *Current Anthropology* 7:51–66.

———. 1968. *The Rise of Anthropological Theory.* New York: Crowell.

Hawkes, David. 1959. *Ch'u Tz'u, Songs of the South.* Oxford: Oxford University Press.

Hayami, Yujiro, and Vernon Ruttan. 1985. *Agricultural Development.* 2d ed. Baltimore, MD: Johns Hopkins University Press.

Heaney, Seamus. 1983. *Sweeney Astray.* London: Faber and Faber.

Hedrick, Kimberly. 2007. Our Way of Life: Identity, Landscape, and Conflict. Ph.D. thesis, Dept. of Anthropology, University of California, Riverside.

Helvarg, David. 1997. *The War Against the Greens: The Wise Use Movement, the New Right, and Anti-Environmental Violence.* San Francisco, CA: Sierra Club.

Herren, Michael W. 2002. "Nature and Culture in Mesopotamian and Greek Myths." In *Thinking About the Environment: Our Debt to the Classical and Medieval Past,* Thomas M. Robinson and Laura Westra, eds. Lanham, MD: Lexington Books. Pp. 3–14.

Hervik, Peter. 1999. *Mayan People within and beyond Boundaries: Social Categories and Lived Identity in Yucatán.* Amsterdam: Harwood Academic Publishers.

Hessel, Dieter, and Rosemary Radford Reuther. 2000. *Christianity and Ecology: Seeking the Well-Being of Earth and Humans.* Cambridge, MA: Harvard University Press for the Center for the Study of World Religions, Harvard Divinity School.

Hillel, Daniel. 2006. *The Natural History of the Bible: An Environmental Exploration of the Hebrew Scriptures.* New York: Columbia University Press.

Ho, Wai-Kam (ed.). 1992. *The Century of Tung Ch'i-ch'ang, 1555–1636.* Kansas City, MO: Nelson-Atkins Museum of Art with University of Washington Press.

Hoang Cam. 2007. On Being "Forest Thieves." (Working paper.) Chiang Mai, Thailand:

Regional Center for Social Science and Sustainable Development, Faculty of Social Sciences, Chiang Mai University.

Hobbes, Thomas. 1950 [1651]. *Leviathan.* New York: Dutton.

Hobsbawm, Eric, and Terence Ranger (eds.). 1983. *The Invention of Tradition.* Cambridge: Cambridge University Press.

Hodder, Ian. 2004. "Women and Men at Catalhoyuk." *Scientific American,* Jan., 77–83.

Hodell, David. 2011. "Maya Megadrought?" *Nature* 479:45.

Hoffman, Werner. 2000. *Caspar David Friedrich.* London: Thames and Hudson.

Hofling, Charles Andrew. 1991. *Itzá Maya Texts with a Grammatical Overview.* Salt Lake City: University of Utah Press.

Hoggan, James, with Richard Littlemore. 2009. *Climate Cover-Up: The Crusade to Deny Global Warming.* Vancouver: Greystone Books.

Hohenstaufen, Frederick II. 1943. *The Art of Falconry.* Tr./ed. Casey A. Wood and Margery Frye (Latin orig. early 13th century). Stanford, CA: Stanford University Press.

Holland, Alan. 2002. "Foreword." In *Thinking About the Environment: Our Debt to the Classical and Medieval Past,* Thomas M. Robinson and Laura Westra, eds. Lanham, MD: Lexington Books. Pp. ix–x.

Holthaus, Gary. 2008. *Learning Native Wisdom: What Other Cultures Have to Teach Us about Subsistence, Sustainability, and Spirituality.* Lexington: University of Kentucky Press.

Holzman, Donald. 1976. *Poetry and Politics: The Life and Works of Juan Chi (A.D. 210–263).* Cambridge: Cambridge University Press.

Homans, George. 1974. *Social Behavior: Its Elementary Forms.* New York: Harcourt, Brace, Jovanovich.

Honour, Hugh. 1975. *The New Golden Land: European Images of America from the Discoveries to the Present Time.* New York: Pantheon Books.

Hordes, Stanley. 2005. *To the End of the Earth: A History of the Crypto-Jews of New Mexico.* New York: Columbia University Press.

Howitt, Alfred William. 1904. *Native Tribes of South East Australia.* London: MacMillan.

Huang, Philip. 1990. *The Peasant Family and Rural Development in the Yangzi Delta, 1350–1988.* Stanford, CA: Stanford University Press.

Huard, Pierre, and Maurice Durand. 1954. *Connaissance du Viet-Nam.* Hanoi: École Française de l'Extrème-Orient. Paris: Imprimerie Nationale.

Huber, Toni. 1999. *The Cult of Pure Crystal Mountain.* New York: Oxford University Press.

Hughes, J. Donald. 1983. *American Indian Ecology.* El Paso: Texas Western University Press.

Hume, David. 1957 [1751]. *An Inquiry Concerning the Prinicples of Morals.* Upper Saddle River, NJ: Prentice-Hall.

Humphrey, Caroline, with Urgunge Onon. 1996. *Shamans and Elders: Experience, Knowledge, and Power Among the Daur Mongols.* Oxford: Oxford University Press.

Humphreys, Macartan, Jeffrey Sachs, and Joseph Stiglitz (eds.). 2007. *Escaping the Resource Curse.* New York: Columbia University Press.

Hunn, Eugene. 1991. *N'Chi-Wana, the Big River.* Seattle: University of Washington Press.

———.2008. *A Zapotec Natural History: Trees, Herbs, and Flowers, Birds, Beasts and Bugs in the Life of San Juan Gbëë.* Tucson: University of Arizona Press.

Hunn, Eugene, Darryll R. Johnson, Priscilla N. Russell, and Thomas F. Thornton. 2003. "Huna Tlingit Traditional Environmental Knowledge, Conservation, and the Management of a 'Wilderness' Park." *Current Anthropology* 44 Supplement: S79–S104.

Huntington, Samuel. 1996. *The Clash of Civilizations and the Remaking of World Order.* New York: Simon & Schuster.

Hutchinson, Peter. 2006. *Thrown Rope.* New York: Princeton Architectural Press.

Hyde, Duncan. 1974. *Yamsi: The Story of a Man's Love for a Ranch in the Oregon Wilderness.* New York: Ballantine.

Hyman, John. 2006. *The Objective Eye: Color, Form and Reality in the Theory of Art.* Chicago, IL: University of Chicago Press.

Hynes, R. A., and A. K. Chase. 1982. "Plants, Sites and Domiculture: Aboriginal Influence Upon Plant Communities in Cape York Peninsula." *Archaeology in Oceania* 17:38–50.

Ibn Luyūn. 1975. *Tratado de Agricultura.* Tr. Joaquina Eguaras Ibáñez. Grenada: Patronato de la Alhambra. Biling.

Idema, Wilt, and Beata Grant. 2004. *The Red Brush.* Cambridge, MA: Harvard University Press.

Imhoff, Daniel. 2012. *Food Fight: The Citizen's Guide to the Nexst Food and Farm Bill.* Healdsburg, CA: Watershed Media.

Ingold, Tim. 2000. *The Perception of the Environment: Essays on Livelihood, Dwelling and Skill.* (Reissued, 2011.) London: Routledge.

Isaacs, Jennifer. 1989. *Australian Aboriginal Paintings.* New York: Dutton Studio.

Israel, Jonathan. 1995. *The Dutch Republic: Its Rise, Greatness, and Fall, 1477–1806.* Oxford: Oxford University Press.

Jackson, Kenneth Hurlstone. 1935. *Studies in Early Celtic Nature Poetry.* Cambridge: Cambridge University Press.

———. 1971. *A Celtic Miscellany.* Harmondsworth, Middlesex: Penguin.

Jacobson, Thorkild. 1987. *The Harps That Once . . . Sumerian Poetry in Translation.* New Haven, CT: Yale University Press.

Jain, Pankaj. 2011. *Dharma and Ecology of Hindu Communities: Sustenance and Sustainability.* Farnham, Surrey, England: Ashgate.

Janzen, Dan. 1998. "Gardenification of Wildland Nature and the Human Footprint." *Science* 279:1312–1313.

Jaramillo, Cleofas. 1980. *The Genuine New Mexico Tasty Recipes, 1942.* Santa Fe, NM: Ancient City Press.

Jarosz, Lucy. 1993. "Defining and Explaining Tropical Deforestation: Shifting Cultivation and Population Growth in Colonial Madagascar (1896–1940)." *Economic Geography* 69:366–379.

Jay, Peter. 1981. *The Greek Anthology and Other Ancient Epigrams.* Harmondsworth, Middlesex, England: Penguin.

———. 2006. *Songs of Experience.* Berkeley: University of California Press.

Jencks, Charles. 2000. "EP, Phone Home." In *Alas, Poor Darwin: Arguments Against Evolutionary Psychology,* Rose, Hilary, and Steven Rose (eds.). NY: Harmony Books. Pp. 33–54; "Bayswater Road art."

Jenness, Diamond. 1955. *The Faith of a Coast Salish Indian.* Victoria: British Columbia Provincial Museum [now Royal British Columbia Museum], Memoir 3.

Johannes, R. E. 1981. *Words of the Lagoon: Fishing and Marine Lore in the Palau District of Micronesia.* Berkeley: University of California Press.

———. 1982. "Traditional Conservation Methods and Protected Marine Areas in Oceania." *Ambio* 11(5):258–261.

Johnsen, D. Bruce. 2009. "Salmon, Science, and Reciprocity on the Northwest Coast." *Ecology and Society* 14:2:43.

Johnson, David, Andrew J. Nathan, and Evelyn S. Rawski (eds.). 1985. *Popular Culture in Late Imperial China.* Berkeley: University of California Press.

Johnson, Leslie Main, and Eugene S. Hunn (eds.). 2010. *Landscape Ethnoecology: Concepts of Biotic and Physical Space.* New York: Berghahn.

Johnson, Vivien. 1994. *The Art of Clifford Possum Tjapaltjarri.* East Roseville, NSW: Gordon and Breach.

Joyce, P. W. 1907. *Old Celtic Romances: Tales from Irish Mythology.* London: Longmans, Green & Co.

Juhasz, Antonia. 2008. *The Tyranny of Oil: The World's Most Powerful Industry—and What We Must Do to Stop It.* New York: William Morrow (HarperCollins).

Juhé-Beaulaton, Dominique. 2008. "Sacred Forests and the Global Challenge of Biodiversity Conservation: The Case of Benin and Togo." *Journal for the Study of Religion, Nature and Culture* 2:351–372.

Kadoi, Yuka. 2009. *Islamic Chinoiserie: The Art of Mongol Iran.* Edinburgh: Edinburgh University Press.

Kahneman, Daniel. 2011. *Thinking, Fast and Slow.* New York: Farrar, Straus and Giroux.

Kant, Immanuel. 1960. *Religion Within the Limits of Reason Alone.* (German original, 1792.) New York: Harper and Brothers.

Karabatzaki, Helen. 2002. "Environmental Issues in Hellenistic Philosophy." In *Thinking About the Environment: Our Debt to the Classical and Medieval Past,* Thomas M. Robinson and Laura Westra, eds. Lanham, MD: Lexington Books. Pp.33–42.

Karlgren, Bernhard. 1950. *The Book of Odes.* Stockholm: Museum of Far Eastern Antiquities.

Kaus, Andrea. 1992. Common Ground: Ranchers and Researchers in the Mapimi Biosphere Reserve. Ph.D. dissertation, Dept. of Anthropology, University of California, Riverside.

Kautilya. 1967. *Arthaśastra.* 8th ed. (Not significantly changed from 3rd ed., 1929.) Mysore: Mysore Printing and Publishing House.

Kay, Charles E., and Randy T. Simmons (eds.). 2002. *Wilderness and Political Ecology: Aboriginal Influences and the Original State of Nature.* Salt Lake City: University of Utah Press.

Kearney, Michael. 1984. *Worldview.* Menlo Park, CA: Chandler and Sharp.

Keen, Ian. 2004. *Aboriginal Economy and Society: Australia at the Threshold of Colonisation.* South Melbourne: Oxford University Press.

Kelly, Fergus. 1999. "Trees in Early Ireland." *Irish Forestry* 56:39–57.

Kemp, Martin. 2009. "Art History's Window Onto the Mind." *Nature* 461:882–883.

Kenin-Lopsan, Mongush B. 1997. *Shamanic Songs and Myths of Tuva.* Ed./Tr. Mihály Hoppál. Budapest: Akadémiai Kiadó.

Kiernan, Ben. 2007. *Blood and Soil.* New Haven, CT: Yale University Press.

Kim Jaihiun. 1994. *Classical Korean Poetry.* Fremont, CA: Asian Humanities Press.

Kinsella, Thomas. 1969. *The Tain.* Oxford: Oxford University Press.

———.1989. *The New Oxford Book of Irish Verse.* Oxford: Oxford University Press.

Kinsley, David. 1995. *Ecology and Religion: Ecological Spirituality in Cross-Cultural Perspective.* Englewood Cliffs, NJ: Prentice-Hall.

Kirby, Peter Wynn. 2011. *Troubled Natures: Waste, Environment, Japan.* Honolulu: University of Hawai'i Press.

Kirch, Patrick V. 1994. *The Wet and the Dry: Irrigation and Agricultural Intensification in Polynesia.* Chicago, IL: University of Chicago Press.

———.1997. "Microcosmic Histories." *American Anthropologist* 99:31–42.

———.2007. "Hawaii as a Model System for Human Ecodynamics." *American Anthropologist* 109:8–26.

Kirk, Ruth. 1986. *Wisdom of the Elders.* Vancouver: Douglas and MacIntyre.

Kirsch, Stuart. 2006. *Reverse Anthropology: Indigenous Analysis of Social and Environmental Relations in New Guinea.* Stanford, CA: Stanford University Press.

Kjaergaard, Thorkild. 1994. *The Danish Revolution, 1500–1800: An Ecohistorical Interpretation.* Cambridge: Cambridge University Press.

Klee, Gary (ed.). 1980. *World Systems of Traditional Resource Management.* New York: V. H. Winston and Sons.

Kleinert, Sylvia, and Margo Neale (eds.). 2000. *The Oxford Companion to Aboriginal Art and Culture.* South Melbourne: Oxford University Press.

Klonk, Charlotte. 1996. *Science and the Perception of Nature: British Landscape Art in the Eighteenth and Early Nineteenth Centuries.* New Haven: Yale University Press.

Kluckhohn, Florence, and Floyd Strodtbeck. 1961. *Variations in Value Orientations.* Cambridge, MA: Harvard University Press.

Koerper, Henry, and A. L. Kolls. 1999. "The Silphium Motif Adorning Ancient Libyan Coinage: Marketing a Medicinal Plant." *Economic Botany* 53:133–143.

Kohen, James L. 1995. *Aboriginal Environmental Impacts.* Sydney: University of New South Wales Press.

Komaroff, Linda, and Stefano Carboni (eds.). 2002. *The Legacy of Cinggis-qan, Courtly Art and Culture in Western Asia, 1256–1353.* New York: The Metropolitan Museum of Art.

Konner, Melvin. 2007. "Evolutionary Foundations of Cultural Psychology." In *Handbook of Cross-Cultural Psychology,* Shigeru Kitayama and Dov Cohen, eds. New York: Guilford Press. Pp. 71–105.

Kovacs, Maureen Gallery. 1985. *The Epic of Gilgamesh.* Stanford, CA: Stanford University Press.

Kramer, Samuel Noah. 1955. "Sumerian Myths and Epic Tales." In *Religions of the Ancient Near East,* Isaac Mendelsohn, ed. New York: Liberal Arts Press. Pp. 3–16.

Krech, Shepard, III. 1999. *The Ecological Indian: Myth and Reality.* New York: W. W. Norton.

Kuhn, Dieter. 2009. *The Age of Confucian Rule: The Song Transformation of China.* Cambridge, MA: Harvard University Press.

Kuo Hsi [Guo Xi]. 1935. *An Essay on Landscape Painting.* Tr. Shio Sakanishi. London: John Murray.

Kwiatkowska, Teresa. 2002. "Perceptions of Nature in Polish Medieval and Early Renaissance Writings." In *Thinking about the Environment: Our Debt to the Classical and Medieval Past,* Thomas M. Robinson and Laura Westra, eds. Lanham, MD: Lexington Books. Pp. 87–98.

Landa, Fray Diego de. 1937. *Yucatan Before and After the Conquest.* Tr./Ed. William Gates. Baltimore, MD: The Maya Society. Dover reprint 1978.

Landgraf, John L. 1954. *Land-Use in the Ramah Area of New Mexico: An Anthropological Approach to Areal Study.* Peabody Museum of American Archaeology and Ethnology, Harvard University, Papers, Vol. 42, no. 1.

Lando, Richard. 1979. The Gift of Land: Irrigation and Social Structure in a Toba Batak Village. Ph.D. dissertation, Dept. of Anthropology, University of California, Riverside.

———. 1983. "The Spirits Aren't So Powerful Any More: Spirit Belief and Irrigation Organization in Northern Thailand." *Journal of the Siam Society* 71:142 ff.

Lansing, Stephen. 1987. "Balinese 'Water Temples' and the Management of Irrigation." *American Anthropologist* 89:326–341.

———. 1991. *Priests and Programmers: Technologies of Power in the Engineered Landscape of Bali.* Princeton, NJ: Princeton University Press.

Lansing, J. Stephen. 2006. *Perfect Order: Recognizing Complexity in Bali.* Princeton, NJ: Princeton University Press.

Lapesa, Rafael. 1981. *Historia de la lengua Española.* 9th ed. Madrid: Editorial Gredos.

Latour, Bruno. 1993. *We Have Never Been Modern.* Cambridge, MA: Harvard University Press.

———. 2004. *The Politics of Nature: How to Bring the Sciences Into Democracy.* Tr. Catherine Porter. Cambridge, MA: Harvard University Press.

———. 2005. *Reassembling the Social: An Introduction to Actor-Network-Theory.* Oxford: Oxford University Press.

Latz, Peter. 1995. *Bushfires and Bushtucker.* Alice Springs, Australia: IAD Press.

Laughlin, Robert M. 1996. *Mayan Tales From Zinacantan: Dreams and Stories From the People of the Bat.* Washington, DC: Smithsonian Institution Press.

Lawrence, Elizabeth Attwood. 1997. *Hunting the Wren: Transformation of Bird to Symbol.* Knoxville: University of Tennessee Press.

Leach, E. R. 1954. *Political Systems of Highland Burma.* Cambridge, MA: Harvard University Press.

Leach, Helen. 1999. "Intensification in the Pacific: A Critique of the Archaeological Critieria and Their Application." *Current Anthropology* 40:311–340.

Leacock, Eleanor. 1981. "Seventeenth-Century Montagnais Social Relations and Values." In *Handbook of North American Indians,* vol. 6, June Helm, ed. Washington: Smithsonian Institution. Pp. 190–195.

Lee, Don. 2005. "Lessons in Harmony Lead to Discord." *Los Angeles Times,* Sept. 27, pp. A1, A20.

Lenkersdorf, Carlos. 1996. *Los hombres verdaderos: Voces y testimonios tojolabales.* Mexico: Siglo veintiuno editores.

———. 1999. *Indos somos con orgullo: Poesía maya-tojolabal.* UNAM.

Lentz, David L. (ed.). 2000. *Imperfect Balance: Landscape Transformations in the Precolumbian Americas.* New York: Columbia University Press.

Leopold, Aldo. 1949. *A Sand County Almanac.* New York: Oxford University Press.

Le Roy Ladurie, Emmanuel. 1978. *Montaillou, the Promised Land of Error.* Tr. Barbara Bray. New York: Braziller.

Lerro, Bruce. 2000. *From Earth Spirits to Sky Gods: The Socioecological Origins of Monotheism, Individualism, and Hyperabstract Reasoning From the Stone Age to the Axial Iron Age.* Lanham, MD: Lexington Books.

Lertzman, Ken. 2009. "The Paradigm of Management, Management Systems, and Resource Stewardship." *Journal of Ethnobiology* 29:339–358.

Levinas, Emmanuel. 1969. *Totality and Infinity.* Tr. Alphonso Lingis (Fr. orig. 1961). Pittsburgh, PA: Duquesne University Press.

Lévi-Strauss, Claude. 1964. *The Savage Mind.* Chicago: University of Chicago Press.

Lewis, Daniel Levering. 2008. *God's Crucible: Islam and the Making of Europe, 570–1215.* New York: W. W. Norton.

Lewis, Martin. 1994. *Green Delusions.* Raleigh: University of North Carolina Press.

Lewis, Paul. 2002. *Akha Oral Literature.* Bangkok: White Lotus Press.

Li, Lillian. 2007. *Fighting Famine in North China: State, Market, and Environmental Decline, 1690s–1990s.* Stanford, CA: Stanford University Press.

Li, Tania Murray. 2007. *The Will to Improve: Governmentality, Development, and the Practice of Politics.* Durham, NC: Duke University Press.

Lieberman, Victor. 2003. *Strange Parallels: Southeast Asia in Global Context, c. 800–1830.* Vol. 1: Integration on the Mainland. Cambridge: Cambridge University Press.

Lin, Pauline. 2009. "Rediscovering Ying Qu and His Poetic Relationship With Tao Qian." *Harvard Journal of Asiatic Studies* 69:37–74.

Lin Yueh-Hwa. 1961. *The Lolo of Liang Shan.* New Haven: HRAF Press.

Liu An. 2010. *Huainanzi.* Tr. and Ed. John Major, Sarah Queen, Andrew Seth Mayer, and Harold D. Roth. New York: Columbia University Press.

Llanes Pasos, Eleuterio. 1993. *Cuentos de Cazadores.* Chetumal: Govt. of Quintana Roo.

Llewellyn, Othman abd-Ar-Rahman. 2011. "The Basis for a Discipline of Islamic Environmental Law." In *Islam and Ecology: A Bestowed Trust,* Richard C. Foltz, Frederick M. Denny, and Azizan Baharuddin, eds. Cambridge, MA: Harvard University Press for the Center for the Study of World Religions, Harvard Divinity School. Pp. 185–247.

Lloyd, G. E. R. 2007. *Cognitive Variations.* Oxford: Oxford University Press.

Longnon, Jean, Raymond Cazelles, and Millard Meiss. 1969. *The Très Riches Heures of Jean, Duke of Berry.* New York: George Braziller.

Louv, Richard. 2005. *Last Child in the Woods: Saving Children from Nature-Deficit Disorder.* Chapel Hill, NC: Algonquin Books of Chapel Hill.

———. 2011. *The Nature Principle: Human Restoration and the End of Nature-Deficit Disorder.* Chapel Hill, NC: Algonquin Books.

Low, Mary. 2007. "Humans and Other Animals in Alexander Carmichael's *Carmina Gadelica.*" *Journal for the Study of Religion, Nature and Culture* 1:371–394.

Lucretius. 1928. *De Rerum Natura.* Tr. W. H. D. Rouse. Latin orig. ca 55 BC. London: William Heinemann.

Maas Colli, Hilaria. 1993. *Leyendas Yucatecas.* Mérida: Universidad Autónoma de Yucatán.

MacCoitir, Niall. 2003. *Irish Trees: Myths, Legends and Folklore.* Wilton, Cork, Ireland: Collins Press.

Machiavelli, Niccolo. 2005. *The Prince.* Tr./Ed. Willima J. Connell (Italian orig. ca. 1515). Boston, MA: Bedford/St. Martin's.

MacKenzie, Lewis. 1957. *The Autumn Wind: A Selection From the Poems of Issa.* London: John Murray.

Magi, Giovanni. 2010. *Avignon.* Florence: Bonechi.

Mair, Victor. 2005. "The Northwest(ern) Peoples and the Recurrent Origins of the 'Chinese' State." In *The Teleology of the Modern Nation-State: Japan and China,* Victor Mair, Nancy Steinhardt, and Paul R. Goldin, eds. Hawai'i Reader in Traditional Chinese Culture. Honolulu: University of Hawai'i Press.

Malhotra, Kailash C., Yogesh Gokhale, Sudipto Chatterjee, and Sanjiv Srivastava. 2007. *Sacred Groves in India: An Overview.* Bhopal: Indira Gandhi Rashtriya Manav Sangrahalaya.

Malinowski, Bronislaw. 1944. *A Scientific Theory of Culture.* Oxford: Oxford University Press.

———. 1948. *Magic, Science and Religion.* Glencoe, IL: Free Press.

Mann, Charles C., photographs by Vincent J. Musi. 2011. "The Birth of Religion." *National Geographic,* June, 34–59.

Manne, Robert (ed.). 2003. *Whitewash: On Keith Wildschuttle's Fabrication of Australian History.* Melbourne: Schwartz.

Marcus, George E. 2002. *The Sentimental Citizen: Emotion in Democratic Politics.* University Park: Pennsylvania State University Press.

Marinatos, Nanno. 2000. *The Goddess and the Warrior: The Naked Goddess and Mistress of Animals in Early Greek Religion.* London: Routledge.

Marks, Robert B. 1998. *Tigers, Rice, Silk, and Silt: Envronment and Economy in Late Imperial South China.* New York: Cambridge University Press.

———. 2009. "Geography Is Not Destiny: Historical Contingency and the Making of the Pearl River Delta. In *Good Earths: Regional and Historical Insights into China's Environment,* Ken-Ichi Abe and James E. Nickum, eds. Kyoto: Kyoto University Press. Pp. 1–28.

———. 2012. *China: Its Environment and History.* Lanham, MD: Rowman and Littlefield.

Marsh, George Perkins. 2003 [1864]. *Man and Nature.* Ed. David Lowenthal. Seattle: University of Washington Press.

Martinez Reyes, José. 2004. Contested Place, Nature, and Sustainability: A Critical Anthropo-Geography of Biodiversity Conservation in the "Zona Maya" of Quintana Roo, Mexico. Ph.D. dissertation, Dept. of Anthropology, University of Massachusetts-Amherst.

Mathews, Andrew. 2008. "State Making, Knowledge, and Ignorance: Translation and Concealment in Mexican Forestry Institutions." *American Anthropologist* 110:484–494.

———. 2009. "Unlikely Alliances: Encounters Between State Science, Nature Spirits, and Indigenous Industrial Forestry in Mexico, 1926–2008." *Current Anthropology* 50:75–102.

———. 2011. *Instituting Nature: Authority, Expertise and Power in Mexican Forests.* Cambridge: MIT Press.

Mathews, Jennifer. 2009. *Chicle: The Chewing Gum of the Americas from the Ancient Maya to William Wrigley.* Tucson: University of Arizona Press.

Maurici, Ferdinando. 2006. *Breve Storia Degli Arabi in Sicilia.* Palermo: Flaccovio Editore.

Mauss, Marcel. 1979. "Techniques of the Body." In *Sociology and Psychology: Essays,* Tr. Ben Brewster. London: Routledge and Kegan Paul.{ Pp. 70–88.

McCabe, J. Terrence. 1990. "Turkana Pastoralism: A Case Against the Tragedy of the Commons." *Human Ecology* 18:81–104.

———. 2003. "Sustainability and Livelihood Diversification Among the Maasai of Northern Tanzania." *Human Organization* 62:100–111.

———. 2004. *Cattle Bring Us to Our Enemies: Turkana Ecology, Politics, and Raiding in a Disequilibrium System.* Ann Arbor: University of Michigan Press.

McCay, Bonnie. 1998. *Oyster Wars and the Public Trust: Property Law, and Ecology in New Jersey History.* Tucson: University of Arizona Press.

McCay, Bonnie, and James Acheson (eds.). 1987. *The Question of the Commons.* Tucson: University of Arizona Press.

McEvilley, Thomas. 2002. *The Shape of Ancient Thought: Comparative Studies in Greek and Indian Philosophies.* New York: Allworth Press.

McNeill, J. R. 1992. *Mountains of the Mediterranean World.* Cambridge: Cambridge University Press.

———. 1998. "China's Environmental History in World Perspective." In *Sediments of Time,* Mark Elvin and Liu Ts'ui-jung, eds. Cambridge: Cambridge University Press. Pp. 31–49.

Medin, Douglas; Norbert O. Ross; Douglas G. Cox. 2006. *Culture and Resource Conflict: Why Meanings Matter.* New York: Russell Sage Foundation.

Melville, Elinor G. K. 1997. *A Plague of Sheep: Environmental Consequences of the Conquest of Mexico.* New York: Cambridge University Press.

Melville, Herman. 2001. *Moby-Dick, or The Whale.* (Orig. ed. 1851.) London: Penguin.

Mencius. 1971. *Mencius.* Tr. D. C. Lau. London: Penguin.

Menzies, Nicholas. 1994. *Forest and Land Management in Imperial China.* New York: St. Martin's.

Merleau-Ponty, Maurice. 2003. *Nature: Course Notes from the Collège de France.* Ed. Dominique Séglard, Tr. Robert Vallier. Evanston, IL: Northwestern University Press.

Metzo, Katherine R. 2005. "Articulating a Baikal Environmental Ethic." *Anthropology and Humanism* 30:39–54.

Mikesell, Marvin. 1961. *Northern Morocco: A Cultural Geography.* Berkeley: University of California Press, Publications in Geography, 14.

Mikhail, Alan. 2011. *Nature and Empire in Ottoman Egypt: An Environmental History.* Cambridge: Cambridge University Press.

Mills, C. Wright. 1959. *The Sociological Imagination.* New York: Grove Press.

Milton, Kay. 2002. *Loving Nature.* London: Routledge.

Minnich, Richard. 1988. *The Biogeography of Fire in the San Bernardino Mountains of California: A Historical Study.* Berkeley: University of California Press. University of California Publications in Geography 28.

Mintz, Sidney. 1985. *Sweetness and Power: The Place of Sugar in Modern History.* New York: Penguin.

Mithen, Steven. 2007. *The Singing Neanderthals: The Origins of Music, Language, Mind, and Body.* Cambridge, MA: Harvard University Press.

Moholy-Nagy, Sybil. 1957. *Native Genius in Anonymous Architecture.* New York: Horizon Press.

Mooney, Chris. 2005. *The Republican War on Science.* New York: Basic Books.

Morphy, Howard. 2000a. "Inner Landscapes: The Fourth Dimension." In *The Oxford Companion to Aboriginal Art and Culture,* Sylvia Kleinert and Margo Neale, eds. South Melbourne: Oxford University Press. Pp. 129–136.

———. 2000b. "Rights in Art." In *The Oxford Companion to Aboriginal Art and Culture,* Sylvia Kleinert and Margo Neale, eds. South Melbourne: Oxford University Press. P. 686.

Morphy, Howard, and Margo Smith Boles (eds.). 1999. *Art From the Land.* Charlottesville: University of Virginia.

Morris, Ian. 2010. *Why the West Rules—For Now: The Patterns of History, and What They Reveal About the Future.* New York: Farrar, Straus and Giroux.

Morwood, M. J. 2002. *Visions From the Past: The Archaeology of Australian Aborigina Art.* Crows Nest, NSW: Allen & Unwin. Basic work.

Moses, A. Dirk (ed.). 2004. *Genocide and Settler Society: Frontier Violence and Stolen Indigenous Children in Australian History.* New York: Berghahn.

Mote, Frederick. 1999. *Imperial China 900–1800.* Cambridge, MA: Harvard University Press.

Mowaljarli, David, in conversation with Anthony James Redmond. 2000. "The Origins of Dance and Song in the Ngarinyin World." In *The Oxford Companion to Aboriginal Art and Culture,* Sylvia Kleinert and Margo Neale, eds. South Melbourne: Oxford University Press. Pp. 346–348.

Murphy, Gerard. 2007. *Early Irish Lyrics.* New ed.; orig. 1956. Dublin: Four Courts Press.

Myers, Fred. 2002. *Painting Culture: The Making of an Aboriginal High Art.* Durham, NC: Duke University Press.

Myers, Norman, with Jennifer Kent. 1998. *Perverse Subsidies: Tax Dollars Undercutting Our Economices and Environments Alike.* Winnipeg: International Institute for Sustainable Development.

Nabhan, Gary Paul. 2008. *Arab/American: Landscape, Culture and Cuisine in Two Great Deserts.* Tucson: University of Arizona Press.

Nabhan, Gary Paul, and Deborah Madison. 2008. *Renewing America's Food Traditions: Saving and Savoring the Continent's Most Endangered Foods.* White River Junction, VT: Chelsea Green Publishing Co.

Nabhan, Gary Paul, and Stephen Trimble. 1994. *Geographies of Childhood: Why Children Need Wild Places.* Boston, MA: Beacon Press.

Nabokov, Peter, and Robert Easton. 1989. *Native American Architecture.* New York: Oxford University Press.

Nadasdy, Paul. 2004. *Hunters and Bureaucrats: Power, Knowledge, and Aboriginal-State Relations in the Southwest Yukon.* Vancouver: University of British Columbia Press.

Nagel, Thomas. 1974. "What Is It Like to Be a Bat?" *Philosophicl Review* 83:435–450.

Nash, Steven A. 1995. *Finding Eden: 100 Years of Landscape Painting in the Bay Area.* San Francisco: Fine Arts Museum of San Francisco and University of California Press.

Nelson, Richard. 1983. *Make Prayers to the Raven.* Chicago, IL: University of Chicago Press.

Netting, Robert McC. 1981. *Balancing on an Alp: Ecological Change and Continuity in a Swiss Mountain Community.* New York: Cambridge University Press.

———. 1986. *Cultural Ecology.* 2d ed. Prospect Heights, IL: Waveland.

———. 1993. *Smallholders, Householders: Farm Families and the Ecology of Intensive, Sustainable Agriculture.* Stanford, CA: Stanford University Press.

New South Wales, Art Gallery. 2004. *Crossing Country: The Alchemy of Arnhem Land Art.* Sidney: Art Gallery of New South Wales.

Nietschmann, Bernard. 1973. *Between Land and Water.* New York: Seminar Press.

Novak, Barbara. 1995. *Nature and Culture: American Landscape and Painting, 1825–1875.* Rev. ed. New York: Oxford University Press.

Nurbakhsh, Javad. 1989. *Dogs From a Sufi Point of View.* London: Khaniqahi-Nimatullahi Publications.

Nyamweru, Celia, and Elias Kimaru. 2008. "Indigenous Beliefs and Biodiverstiy Conservation: The Effectiveness of Sacred Groves, Taboos and Totems in Ghana for Habitat and Species Conservation." *Journal for the Study of Religion, Nature and Culture* 2:309–326.

Nyamweru, Celia, and Michael Sheridan (eds.). 2008. "African Sacred Ecologies." Special issue, *Journal for the Study of Religion, Nature and Culture* 2:3.

Nyerges, A. Endre (ed.). 1997. *The Ecology of Practice: Studies of Food Crop Production in Sub-Saharan West Africa.* Amsterdam: Gordon and Breach.

O'Croinin, Daibhi. 1995. *Early Medieval Ireland, 400–1200.* London: Longmans.

O'Faoláin, Seán. 1968. *The Silver Branch.* Freeport, NY: Books for Libraries Press. (Original: New York: Viking, 1938.)

O'Keeffe, J. G. 1913. *Buile Suibne (The Frenzy of Suibne), Being the Adventures of Suibne Geilt, a Middle-Irish Romance.* London: Irish Texts Society.

Oliver, Paul. 1987. *Dwellings.* Austin: University of Texas Press.

Olson, Mancur. 1965. *The Logic of Collective Action.* Cambridge, MA: Harvard University Press.

Oreskes, Naomi, and Erik M. Conway. 2010. *Merchants of Doubt: How a Handful of Scientists Obscured the Truth on Issues From Tobacco Smoke to Global Warming.* New York: Bloomsbury Press.

Orians, Gordon, and Judith H. Heerwagen. 1992. "Evolved Responses to Landscapes." In *The Adapted Mind*, J. Barkow, L. Cosmides, and J. Tooby, eds. New York: Oxford University Press. Pp. 555–580.

O'Shea, Stephen. 2002. *The Perfect Heresy: The Revolutionary Life and Death of the Medieval Cathars*. New York: Walker and Co.

Ostrom, Elinor. 1990. *Governing the Commons: The Evolution of Institutions for Collective Action*. New York: Cambridge University Press.

———. 2005. *Understanding Institutional Diversity*. Princeton: Princeton University Press.

———. 2009. "A General Framework for Analyzing Sustainability of Social-Ecological Systems." *Science* 325:419–422.

Ovid. 2000. *Metamorphoses*. Tr. Arthur Golding, ed. John Frederick Nims. (Orig. ca. 1 AD; translation 1567.) Philadelphia, PA: Paul Dry Books.

Painter, Michael, and William Durham (eds.). 1995. *The Social Causes of Environmental Destruction in Latin America*. Ann Arbor: University of Michigan.

Painter, Muriel. 1986. *With Good Heart*. Tucson: University of Arizona Press.

Parkinson, Gavin. 2008. *Surrealism, Art and Modern Science*. New Haven, CT: Yale University Press.

Peet, Richard, and Michael Watts (eds.). 1996. *Liberation Ecologies: Environment, Development, Social Movements*. London: Routledge.

Pei Shengji. 2010. "The Road to the Future? The Biocultural Values of the Holy Hill Forests of Yunnan Province, China." In *Sacred Natural Sites: Conserving Nature and Culture*, Bas Verschuuren, Robert Wild, Jeffrey A. McNeely, and Gonzalo Oviedo, eds. London: Earthscan. Pp. 98–106.

Peluso, Nancy Lee. 1992. *Rich Forests, Poor People: Resource Control and Resistance in Java*. Berkeley: University of California Press.

Perdikaris, Sophia, and Thomas H. McGovern. 2008. "Codfish and Kings, Seals and Subsistence: Norse Marine Resource Use in the North Atlantic." In *Human Impacts on Ancient Marine Ecosystems: A Global Perspective*, Torben C. Rick and Jon M. Erlandson, eds. Berkeley: University of California Press. Pp. 187–214.

Perezgrovas Garza, Raúl (ed.). 1990. *Los carneros de San Juan: Ovinocultura indígena en los Altos de Chiapas*. San Cristóbal de Las Casas: Universidad Autónoma de Chiapas.

Perramond, Eric P. 2010. *Political Ecologies of Cattle Ranching in Northern Mexico*. Tucson: University of Arizona Press.

Pierotti, Raymond. 2011. *Indigenous Knowledge, Ecology, and Evolutionary Biology*. New York: Routledge.

Pierotti, Raymond, and Daniel R. Wildcat. 1999. "Traditional Knowledge, Culturally-based World-views and Western Science." In *Cultural and Spiritual Values of Biodiversity*, Darrell Posey, ed. London: UN Environment Programme. Pp. 192–199.

Pinkaew Laungaramsri. 2001. *Redefining Nature: Karen Ecological Knowledge and the Challenge to the Modern Conservation Paradigm*. Chennai, India: Earthworm Books.

Pinkerton, Evelyn (ed.). 1989. *Cooperative Management of Local Fisheries: New Directions for Improved Management and Community Development*. Vancouver: University of British Columbia.

Pinkerton, Evelyn, and Martyn Weinstein. 1995. *Fisheries That Work: Sustainability Through Community-Based Management*. Vancouver, BC: David Suzuki Foundation.

Pitarch, Pedro. 2010. *The Jaguar and the Priest: An Ethnography of Tzeltal Souls*. Austin: University of Texas Press.

Pliny the Elder. 2004. *Natural History: A Selection*. New York: Penguin.

Posey, Darrell Addison. 2004. *Indigenous Knowledge and Ethics: A Darrell Posey Reader*. New York: Routledge.

Posey, Darrell (ed.). 1999. *Cultural and Spiritual Values of Biodiversity*. London: UN Environment Programme.

Potter, Jack. 1976. *Thai Peasant Social Structure.* Chicago, IL: University of Chicago Press.

Potts, D. T. 1997. *Mesopotamian Civilization: The Material Foundations.* Ithaca, NY: Cornell University Press.

Powell, James Lawrence. 2011. *The Inquisition of Climate Science.* New York: Columbia University Press.

Preece, R. 1999. *Cultural Myths, Cultural Realities.* Vancouver: University of British Columbia Press.

Presicce, Claudio Parisi. 2000. *La Lupa Capitolina.* Roma: Comune di Roma, Musei Capitolini.

Psilakis, Michael. 2009. *How to Roast a Lamb: New Greek Classic Cooking.* New York: Little, Brown.

Putnam, Robert D. 1993. *Making Democracy Work.* Princeton, NJ: Princeton University Press.

Pyne, Stephen J. 1991. *Burning Bush: A Fire History of Australia.* New York: Henry Holt & Co.

Radin, Paul. 1916. *The Winnebago Tribe.* Washington, DC: Bureau of American Ethnology, Annual Report 37, pp. 33–550.

———. 1957a. *Primitive Man as Philosopher.* Rev. ed. New York: Dover.

———. 1957b. *Primitive Religion.* Rev. ed. New York: Dover.

Ramsey, Jarold. 1980. *Coyote Was Going There: Indian Literature of the Oregon Country.* Seattle: University of Washington Press.

Randall, Robert A. 1977. Change and Variation in Samal Fishing: Making Plans to 'Make a Living' in the Southern Philippines. Ph.D. thesis, Dept. of Anthropology, University of California, Berkeley.

Rangan, Haripriya. 1996. "From Chipko to Uttaranchal." In *Liberation Ecologies: Environment, Development, Social Movements,* Richard Peet and Michael Watts (eds.). London: Routledge. Pp. 205–226.

Rappaport, Roy A. 1984. *Pigs for the Ancestors.* New Haven, CT: Yale University Press.

———. 1999. *Ritual and Religion in the Making of Humanity.* New York: Cambridge University Press.

Red Pine (William Porter). 2000. *The Collected Songs of Cold Mountain.* Port Townsend, WA: Copper Canyon Press.

Redfield, Margaret Park. 1935. *The Folk Literature of a Yucatecan Town.* Carnegie Institution of Washington, Contributions to American Archaeology, 13.

Redfield, Robert, and Alfonso Villa Rojas. 1934. *Chan Kom, A Maya Village.* Carnegie Institution of Washington.

Redford, Kent. 1990. "The Ecologically Noble Savage." *Orion Nature Quarterly* 9:25–29.

Redman, Charles. 1999. *Human Impacts on Ancient Environments.* Tucson: University of Arizona Press.

Reed, Richard K. 1995. *Prophets of Agroforestry: Guaraní Communities and Commercial Gathering.* Austin: University of Texas Press.

———. 1997. *Forest Dwellers, Forest Protectors: Indigenous Models for International Development.* Boston, MA: Allyn and Bacon.

Rees, Alwyn, and Brinley Rees. 1995. *Celtic Heritage.* (Orig. ed. 1961.) London: Thames and Hudson.

Reichel-Dolmatoff, G. 1971. *Amazonian Cosmos: The Sexual and Religious Symbolism of the Tukano Indians.* Chicago, IL: University of Chicago Press.

———. 1976. "Cosmology as Ecological Analysis: A View from the Rain Forest." *Man* 11:307–316.

———. 1996. *The Forest Within: The World-View of the Tukano Amazonian Indians.* Foxhole, Dartington, Totnes, Devon: Themis, imprint of Green Books.

Reid, Anthony. 1988. *Southeast Asia in the Age of Commerce.* Vol. I: *The Lands Below the Winds.* New Haven, CT: Yale University Press.

———. 1994. *Southeast Asia in the Age of Commerce.* Vol. II: *Expansion and Crisis.* New Haven, CT: Yale University Press.

Remes, Pauliina. 2008. *Neoplatonism.* Berkeley: University of California Press.

Remmers, Gaston G. A. 1998. *Con Cojones y Maestría.* Amsterdam: Thela.

Remotti, Francesco. 1987. "Catégories sémantiques de l'éros chez les Wanande du Zaïre." *L'Homme* 27:73–92.

Restall, Matthew. 1997. *The Maya World: Yucatec Culture and Society, 1550–1850.* Stanford, CA: Stanford University Press.

———. 1998. *Maya Conquistador.* Boston, MA: Beacon Press.

Reyes, Lawney L. 2002. *White Grizzly Bear's Legacy: Learning to be Indian.* Seattle: University of Washington Press.

Reynolds, Peter J. 1995. "Rural Life and Farming." In *The Celtic World,* Miranda Green, ed. London: Routledge. Pp. 176–208.

Rick, Torben C., and Jon M. Erlandson (eds.). 2008. *Human Impacts on Ancient Marine Ecosystems: A Global Perspective.* Berkeley: University of California Press.

Robb, John Donald. 1980. *Hispanic Folk Music of New Mexico and the Southwest: A Self-Portrait of a People.* Norman, OK: University of Oklahoma Press.

Robbins, Paul. 2004. *Political Ecology.* Oxford: Blackwell.

Robinson, Thomas M., and Laura Westra. 2002. *Thinking About the Environment: Our Debt to the Classical and Medieval Past.* Lanham, MD: Lexington Books.

Robotham, Tom. 1993. *Albert Bierstadt.* New York: Crescent Books.

Rogers, Carl. 1961. *On Becoming a Person.* Boston, MA: Houghton Mifflin.

Rose, Deborah. 2000a. *Dingo Makes Us Human: Life and Land in an Australian Aboriginal Culture.* New York: Cambridge University Press.

———. 2000b. "The Power of Place." In *The Oxford Companion to Aboriginal Art and Culture,* Sylvia Kleinert and Margo Neale, eds. South Melbourne: Oxford University Press. Pp. 40–49.

———. 2005. "An Indigenous Philosophical Ecology." *Australian Journal of Anthropology* 16:294–305.

Rosenberg, Melrich V. 1939. *The Ark of Heraldry.* New York: Henry Holt & Co.

Roumasset, James A. 1976. *Rice and Risk.* Amsterdam: North Holland Pub Co.

Ruddle, Kenneth, and Tomoya Akimichi (eds.). 1984. *Maritime Institutions in the Western Pacific.* Senri Ethnological Studies 17. Osaka: National Museum of Ethnology.

Ruddle, Kenneth, and R. E. Johannes, eds. 1983. *The Traditional Knowledge and Management of Coastal Systems in Asia and the Pacific.* Jakarta: UNESCO, Regional Office for Science and Technology for Southeast Asia.

Rudofsky, Bernard. 1965. *Architecture Without Architects.* New York: Museum of Modern Art.

Ruiz de Alarcón, Hernando. 1982. *Aztec Sorcerers in Seventeenth Century Mexico: The Treatise on Superstitions by Hernando Ruiz de Alarcón.* Albany: Institute for Mesoamerican Studies, State University of New York at Albany.

Rumsey, Alan, and James F. Weiner (eds.). 2001. *Emplaced Myth: Space, Narrative, and Knowledge in Aboriginal Australia and Papua-New Guinea.* Honolulu: University of Hawai'i Press.

Runciman, Stephen. 1955. *The Medieval Manichee.* Cambridge: Cambridge University Press.

Rustagi, Devesh, Stefanie Engel, and Michael Kosfeld. 2010. "Conditional Cooperation and Costly Monitoring Explain Success in Forest Commons Management." *Science* 330:961–965.

Ruttan, Lore, and Monique Borgerhoff Mulder. 1999. "Are East African Pastoralists Truly Conservationists?" *Current Anthropology* 40:621–653.

Sahagun, Bernardino de. 1950–1982. *Florentine Codex.* Tr. Charles E. Dibble and Arthur J. O. Anderson. (Spanish original late 16th century.) Salt Lake City: University of Utah Press.

Sahlins, Marshall. 1972. *Stone Age Economics.* Chicago, IL: Aldine.

———. 1976. *Culture and Practical Reason.* Chicago, IL: University of Chicago Press.

Salick, Jan, Yang Yongping, and Anthony Amend. 2005. "Tibetan Land Use and Change Near Khawa Karpo, Eastern Himalayas." *Economic Botany* 59:312–325.

Sanday, Peggy Reeves. 2007. *Aboriginal Paintings of the Wolfe Creek Crater: Track of the Rainbow Serpent.* Philadelphia: University of Pennsylvania Museum.

Santangelo, Paolo. 1998. "Ecologism Versus Moralism: Conceptions of Nature in Some Literary Texts of Ming-Qing Times." In *Sediments of Time: Environment and Society in Chinese History,* Mark Elvin and Liu Ts'ui-Jung (eds.). Cambridge: Cambridge University Press. Pp. 617–656.

Sauer, Carl. 1963. *Land and Life, a Selection from the Writings of Carl Ortwin Sauer,.* Ed. John Leighly. Berkeley: University of California Press.

Scarborough, Vernon. 2003. *The Flow of Power: Ancient Water Systems and Landscapes.* Santa Fe, NM: SAR Press.

———. 2009. "Beyond Sustainability: Managed Wetlands and Water Harvesting in Ancient Mesoamerica." In *The Archaeology of Environmental Change: Socionatural Legacies of Degradation,* Christopher T. Fisher, J. Brett Hill, and Gary M Feinman, eds. Tucson: University of Arizona Press. Pp. 62–83.

Schmitt, Jean-Claude. 1983. *The Holy Greyhound: Guinefort, Healer of Children Since the Thirteenth Century.* Tr. Martin Thom; Fr. original 1979. Cambridge: Cambridge University Press.

Schneider, Norbert. 1992. *Naturaleza muerte.* Kőln: Benedikt Taschen.

Schwartz, Norman B. 1990. *Forest Society: A Social History of Peten, Guatemala.* Philadelphia: University of Pennsylvania Press.

Scott, James C. 1985. *Weapons of the Weak.* New Haven, CT: Yale University Press.

———. 1990. *Domination and the Arts of Resistance: Hidden Transcripts.* New Haven: Yale University Press.

———. 1998. *Seeing Like a State.* New Haven, CT: Yale University Press.

———. 2009. *The Art of Not Being Governed: An Anarchist History of Upland Southeast Asia.* New Haven, CT: Yale University Press.

Scudder, Thayer. 2005. *The Future of Large Dams: Dealing With Social, Environmental, Institutional and Political Costs.* London: Earthscan.

Searcy, Michael T. 2011. *The Life-Giving Stone: Ethnoarchaeology of Maya Metates.* Tucson: University of Arizona Press.

Seaton, Jerome P., and Dennis Maloney. 1994. *A Drifting Boat: Chinese Zen Poetry.* Fredonia, NY: White Pine Press.

Secaira, Estuardo. 2000. *La conservación de la natura, el pueblo y movimiento Maya, y la espiritualidad en Guatemala: Implicaciones para conservacionistas.* Guatemala: PROARCA/ CAPAS/AID, IUCN, Fideicomiso para la Conservación de Guatemala, and The Nature Conservancy.

Sen, Amartya. 1992. *Inequality Reconsidered.* Cambridge: Harvard University Press and Russell Sage Foundation.

———. 2009. *The Pursuit of Justice.* Cambridge, MA: Harvard University Press.

Shandra, John M., Laura A. McKinney, Christopher Leckband, and Bruce London. 2010. "Debt, Structural Adjustment, and Biodiversity Loss: A Cross-National Analysis of Threatened Mammals and Birds." *Journal of Human Ecology* 17:18–33.

Sharp, Henry. 2001. *Loon: Memory, Meaning and Reality in a Northern Dene Community.* Lincoln: University of Nebraska Press.

Sheridan, Thomas E. 1988. *Where the Dove Calls: The Political Ecology of a Peasant Corporate Community.* Tucson: University of Arizona Press.

———. 2007. "Embattled Ranchers, Endangered Species, and Urban Sprawl: The Political Ecology of the New American West." *Annual Review of Anthropology* 36:121–154.

Shields, Scott. 2006. *Artists at Continent's End: The Monterey Peninsula Artists' Colony, 1875–1907.* Berkeley: University of California Press.

Shishkin, Ivan. 2008. *Ivan Shishkin.* St. Petersburg: Ruskii Muzei.

Sillitoe, Paul. 2010. *From Land to Mouth: The Agriculural "Economy" of the Wola of the New Guinea Highlands.* New Haven, CT: Yale University Press.

Simoons, Frederick. 1979. "Questions in the Sacred Cow Controversy." *Current Anthropology* 20:3:467–493.

———. 1994. *Eat Not This Flesh: Food Avoidances From Prehistory to the Present.* 2d ed. Madison: University of Wisconsin.

Slicher von Bath, B. H. 1963. *The Agrarian History of Western Europe, 500–1850.* New York: St. Martin's.

Slive, Seymour. 1995. *Dutch Painting 1600–1800.* Revised edition. New Haven, CT: Yale University Press.

———. 2005. *Jacob van Ruisdael.* London: Royal Academy of Arts.

Smil, Vaclav. 2004. *China's Past, China's Future: Energy, Food, Environment.* New York: RoutledgeCurzon.

———. 2013. *Harvesting the Biosphere: What We Have Taken from Nature.* Cambridge: MIT Press.

Smith, Eric A., and Mark Wishnie. 2000. "Conservation and Subsistence in Small-Scale Societies." *Annual Reviews in Anthropology* 29:493–524.

Smith, J. Russell. 1950. *Tree Crops: A Permanent Agriculture.* New York: Devin Adair.

Snyder, Gary. 1979. *He Who Hunted Birds in His Father's Village: The Dimensions of a Haida Myth.* Bolinas, CA: Grey Fox Press.

Spencer, J. E. 1966. *Shifting Cultivation in Southeast Asia.* Berkeley: University of California Press.

Spencer, W. Baldwin, and Frank J. Gillen. 1889. *The Native Tribes of Central Australia.* London: MacMillan.

———. 1904. *Northern Tribes of Central Australia.* London: MacMillan.

Sponsel, Leslie. 2012. *Spiritual Ecology: A Quiet Revolution.* Santa Barbara, CA: Praeger.

Stafford, Anthony. 1615. *Stafford's Heavenly Dogge.* London: "Printed by George Purslowe for John Budge."

Stauber, John, and Sheldon Rampton. 1996. *Toxic Sludge Is Good for You: Lies, Damn Lies and the Public Relations Industry.* Monroe, ME: Common Courage.

Stein, Rolf A. 1990. *The World in Miniature: Container Gardens and Dwellings in Far Eastern Religious Thought.* Tr. Phyllis Brooks (French orig. 1987). Stanford, CA: Stanford University Press.

Steward, Julian H. 1955. *Theory of Culture Change.* Urbana: University of Illinois Press.

———. 1977. *Evolution and Ecology: Essays on Social Transformation.* Ed. Jane Steward and Robert Murphy. Urbana: University of Illinois Press.

Stewart, Omer C., Henry Lewis, and Kat Anderson. 2002. *Forgotten Fires: Native Americans and the Transient Wilderness.* Norman: University of Oklahoma Press.

Stiglitz, Joseph. 2003. *Globalization and Its Discontents.* New York: W. W. Norton.

Stokes, Whitley. 1890. *Lives of Saints, From the Book of Lismore.* Oxford: Oxford University Press.

Stonich, Susan C. 1993. *"I Am Destroying the Land!" The Political Ecology of Poverty and Environmental Destruction in Honduras.* Boulder, CO: Westview.

Stuart, David, and George Stuart. 2008. *Palenque, Eternal City of the Maya.* London: Thames and Hudson.

Studley, John. 2010. "Uncovering the Intangible Values of Earth Care: Using Cognition to Reveal the Eco-Spiritual Domains and Sacred Values of the People of Eastern Kham." In *Sacred Natural Sites: Conserving Nature and Culture,* Bas Verschuuren, Robert Wild, Jeffrey A. McNeely, and Gonzalo Oviedo, eds. London: Earthscan. Pp. 107–118.

Sturgeon, Janet. 2005. *Border Landscapes: The Politics of Akha Land Use in China and Thailand.* Seattle: University of Washington Press.

Sukhdev, Pavan. 2009. "Costing the Earth." *Nature* 462:277.

Sukhu, Gopal. 2012. *The Shaman and the Heresiarch: A New Interpretation of the Li Sao.* Albany: SUNY Press.

Sullivan, Michael. 1962. *The Birth of Landscape Painting in China.* Berkeley: University of California Press.

———. 1980. *Chinese Landscape Painting in the Sui and T'ang Dynasties.* Berkeley: University of California Press.

———. 2008. *The Arts of China.* 5th ed. Berkeley: University of California Press.

Sutton, Peter (ed.). 1988. *Dreamings: The Art of Aboriginal Australia.* New York: George Braziller.

Swartz, Wendy. 2008. *Reading Tao Yuanming: Shifting Paradigms of Historical Reception, 427–1900.* Cambridge, MA: Harvard University Asia Center, distributed by Harvard University Press.

———. 2010. "Naturalness in Xie Lingyun's Poetic Works." *Harvard Journal of Asiatic Studies* 70:355–386.

Tamisari, Franca. 2000. "Knowing the Country, Holding the Law: Yolngu Dance Performance in North-Eastern Arnhem Land." In *The Oxford Companion to Aboriginal Art and Culture,* Sylvia Kleinert and Margo Neale, eds. South Melbourne: Oxford University Press. Pp. 146–152.

Taube, Karl. 2004. "Flower Mountain: Concepts of Life, Beauty and Paradise Among the Classic Maya." *Anthropology and Aesthetics* 45:69–98.

Taylor, Bron. 2010. *Dark Green Religion: Nature, Spirituality and the Planetary Future.* Berkeley: University of California Press.

Telfer, Wendy R., and Murray J. Garde. 2006. "Indigenous Knowledge of Rock Kangaroo Ecology in Western Arnhem Land, Australia." *Human Ecology* 34:379–406.

Terán, Silvia; Christian H. Rasmussen. 1993. *La milpa de los Mayas.* Mérida: authors.

Terborgh, John. 1989. *Where Have All the Birds Gone?* Princeton: Princeton University Press.

———. 1999. Requiem for Nature. Washington, DC: Island Press.

Thick, Malcolm. 2010. *Sir Hugh Plat: The Search for Useful Knowledge in Early Modern London.* Totnes, Devon: Prospect Books.

Thomas, Lynn L. 1977. Kinship Categories in a Minangkabau Village. Ph.D. thesis, Dept. of Anthropology, University of California, Riverside.

Thomas, Lynn L. (ed.). 1985. *Change and Continuity in Minangkabau: Local, Regional and Historical Perspectives on West Sumatera.* Athens: Ohio University, Center for International Studies.

Thompson, E. P. 1975. *Whigs and Hunters: The Origins of the Black Act.* New York: Pantheon.

Thompson, Stith. 1955–1958. *Motif-Index of Folk-Literature.* Bloomington: Indiana University Press.

Thornton, Thomas F. 2008. *Being and Place Among the Tlingit.* Seattle: University of Washington Press.

Tilt, Bryan. 2009. *The Struggle for Sustainability in Rural China: Environmental Values and Civil Society.* New York: Columbia University Press.

Tirosh-Samuelson, Hava (ed.). 2002. *Judaism and Ecology: Created World and Revealed Word.* Cambridge, MA: Harvard University Press for the Center for the Study of World Religions, Harvard Divinity School.

Toledo, Victor. 1992. "What Is Ethnoecology? Origins, Scope and Implications of a Rising Discipline." *Etnoecologia* 1:5–21.

Toledo, V. M. 2002. "Ethnoecology: A Conceptual Framework for the Study of Indigenous Knowledge of Nature." In *Ethnobiology and Biocultural Diversity,* J. R. Stepp, F. S. Wyndam, and R. K. Zarger, eds. Pp. 511–522. Athens, GA: International Society of Ethnobiology.

Totman, Conrad. 1989. *The Green Archipelago: Forestry in Preindustrial Japan.* Berkeley: University of California Press.

Trenton, Paricial, and William H. Gerdts. 1990. *California Light, 1900–1930.* Laguna Beach, CA: Laguna Art Museum.

Tsing, Anna Lowenhaupt. 2005. *Friction: An Ethnography of Global Connection.* Princeton, NJ: Princeton University Press.

Tuan, Yi-Fu. 1969. *China.* Chicago, IL: Aldine.

Tuchman, Barbara. 1978. *A Distant Mirror: The Troubled Fourteenth Century.* New York: Knopf.

Tucker, Mary Evelyn, and John Berthrong (eds.). 1998. *Confucianism and Ecology: the Inter-relation of Heaven, Earth and Humans.* Cambridge, MA: Harvard University Press for the Center for the Study of World Religions, Harvard Divinity School.

Tucker, Mary Evelyn, and John A. Grim (eds.). 1994. *Worldviews and Ecology: Religion, Philosophy, and the Environment.* Maryknoll, NY: Orbis Books.

Tucker, Mary Evelyn, and Duncan R. Williams (eds.). 1997. *Buddhism and Ecology: The Interaction of Dharma and Deeds.* Cambridge, MA: Harvard University Press for the Center for the Study of World Religions, Harvard Divinity School.

Turchin, Peter, and Sergey Zefedov. 2009. *Secular Cycles.* Princeton: Princeton University Press.

Turner, Nancy J. 2005. *The Earth's Blanket.* Vancouver: Douglas and MacIntyre.

Turner, Nancy J., Yilmaz Ari, Fikret Berkes, Iain Davidson-Hunt, Z. Fusun Ertug, and Andrew Miller. 2009. "Cultural Management of Living Trees: An International Perspective." *Journal of Ethnobiology* 29:237–270.

Turpin, Myfanwy, Alison Ross, Veronica Dobson, and M. K. Turner. 2013. "The Spotted Nightjar Calls When Dingo Pups Are Born: Ecological and Social Indicators in Central Australia." *Journal of Ethnobiology* 33:7–32.

Uleman, James S., and S. Adil Saribay. 2012. "Initial Impressions of Others." In *The Oxford Handbook of Personality and Social Psychology,* Kay Deaux and Mark Snyder, eds. New York: Oxford University Press. Pp. 337–366.

Underwood, Paul. 1966. *The Kariye Djami.* New York: Pantheon Books for Bollingen Foundation.

Varro (Marcus Terentius Varro). 1935. "Marcus Terentius Varro on Agriculture." In *Cato and Varro.* Tr. William Davis Hooper, revised by Harrison Boyd Ash. Cambridge, MA: Harvard University Press, Loeb Classical Library. Pp. 159–529.

Vayda, Andrew P. 2008. "Causal Explanations as a Research Goal: A Pragmatic View." In *Against the Grain: The Vayda Tradition in Ecological Anthropology,* Bradley Walker, Bonnie McCay, Paige West, and Susan Lees, eds. Lanham, MD: AltaMira (division of Rowman and Littlefield). Pp. 317–367.

———. 2009. "Causal Explanation as a Research Goal: Do's and Don't's." In *Explaining Human Actions and Environmental Changes.* Lanham, MD: AltaMira (division of Rowman & Littlefield). Pp. 1–48.

Vayda, Andrew P., and Bradley Walters. 1999. "Against Political Ecology." *Human Ecology* 27:167–179.

Veblen, Thorstein. 1912. *The Theory of the Leisure Class: An Economic Study of Institutions.* New York: MacMillan.

Verschuuren, Bas, Roert Wild, Jeffrey A. McNeely, and Gonzalo Oviedo (eds.). 2010. *Sacred Natural Sites: Conserving Nature and Culture.* London: Earthscan.

Villa Rojas, Alfonso. 1945. *The Maya of East Central Quintana Roo.* Washington, DC: Carnegie Institution of Washington. Publ. 559.

Vincent, Stephen (ed.). 1990. *O California! Nineteenth and Early Twentieth Century California Landscapes and Observations.* San Francisco: Bedford Arts.

Vincenti, Valentina. 2002. "La tutela ambientale del lago Trasimeno in eta medioevale." In *Thinking About the Environment: Our Debt to the Classical and Medieval Past,* Thomas M. Robinson and Laura Westra, eds. Lanham, MD: Lexington Books. Pp. 131–141.

Virgil (Publius Vergilius Maro). 1999. *Virgil I: Eclogues, Georgics, Aeneid I-VI.* Tr. H. Rushton Fairclough, rev. G. P. Goold (Latin orig. ca. 38 BC). Cambridge, MA: Harvard University Press, Loeb Classical Library.

———. 2006. *Georgics.* Tr. Peter Fallon, intro. Elaine Fantham (Latin orig. ca. 38 BC). Oxford: Oxford University Press.

Vlach, John Michael. 2002. *The Planter's Prospect: Privilege and Slavery in Plantation Paintings.* Chapel Hill: University of North Carolina Press.

Vogt, Evon Z. 1993. *Tortillas for the Gods: A Symbolic Analysis of Zinacanteco Rituals.* Norman: University of Oklahoma Press.

Vogt, Evon Z., and Ethel Albert. 1966. *People of Rimrock: A Study of Values in Five Cultures.* Cambridge, MA: Harvard University Press.

Wack, Mary Frances. 1990. *Lovesickness in the Middle Ages: The Viaticum and Its Commentaries.* Philadelphia: University of Pennsylvania Press.

Wagner, Donald. 2008. *Science and Civilisation in China. Vol. V: Chemistry and Chemical Technology. Part 11: Ferrous Metallurgy.* Cambridge: Cambridge University Press.

Wagner, John, and Maia Talakai. 2007. "Customs, Commons, Property and Ecology: Case Studies from Oceania." *Human Organization* 66:1–10.

Waldau, Paul, and Kimberly Patton (eds). 2007. *A Communion of Subjects: Animals in Religion, Science, and Ethics.* New York: Columbia University Press.

Waley, Arthur. 1955. *The Nine Songs.* London: George Allen & Unwin.

———. 1961. *Chinese Poems.* 2d ed. London: George Allen & Unwin.

Walker, William. 1854. *The Southern Harmony.* Revised ed. Philadelphia, PA: E. W. Miller.

Wang Jianhua "Ayoe." 2007. Landscapes and Natural Resource Management of Akha People in Xishuangbanna, Southwestern China. Paper, Society of Ethnobiology, annual meeting, Berkeley, CA.

———. 2008. Cultural Adaptation and Sustainability: Political Adaptation of Akha People in Xishuangbanna, Southwestern China. Final Report to Sumernet Foundation. Ms.

———. 2013. Sacred and Contested Landscapes. Ph.D. dissertation, Dept. of Anthropology, University of California, Riverside.

Wapner, Paul. 2010. *Living Through the End of Nature: The Future of American Environmentalism.* Cambridge: MIT Press.

Warner, Lloyd. 1953. *American Life: Dream and Reality.* Chicago, IL: University of Chicago Press.

Watson, Andrew. 1983. *Agricultural Innovation in the Early Islamic World: The Diffusion of Crops and Techniques, 700-1100.* 2nd ed. Cambridge: Cambridge University Press.

Weber, Max. 1946. *From Max Weber: Essays in Sociology.* Ed. and tr. Hans Gerth and C. Wright Mills. New York: Oxford University Press.

———. 2002. *The Protestant Ethic and the "Spirit" of Capitalism.* Tr. Peter Baehr/Gordon Wills. New York: Penguin. Tr. of the 1907 edition.

Webster, David. 2002. *The Fall of the Ancient Maya.* New York: Thames and Hudson.

Webster, Jane. 1995. "Sanctuaries and Sacred Places." In *The Celtic World,* Miranda Green, ed. London: Routledge. Pp. 445–464.

West, Paige. 2006. *Conservation Is Our Government Now: The Politics of Ecology in Papua New Guinea.* Durham, NC: Duke University Press.

West, Paige, James Igoe, and Dan Brockington. 2006. "Parks and Peoples: The Social Impact of Protected Areas." *Annual Review of Anthropology* 35:251–277.

West, Rebecca. 1941. *Black Lamb and Grey Falcon.* London: MacMillan.

Westen, Drew. 2007. *The Political Brain: The Role of Emotion in Deciding the Fate of the Nation.* New York: PublicAffairs.

Whicher, George. 1949. *The Goliard Poets.* Cambridge, MA: author.

White, Lynn, Jr. 1967. "The Historical Roots of Our Ecologic Crisis." *Science* 155:1205–1206.

Wilke, Philip J. 1988. "Bow Staves Harvested From Juniper Trees by Indians of Nevada." *Journal of California and Great Basin Anthropology* 10:3–31.

Wilken, Gene. 1987. *Good Farmers.* Berkeley: University of California Press.

Willerslev, Rane. 2007. *Soul Hunter: Hunting, Animism, and Personhood Among the Siberian Yukaghirs.* Berkeley: University of California Press.

Williams, Nancy, and Hunn, Eugene (eds.). 1982. *Resource Managers.* Boulder: Westview.

Winnington, Alan. 1962. *Slaves of the Cool Mountains.* Berlin: Seven Seas Press.

Witherspoon, Gary. 1977. *Language and Art in the Navajo Universe.* Ann Arbor: University of Michigan Press.

Wolf, Eric. 1972. "Ownership and Political Ecology." *Anthropological Quarterly* 45:201–205.

Wolstein, Diana, and Samuel Noah Kramer. 1983. *Inanna, Queen of Heaven and Earth*. New York: Harper and Row.

Wolverton, Steve, R. Lee Lyman, James H. Kennedy, and Thomas W. La Point. 2009. "The Terminal Pleistocene Extinctions in North America, Hypermorphic Evolution, and the Dynamic Equilibrium Model." *Journal of Ethnobiology* 29:28–63.

Xenophon. 1990. "The Estate-Manager." In *Conversations of Socrates*, Xeonphon, tr./ed. Hugh Tredennick and Robin Waterfield (Greek original early 4th century BC). London: Penguin. Pp. 271–359.

Yeldham, Caroline. 2007. "Living History: Cooking and Fire." *Petits Propos Culinaires* 84:121–126.

Yos Santasombat. 2003. *Biodiversity, Local Knowledge and Sustainable Development*. Chiang Mai, Thailand: Regional Center for Social Science and Sustainable Development, Chiang Mai University.

———. 2008. *Flexible Peasants: Reconceptualizing the Third World's Rural Types*. Chiang Mai, Thailand: Regional Center for Social Science and Sustainable Development, Chiang Mai University.

Yuan Mei. 1997. *I Don't Bow to Buddhas: Selected Poems of Yuan Mei*. Tr. J. P. Seaton. Port Townsend, WA: Copper Canyon Press.

Zambrano, Isabel, and Patricia Greenfield. 2004. "Ethnoepistemologies at Home and at School." In *Culture and Competence: Contexts of Life Success*, Robert J. Sternberg and Elena L. Grigorenko, eds. Washington: American Psychological Association. Pp. 251–272.

Zeitlin, Judith. 1991. "The Petrified Heart: Obsession in Chinese Literature." *Late Imperial China* 12:1–26.

Zenith, Richard. 1995. *113 Galician-Portuguese Troubadour Poems*. Manchester: Carcanet, with Calouste Gulbenkian Foundation.

Zhou, Yichun. 2013. "*Honglou Meng* and Agrarian Values." *Late Imperial China* 34:28–66.

Zozayong. 1975. *Diamond Mountain*. 2v. Seoul: Emillle [*sic*] Museum.

INDEX

ABOUT THE AUTHOR

E. N. Anderson is professor of anthropology, emeritus, at the University of California, Riverside. He has done research on ethnobiology, cultural ecology, political ecology, and medical anthropology in several areas, especially Hong Kong, British Columbia, California, and the Yucatan Peninsula of Mexico. His books include *The Food of China* (Yale University Press, 1988), *Ecologies of the Heart* (Oxford University Press, 1996), *Political Ecology of a Yucatec Maya Community* (University Press of Arizona Press, 2005), and *The Pursuit of Ecotopia* (Praeger, 2010). In 2013 he received the Distinguished Ethnobiology Award from the Society for Ethnobiology.